Contents

Contributors

"It's a Whole Family of Supers"

Frauke Albersmeier is a research fellow at Heinrich Heine University, Duesseldorf. Her research focuses on animal ethics (speciesism; abolitionism in the animal rights debate; interspecies solidarity), metaethics, and philosophical methodology. In her PhD thesis, she argues that progress must culminate in a zootopian wonderland, where the fortunes of overthrown monarchs are used to finally reimburse the animals of the forest (and under the sea) – for their selfless service to animatic princesses and to build a functioning interspecies democracy based on liberty, justice, equality, and of course, catchy tunes. Lots and lots of catchy tunes.

Steve Bein is associate professor of philosophy at the University of Dayton, where he is a specialist in Asian thought. He is the author of *Purifying Zen* and *Compassion and Moral Guidance*, both from University of Hawai' i Press (2011, 2013), and numerous chapters and articles on Japanese, Buddhist, and comparative East–West philosophy. Steve is a regular contributor to the Blackwell Philosophy and Pop Culture Series, including *LEGO and Philosophy* (Wiley, 2017), *Wonder Woman and Philosophy* (Wiley, 2017), and *The Ultimate Star Trek and Philosophy* (Wiley, 2016). He is also a sci-fi and fantasy writer, and some of his short stories are used in college classes across the country. For his chapter in this book, his nieces Kalyn and Audrey are responsible for much of the research. A PhD in philosophy is nothing compared to their combined 24 years of expertise.

Armond Boudreaux is an Associate Professor of English at East Georgia State College. His publications include *Titans: How Superheroes Can Help Us Make Sense of a Polarized World*, *That He May Raise*, and a chapter in *Doctor Strange and Philosophy* (Wiley, 2018). Whenever someone mentions Pixar movies in his presence, people who know him say, "Oh, no – don't get him started on that again!"

Timothy Brown is the director of Southern Evangelical Bible College, and an Assistant Professor of Philosophy and Theology at Southern Evangelical Seminary. He has for some time been trying to drink less coffee, with little to no success. Courses he has instructed include Logic, Moral Philosophy, and Philosophy of Religion. He holds degrees in both Political Science and Philosophy of Religion, which guarantees there is much he can talk about at parties. From what he has observed, he has concerns about what is being taught by the Buy n Large NAN·E bots.

Elizabeth Butterfield is Associate Professor of Philosophy at Georgia Southern University, where she teaches classes on existentialism, ethics, religion, and happiness. She is the author of *Sartre and Post-Humanist Humanism*, and has also published articles on Dr. Seuss, James Bond, and Roald Dahl. Beth's true calling is to be a Jungle Cruise skipper, to share with all her guests the joys of her favorite jungle plants (the hibiscus and the low biscus), her favorite rock formations (that so many people take for granite!), and the one – the only – backside of water! O2H! O2H!

Alexander Christian is a bewitched herbivorous red fox, cursed to act as the assistant director of the Düsseldorf Center for Logic and Philosophy of Science, and Lecturer at the Westfälische Wilhelms-Universität Münster. In his research he is particularly concerned with scientific misconduct and questionable research practices in biomedical research. During twilight, Alex can sometimes be seen hunting for vegan take-out dishes in downtown Düsseldorf. Some people say that he is slightly snappy when it comes to students – what he considers a totally untrue defamatory statement based on speciesist stereotypes.

Louis Colombo is Associate Professor of Philosophy at Bethune-Cookman University in Daytona Beach, where he teaches courses in ethics and the history of Western philosophy. His research interests include Hegel, critical theory, and American pragmatism, although living and teaching in sunny Florida makes the call of the beach almost irresistible. He is currently attempting to recruit a trombonist for his death metal band, "ball of death."

Kody Cooper is UC Foundation Assistant Professor of Political Science & Public Service at the University of Tennessee at Chattanooga. He is the author of *Thomas Hobbes and the Natural Law* (University of Notre Dame Press, 2018). His life goal is to have 15 biological children, adopt 86 more, and then write a catchy jingle that will bring home enough bacon to feed, clothe, and house them all in style.

Timothy Dale is an Associate Professor of Political Science at the University of Wisconsin–La Crosse. He teaches in the area of political philosophy, and his research interests include democratic theory, political messaging in popular culture, and the scholarship of teaching and learning. He is co-editor of several books on popular culture and politics, including *Jim Henson and Philosophy* (2015), *Homer Simpson Ponders Politics* (2013), and *Homer Simpson Marches on Washington* (2010). In addition to spending time in line at Animal Kingdom for the *Avatar* Flight of Passage ride, he also likes roaming Epcot with a beer while his family rides on Test Track.

Richard B. Davis is Professor and Chair of Philosophy at Tyndale University in Toronto, Canada. He is the editor of *Alice in Wonderland and Philosophy* (Wiley, 2010), and co-editor (with Jennifer Hart Weed and Ronald Weed) of *24 and Philosophy* (Wiley, 2007). His philosophical musings have also appeared in *The X-Men and Philosophy* (Wiley, 2009). Like baby Jack-Jack, Davis has the much sought-after super power of transporting himself to other dimensions. For some reason this takes place spontaneously during faculty meetings.

William J. Devlin is Associate Professor of Philosophy at Bridgewater State University, offering classes in existentialism, nineteenth century philosophy, the philosophy of Friedrich Nietzsche, and philosophy of science. His publications include chapters in *Westworld and Philosophy* (Wiley, 2018), *Game of Thrones and Philosophy* (Wiley, 2012), and *The Walking Dead and Philosophy* (Wiley, 2012). He finds himself closely resembling Moana's father, Chief Tui – overly confident in his family rules, which are constantly undermined as his mother encourages and instigates his daughter's existential rebellion.

George A. Dunn has taught Philosophy and Religion in both the United States and the People's Republic of China. He is the editor or co-editor of six books on philosophy and popular culture, including *The Philosophy of Christopher Nolan* (Lexington Books, 2017) and *Sons of Anarchy and Philosophy* (Wiley, 2013), and *The Hunger Games and Philosophy* (Wiley, 2012). Like Mulan, he's visited the Forbidden City in Beijing, though he didn't arrive on horseback and he missed the fireworks display.

Joseph Foy is the editor of *Homer Simpson Goes to Washington*, and *SpongeBob SquarePants and Philosophy*. He is also co-editor of *Homer Simpson Marches on Washington* and *Homer Simpson Ponders Politics*. Foy has also contributed essays in over fifteen popular culture anthologies. He is currently serving as the Dean of the College of Arts, Sciences and Letters at Marian University in Fond du Lac, Wisconsin, which is, of course, the *second* happiest place on Earth.

Robert K. Garcia is an Associate Professor of Philosophy at Texas A&M University, where he works in analytic metaphysics and philosophy of religion. He is the co-editor of *Is Goodness without God Good Enough?* and is writing a book on C. S. Lewis's views about the uniqueness of persons. His dream is to cameo in a Disney film as the philosopher who solved two seemingly intractable conundrums: Pluto's *Euthyphro Dilemma* (Is Mickey unable to be mad at Pluto because Pluto is cheerful or is Pluto cheerful because Mickey is unable to be mad at him?) and the lesser-known Goofy Dilemma (Is the talking dog goofy because he is "Goofy" or is he "Goofy" because he is goofy?).

J. Edward Hackett is a full-time Lecturer at Savannah State University, where he teaches courses in the Humanities and Philosophy. He is the author of *Persons and Values in Pragmatic Phenomenology*, and co-edited *Phenomenology for the 21st Century*. He works in ethical theory, American philosophy, and continental philosophy. Apart from his scholarly writings, he's published a novel, *Flight of the Ravenhawk* with Ink Smith Press. He writes public philosophy and has edited *House of Cards and Philosophy* (Wiley, 2015). Unlike Wall·E, Hackett would much rather find a faster-than-light vehicle and leave earth for adventure.

Jamey Heit's interest in cultural studies grew out of his PhD work at the University of Glasgow. In addition to his dissertation on John

Donne and Emily Dickinson, he has written about a range of cultural topics: representations of evil, *Calvin and Hobbes*, and *The Hunger Games*. He taught extensively before co-founding an educational technology company. He still teaches online at Walden University. Someday, his daughters would like to visit Arendelle with him. Disney World will probably have to suffice.

Steve Jones is Associate Professor of Humanities at Bethune-Cookman University, where he teaches interdisciplinary humanities and Greek and other related things. Current projects include "Straight from the Dragon's Mouth," an investigation of the "Roswell of 888," in which Alfred the Great directed a cover-up of frequent and devastating dragon attacks on Wessex by claiming they actually were Viking raids. Also planned is "Don't Steiff That Teddy," a Jungian analysis of the synchronous emergence of the teddy bear archetype in early twentieth-century Germany and America.

Dean A. Kowalski is a Professor of Philosophy and the inaugural chair of the Arts & Humanities Department in the College of General Studies at the University of Wisconsin-Milwaukee. He is the author or editor of eight books, each exploring philosophical connections to film or television, including *The Philosophy of The X-Files* (2009), *The Big Bang Theory and Philosophy* (Wiley, 2012), *Classic Questions and Contemporary Film* (Wiley, 2016), and *Joss Whedon as Philosopher* (2017). He would have given anything for Chef Kronk to utter: "Hey, how come people don't have dip for dinner? Why is it only a snack?"

Mark D. Linville is Senior Research Fellow and Philosophy Tutor for Faulkner University's PhD program in the Humanities. He has edited (with Dave Werther) *Philosophy and the Christian Worldview* (Bloomsbury) as well as numerous journal articles and book chapters on moral philosophy and philosophy of religion, including "The Moral Argument" in the *Blackwell Companion to Natural Theology*. He is the co-founder (with Dave Werther) of Cody State University – a quite imaginary institution "Where Seldom is Heard a Discouraging Word" – where he also holds the Zane Grey Chair of Western (i.e. Rootin' Tootin') Philosophy. He is more likely to feed the birds with his tuppence than invest it and wants to be a chimney sweep when he grows up.

Megan S. Lloyd is the Manus Cooney Distinguished Professor of English at King's College in Wilkes-Barre, Pennsylvania, and the author of *The Valiant Welshman, the Scottish James, and the Formation of Great Britain* and "*Speak it in Welsh*": *Wales and the Welsh Language in Shakespeare*. She would like to thank her research assistants, Daniel and Kate, who encouraged her to watch hundreds of hours of Disney videos, especially Disney's *Sing-Along-Songs* and *The Little Mermaid II: Return to the Sea*.

Tuomas W. Manninen is a Senior Lecturer in Philosophy at Arizona State University, West Campus, where he teaches courses in critical thinking, philosophy of mind, political philosophy, and other related topics. A lifelong enthusiast of most things Disney, he taught himself to read with the help of Donald Duck comics. Although it is probably for this reason he believes that the Mouse is overrated. He lives in Phoenix, Arizona with his wife, Bertha (with whom he fell in love on a trip to Disney World), and two daughters, Michelle and Julia.

C. A. McIntosh is a PhD candidate in Philosophy at Cornell University. He uses his initials not because he's a pretentious Brit, but because he hates his first name (Chad). McIntosh has written extensively on a wide range of topics in philosophy including metaphysics, epistemology, ethics, philosophy of religion, and political philosophy, most of which sit stillborn on his computer's hard drive. His goal in life is to cultivate his masculinity to be at least as toxic as that of Prince Phillips'.

Robert M. Mentyka is an Independent Scholar who squeezes in philosophical writing after spending the day working in retail and watching reruns of *The Disney Afternoon* over his lunch break. A life-long Disney fan, he received his MA in Philosophy from the Franciscan University of Steubenville, Ohio, and considers vacationing in Disney World a prerequisite for a truly well-rounded education in the humanities. His previous contributions to the Blackwell Philosophy and Pop Culture Series include articles for *Bioshock and Philosophy* (Wiley, 2015), *Alien and Philosophy* (Wiley, 2017), and most recently, *LEGO and Philosophy* (Wiley, 2017).

Ellen Miller is Associate Professor of Philosophy at Rowan University in Glassboro, New Jersey. Her book, *Releasing Philosophy, Thinking Art: A Phenomenological Study of Sylvia Plath's Poetry* (Davies Group Publishers), is the first full-length philosophical examination of Sylvia Plath's poetry. Her other publications and presentations focus on topics in ethics, philosophy of art, and feminist philosophy. She is actively involved in pre-college philosophy programming and research. In her article (in press) for Volume 10 of *Plath Profiles: An Interdisciplinary Journal for Sylvia Plath Studies*, she examines how Plath's writings can help us better understand mental health care and case studies in ethics. Unlike Riley, she is not disgusted by broccoli on pizza; like Riley, she tries to preserve her childhood memories and emotions as long as possible.

Jessica Miller is Professor of Philosophy and Associate Dean for Faculty Affairs at the University of Maine. She has previously contributed to *Buffy the Vampire Slayer and Philosophy* and *The Hunger Games and Philosophy* (Wiley, 2012). When she is not working on a project in bioethics or pop culture, she can be found in her doom buggy, trying to count all 999 ghosts in the Haunted Mansion ride at Walt Disney World.

Kevin Mintz is a PhD candidate at Stanford University. A disability scholar and lifelong, die-hard Disney fan, he grew up going to Disney World with his brothers regularly. His research interests include sexuality politics and the philosophy of disability. His not-so-secret hedonistic fantasy is to eventually make enough money to buy a Disney Premier Passport and move into a room at the Hollywood Tower Hotel. His more realistic goal is to help make Disney magic accessible to all dreamers with disabilities.

Leilani Mueller teaches competitive drama and British literature to high-school students. Her philosophy comes via osmosis both from her philosopher husband and lots of attention to Plato and Aquinas. Her expertise in fairy-tales in general and Disney stories in particular was gained through countless visits to Disneyland and memorizing the soundtracks to many Disney films. She strives to avoid being spellbound by loving beauty wherever she finds it.

Nathan Mueller is a doctoral student in philosophy at Baylor University. His research interests center on issues in social epistemology and philosophy of education. Pursuant to the former interest he wonders what beliefs were had by the mob which set out to kill the Beast, and how that collective belief was formed. He was reminded by his co-author, however, of the role of the true, the good, and, specifically, the beautiful and now he is pondering the spell-breaking power of beauty and its powerful role in the process of education.

Originally the eighth dwarf, **Edwardo Pérez** spent his childhood toiling away in the mines with Sneezy and Dopey. After an ill-fated romance with Tinkerbell (and a trip to Vegas with Mushu and Genie that cannot be put into words), Edwardo earned his PhD in English while doing odd jobs in Beast's castle as a feather quill, and while working summers lifeguarding in Motunui with Tamatoa (before he went glam). Eventually settling down as an Associate Professor of English at Tarrant County College in Hurst, TX (though never forgetting his time spent hitting the slopes in Arendelle with Olaf), Edwardo writes blogs for AndPhilosophy.com, manages the website lightsabertoss.com, and contributes essays to magical texts like the one you're holding in your hand.

Timothy Pickavance is Associate Professor of Philosophy and Chair of the Talbot Department of Philosophy at Biola University. His philosophical interests are all over the map. But his published work is mostly in metaphysics, and include *Metaphysics: The Fundamentals* and *The Atlas of Reality: A Comprehensive Guide to Metaphysics* (both Wiley Blackwell, and both co-authored with Robert Koons). Fun fact: an anagram of "Tim Pickavance" is "pancake victim." So if Tim were a character in a Disney film, he assumes it would be a bit part that involves being assaulted with breakfast food.

Read Mercer Schuchardt is the great-nephew of Johnny Mercer, who wrote "Zip-A-Dee-Doo-Da" and other Disney tunes, as well as the soundtrack for Seven Brides for Seven Brothers and the Breakfast At Tiffany's hit song, "Moon River." He is Associate Professor of Communication at Wheaton College, and hopes to become the world's leading scholar of the Star Wars Y-Wing Fighter.

Shawn White has an MA in Christian Apologetics from Biola University, and is currently pursuing a PhD at Faulkner University studying Philosophy of Humanities. His academic interests include G.K. Chesterton and Chesterton's writings on gratitude, wonder, and humility. His non-academic interests include having a wife, having a dog, playing board games, and having a wooden leg named Smith. He is grateful for being practically imperfect in every way.

Acknowledgments
It Takes People to Make a Dream Reality

Sincere thanks are due to Marissa Koors at Wiley Blackwell who, while waiting for this book to finally arrive, was no doubt consoled by the magical words of Cinderella's fairy godmother: "Even miracles take a little time." And to Megan S. Lloyd whose generosity of spirit and contributions to this volume truly went "to infinity and beyond." And finally to Mr. Incredible, Bill Irwin: author, editor, and colleague *extraordinaire*. Bill has an inexplicable knowledge of pop culture's (and this book's) inner workings, exploiting every loophole, dodging every obstacle. In my books, he's a Super – with or without the Supersuit.

The book you are holding is fondly dedicated to the memory of Walt Disney, who if he were reading these words would promptly decree, "The way to get [a book] started is to quit talking and begin doing." So off we go; enjoy the ride!

Introduction
Philosophy Begins in Wonder

"First, think. Second, believe. Third, dream. And finally, dare"
—Walt Disney

If you've ever experienced the feeling of *wonder* – if you've ever asked who you are, what your purpose is, or how you might function freely, happily, and creatively in the circle of life – this book is for you. You don't have to take my word for it. For the greatest of *all* philosophers, Socrates (470–399 BCE) himself, declared once and for all time: "*wonder* is the feeling of a philosopher, and philosophy begins in *wonder*." There is no better place to start the philosophical journey than with the often animated, indisputably *wonder*-ful world created for us by Walt Disney – through television, motion pictures, theme parks, and much else. Without a doubt, Disney has made the world (parts of it at least) a "Magic Kingdom," where time stands still and we can escape, dream, and (for one tiny moment) be special.

The 27 chapters in this book explore issues that affect each one of us: freedom, fatalism, friends, family, ethics, identity, disabilities, and ultimately death. In these pages the great sages of the ages meet Disney at its cinematic best: from the early days of *Mickey Mouse, Goofy*, and *Sleeping Beauty*, to recent blockbusters such as *The Little Mermaid*, *Toy Story*, *Mulan, The Incredibles*, *Frozen*, and more. It's all here. All the uncommon wisdom spun out of these wonderful tales – plus, a few unexpected insights into the philosophy of Disney, its media impact, and theme parks – is illuminated and explained by 32 of the world's most Disney-loving philosophers. You'll consider the feminist evolution of Disney princesses from passive, shy, and petite to passionate, outspoken, and proud. You'll confront the question of whether those

"Hidden Mickeys" at Walt Disney World tell us anything about God. And you'll journey through *Inside Out*'s complex inner world of emotions into *Finding Dory*'s equally challenging outer world of the social stigmas facing those for whom disability is "part of their world."

So whether you grew up with *The Wonderful World of Disney* in the 1970s, raised your kids in front of *Beauty and the Beast* and *The Lion King* in the 1990s, or (like philosopher Elizabeth Butterfield) are just getting home from yet another Disney vacation, you'll want *Disney and Philosophy* to help chart your course through the philosophical world of Disney. All it takes is truth, trust, and a little bit of pixie dust.

Part I

"THE SEAWEED IS ALWAYS GREENER IN SOMEBODY ELSE'S LAKE"

Unruly Ariel

Not Born but Made a Woman

Megan S. Lloyd

Molly, my five-year-old niece, is going to Disney World soon. Of course, she's very excited. But she doesn't care at all about princesses, and that disappoints me. After all, Disney *is* princesses. Beginning with *Snow White* (1937), then *Cinderella* (1950), and *Sleeping Beauty* (1959), Disney marketed the favorite fairy tales of days gone by. Lovely ladies wished that "someday my prince will come" to move them out of or awaken them from a deathlike existence to live happily ever after in a new kingdom.

I don't think for a moment that my five-year-old niece is rejecting the gender stereotypes of Disney princesses. Molly is just a unique little girl who likes what she likes. But if she were concerned about the way Disney portrays women, she would do well to consider *The Little Mermaid*. As we'll see, Ariel represents a major step forward from Snow White.

After *Sleeping Beauty*, Disney experienced a lull in princess traffic. A long 30 years later, after the successes of such classics as *One Hundred and One Dalmatians* (1961), *The Jungle Book* (1967), and *Robin Hood* (1973), Disney revisited its princess roots with *The Little Mermaid* (1989), giving us a fairy tale with a determined heroine, ushering in a new kind of princess with a voice. Assertive Ariel clones followed with Belle from *Beauty and the Beast* (1991), *Pocahontas* (1995), and *Mulan* (1998). But does Ariel fix Disney's princess problem? Probably not. However, she does point the way forward.

Disney and Philosophy: Truth, Trust, and a Little Bit of Pixie Dust, First Edition.
Edited by Richard B. Davis.

Flip the Script

Ariel is a departure from the man-requiring damsel in distress that made Disney famous. Our favorite mermaid is precocious, curious, and interested in all the world around her – above and below sea level. Beyond that, she can take care of herself. In her opening scene, Ariel swims, surveying the wreckage of a downed galleon with her friend, Flounder, and disregards the shark that swims nearby. Aristotle (384–322 BCE) famously said, "All men by nature desire to know."[1] Ariel shows that the philosopher's observation was too narrow. Women, including mermaids, have innate curiosity, too. Ariel desires to know. In fact, everything about the world excites her. To nurture her curiosity, she collects all she can from beyond. Finding a fork in the wreckage she gleefully expounds with, "Oh my gosh! Oh my gosh! Have you ever seen anything so wonderful in your entire life?" Aristotle would approve of her excitement. After all, he believed that philosophy begins in wonder.[2]

Ariel's treasure trove is full of dinglehoppers and snarfblats, but once she lays eyes on Prince Eric, the young man is the prize she wants most. When the Prince's ship splits, *The Little Mermaid* flips the script. Ariel saves her own Prince Charming. Roles continue to be reversed as Ariel drags him from the sea and gazes on him longingly as he lies there, unconscious or asleep, reminiscent of other Disney princesses, Snow White and Sleeping Beauty. Instead of Prince Charming, it is Princess Ariel who does the ogling. Not only does Ariel save Eric, but throughout the film she is the hero.

Like the epic heroes of literature, Ariel overcomes naysayers – like Sebastian; sacrifices part of her self – her voice; ventures into a whole new world – Eric's kingdom; and unites both worlds – land and sea. None of this comes easily, of course. To get what she wants Ariel makes an unholy alliance. In a nod to the Faustus story – you know the one where you sell your soul to the devil – Ariel makes a pact with the sea witch, Ursula. What could possibly go wrong?

Silencing Women and a Mermaid

Under the sea, Ariel has her voice and is even extolled for it. Indeed, her voice is the best in the kingdom. At the pageant for King Triton, her sisters sing well. In fact, all Ariel's sisters have voices, good voices, but Ariel is the star … fish. Early in the film, all are gathered for the premiere of the newest composition by the distinguished court composer, Horatio Thelonious Ignatius Crustaceous Sebastian. The new song will feature the talents of Ariel. Her sisters sing her in with, "And then there is the youngest in her musical debut, / Our seventh little sister, we're presenting her to you, / To sing a song Sebastian wrote, her voice is like a bell, / She's our sister, Ar -I ..." Truly, her voice is like a bell, but the little mermaid has gone missing.

Ariel is so busy with her pursuit of human artifacts that she misses the big premiere. It's not just her singing voice that is strong. She is outspoken, assertive, doing her own thing, without regard for other family obligations. She is a young woman with a mind of her own and a voice of her own – in the best sense. Ariel's behavior may be negligent as she misses the premiere, but it is not conceited. This youngest and motherless daughter of King Triton has the strength of character to know who she is and what she wants. Ariel doesn't want to be subject to the rules under the sea. As she sings, Ariel wants to "go where the people go." But why?

As Sebastian's lyrics remind us, "Under the Sea" all is well. In her father's kingdom, Ariel could live happily ever after. Sebastian's famous song, catchy tune and all, describes a submerged peaceable kingdom where all forms of sea-life jam together and make beautiful music, with no hint of a food chain in sight. He describes a happy, content world with no troubles. No mention of the sharks lurking nearby, like the one who tries to attack Flounder. Triton's peaceable kingdom does not extend beyond the depths. Yet, Ariel is drawn upward. She should heed Sebastian's advice: "The seaweed is always greener / In somebody else's lake." Part of her problem with the sea is teen angst and opposition to her father, as she believes that on land, people don't "reprimand their daughters." Ariel assumes that on land, they "understand their daughters," and they acknowledge "bright young women" like herself, "ready to stand."

The desire to move beyond one's place often gets people into trouble. For women, especially, that trouble comes through their voices. In the Bible, Eve's tongue was the trap that led humanity to sin. In Greek mythology, the first woman, Pandora, was sent from the gods as a punishment to mankind after Prometheus stole fire. Her curiosity posed a problem for the whole earth. In another myth, Cassandra said no to the advances of Apollo who cursed her to speak the truth no one would believe.

A woman's voice was problematic in medieval times when a strident female, gossiping or challenging male authority, could be labeled a witch. In fact, *The Little Mermaid* supports the connection between assertive female behavior and witchcraft. Ariel and the sea witch herself, Ursula, share some significant things in common. Both are collectors. Ariel collects what she can from the land and contains her collection in a treasure trove under the sea. Ursula also collects, poor unfortunate souls, that she gathers in a cave treasury as well. Both want the power and the voice to do what they please.

In early modern Europe, the outspoken woman was considered a shrew to be tamed (as in the play). In Shakespeare's day, women who were talkative – and more importantly not following male hierarchy, like the rules Ariel's father gives her – were disciplined for their assertiveness. Many of these punishments were physically abusive, such as the cucking stool, where the shrew was taken to a body of water, strapped to a chair, and dunked in the water a few times, something close to waterboarding today. Another punishment was for her to be led around by the scold's bridle, a metal contraption put over her head complete with a barbed bit, as one might use on a horse. Both of these taming methods targeted the woman's voice as the source of evil. Because a woman's tongue gave way to ideas and potential power, it had to be restrained.

With this history in mind, we should shudder when Ursula offers to make Ariel human in exchange for her voice. The deal specifies that if Eric kisses Ariel before sunset on day three, she will remain human. Otherwise, Ariel's soul will belong to Ursula. To lure Ariel into her trap, Ursula minimizes the value of Ariel's voice, saying, "I'm not asking much. Just a token, really, a trifle. You'll never even miss it. What I want from you is … your voice." But Ursula, of all creatures, understands the power of a woman's voice. She, herself, a commanding voice, has been ostracized, cast out and named the sea witch. Ursula knows that Ariel's singing voice is what first attracted Eric, and later Ursula uses Ariel's voice to lure him to her, the sea witch in disguise. To coax Ariel further, Ursula sings about how men on land don't want a woman with a voice: "The men up there don't like a lot of blabber / They think a girl who gossips is a bore / Yes, on land it's much preferred / For ladies not to say a word / And after all, dear, what is idle prattle for? / Come on, they're not all that impressed with conversation / True gentlemen avoid it when they can / But they dote and swoon and fawn / On a lady who's withdrawn / It's she who holds her tongue who gets her man." Heading off the objection that without her voice, Ariel could not procure a kiss from Eric, Ursula reminds her, "You'll have your looks! Your pretty face! And don't underestimate the importance of body language! Ha!" Ursula says the prince will "never" miss her voice – she's got looks, a pretty face, and body language to get the kiss. So when Ursula snatches Ariel's voice in payment for legs, the sea witch gives Eric the epitome of stereotypical male desire – the beautiful silent female.

You Don't Complete Me

Ursula is right in at least one way, namely that Ariel is drawn to please the eye. Beginning with Laura Mulvey in 1975, feminist theorists have criticized the "male gaze" in film, the tendency to depict women in a way that caters to male desire.[3] In the case of Ariel, it's not costuming and camera angles, but animation that does the trick. She is the sexiest of the Disney princesses, scantily clad with strategically placed sea shells. What's the harm? When my daughter, Kate, was little, around age five like her cousin Molly is now, I would sometimes find her with her nightgown pulled down around her shoulders. Asked what she was doing, Kate would reply "playing princess." My daughter had gotten the message from Ariel and others that to be a princess was to put flesh on display.

As much as I love Disney, this was not a lesson I wanted my daughter to learn. In fact, it was the kind of thing that led the philosopher Simone de Beauvoir (1908–1986), one of the mothers of modern feminism, to remark that, "One is not born but becomes a woman."[4] Beauvoir's message – that biology is not destiny – was radical in 1949. Really, we owe a debt to those who fought for women's rights in prior years, because Beauvoir's words sound obvious today. A woman does not have to wear clothes that will attract the eye of a man, and she does not have to play dumb.

The concept of the male gaze was inspired by "the look," an integral part of the philosophy of Jean-Paul Sartre (1905–1980). In Sartre's existentialism, we experience the look when another person objectifies us, seeing us as a thing rather than as a conscious being. The liberating truth, according to Sartre, is that we are all free. We do not need to conform to the expectations that "the look" of the other person places upon us, and we certainly do not need to dress or act in ways that anticipate those expectations. Indeed, this is what Beauvoir meant by her famous quote, and she would have approved of Ariel's curiosity, sense of adventure, and willingness to defy her father's wishes.

But Beauvoir would not have approved of the little mermaid's apparel. Yes, a bathing suit is appropriate for someone who spends so much time in the water, but come on. There is nothing wrong with a woman proudly displaying her body, but Ariel the little mermaid is not Beyoncé the diva. Disney should know better. Ariel was more modestly attired in Hans Christian Anderson's original story, and the animators could have followed suit. Beauvoir would likewise have disapproved of Ariel's need for a man and desire to marry, especially at such a young age. Jerry Maguire sounded romantic when he told Dorothy Boyd, "You complete me," but Beauvoir was firmly of the mind that a woman does not need a man to complete her. Jean-Paul Sartre and Simone de Beauvoir were romantically involved from the time of their "dangerous liaison" as students until Sartre's death in 1980, but they never married. Their relationship would best be described as "it's complicated."

At the beginning of *The Little Mermaid*, Ariel is inquisitive and curious about everything the land has to offer. After setting eyes on Eric, though, she falls prey to love at first sight or to the stereotypical romantic notions of a traditional patriarchal storyline. No longer is everything under the sun interesting, only Eric. That's not to knock love at first sight, but with Ariel, Disney initially creates a formidable female role model, a woman who stands up for herself and wants what she wants. Once the little mermaid sees and falls in love with Eric, Ariel – and Disney – succumb to the typical format, a princess searching for a prince charming who will take her away to a life new, unknown, and exciting to her. When Ariel finds a man, she loses her voice, both figuratively and literally – the feminist nightmare. Even though Ariel eventually gets her voice back, it's a shame that the story doesn't follow through with a stronger depiction of the little mermaid. Instead, it gives us a heroine that I wouldn't want my daughter or niece to emulate fully.

It might be tempting to think that I'm making too much of Ariel's appearance and choice to marry. It's just a cartoon! Lighten up! But consider that Disney recognizes they haven't always done well with the way they have depicted people. In 1946 Disney released *Song of the South*, featuring the stereotypical Uncle Remus speaking in cringe-worthy black vernacular. If you want to see how bad it is, you can watch some clips on YouTube, but you can't watch a tape or DVD. Disney, to its credit, has never released the movie on video.

When we're first introduced to Eric, he is returning from a failed attempt to secure himself a princess. Later, when Grimbsy continues to look for a suitable wife for Eric, he encourages the prince to go after the beauty that's in front of him, the voiceless Ariel. "Eric, if I may say, far better than any dream girl, is one of flesh and blood, one warm and caring, and right before your eyes." Thus, the culture surrounding Eric also buys into the "the look." But Eric, too, subverts convention. He plays the damsel in distress attracted to his savior, saying, "A girl – rescued me.... She was – singing ... she had the most – beautiful voice." Eric is captivated by her voice – he hears her. Her. That's significant. Prince Eric wants more than just a pretty face and a hot body.

OK, Eric likes Ariel's voice, her singing voice, and as a sea creature, her voice makes her a siren that may lure men to their death. Let's forget that sea myth. Instead, let's listen to Ariel's voice another way. Eric is interested in her voice and thus is interested in what makes Ariel who she is. Her voice is the means to her confidence, her outgoing nature, her curiosity, her very self. The outside packaging is a benefit, but he rejects it in search of something more than what's on the outside. Sebastian croons in an attempt to get the prince to "kiss the girl," and Eric almost does until Flotsam and Jetsam, Ursula's hench eels, land both Eric and Ariel in the water. Despite his amorous intent, the prince is not some kind of predator. Ariel's eyes convey that she wants to be kissed, and the bargain with Ursula precludes Ariel kissing him.

A Hope for the Future

At the beginning of the movie, under the sea, Ariel is a fish out of water, so to speak. Like a bell, Ariel's voice tolls as an injunction for all to experience the larger world around them. But when she tells her father that another reality exists, he thunders, "Down HERE is your home!" Ariel, who has seen beyond and understands another reality, wants desperately for others, especially her father, to see the world the way she does. Triton is not an ogre. He is a protective parent, concerned for the well-being of his daughter, setting rules to make sure she is safe and secure. Luckily for us and for her, Ariel is unruly. Ultimately her rule-breaking leads not just to her own happiness but to peace between the worlds of land and sea.

It would be tempting to imagine that Ariel would become the kind of mother who encourages her daughter to take risks and walk her own path. But, as I can attest from my own experience, parenthood has a way of making us risk-averse. Sure, I don't want my daughter or niece to feel like they need to flaunt themselves or follow traditional paths. But most of all I want them to be safe and happy. Despite myself, I want to save them from making mistakes even though I know they need to make their own mistakes to learn who they are and become strong women.

Ariel, too, succumbs to the rules eventually. In *Little Mermaid II: Return to the Sea* (2000), released straight to DVD, she has become her father, as children often do, even ones who rebel and alter themselves when they first start out in life. Despite her best intentions, Ariel becomes the purveyor of stereotypes, especially as a protective parent to her little girl, Melody, not telling her that she is half mermaid. Unfortunately, this rings true. It's much easier to be a rebel and a critic, than it is to be a caretaker and a creator.

For all her shortcomings from a feminist perspective, unruly Ariel represents a move in the right direction. *The Little Mermaid* does not belong in the hall of shame, like *Song of the South*. Adolescent Ariel sings and leads a viewing public into a new, fresh take on Disney princesses, with a voice reminding everyone to be assertive, speak their minds, and do what they want to do. Hopefully, in the years to come, my daughter and niece will have newer, better Disney heroines to discuss with their own daughters.

Notes

1. *Metaphysics* Book 1, http://classics.mit.edu/Aristotle/metaphysics.1.i.html
2. Ibid.
3. Mulvey, L. (1975). Visual pleasure and narrative cinema, *Screen* 16: 6–18.
4. de Beauvoir, S. (2011). *The Second Sex*, 283. New York: Vintage.

"True to Your Heart"
Honor and Authenticity in *Mulan*

George A. Dunn

Disney's animated *Mulan* was not a hit in mainland China. Despite being one of the studio's most financially successful and critically acclaimed films, it was a box-office flop in the country where its legendary heroine was born. The movie's feisty protagonist may have defeated the Hun army almost single-handedly – aided only by a trio of cross-dressing male comrades, her wisecracking dragon sidekick, and a cricket – but, somehow, she failed to conquer the hearts of mainland Chinese audiences.

That's not to say that the Chinese public doesn't love the Mulan of legend, the brave young woman who disguised herself as a man to take the place of her aging father when he was called up in the draft. Making its first appearance in a sixth century poem, Mulan's story has been retold countless times in the form of poems, novels, plays, operas, and, in recent years, nearly a dozen film and television series from Chinese studios.[1] It is one of China's most beloved folktales, yet Disney's *Mulan* was unable to cash in on that love, despite the studio's success on the Chinese mainland with such earlier releases as *The Lion King* and *Toy Story*.

To be fair, *Mulan*'s poor box office wasn't entirely the movie's fault. As Disney's Mulan learned when bathing in the river near camp, timing is everything. The movie's release date in China wasn't exactly auspicious. Because the Chinese government insisted on keeping *Mulan* out of theaters until after the Spring Festival (the Chinese New Year),

Disney and Philosophy: Truth, Trust, and a Little Bit of Pixie Dust, First Edition.
Edited by Richard B. Davis.

Disney's first Chinese heroine didn't hit the multiplexes until after the holiday, just as children were returning to school. That's not unlike releasing a movie in the United States right *after* the end of the Christmas holidays. The year was 1999, the 50th anniversary of the founding of the People's Republic of China, and the government wanted to spotlight its own domestic movie industry during the prime moviegoing season, rather than cede its screens to the marauding armies of Hollywood (the cultural equivalent of the Huns). By the time *Mulan* finally made it to Chinese theaters, so many pirated copies were in circulation that not even the luckiest cricket could undo the damage.

Yet, more may have been in play than just bad timing. Part of the problem may have been Disney's depiction of its heroine. The movie did an impressive job of creating the *look* of China with its gorgeous images of the Great Wall, Chinese lanterns, pagodas, calligraphy, fireworks, a lineage temple, and more. Still, some viewers found Disney's Mulan far too Western in her attitudes and behavior. In turns out that China's ancient heroine of filial piety and patriotism had, in the process of being translated from one culture to another, acquired a new motivation unknown to the original Mulan. Though she loves her family and her country no less than the Mulan of Chinese legend, Disney's Mulan also has a burning need to express her authentic self, to break free of the constricting social role she has been assigned by tradition. As joyfully celebrated in the movie's theme song, she has an overriding need to be "true to her heart."

"Honor to Us All"

One of the first things we learn about Disney's Mulan is what a clever and resourceful young woman she is, a trait she shares with many Disney princesses. These are the qualities she will draw upon to save her country from the invading Huns, but when we're first introduced to Mulan she's deploying her wit to save time doing her chores. To give herself more time to prepare for her visit to the matchmaker, she has enlisted the help of her canine companion Little Brother,[2] tying a bag of chicken feed to his tail and sending him running off in the direction of the chicken pen. We see more evidence of Mulan's ample intelligence as her family hurries her to the dressmaker to be outfitted for her interview with the matchmaker. Pausing for only a moment to ponder a game of checkers played by two old men in the public square, she transfers a piece from one square to another, making a winning move. While being ushered to the makeup artist, she also exhibits her keen sense of fair play, snatching a doll from the hand of a mischievous boy and returning it to the girl from whom he had stolen it.

But these aren't virtues that matter to the matchmaker. Despite all of Mulan's superior brainpower and her earnest desire to honor her family, she just can't seem to master the art of performing the role she's been assigned by her society. As she laments in the song "Reflection,"[3] she "will never pass for a perfect bride" or even, she fears, "a perfect daughter." The measure of such perfection is the list of traditional feminine virtues that Mulan had scrawled on her arm as a reminder of how to conduct herself with the matchmaker: "quiet and demure, graceful, polite, delicate, refined, poised, punctual" – all of which she fails miserably at exemplifying. To call her meeting with the matchmaker a disaster would be a massive understatement. "You are a *disgrace*!" she screams at Mulan, as our heroine makes her embarrassed exit after having set the matchmaker's dress on fire and then drenched the poor woman in tea to extinguish the flames. "You may *look* like a bride, but you will *never* bring your family honor!"

It's that failure to bring honor to her family that marks Mulan as a disgrace according to the standards of her traditional Chinese culture. The supreme importance of honor is underscored by the song "Honor to Us All,"[4] sung as she's bathed, dressed, made-up, and marched to her fate in a procession of other young women, "each a perfect porcelain doll." The influence of Asian culture is more prominent in this song than in any other musical number in the movie, with its pentatonic scales and Chinese instruments used to reinforce the cultural setting.[5] But the lyrics could easily be heard as mocking traditional Chinese culture and the highly restricted social roles it allots to men and women. "A girl can bring her family / Great honor in one way / By striking a good match / And this could be the day / Men want girls with good taste / Calm, obedient, who work fast-paced / With good breeding and a tiny waist / You'll bring honor to us all." As they sing this song, the older women set themselves to work at the ultimately futile task of sculpting Mulan into the ideal image of traditional womanhood. But, as the lyrics remind us, the charming attire and makeup of a prospective bride primarily serve as outward signs of an important set of inner virtues: good taste, good breeding, calmness, obedience. Mulan fails to exhibit these virtues, no matter how much she may "*look* like a bride." The irony of the song is that most of us in the modern West would rank these items quite low on our list of cardinal virtues, if we would even count them as virtues at all. And the irony is a bitter one, due to our awareness of Mulan's other virtues, her intelligence and courage, which are somehow overlooked or discounted by everyone around her, though most of us would value them much more highly than superficialities like beauty and grace.

Yet, according to the ethics of the ancient sage Confucius (551–479 BCE), whose thought profoundly shaped Mulan's society, the beautification of the surface of our world through 礼乐 (*lǐyuè*), the social graces and the arts, is what makes civilization possible in the first place. From a Confucian perspective, knowing how to pour the tea with what the matchmaker describes as "a sense of dignity and refinement" is nothing to sneer at. But if the virtues of a woman pertain to the surface of human life – adding elegance, refinement, and some cultural polish to our social interactions – the virtues of a man are compared to the roiling depths of nature. As Captain Li Shang instructs his recruits in the song "Make a Man Out of You"[6]: "We must be swift as the coursing river … / With all the force of a great typhoon … / With all the strength of a raging fire / Mysterious as the dark side of the moon." Swift, forceful, strong, mysterious (stealthy) – these are the virtues that make a man a great warrior and offer a route to winning honor denied to women, who have their own prescribed way of supporting the war effort. "Honor to Us All" outlines this gendered division of labor in a traditional society defined by the needs of warfare: "We all must serve our emperor / Who guards us from the Huns / A man by bearing arms /A girl by bearing sons." In ancient China, as in most traditional societies, gender roles were strictly demarcated, with loss of honor being the penalty for failing to perform them properly. Being literally out step with her peers as they promenade to the matchmaker's residence may endear Mulan to modern audiences, who tend to put a premium on individuality and quirkiness, but it doesn't bode well for her future in a society that has decided in advance what form her contribution to the common good must take.

No doubt these gender roles strike us today as oppressively rigid, but almost equally foreign to the modern Western mind is the preoccupation with honor and, in particular, how whatever dishonor you suffer as an individual can stain your family as well. If Mulan fails to cultivate the virtues that correspond to her allotted role in her society, she fears that she might just "uproot the family tree," not only because she might fail to find a husband and produce some of those highly sought-after sons, but also because she will disgrace her family name.

But to understand how that works, we need first to look at the significance of family in traditional honor-based cultures and in traditional Chinese thought in particular.

"Protect My People"

Later on the same day as the matchmaker debacle, the Emperor's trusted advisor Chi Fu rides into Mulan's village flanked by two soldiers hoisting dragon banners to recite a proclamation from the emperor. To repel the invasion of the Huns, one man from each family is ordered to report the next day for military service. Why does the Chinese army obtain its conscripts in this way, requiring each *family* to contribute one man, rather than just round up all the able-bodied men of a certain age?

In the modern West, we tend to think of the individual as the basic unit of society – or at least of a *just* society. It's as individuals, each with his or her own unique identity, that we're the bearers of rights and duties. So, our draft notices are addressed to individuals, each identified by his or her full proper name. When we cast our ballots in elections, we follow the rule of *one person, one vote*. And when jurists and philosophers in the modern West developed systems of laws and ethics, they were generally predicated on a belief in the inherent dignity of each individual, seen as autonomous, independent, and one of a kind. It has become so natural for us to view ourselves in this way that we may be surprised to learn that these ideas about the sanctity of the individual emerged from a revolution in thought that dates back only a few hundred years. From the perspective of traditional societies like ancient China, this focus on the individual is downright weird,[7] as weird as a pocket-sized, wise-cracking Chinese dragon or a sad-eyed lucky cricket, since everyone knows that a solitary individual doesn't exist. To be human is always to be part of something larger than yourself.

The social psychologist Jonathan Haidt has described how people in East Asian cultures tend to identify themselves primarily in terms of their significant relationships and group affiliations:

> For example, when asked to write twenty statements beginning with the words "I am …," Americans are likely to list their own internal psychological characteristics (happy, outgoing, interested in jazz), whereas East Asians are more likely to list their roles and relationships (a son, a husband, an employee of Fujitsu).[8]

Imagine if Mulan's father, Fa Zhou, had been asked to write 20 such statements. He would surely mention his role as a husband and a father, as well as his distinguished record of service to the emperor as a soldier. And he would also almost certainly mention his ancestors, to whom we see him praying at the lineage temple on his estate, entreating them to *please* help Mulan. The family to which Fa Zhou belongs includes those departed spirits, who are still very much present for him, looking over him and his loved ones in return for his obeisance and the offerings he bestows on them.

What holds that extended family together is the virtue of 孝 (*xiào*) or filial piety, the respect owed to parents, elders, and ancestors. It's a cornerstone of traditional Chinese ethics. Fa Zhou's entire identity is bound up with that rich network of familial relationships. He's the product of a society whose basic building blocks are not solitary individuals, as in the modern West, but extended families bound together by mutual obligations. And it's on these families, rather than on isolated individuals, that the duty to defend against the Huns falls. Since one always acts as a member of this larger group, one's actions reflect on the group.

This way of thinking about the self is graphically represented in the Chinese character that signifies the acme of human goodness, 仁 (*rén*). Being the virtue of the truly humane person who cares for others in the right way, 仁 (*rén*) combines the character for human being, 人 (also pronounced *rén*), with a character meaning two or another, 二 (*èr*), indicating that human beings can achieve the moral perfection proper to us only by fostering the right kind of relationships with others. 仁 (*rén*) emphasizes that we are *not* individuals first and foremost, possessing the same generic rights as everyone else, but rather members of larger groups – families, army units, nations – that prescribe duties to each of us that correspond to our assigned roles and relationships to others in the group.

Because we all have different roles to play, equality is not the norm. The Emperor of China demands obedience from his subjects, Li Shang from his troops, and Fa Zhou and Fa Li from their child. But superiors also have duties to those who are in their care. The Emperor brushes away the suggestion that troops should be deployed to protect his palace from the Huns, ordering General Li instead to "send your troops to protect my people"; Li Shang takes seriously his duty to turn his rag-tag batch of recruits into a formidable fighting force, as challenging as that task proves to be given what he has to work with; and Mulan's father and mother love her deeply and have been doing all they can to ensure a good future for her as a bride, as unpromising as her prospects seem to be. These are all instances of 仁 (*rén*), a remarkably protean virtue since its form varies depending on the position or rank of the person exercising it. But whatever form it takes, its function is always to bind people together to form larger wholes that can provide their lives with meaning and direction. And a sense of honor is crucial to making the system work.

"Mulan, You Dishonor Me"

Let's return to the scene with Chi-Fu reciting the Emperor's proclamation. As Chi-Fu calls out the name of each family in the village, one male family member steps forward and proudly accepts the recruitment notice. Hearing his own family name called, Mulan's father bravely sets his crutch aside and marches up to receive his notice, gamely trying to hide a limp that may very well be from an injury he suffered during his earlier military service. One gets the impression that Fa Zhou would regard it as dishonorable to plead disability as a reason to be exempted from the draft. "I am ready to serve the emperor," he solemnly declares. But Mulan, who has been watching clandestinely, will hear nothing of it. She darts out from her hiding place and thrusts herself between her father and Chi-Fu, crying, "Father, you can't go!" "Please, sir, my father has already fought bravely," she entreats Chi-Fu, but he cuts her off, demanding her silence and admonishing Fa Zhou to teach his daughter to "hold her tongue in a man's presence." Fa Zhou is traditional enough to sympathize with Chi-Fu's indignation at the impropriety of Mulan's outburst. "Mulan, you dishonor me," he softly groans as he turns his face away from her.

Honor becomes a topic of discussion at the dinner table that evening, as Mulan once again speaks out of turn, failing to show the deference to elders required by 孝 (*xiào*), filial piety. Angrily slamming her tea cup down on the table, she bolts up out of her chair and begins to remonstrate with her father. Quiet and demure – hardly!

MULAN: You shouldn't have to go! … There are plenty of young men to fight for China!
FA ZHOU: It is an honor to protect my country and my family.
MULAN: So, you'll *die* for honor.
FA ZHOU: I will die doing what's right. […] I know my place. It is time you learned yours.

Honor demands that Fa Zhou not only know his place and submit to his superiors, but that he come to see the value of his own life as negligible compared to the overriding good of protecting his country and family, the two larger wholes it is his duty to serve. His sense of honor ennobles and gives meaning to his existence by pressing it into the service of a greater good. But there's a downside, as Mulan hastens to point out – it's likely to get him killed.

Mulan is equal parts furious and grief-stricken when her father resigns himself to the prospect of dying for honor, but honorable conduct isn't something entirely foreign to Mulan, both the Mulan of legend and the Disney version. After all, she displays the same honorable willingness to sacrifice herself when she dons her father's armor and rides off in the night to take his place at the army camp, risking her life to save his. It's her courage and self-sacrifice that made Mulan a folk hero to countless generations of Chinese admirers, an exemplar of honorable conduct, even if it's not the sort of conduct ordinarily associated with Chinese womanhood. We see Mulan honorably throw herself into the path of danger on the battlefield and save the life of her commanding officer, among other heroic deeds.

And when, after an adoring multitude prostrates itself before her in reverence and gratitude outside the Emperor's palace, she at last returns home bearing "gifts to honor the Fa family," the sword of the Hun chieftain Shan-Yu and the Crest of the Emperor, she is followed by a handsome suitor. There can be little doubt that she has brought considerable honor to her family, despite the matchmaker's shrill prediction to the contrary. We learn that the chorus in the opening musical number was wrong when it declared: "A girl can bring her family / Great honor in one way / By striking a good match ..." Mulan has indeed struck a good match, but she's also brought her family great honor in a way that would normally be barred to someone like her – through her spectacular military success in the war against the Huns.

"What Do You Mean You're Not Lucky?"

The idea of Mulan bringing honor or disgrace to her family through her actions, either matrimonial or military, is hard to square with the individualistic assumptions of modern Western thought, which leads to the belief that we can be blamed or praised only for actions we *ourselves* have personally performed. How can one person's actions honor or dishonor someone else? Why should Fa Zhou and Fa Li bask in the glory of Mulan's accomplishments? And what if things had gone differently? What if, after Mulan's ruse had been discovered and she had been sent home in disgrace, she had not had the opportunity to redeem herself by saving China? Would "Fa Zhou [...] be forever shamed" and would "dishonor [...] come to the family," as forecasted by one of the ancestors?

That events took a different turn is fortunate for Mulan and her family honor, but it also tells us something else about honor cultures that may not sit well with our modern Western moral sensibilities – namely, that whether your actions bring you (or your family) honor or shame may sometimes depend, at least in part, on the fickle nature of *luck*.[9] In an early scene, Mulan's mother, Fa Li, reports that she's been praying to the ancestors to bring her daughter some much needed luck when she meets with the matchmaker. Grandmother Fa, who's skeptical that those who bear the misfortune of being dead could possibly bring luck to the living, suggests that Mulan might be better off trusting her fate to the lucky cricket Cri-Kee. Neither Cri-Kee nor the ancestors come through for Mulan with the matchmaker – indeed, the honor-decimating fiasco was largely Cri-Kee's fault – though, in due course, the ancestors do end up sending Mulan some luck in the form of Mushu, who proves himself useful once or twice, and even Cri-Kee plays a decisive role in helping Mulan to defeat Shan Yu.

That family honor should depend on something as capricious as luck is yet another way in which traditional honor cultures run afoul of modern assumptions. Rightly or wrongly, modern philosophers, legal theorists, and even ordinary people generally agree that we can be neither praised nor blamed for things outside our control. It's not Mulan's fault that Cri-Kee leaped into the teacup and then down the matchmaker's blouse, and it's certainly no reflection on Fa Zhou and Fa Li that their daughter suffered the misfortune of being saddled with a cricket who turned out to be the opposite of lucky. Yet, as philosopher Tamler Sommers notes, "In honor cultures, you can be blamed for actions that weren't intentional, for actions committed by relatives, ancestors, or other members of your group."[10] The strong identification with the group found in such cultures tends to underwrite a powerful sense of collective responsibility. But Disney's *Mulan* points to an alternative conception of the self and its relationship to institutional roles, one that we in the individualistic West are likely to find much more agreeable.

"Who is that Girl I See?"

In the traditional legend of Mulan, Mulan's motivation for joining the army was completely in line with traditional Chinese values, even if the ruse she employed was not. She sought to protect her father, which makes her a model of 孝 (*xiào*), filial piety, and her devotion to defeating the enemies of China underscores her loyalty to the Emperor and the nation. But Disney's Mulan confesses to a different motivation, one quite foreign to traditional Chinese culture, since it implicitly rejects many of the assumptions about self and society on which that honor culture rests. Exposed as a woman and abandoned by her former comrades, Mulan sits despondently in the snow, huddled in a blanket and openly ruing her decision to leave home. Mushu attempts to console her, albeit quite artlessly.

MUSHU: Hey, come on. You went to save your father's life. Who knew you'd end up shaming him, disgracing your ancestors, and losing all your friends? [...]

MULAN: Maybe I didn't go for my father. Maybe what I really wanted was to prove that I could do things right. So, that when I looked in the mirror, I'd see someone worthwhile.

The reference to viewing herself in the mirror harks back to another low moment for Mulan, when she returned from her humiliating meeting with the matchmaker. Having been told she would never bring honor to her family, a mortified Mulan slinks through the gate of her family's estate, still wearing her makeup and elegant costume. She ducks behind her horse Kahn when she sees her father, so his eyes won't fall upon her shame. But she's not afraid to look at herself, perhaps because she doesn't recognize her outward appearance as who she really is.

After leading Kahn into his corral, she gazes at her own reflection in the trough and begins singing the wistful song "Reflection": "Look at me / I will never pass for a perfect bride or a perfect daughter / Can it be I'm not meant to play this part?" As she sings these lines, she slowly removes her jewelry and gazes off in the distance to spy her parents, their heads hung low. Sorrow floods over her. But as she continues singing, we learn that her regret is twofold – she's pained at having disappointed her parents, but no less at the necessity of performing a social role that she feels is false, that doesn't truly reflect who she is inside. "Now I see that if were truly to be myself, / I would break my family's heart" Crossing a footbridge, she executes a graceful but tomboyish leap onto one of its railings, skipping briefly from post to post as she sings "truly to be myself." This agile but unladylike move makes it clear that at least part of the reason her "true self" is such a poor fit with her society's expectations has to do with its stifling gender roles. As she continues past the pond that lies at the base of the path leading up to the family's lineage temple, her reflection again appears in its waters. She then proceeds up the hill. "Who is that girl I see, staring straight back at me? / Why is my reflection someone I don't know?" Her "reflection" is her outward self-presentation, but it's a façade or a mask, a costume she dons to conform to the expectations of others. As such, it's alien to who she really is.

Multiple reflections appear as she enters the lineage temple, mirrored on each of the shiny surfaces of the ancestors' headstones. It is a felicitous mise en scène, underscoring the idea that these images do not reflect Mulan's "true self," but rather expectations handed down from the (dead) past. Prostrating herself before one of the stones in a properly filial manner, she finishes the song. "Somehow, I cannot hide / Who I am, though I've tried / When will my reflection show who I am inside?" As the song concludes, she uses the sleeve of her garment to wipe away her white makeup, a symbolic abandonment of the disguise behind which oppressive social expectations had required her to hide. Multiple images of her unadorned face reflect back from the gravestones in all their nakedness and melancholy yearning.

It's a beautiful song, accompanied by stunning images, and it's no doubt highly relatable to many young people, including or especially those who are gender non-conforming.[11] Given Mulan's later efforts to disguise herself as a man, it's interesting that the theme of this song, as well as many of the early scenes of the movie leading up to it, is the painful experience of trying to pass yourself off as something you're not – and failing miserably at it. If we are to believe Mulan's confession to Mushu, she joins the army not just – or even primarily – for her father, but out of a need to give expression to the yearnings of her authentic self, which traditional Chinese culture with its rigidly defined social roles requires her to suppress. Her unique potential lies within her, independent of her family or her lucky or unlucky external circumstances. It beckons her to an adventure of self-discovery, in which the greatest danger is self-betrayal by succumbing to the pressures of outward conformity or by looking outside herself for models of how to live. And the plaintive question Mulan poses at the end of the song – "When will my reflection show who I am inside?" – points to her need not just to discover and express her authentic self, but to have it recognized and affirmed by others, for, despite everything, we're still social creatures who need to have our worth validated by those around us.

"Your Heart Knows"

These are sentiments that most of us in the modern West would applaud, which is surely a big part of the reason Disney's *Mulan* was such a box office success *outside* of China. But Mulan is an ancient Chinese woman, the product of a society in which one's filial relationships and assigned social roles comprise the most essential parts of one's identity. There's something jarringly anachronistic about this ancient Chinese woman treating those roles and relationships as not only inessential to who she is, but indeed even as roadblocks to self-discovery. In the song that accompanies the closing credits of *Mulan*, Stevie Wonder gets to the crux of the matter for those who hold the Romantic view of the self that emerged in the modern West as the antithesis of the tradition against which Mulan rebels. "Your heart knows what's good for you," he sings, so "let your heart show you the way," trusting in "what feels so right," rather than external authorities.[12] Ignore the promptings of your heart and imitate others at your own peril.

I began and finished work on this chapter while in China, which gave me the opportunity to discuss *Mulan* with a number of Chinese students. What I discovered may be telling. It turns out that this same movie that was a box office bomb twenty years ago has found a much more appreciative audience among the current generation of Chinese youth, a sign perhaps that our Western ideas of selfhood are going global. Whether this development is a good or a bad thing may depend on whether we believe our individualistic conception of selfhood reflects what human beings really are, as opposed to being just a weird outlook of the modern West that, like the Huns of *Mulan*, has scaled the Great Wall of China with global conquest in its heart.[13]

Notes

1. For a good introduction to the sources and history of the legend of Mulan, see Kwai, S. (ed.) (2010). *Mulan: Five Versions of a Classic Chinese Legend, With Related Texts*, xi–xxxii. Indianapolis: Hackett Publishing Company.

2. The Mulan of Chinese legend had an actual little brother, too young to take his father's place in the army. In what may be a nod to that legend, Disney has given Mulan a canine Little Brother.
3. "Reflection," music Matthew Wilder, lyrics David Zippel, 1998.
4. "Honor to Us All," music Matthew Wilder, lyrics David Zippel, 1998.
5. Its melody also accompanies the opening credits.
6. "Make a Man Out of You," music Matthew Wilder, lyrics David Zippel, 1998.
7. Social psychologists have coined the acronym WEIRD to describe subjects from societies that are Western, Educated, Industrialized, Rich, and Democratic. It turns out that the psychology of such subjects – people like me and most likely you as well if you're reading this book – really is weird compared to the rest of the world, especially when it comes to how we think about the self. See Haidt, J. (2013). *The Righteous Mind: Why Good People Are Divided by Politics and Religion*, 112–114. New York: Vintage Books.
8. Haidt, 113.
9. For an excellent collection of essays on the relationship of luck to ethics, see Statman, D. (ed.) (1999). *Moral Luck*. Albany: State University of New York Press.
10. Sommers, T. (2018). *Why Honor Matters*, 6. New York: Basic Books.
11. Some commentators suspect a LGBT subtext in this song's theme of hiding who you really are, a suspicion that gains some support from Mulan's subsequent cross-dressing (not to mention how her plan to save the Emperor involved the cross-dressing of her trio of male comrades), though there is no other evidence that Mulan is anything but straight. In ABC-Disney's television series *Once Upon a Time*, however, Mulan is bisexual, in love with *Sleeping Beauty* princess Aurora. This theme points to another problem with traditional honor cultures – with few exceptions, they don't make a place for LGBT people.
12. "True to Yourself," music Matthew Wilder, lyrics David Zippel, 1998.
13. In the modern West, most of us believe our desires to be authentically our own, but the social theorist René Girard (1923–2015) has argued that even today society retains a deep hold on our longings. Though we imagine our desires springing up spontaneously from some mysterious place deep within, their true source is often unacknowledged envy of others. See Girard, R. (1966). *Deceit, Desire and the Novel: Self and Other in Literary Structure*. Baltimore: Johns Hopkins University Press.

3

Zen and the Art of Imagineering

Disney's Escapism Versus Buddhism's Liberation

Steve Bein

Syndrome, that self-styled nemesis of Mr. Incredible, has a retirement plan worthy of Walt Disney himself. Both he and Disney created products that just about everyone in the world wants to have. While Disney sold escapism and wonder, Syndrome wants to sell super powers. As he famously quipped, "Everyone can be super. And when everyone's super, no one will be."

Strangely enough, Syndrome's decree lines up with a basic tenet of Zen Buddhism. Zen says all beings possess something called "buddha-nature," the intrinsic potential to become a buddha – that is, an enlightened being, a paragon of wisdom and compassion. Zen says enlightenment is latent in buddha-nature itself, so in effect everyone *is* super. The trick is just figuring out how that's true.

Obviously that's not what Syndrome had in mind. Originally his decree was probably just a commentary about the modern parenting ideal that every child is equally special. (*The Incredibles* itself is the extended commentary.) But the keen philosophical ear detects a deeper message, one that resonates in so many of Disney's most enduring films. It's the dream that any kid can be a hero. One trait many Disney heroes have in common is that they're children, and whether they're royalty or just ordinary schmoes, they don't really get to be heroes until they escape the fetters of adult supervision. (Sane parents don't allow their children to sail off alone to Te Fiti or shack up in the woods with seven short-statured strangers.) The characters resonate

Disney and Philosophy: Truth, Trust, and a Little Bit of Pixie Dust, First Edition.
Edited by Richard B. Davis.

especially well with children because all of us dreamed – and some of us still do – of what epic adventures we'd have if only we weren't held back by all the adults.

This, too, bears a certain similarity to a fundamental teaching of Zen Buddhism. Zen advocates returning to a childlike state of mind, unburdened by the conceptual baggage that marks what we typically call "adult" and "mature" thinking – baggage that includes concepts of the self, of the future, and of hoarding worldly goods so your future self will live comfortably. Just as Mulan and Moana become heroes only after escaping the constraints placed on them by adults, so the childlike mind has its best chance to understand buddha-nature only after freeing itself of worldly assumptions.

Disney says, "Hey, kid, you can be a hero," while Zen says, "Hey, kid, you can be a buddha." But though they might not seem that way, those two maxims are actually direct opposites of one another. Escapism is the very opposite of liberation. To see how that's true – and to see why you might prefer one over the other – let's begin with a Zen master whose own life story is worthy of a Disney movie. His name is Dōgen Kigen.

When You Wish upon a Bodhi Tree

Like Elsa, Ariel, and Tarzan, Dōgen was of noble birth. (The year was 1200, and he was born near Kyoto, Japan. His parents were aristocrats with links to the Imperial house.) Like Bambi, Cinderella, and Belle, he lost his mother at a young age. (That was c. 1208,[1] and legend has it he got his first inkling of the impermanence of all things while watching the smoke rise from the incense at her funeral.) Like Wall·E and Moana, he boarded a ship on an epic voyage that would ultimately reshape the history of his homeland. Unlike any of those characters, you can't buy pajamas with Dōgen's face on them, but like them, he did inspire some catchy tunes. (He was an accomplished poet, and various musicians have put his poems to song.)

If we wanted to tell the story of Dōgen as a Disney character, we'd start with his fateful choice at the tender age of 12 or 13: he had to decide whether to become the wealthy heir of his aristocratic uncle or to fulfill his mother's dying wish and become a monk. Then we'd take Dōgen through his formative years in the monastery, where he might break into a musical number about the people he saw violating their monastic vows. He'd sing about the monks who, after taking their vow of poverty, built secret cubbyholes in the walls to hide their riches. Then comes a verse about the vow of nonviolence, and the private armies that some of these monasteries mustered to defend their growing wealth. Then a verse about the vow of temperance, and about the debauchery and drunkenness and even orgies Dōgen saw in the temples. (On second thought, to keep our movie rated G maybe we'll leave out the orgies.)

The musical number would end with a dramatic verse about wanting to seek out the Buddha's teachings as they were really meant to be. So after he sings his big solo, young Dōgen joins a Zen temple that emphasizes seated meditation, following the practice of the historical Buddha himself.[2] In this temple he meets the Raffiki of our movie, a wizened Zen master named Myōzen who tells him he'll find what he seeks in China. Braving storms that would challenge even Moana and Maui, Dōgen and Myōzen cross the sea together, and Dōgen ultimately comes to study at the feet of another great Zen master named Rujing. In our movie it will be Rujing who opens young Dōgen's eyes to what Buddhism is really all about.

Let's start with the basics. The Buddha said everything in existence has three qualities in common: it's *empty*, it's *impermanent*, and it's *frustrating*. These are the so-called Three Marks of Existence, and Mickey Mouse himself happens to be a perfect illustration of them.

Mickey became famous in *Steamboat Willie*, the first of Walt Disney's cartoons to feature synchronized sound. Mickey[3] spends most of his time making music. In the opening sequence he's whistling to himself, and by the end he and his girlfriend Minnie play music by tormenting various farm animals. (We might interpret this as the first instance of Disney's animal abuse, presaging the infamous incident with the lemmings.) But of course we know Mickey himself makes no sound at all. His whistling is just an illusion; the whistles come from a speaker, not the black-and-white figure on the screen. Even that figure is just an illusion. He looks like he's tapping his foot and whistling, but in fact he never moves at all. There isn't even a *he*; there's only a series of images, each one perfectly still, run through a projector so fast that there appears to be a mouse rocking out on a steamboat.

The Buddha says you're just like Mickey. What we think of as *you* is really just a bundle of mental and physical processes, not so different from still images running past a projector bulb, except that yours are a lot more complex and they change a lot faster than twenty-four frames per second.[4] Neither your molecules nor your thoughts are the exactly same as they were when you opened this book. Memories don't stay constant either – if they did, you'd never forget anything – and as for a soul or spirit that lives in the body and goes somewhere after death, the Buddha said he looked for one but couldn't find it. He thinks this is good news; if you don't have one of these things, you don't have to worry about taking care of it.

Now notice two important facts about you and Mickey, according to this view. First, you're *empty*. There's no self, no unchanging core that all of these ever-changing processes happen to; you yourself are nothing other than the processes all bundled together. Second, you're *impermanent*. In fact, you're so impermanent that the you who started reading this sentence is already gone by the time you finish it. A little while ago, there was a you who began reading this paragraph in what was then the present moment. That you is gone, just as that moment is gone; they exist now only as memories of the current you. Except – *whoops!* – now we've lost that you too. Dead and gone.

Depressed yet? It gets worse. Because everything you love in this world is just as empty and impermanent as you are. And for that reason, everything is *frustrating*. It's all *duḥkha*, to use the Sanskrit term, which is sometimes translated as *suffering*. Our lives are frustrating through and through, because even the most supercalifragilisticexpialidocious parts still don't last. According to the Buddha, everything that exists is characterized by these three marks of existence – emptiness, impermanence, and frustration – and until we make peace with that fact, we're bound to be miserable.

Under the Sea or Part of your World?

So how *do* you make peace with that? One really popular approach is to just pretend it isn't true. That's what the drunken bacchanals in the monasteries were for. If that's not your style, you could try … well, pretty much everything the Walt Disney Company sticks its label on. Movies, toys, theme parks, video games, entire TV channels, all perfectly calibrated for you to distract yourself from the here and now.

We can't single out Disney, of course. The fact is, day-to-day living in the modern world is mostly directed at seeking temporary distractions from the present moment. Disney is just one storefront in the distraction mega-mall. There's more to be said on this later, but for now let's just note that keeping yourself distracted from the here and now isn't just a twenty-first century pastime; Dōgen saw plenty of it in his day too.

He sailed to China to get away from it, and there, under Rujing's tutelage, he devoted himself day and night to seated meditation. This, he says, is the key to making peace with the empty, impermanent, frustrating nature of everything: you look right at it, you accept it for what it is, and you stop wanting it to be different. The problem isn't that you're impermanent, it's that you don't want to be. So you can either satisfy that want (by becoming immortal) or stop wanting it (which is a whole lot easier by comparison).

Ditto for those other two marks of existence, emptiness and frustration. It's perfectly natural to want an independent, blissful existence, just as it's natural to want that existence to endure indefinitely. But that's about as practical as wanting to become a mermaid. It's a pleasant fantasy, but by clinging to such fantasies you only set yourself up for disappointment. In Disney's version of *The Little Mermaid*, Ariel gets off light; in the original fairy tale from Hans Christian Andersen, her new human feet bleed terribly. She's doomed to feel like she's walking on knives for the rest of her life. She doesn't even get to marry her prince.

Dōgen would say Ariel ought to listen to her little crustacean buddy, Sebastian. Instead of wishing to be part of another world, accept the world you're in. It sounds paradoxical, but by embracing the idea that everything's frustrating, you're less likely to feel frustrated. (Maybe you've had this experience. If I go to the Department of Motor Vehicles expecting it'll take forever, I'm pleasantly surprised when it only takes 10 minutes. If I go expecting I'll get out lickety-split, 10 minutes feels like forever.) Similarly, by accepting that everything is impermanent, you're better able to make the most of every moment. And by accepting that nothing has independent existence, you're better at noticing the interdependence and interconnections between everything and everything else.

And that's pretty cool, because when you fully embrace these ideas you arrive at a new understanding of yourself. As a complex bundle of ever-changing processes, you realize that you're inextricably intertwined with the processes of others. For instance, you and I are bound up with each other right now. You've got my words bouncing around in your head, but as I'm choosing these words I've got you, my future reader, foremost in mind. Even Walt Disney and Hans Christian

Andersen are bound up in us, as creators of the ideas we've just been thinking about. The upshot of all of this is that there's a meaningful sense in which I *am* you – or at least part of me is. The rest of me is bound up in all the other people, animals, objects, and ideas I interact with. I'm one with all of it, and so are you.

If that's how you think of yourself, then compassion should come pretty easily to you. You become like Tramp, whose immediate instinct when he sees Lady upset is to make her feel better. Or like Woody and Buzz and the rest of Andy's toys, who think nothing of self-sacrifice so long as they can make their boy happy. In a moment like that, a moment of perfect selflessness, you may catch your first glimpse of your own buddha-nature. Hey kid, you can be a buddha.

Dōgen says that if you spend long enough in this mode of selfless awareness, a couple of things become clear. First, acquiring more stuff doesn't really make people happier. Second, being attached to your *you* is just as toxic as being attached to your stuff. In fact, those two things are closely connected. It's a short leap from "you" to "yours" – that is, from *self* to *property* – and once we start thinking in terms of "mine" and "yours" we invite misery. On the smallest scale it's picking someone's pocket; on the largest scale it's conquering someone's country.

Dōgen said the best way to protect yourself from robbers is to simply not own anything, and the best way to protect yourself from murderers is to not mind being killed.[5] This is the ultimate liberation: to shed all sense of self and fully grasp your interconnected interdependence with all things. If you can do that, you realize your buddha-nature and *voilà*, you're a buddha. And if you can do *that*, then you can lead a life like one of Disney's most recent acquisitions: Yoda.

May the Cash Be with You

Yoda, shortest and coolest of all the Jedi Masters, was originally a Buddhist master. His home planet, Dagobah, is named for a type of Buddhist shrine called a pagoda, the Tibetan spelling for which is *dagoba*. (Yoda's creator, George Lucas, was on an eastern philosophy kick while he was writing *The Empire Strikes Back*.) When we first encounter Yoda, he lives a life of peace and contentment on his planet-sized pagoda, as far from the materialistic life as he can possibly get. He's quite impish, even childish, for he's overthrown many of those "mature," "adult" assumptions that everyone else in the movie takes as bedrock. (He tries to pass the childlike mind on to Luke Skywalker: "Unlearn what you have learned.") Yoda has no interest in political power or material things, just as Dōgen himself claimed to have no interest in them; when he returned to Japan Dōgen ultimately founded his temple deep in the mountains.[6] The great irony of Yoda's life is that he's quite literally the puppet of people who used him to make billions of dollars.

Lucas caught lightning in a bottle with *Star Wars*, but his real genius lay in merchandising. Star Wars films smashed one box office record after the next, but it's toys, not tickets, that created the world's most valuable movie franchise. Toy sales have roughly doubled ticket sales, and that's to say nothing of the other merch, everything from area rugs to zipper-lock bags. All told, for every dollar generated at the box office there's another four dollars in sales of Star Wars loot.[7] To a company like Disney this ratio made a lot of sense – it too built an empire on its brand, not just its film studio – and so in 2012 it bought Lucasfilm for just over $4 billion. That drew a giant collective incredulous gasp at the time, but Disney had a plan: make Star Wars an annual event. No more three-year waits between films; Disney's ambition was to make one or two Star Wars movies every year. And it's working. By 2017 the new Star Wars movies had already surpassed $4 billion in ticket sales alone.

This was no wish upon a star. Disney simply applied its time-tested formula: if it makes money, make a sequel. Almost all of Disney's animated films get a sequel or two. Some of these make it to the big screen, but there are dozens more that even many diehard Disney fans have never heard of. These aren't big-budget films but the direct-to-video efforts of Walt Disney Studios Home Entertainment. They're produced quickly and on the cheap, and audiences aren't fooled. They know the difference between a *Toy Story 3* and a *Cinderella III*. (Wait, there's a *Cinderella III*?) But the filmmakers aren't *trying* to fool the audience. Everyone's in on the scheme: it's a cash grab, plain and simple, but if it keeps the audience entertained everyone's happy.

This, of course, is the opposite of everything a countercultural minimalist like Yoda stands for. He's more a Baloo sort of guy, seeking contentment in the bare necessities. Dōgen agrees with Yoda and Baloo. In fact, he said money is akin to poison, and he once praised a wealthy Chinese layman for throwing all his riches into the sea. When asked why he didn't give everything to the poor, the man said, "I threw it all away because I knew it was harmful. Why would I give something to another person if I knew it to be harmful?"[8]

Compare this attitude to the mission statement of the Walt Disney Company: "to be one of the world's leading producers and providers of entertainment and information." Dōgen would object to every part of that. Being a producer and provider of entertainment is already objectionable, if the primary function of such entertainment is to distract people from more important concerns. Being one of the world's *leading* producers is even worse; the goal should be detachment from self, not self-aggrandizement through victory in the marketplace. Put another way, the ideal goal is to be "at one with," not to be number one.

Now maybe all of this sounds high-minded to you. Maybe you're thinking Dōgen would have made a really bad capitalist. I'd agree with you on both counts. But as a counterpoint I'd ask what we the audience might think of a Disney character whose behavior was modeled on the marketplace behavior of the Walt Disney Company. Being the biggest wouldn't be enough; the character's central motivation would be to *keep getting bigger*. It wouldn't be content to grow by its own efforts; it would seek out other characters to gobble up. The character does this over and over, no matter how big it gets.[9]

It's not hard to imagine such a character, but it's impossible to cast this character as the *hero*. More like the White Witch banishing spring, summer, and fall from Narnia, plunging all the realm into the Long Winter. Or perhaps this character isn't evil at all, but rather an amoral force, like Te Kā blighting one island after the next. He doesn't consume them because he's wicked; it's just in his nature. His heart's been stolen.

Even so, it's awfully hard to root for him.

Hakuna Matata, Bodhisattva

Perhaps you want to say that while Dōgen's idealism may be admirable, it's just not practical in the twenty-first century. Who has the luxury to sit around and meditate anymore? We have bills to pay. Bosses to please. Clients or customers to satisfy, or else risk their wrath in online reviews. Try telling your boss you have no intention to be the best because striving to outdo the competition just builds attachment to self. See if that gets you the promotion you were hoping for.

Such objections were just as relevant in Dōgen's day. Remember, he was faced with the same choice himself: become rich and powerful or become a monk. The life of luxury was just as glamorous back then as it is today. But I choose the word *glamorous* carefully: it derives from the root word *glamer*, a magical spell meant to deceive. Wealth and power promise happiness, but the promise is empty. If it weren't, then we wouldn't be able to find any examples of people who are wealthy or powerful and also unhappy. But of course the world is full of such examples, so Dōgen would have us ask why.

Here's a possible answer: if you return to the childlike mind, you understand wealth and power as mere distractions. Trying to enrich yourself or empower yourself is doomed to failure if you don't actually have a self. Remember, there's no *yours* without *you*, so if your *you* is really just a set of turbulent, ever-changing, interconnected processes, then so are any traits it could possess. Affluence and influence are just as frustrating as everything else.

The truth is, fantasizing about being better off is just another form of escapism, the kind Disney sells so expertly. And like all forms of escapism, the rewards are just imaginary. Sure, kid, you can be a hero, but the highest flights of heroic fantasy still come to an end. Emptiness, impermanence, and frustration will always be waiting for you when you come back down to the here and now.

Dōgen chose the monastic path because he wanted the opposite of escape: liberation. If the three marks of existence are the problem, the solution isn't to flee them. Rather, it's to make peace with them. If you can do that, maybe you can even reach a deeper level of insight: they were never the problem in the first place. They're just so. The only real problem is that we wish they weren't so. If you can stop wishing that, they don't bother you anymore. You're liberated. Hakuna matata for the rest of your days.

That's not to say the path of Zen is easy. Quite the contrary: it took the Buddha three uninterrupted years to get it right. But maybe we can forgive Timon and Pumbaa for making it sound too simple. After all, they were singing about excessive flatulence, not liberation writ large. But the heart of the path of Zen is in their song, if we're mindful enough to hear it. If you want no worries for the rest of your days, you've got two choices. Turning your attention inward, you can notice that worry is a subjective response, not an objective fact, and bit by bit you can recondition that response. By returning to the childlike mind you can come to terms with the three marks of existence, thereby liberating yourself from them. Or, turning your attention outward, you can try to escape the three marks of existence, and with them you escape everything in life that might cause you to worry. I think I speak for Dōgen when I say good luck with that.[10]

Notes

1. Scholars disagree on the exact dates in his life. We don't even know his name at birth; Dōgen Kigen is his monastic name, the name he took on when he first shaved his head and entered the monastery.
2. Siddhartha Gautama, whose biography is subject to much more debate than we can handle in a footnote. For our purposes I'll just note that traditionally he's said to have been an Indian prince whose dates are around 563–483 BCE, though modern scholars say all of that is almost certainly wrong. But historians agree that he was a real guy, and Buddhist tradition has held from the beginning that he sat for three years under what's now called the Bodhi Tree, the Tree of Enlightenment.
3. Fun fact: Steamboat Willie is his nickname. The movie is a parody of Buster Keaton's *Steamboat Bill, Jr.*
4. In fact they're said to change thousands of times per second. If you want to read more about them – or about anything else in the basics of Buddhism – an accessible introduction is Rahula, W. (1959). What the Buddha Taught. New York: Grove Press.
5. *Shōbōgenzō Zuimonki* 3.4, translated into English by Reihō Masunaga as *A Primer of Sōtō Zen* (Honolulu: University of Hawaii Press, 1971).
6. I say "claimed" because there's reason to believe he didn't have much choice in the matter. He tried founding his temple in the capital city of Kyoto, and when that failed he chose instead to accept the mountainous land donated to him by a student.
7. This according to *Forbes* (Aswath Damodaran, "Intergalactic Finance: Why The Star Wars Franchise Is Worth Nearly $10 Billion To Disney" [January 6, 2016]).
8. Dōgen recounts this story in *Shōbōgenzō Zuimonki* 3.11. The passage here is quoted from Bein, S. (2011). *Purifying Zen: Watsuji Tetsurō's* Shamon Dōgen, 80. Honolulu: University of Hawaii Press.
9. The Star Wars acquisition was hardly a unique occurrence. Disney also bought Marvel Entertainment and most of 21st Century Fox. That means one company – Disney – now owns about one-third of the entire film industry. With Fox it also acquired a majority share of Hulu. As of this writing, plans are underway to pull its content from all other online streaming services, re-releasing its family-friendly material on a new Disney streaming service and its edgier stuff (e.g. *Deadpool*) on Hulu.
10. Thanks to Jared and Chrissa McPherson for their help in conceptualizing this chapter, and to Kalyn and Audrey Embry for their invaluable work as research assistants.

Hidden Mickeys and the Hiddenness of God

Robert K. Garcia and Timothy Pickavance

Professional Hidden Mickey hunter Steven Barrett says that a Hidden Mickey is "a partial or complete image of Mickey Mouse that has been hidden by Disney's Imagineers and artists in the designs of Disney attractions, hotels, restaurants, and other areas."[1] Usually, Hidden Mickeys take the iconic shape of Mickey Mouse's head: one larger circle representing Mickey's face capped by two smaller circles representing his ears. The hiddenness of God, on the other hand, is the fact that, even if God exists, sometimes God *seems* distant, absent, or even non-existent. As we'll see, Hidden Mickeys can help us come to terms with the hiddenness of God.

Emphatic Silence: the Experience of Divine Hiddenness

Believers in a personal, loving God struggle with God's seeming absence from their lives, with God's silence, with what is sometimes called God's "hiddenness." This doesn't square with how we expect a loving, personal God to relate to us. When someone loves us, we expect them to be present and available to us, to care for us; in short, we expect those who love us to be available to us when there is nothing keeping them away. God, we are told, loves us more than we can imagine, and God cannot be hindered in the ways ordinary humans can. So it seems that

Disney and Philosophy: Truth, Trust, and a Little Bit of Pixie Dust, First Edition.
Edited by Richard B. Davis.

there is nothing to prevent God from being personally present to us. Thus, when God seems absent or distant or unloving toward us, our expectations are violated. We are left wondering whether God really does love us, and sometimes whether God exists at all.

God's hiddenness has plagued even the most devout believers. Mother Teresa (1910–1997), for example, lived through a decades-long struggle with God's absence:

> Lord, my God, who am I that You should forsake me? The Child of your Love – and now become as the most hated one – the one – You have thrown away as unwanted – unloved. I call, I cling, I want – and there is no One to answer – no One on Whom I can cling – no, No One. – Alone ... Where is my Faith – even deep down right in there is nothing, but emptiness & darkness – My God – how painful is this unknown pain – I have no Faith – I dare not utter the words & thoughts that crowd in my heart – & make me suffer untold agony. So many unanswered questions live within me afraid to uncover them – because of the blasphemy – If there be God – please forgive me – When I try to raise my thoughts to Heaven – there is such convicting emptiness that those very thoughts return like sharp knives & hurt my very soul. – I am told God loves me – and yet the reality of darkness & coldness & emptiness is so great that nothing touches my soul. Did I make a mistake in surrendering blindly to the Call of the Sacred Heart?[2]

Teresa's experience of God's seeming absence was "untold agony," an "unknown pain" that was dark, cold, and empty. She felt as though God hated her, that she was unwanted and unloved. She longed for God's presence, and expected God to come to her. But God seemed not to care. And so Teresa was left wondering whether there is a God at all.

C. S. Lewis (1898–1963) also wrestled with the hiddenness of God. In *A Grief Observed*, Lewis reflects on the death of his wife, Joy. He recounts God's "silence" in the midst of our loneliness or grief:

> Meanwhile, where is God? This is one of the most disquieting symptoms. When you are happy, so happy that you have no sense of needing Him, so happy that you are tempted to feel His claims upon you as an interruption, if you remember yourself and turn to Him with gratitude and praise, you will be – or so it feels – welcomed with open arms. But go to Him when your need is desperate, when all other help is vain, and what do you find? A door slammed in your face, and a sound of bolting and double bolting on the inside. After that, silence. You may as well turn away. The longer you wait, the more emphatic the silence will become. There are no lights in the windows. It might be an empty house. Was it ever inhabited?[3]

Lewis experienced rejection in the midst of his grief – "A door slammed in [his] face." Where Lewis expected God to meet him and care for him, there was only silence and absence. And this led him to wonder whether God's house was simply empty.

There's a clear common thread. Both Teresa and Lewis sensed an incongruity between their *expectations* about how God would relate to them and their *experience* of God's activity. And both moved from that incongruity to questioning whether God exists. What should we make of this movement? And what do Hidden Mickeys have to do with it?

We hope to show that reflecting on Hidden Mickeys can take us at least part of the way to a solution to the problem of divine hiddenness. Here is the basic idea: it is often ambiguous whether some constellation of shapes is a Hidden Mickey, and similarly, it is often ambiguous whether some experience is an experience of God's presence and love. In order to develop this idea, we'll have to step away from Hidden Mickeys in order to develop the problem of divine hiddenness in a bit more detail. We promise to return to them as soon as possible!

The Argument from Divine Hiddenness

Philosophers have expanded Teresa's and Lewis's type of worry into an argument against the existence of God. J. L. Schellenberg is the most prominent contemporary defender of such an argument. He puts the heart of the hiddenness argument like this:

> Many religious writers, sensitive to the difficulties in which our evidence for God is involved, have held that God would wish (or at any rate, permit) the fact of his existence to be obscure. God, so it is said, is a *hidden* God. But upon reflection, it may well appear otherwise. Why, we may ask, would God be hidden from us? Surely a morally perfect being – good, just, loving – would show himself more clearly. Hence the weakness of our evidence for God is not a sign that God is hidden; it is a revelation that God does not exist.[4]

According to Schellenberg, the fact that God's existence is not more clear violates our expectations of what sort of evidence God would supply regarding his existence. So the fact that God's existence is not rationally mandatory for everyone is actually evidence that a perfectly loving God doesn't exist. Lewis seems to agree: maybe God's house has never been inhabited. Of course there are aspects of Teresa's and

Lewis's experiences and accounts that are left untouched by Schellenberg's argument. But Schellenberg is isolating the properly philosophical concern embedded in those deeply personal reflections. Our discussion, therefore, will focus on Schellenberg's presentation of the hiddenness worry.

It will help to formulate Schellenberg's argument a bit more precisely:

1. If a perfectly loving God exists, then anyone who fails to believe in God is resistant to relationship with God.[5]
2. There are people who fail to believe in God but who aren't resistant to relationship with God.[6]
3. Thus, no perfectly loving God exists.

The first premise (1) contains something new, namely, the idea of being *resistant to relationship with God*. Let's unpack this a bit. The first premise connects the idea of a perfectly loving God to expectations about how God would relate to us. Here's the connection: if God loves us perfectly, then God's existence would be abundantly clear, so clear that only resistance on the part of a creature would prevent her from believing in God's existence. The motivation for this premise is simple reflection on the nature of love. For example, it would be odd to say that a mother loves her son while not making herself relationally available to him. Suppose the son desired a close, personal relationship with his mother. If she loves him, then she would be available to him. If she could help it, she would not remain hidden from him. Of course, if the son chose to reject his mother, she might let him do so. She might remain distant in order to respect his desires. Indeed, that may be an expression of her love for him. But only this kind of resistance to relationship would keep the mother at bay.

We see this dynamic in the timeless stories of the Disney universe. *Finding Nemo*, for example, is a story about Marlin relentlessly pursuing his lost son, Nemo, a pursuit fueled by a father's love. In *Frozen*, Anna, with the help of Kristoff, Sven, and Olaf, pursues Elsa into the mountains because of her love for her sister. There are barriers along the way, obstacles to be overcome. But that's the beauty of the stories! Love drives us to overcome these barriers and obstacles to restore relationships to the kind of intimacy that love requires.

You might notice that we are discussing two interrelated ideas: believing in God's existence and being in a relationship with God. Merely believing that God exists is much weaker than being in a full-blooded personal relationship with God. Believing that God exists, however, is necessary for being in a personal relationship with God. This is true for all relationships. You cannot be in a relationship with another person if you don't believe that person exists. The hiddenness argument uses this idea to strengthen its case against the existence of God. If God really loves us, then God's existence would be absolutely obvious, since love strives for relationship and relationship requires that one knows the other exists. Imagine a mother who says she loves her son, but who avoids letting her son know that she exists. Unless the mother has some excellent reason for hiding, her avoidance seems at odds with her professed love.

When we love one another, we strive for relational intimacy. The same goes for God, according to premise (1). If God is perfectly loving, then God would do anything to be near God's creatures and would therefore create a world that makes God's existence obvious. Merlin of course pursued Nemo, but importantly Nemo *wanted* to be found. Between them, there were barriers that Marlin had to overcome, just like there were barriers Anna had to overcome in her pursuit of Elsa. Unlike Marlin and Anna, however, God cannot be put off by barriers to God's creatures. God is all-powerful, so there is nothing that can keep God away. Well, almost nothing. God respects our desires. So there is *one* reason a creature could fail to be in a relationship with God: the creature's *unwillingness* to be found, the creature's *resistance* to such a relationship.

The second premise (2) asserts that there are people who fail to believe in God while being open to relationship with God. Following Schellenberg, let's call any such person a non-resistant non-believer. Most of us probably know at least one non-resistant non-believer. Maybe you are one yourself! But notice: given the first premise, the existence of a perfectly loving God is incompatible with the existence of a single non-resistant non-believer! The existence of one implies the non-existence of the other. It's all the more striking, then, that so many people seem to be non-resistant non-believers. If God were so loving, why would so many people non-resistantly fail to believe in God?

When Is a Hidden Mickey a Hidden Mickey?

Schellenberg gives a powerful argument. It has plausible premises, and the conclusion clearly follows from those premises. But Hidden Mickeys highlight a potential problem for the first premise. Whether a particular arrangement of shapes is a Hidden Mickey is sometimes ambiguous, and this is at least in part because it is sometimes unclear how that arrangement of shapes came to be.

Here's an example, so you can see what we mean. In Disney Springs, near Disney World, there is a *Once Upon a Toy* store. At the entrance to the store are two pillars made out of what appear to be giant-sized Lincoln Logs: interlocking wooden beams like one would find in a traditional log cabin. Let's suppose we're looking at the right pillar. The log at the top of the pillar is arranged so that the end of the log faces you as you are walking into the store, and sitting atop the log is a yellow toy dump truck. The result of this arrangement is that the end of the log (a large circle), together with the front and back wheels of the truck (two smaller circles) form what many count as a Hidden Mickey. (You might do a Google image search for "Once Upon a Toy store" to see pictures.)

Although many *count* the log-and-truck arrangement as a Hidden Mickey, it's not obvious that it actually *is* a Hidden Mickey. To be a Hidden Mickey, an arrangement of objects or shapes must have been arranged that way to, as it were, hide a Mickey. Hidden Mickeys cannot be produced by accident. Hidden Mickeys must be created *as* Hidden Mickeys. In some cases, it is fairly clear that the arrangement of objects constituting the Hidden Mickey was produced intentionally, that the designer of that Disney artifact meant to hide a Mickey. For example, in the Downtown Disney D Street Store in Anaheim, California, there is a brick wall overlaid with stucco. Part of the stucco is missing, and it is missing in such a way that the brick underneath forms the iconic Mickey head characteristic of Hidden Mickeys. It would be hard to believe, given how meticulously maintained Disney properties are, that the missing stucco happened unintentionally. And if the stucco is missing unintentionally, it would be even harder to believe that it just so happened to be missing in a perfect Mickey shape. The point here is that it is very hard to imagine that this particular arrangement of objects could have come to be without intention on the part of a designer to produce a Hidden Mickey.

By contrast, there are plausible stories to tell about the log-and-truck arrangement that have nothing to do with Hidden Mickeys. Most simply, the log-and-truck arrangement might have resulted from an attempt to decorate the Once Upon a Toy store with toys. The logs serve to frame the door, and adorning them with trucks on top might have seemed a natural, playful, fitting cap for the log pillars. No need for the designers to be thinking about Hidden Mickeys. It is therefore not obvious that the log-and-truck arrangement is a Hidden Mickey.[7]

Relatedly, it's also clear that someone could be well-acquainted with the log-and-truck arrangement and yet fail to believe that it's a Hidden Mickey. There are lots of reasons this might be. There are the points made above. Maybe, for example, the person finds the story according to which the arrangement was just a matter of decorative accident more plausible than the story according to which the arrangement is a Hidden Mickey. But also, the person may not be aware that Hidden Mickeys exist at all. Someone might even lack the relevant concept. Such a person could stare for hours at the log-and-truck arrangement, consider the evidence of their eyes in painstaking detail, with precision and attention, and yet fail to believe there is a Hidden Mickey there. Such a belief is simply unavailable to them because they aren't positioned to even consider the possibility. (Again, this is not equivalent to the claim that no one can reasonably believe that the log-and-truck arrangement is a Hidden Mickey.)

To recap: the log-and-truck arrangement may not even *be* a Hidden Mickey, and the evidence we have doesn't rationally mandate the belief that it *is* a Hidden Mickey. These two points together suggest that sometimes the traces left behind by the intentional actions of agents are ambiguous in two senses. First, sometimes those traces can be mimicked by events in the world brought about by agents without the needed intentions or even by entirely mindless forces. The Lego chaos on the floor of a child's room might have been caused by the child's truncated attempt to organize her Legos, by the family puppy's latest rampage through the child's room, or by an earthquake that caused the child's prized Lego creations to crash from the shelves and shatter into pieces. Second, sometimes we can have all the evidence that is available to be had and still not be rationally required to believe that some trace was left by the intentional activity of an agent (even if the trace was in fact left by such activity). This can happen when we have no insight into the source of the situation in question. Maybe no one is around to speak to about whether the child was organizing her Legos, or whether the puppy got past the baby gate meant to keep him from the child's room, or whether there was an earthquake recently.

We can apply this to the problem of divine hiddenness. Because of the ambiguities noted above, someone might be open to believing that something is a Hidden Mickey and yet might rationally fail to believe that the arrangement of objects they are observing actually is a Hidden Mickey. More generally, you might be open to believing that some situation is the result of an action of an agent with a particular set of intentions, and yet you might rationally fail to believe that the situation is the result of an action of an agent. God's activities in the world are simply activities of a very particular agent. And it shouldn't surprise us that sometimes the activities of other forces in the world, whether other agents or just mindless forces like earthquakes, might leave behind situations of just the sort we would expect to find if God acted in a particular way. A situation can be ambiguous: you could reasonably take it to be the result of a mindless cause and just as reasonably take it to be the result of God's activity. If that is so, then it is possible that someone could be open (that is, not resistant) to believing that God is involved in a particular situation and yet rationally fail to believe that God is involved. Reflecting on Hidden Mickeys helps to sever the connection between openness (non-resistance) to relationship with God and belief in God's existence. It thereby challenges the first premise of the hiddenness argument articulated above.

The Disanalogy Between Hidden Mickeys and Divine Hiddenness

Then again, there is a crucial disanalogy between the problem of divine hiddenness and Hidden Mickeys. We have overwhelming evidence, unrelated to Hidden Mickeys, that intentional agents run the Disney corporation. There is no doubt that the presence of Hidden Mickeys is due to the intentional activities of various people. The hiddenness problem, on the other hand, leaves us doubting the very existence of God, not just whether some situation in the world is the result of God's intentional activity. Hidden Mickeys, therefore, don't take us all the way to a solution to the problem of divine hiddenness.

One way to bridge the divide is to try out the idea that God simply *cannot* make his existence as apparent to us as the Disney corporation can make it apparent that it is run by agents acting intentionally. God isn't like Disney in this way. For some reason God is less accessible to us. Maybe, for instance, the fact that God's activity is ubiquitous means that all of God's actions have the same degree of accessibility to us. Thus, if *any* event can be reasonably seen as not involving divine action, then *every* event can reasonably seen as not involving divine action.

The problem with this avenue is that the major theistic religions all assert both that God's activity is ubiquitous and that God, at least on occasion, makes his existence rather undeniable. Consider the latter. According to Judaism, Moses encountered a burning bush that was not consumed, and so Moses was compelled to believe that God was speaking to him. According to Christianity, Paul encountered the risen Jesus on the road to Damascus and transformed from a persecutor of Jesus-followers to one of their principle leaders. According to Islam, God dictated the Quran to the prophet Muhammad. Thus, according to these religions, the ubiquity of divine action is compatible with special acts being undeniably revelations of God's existence. But if God can do these sorts of things for Moses, Paul, and Muhammad, why would God not do this for the rest of us? The idea that God wouldn't do so is difficult to square with God's love, at least when coupled with God's omnipotence. So, we're right back at the problem of hiddenness.

Might God Be Hidden for Love's Sake?

How might a defender of God's existence respond? One response appeals to facts about the connection between human free will and true love. C. S. Lewis seems to advocate for this sort of idea in *The Screwtape Letters*. Here is the demon Screwtape writing to his understudy Wormwood:

> You [Wormwood] must have often wondered why the Enemy [God] does not make more use of His power to be sensibly present to human souls in any degree He chooses and at any moment. But you now see that the Irresistible and the Indisputable are the two weapons which the very nature of His scheme forbids Him to use. Merely to override a human will (as His felt presence in any but the faintest and most mitigated degree would certainly do) would be for Him useless. He cannot ravish. He can only woo. For His ignoble idea is to eat the cake and have it; the creatures are to be one with Him, but yet themselves…"[8]

Lewis's idea is that God cannot overwhelm people with his existence because doing so would override their freedom. One reason this might be so, according to the Christian tradition from which Lewis is writing, is that God simply *is* love. Thus, an experience of God is an experience of the purest form of love, and this experience would of necessity compel a particular response. But the purest expressions of love are those that are *freely* chosen. So God desires a *free* response. That is, God desires for creatures to freely choose to love him. But to make our free response possible, the traces of God's existence must be ambiguous for us. That is, it must be possible for us to reasonably fail to believe. Here again, we have a challenge to premise (1) of Schellenberg's argument. Schellenberg's argument demands that God's love requires God's existence to be undeniable. Lewis suggests that God's love requires the opposite: in order for God to have a loving relationship with us, God's existence must be ambiguous.

Of course, questions remain. How plausible is Lewis's strategy? Is it really true that, for love's sake, God cannot make his existence obvious? Not even Mickey Mouse can help us answer these questions in a way that will make everyone happy.

Notes

1. Barrett, S. (2017). *Disneyland's Hidden Mickeys*, 6e, 9. Lake Mary, FL: SMB Books.
2. Brian Kolodiejchuk, M. C. (ed.) (2007). *Come Be My Light: The Private Writings of the "Saint of Calcutta"*, 186–187. New York: Crown Publishing.
3. Lewis, C. S. (2001). *A Grief Observed*, 5–6. New York: HarperCollins Publishers.
4. Schellenberg, J. L. (2006). *Divine Hiddenness and Human Reason*, 1. Ithaca, NY: Cornell University Press.
5. This combines two premises on pp. 52, 53 of Schellenberg, J. L. (2015). *The Hiddenness Argument: Philosophy's New Challenge to Belief in God*. Oxford: Oxford University Press.
6. This is similar to another of Schellenberg's (2015) premises.
7. Note that this is different from the claim that one can't reasonably believe that the log-and-truck arrangement is a Hidden Mickey. We reasonably believe all sorts of non-obvious things! A quick example: it's reasonable to believe – indeed we *know* – that the shortest distance between two points on a sphere is the path traced by the great circle defined by those two points, but that claim is nowhere near obvious.
8. Lewis, C. S. (2001). *The Screwtape Letters*, 39. New York: HarperCollins Publishers.

Part II

"I'LL BE SHOOTING FOR MY OWN HAND"

"Everyone's Special Dash"

Tolerance and Conformity in a World of Incredible Differences

Richard B. Davis

It is a truth universally acknowledged, that a superhero in possession of a good power must be in want of a secret identity. This truth is so well fixed in the minds of Supers that, without the slightest fear of refutation, Mr. Incredible can boldly declare: "Every superhero has a secret identity. I don't know a single one who doesn't." If by night you listen to police scanners, save folks from burning buildings – *yes*, knocking them down, but they were structurally unsound anyway! – and stop the Omnidroid 8000 in its tracks without completely destroying it, then by day you are Robert Parr, insurance adjuster, whose only claim to fame is helping customers penetrate the bureaucracy at Insuricare.

Just why superheroes and secret identities go hand-in-hand is a matter of spirited debate. Some experts point to the pressure of being a super. You always have to be *on*. Well, no one really wants that 24/7. Even a Super needs to "clock out" once in a while. If Helen Parr wears her super suit to the supermarket, how will the groceries get done? All her time will be taken up signing autographs, taking selfies, and answering the question, "What's it like to be a Super?" Clearly, a secret identity is a matter of practical necessity – and not just, as Frozone would have us believe, a lure Superladies dangle in front of their love interests to make them wonder who's under that mask.

So if a Super can strike the right hero work/secret life balance, it's a win. More than that, it's a win-win since society also gets the benefit

Disney and Philosophy: Truth, Trust, and a Little Bit of Pixie Dust, First Edition.
Edited by Richard B. Davis.

of crime fighting the likes of which they've never seen. The cops might be able to handle Bomb Voyage on their own, but they're no match for Syndrome and his zero-point energy device, or Evelyn Deavor and her Screenslaver scheme. You need a Super – or rather a whole family of Supers – to bring the likes of those two down.

But here we strike a problem. Including Supers in public life comes at a cost. Society loses a measure of control over a few of its more powerful members. Supers are incredibly different from us. Because they *are* super; they may do as they please. You can't *make* them do anything – not if they don't want to. They can march to the beat of their own drummers. If Mr. Incredible personally believes *No one has a right to take his own life*, and decides to act on that belief, thereby foiling Oliver Sansweet's attempted suicide, there's not much society can do about it. Sure, you can file suit in Superior Court; but Mr. Incredible doesn't *have* to show up. If he believes the lawsuit is unjust, he can simply ignore the subpoena, assume his secret identity, and slip away. That's at least a possibility. Can a society with Supers tolerate this sort of thing? You can hardly blame the authorities for thinking the freedom of Supers to fight crime on their own terms needs to be restricted (even if it can't be enforced).

Immediately, however, difficult questions arise: When can a society rightly exercise its authority to restrict the freedoms of its members? On what basis are these restrictions to be made? How far should they go? With a little help from British philosophers John Locke (1632–1704) and John Stuart Mill (1806–1873), I believe we can recover from *The Incredibles* a treasure trove of ideas that can help us think more clearly about tolerance, individual freedoms, and cultural conformity in our own world of incredible differences.

"Join Us or Go Away!"

Once upon a time there was a Golden Age of Supers. Supers saved the world from the dark forces of evil and their reign of terror. Super deeds were emblazoned on the front-pages of newspapers. They made the cover of *TIME*. *LIFE* magazine devoted an entire issue to the "Outstanding Citizen and Superhero of the Year." Action figures were created after them; school children worshipped them. The Supers were beloved: veritable gods among humans. The only bump in the road, it seems, were those *capes*: Dynaguy snagged on takeoff, Stratogale caught in a jet turbine, Splashdown sucked into a vortex!

Now fast forward to the present and the all-out war on Supers: "dozens of superhero lawsuits the world over" and "tremendous public pressure" has resulted in an imposed "relocation program" – in effect, a government ban. Their secret identities must become their only identity. While they will always *be* Supers (they can hardly help that), the *use* of their super powers in public service will no longer be tolerated. They must agree under the penalties of law to act only as "average citizens, average heroes." Not super, just average. "Time for them to join us, or go away!"

Seriously? That's it? I'm sure villains across the globe will be delighted. By what infallible mode of reasoning, however, did society come to this calamitous decision? It won't surprise you, I suspect, to discover that it *wasn't* by appeal to solid facts and sound reasoning at all. Just consider this short but highly illuminating exchange between Mr. Incredible and Winston Deavor – head of DevTech and PR man extraordinaire:

DEAVOR: Let me ask you something. What is the main reason you were all forced underground?

MR. INCREDIBLE: Ignorance.

DEAVOR: Perception. When you fight bad guys like today, people don't see the fight or what led up to it. *They see what politicians tell them to see.* They see destruction and they see you.

There you have it. Those in political power filter what they want the general public to *see* and therefore manufacture how they will *feel* about the Supers. Edit out all the good stuff and you're left with visceral images of collapsed buildings, blown out train lines, and angry citizens in neck braces ("You didn't save my life; you ruined my death!"). If you cap it off by telling everyone they can expect a tax hike to cover the "crushing financial burden" of all these lawsuits and repairs, you've got a sure-fire recipe for explosive social conflict. And then a full-scale ban on Supers can seem like just what the doctor ordered to defuse the tensions.

But is that the script a *philosophical* doctor would write? Well, perhaps not. According to famed political philosopher and physician, John Locke, for example, the very first thing an enlightened society would do at this point is not rush to judgment. Locke himself lived in a turbulent time filled with "factions, tumults, and civil wars."[1] Invariably, political turmoil (assassination plots, tower imprisonments, exiles, and the like) centered around fever-pitched disagreements over Christian doctrine and practice. Now if the Christian religion really were "destructive of the civil peace," Locke tells us, it would be "the worst of all religions" and not to be "tolerated by any commonwealth."[2] We should ban it outright. However, since Christianity in itself is "modest and peaceable," we must look elsewhere for the true cause of political and civil unrest:

> It is not the diversity of opinions, which cannot be avoided; but the refusal of toleration to those that are of different opinions, which might have been granted, that has produced all the bustles and wars, that have been in the Christian world, upon account of religion.[3]

So in Locke's mind, intolerance is the real disease, and thus the good doctor prescribes a healthy dose of *tolerance* as the cure. Initially at least, this sounds like a promising step forward in resolving the Supers controversy.

It turns out, however, that there's a loophole. Locke doesn't think we should tolerate everyone's opinions and practices – an escape clause I can well imagine adversaries of the Supers wanting to exploit. Here Locke singles out Catholics and atheists as proper objects of our *intolerance*: the former because they owe their allegiance to "another prince"[4] (the Pope); the latter because "Promises, covenants, and oaths, which are the bonds of human society, can have no hold upon an atheist."[5] For the "taking away of God, though but even in thought, dissolves all."[6] Locke thinks that if you're of the opinion that there is no God, then you won't believe in an afterlife in which rewards and punishments are meted out. Hence, you won't be afraid to lie under oath.

Now Locke's argumentation here is flimsy *in excelsis*. To be sure, Catholics owe their *religious* allegiance to "another prince," but it doesn't follow that they also owe him their *political* allegiance, which, I take it, is Locke's main worry. And there's no reason at all to think that an atheist's only motivation for telling the truth is fear of punishment in an afterlife. Indeed, she might think that since promises, covenants, and oaths *are* "the bonds of human society," we shouldn't break our promises because that would ultimately erode societal cohesion and happiness.

In any event, if you're a Super, John Locke is definitely not your man. For then (using Locke's logic) it could be argued that your allegiance is in dispute. It isn't really to the Superior Court, but rather the "Supers Club"[7] – more exactly, the personal opinions of its members about whether to cooperate with the "Join Us or Go Away" imperative. Moreover, like Locke's atheist, it might be said that a Super doesn't have a proper fear of punishment ("Hey, come on. We're superheroes. What could happen?"), and therefore will incline to breaking the law every Wednesday on Bowling Night, if it affords the opportunity to "relive the glory days." If Locke is right, then, the Supers fall into the same camp as his Catholics and atheists, in which case they shouldn't be tolerated at all. Nice.

Mill's Maxims

Still, perhaps all hope is not lost. For there is another British philosopher the Supers might retain to handle their legal woes – one who (ironically given Locke's comments on atheism) "did not throw off religious belief but never had it."[8] I am speaking, of course, of John Stuart Mill: prominent utilitarian, near atheist, and the author of the classic work on tolerance, *On Liberty*.[9] According to Mill, any society worth its salt will adhere to two maxims:

M1: "All that makes existence valuable to any one, depends on the enforcement of restraints upon the actions of other people"[10]

and therefore

M2: "Some rules of conduct … must be imposed."[11]

Some of these rules will be implemented "in the form of legal penalties"; others by "the moral coercion of public opinion."[12] (Hey listen, group peer pressure is a powerful thing. Think Twitter!) Each is a way of safeguarding social order.

So far so good. Next we'll need to decide what these rules should be. That's actually a bit tricky. For the general public, says Mill, has convinced itself that *reasons* needn't be given at all for imposing these restraints. Thus Mill observes:

> People are accustomed to believe, and have been encouraged in the belief by some who aspire to the character of philosophers, that their feelings, on subjects of this nature, are better than reasons, and render reasons unnecessary.[13]

As a result,

> The practical principle which guides them to their opinions on the regulation of human conduct, is the feeling in each person's mind that everybody should be required to act as he, and those with whom he sympathizes, would like them to act.[14]

Well, that's exactly what Winston Deavor would say! Laws and rules of conduct are generated by public opinion which, in turn, is birthed out of our individual *feelings* about how we *want* others to behave. Consequently, you don't change laws by presenting the public with principled reasons for thinking a Supers ban is unfair. You change them by altering the way Supers are perceived. You have to make them *likable*. You need to embed tiny cameras in their super suits:

DEAVOR: If we want to change people's perceptions about superheroes, we need you to share your perceptions with the world.
ELASTIGIRL: How do we do that?
DEAVOR: With cameras. We need you to share your perceptions with the world.

Brilliant idea. Just make sure the camera isn't clipped to Mr. Incredible's suit! You might not like what you see. Elastigirl is clearly your poster girl. She'll get the job done but without destroying a stitch of public property. The public will fall in love her, and then (as Elastigirl herself says) "public pressure" will "[change] all the right minds" – the minds that pass the laws. That's the way things work; there's no sense fighting it.

Mill and Deavor are on the same page in one respect. They both agree that human nature being what it is, a society will operate – almost by default – on what we might call the "PREFER" principle:

PREFER: "The likings and dislikings of society, or some powerful portion of it," are the standard for determining "the rules laid down for general observance, under the penalties of law or opinion."[15]

If society likes the Supers, they're good to go; they can be Supers with little (if any) interference from the law or public opinion. If, on the other hand, society takes a particular dislike to the Supers, an out-and-out ban could be perfectly in order, if that's what the people desire. The one big difference between Deavor and Mill is that Deavor seems to think PREFER, along with the right PR campaign, will produce a fair and just law. As he says at the signing of the *International Superhero Accord*:

> We agree to undo a bad decision, to make sure a few extraordinarily gifted members … of the world's many countries are *treated fairly*. To invite them once again to use their gifts … to benefit the world.

But why think it was a *bad* decision in the first place? If it was in accord with the likings of society, then PREFER tells us it wasn't bad; it was the gold standard. It's worth noting that Deavor himself *never* gives us a reason for thinking the Supers have been treated unfairly. He tells us his father loved the Supers, that he loves the Supers, and that he feels the world would be more dangerous without them. But none of these statements of preference show that the Supers have been treated unfairly. And they haven't been, if PREFER is true.

Deavor is a realist. He's not going to challenge the PREFER principle. He's going to work with it. He's a marketer, not a philosopher. But after he gets what he wants, he really does need to sit down and rethink the principle. He needs to study some Mill, not just the latest market trends. Those who cleave to PREFER, Mill notes, typically busy themselves with telling us what we should all like or dislike. But they fail to ask whether society's likings and dislikings "should be a law to individuals."[16] In fact, they shouldn't.

Note first, he says, that "an opinion on a point of conduct, not supported by reasons, can only count as one person's preference."[17] But as we all know, our preferences are infected by a multitude of base influences: "prejudices," "superstitions," "envy," "jealousy," "arrogance or contemptuousness," but more often than not individuals' "desires or fears for themselves."[18] In a comment absolutely dripping with envy, Buddy (Incrediboy) tells Mr. Incredible in censorious tones: "Well not every superhero has powers, you know. You can be super without them." You don't think that's influencing his bad opinion of the Supers?

Or take the politicians. Why do you think they pressed the case against the Supers in the first place? Is it really just about "Money, money, money, money, money," as Rick Dicker claims? I don't believe it. Sure, Mr. Incredible knocked down a building. But he's right. It was on fire and it was coming down anyway. The insurance company was paying either way. More than that, he actually saved them money, since he saved the lives of everyone in the building (no deaths = no life insurance policies to pay out). What's really driving the political winds is something more like *fear* – of a small but powerful segment of society (the Supers) conducting themselves in ways we can't control.

At any rate, Mill bids us to ask just how likely it is that the "rules of conduct" necessary for having a valuable life are going to come out fair and reasonable, if they emerge from this irrational cesspool. The prospects aren't heartening. Indeed, if a society likes and dislikes the wrong things, PREFER might be employed to curtail (say) our freedom of conscience to think and feel as we please in moral, political, and theological matters – and to publish our opinions without fear of reprisal. It might curtail "framing the plan of our life to suit our own character"[19] – as it does with the Supers. And it could even be used to block our "freedom to unite, for any purpose not involving harm to others."[20] So the short-lived "Supers Club," which had just such a purpose, would be ruled out of court. Mill is right. Rules of conduct that enforce social order at the expense of these freedoms are not only unfair, they're tyrannical.

"Cogs that Fit, that Cooperate by Design"

There is yet another price to be paid for building a society on preference rather than principle, on feelings rather than reasons. The price is philosophical in nature, and not what any society wants to pay. Let me explain. On Mill's view, the "only purpose for which power can be rightfully exercised over" a member of society (against her will) "is to prevent harm to others."[21] Thus, for example, we don't legislate against drinking; but we do prohibit *drinking on duty*. Elastigirl asks Evelyn Deavor: "Are superheroes allowed to drink on duty? I'm definitely not on duty. Ignore the custom." She thereby implicitly endorses Mill's *prevention of harm principle*. An inebriated Super "on duty" is tantamount to a DUI (driving under the influence); they're a danger to themselves and others. Exactly right.[22]

If we follow Mill, we have a reasonable but not overly restrictive principle for guiding human life and conduct. There is room to hold unpopular opinions, publish unpopular views, and belong to unpopular groups – even if society disapproves. These things are to be tolerated unless they have as their purpose harming others. But the PREFER principle won't give us that. Since intolerance in "whatever [we] really care about" is "so natural"[23] to us, Mill remarks, we face a powerful temptation to brand those who disagree with us – who fail to share our likings and dislikings (or even worse: who publicly speak against them) – as being *intolerant*. They are the ones who violate societal rules of conduct, and should therefore be silenced by "the penalties of law," stinging rebukes on social media, or perhaps even violent protest if a controversial speaker is invited to a college campus.

In Mill's books, however, all of this is a "peculiar evil" guilty of "robbing the human race"[24] of great philosophers and thinkers. For "No one can be a great thinker who does not recognize, that as a thinker it is his first duty to follow his intellect to whatever conclusions it may lead."[25] But that's just the thing. You can't do that in a culture that suppresses unpopular speech or conduct just because society as a whole, "or some powerful portion of it," doesn't *like* it. A society like that will never produce a Galileo, Newton, or Darwin. It produces intellectual pacifists, who keep their opinions to themselves, thank you very much, lest they are branded heretics and set upon by the mob. They stay off society's radar by "narrowing their thoughts and interest to things"[26] which can be said and done without offending the gatekeepers of culture. This truth is portrayed in dramatic fashion in this (much beloved) exchange between Dash and his mother (Helen Parr) after meeting with the school principal:

DASH: You always say, "Do your best." But you don't really mean it. Why can't I do the best that I can do?
HELEN: Right now, honey, the world just wants us to fit in, and to fit in, we just gotta be like everybody else.
DASH: Dad always said our powers were nothing to be ashamed of. Our powers made us special.
HELEN: Everyone's special, Dash.
DASH: Which is another way of saying no one is.

Under the withering effects of the PREFER principle, Elastigirl has given in. And now she's pressuring her son to give in as well. It's this same pressure to conform that Mr. Incredible faces at Insuricare. A company, his boss – the dimunutive, Mr. Huph – tells him, is like an enormous clock. "It only works if all the little cogs mesh together ... cogs that fit, that cooperate by design ... You know what I mean by cooperative cogs?" Yes, he knows. It means returning to his desk, and letting the guy in the alley get robbed. But Mr. Incredible won't have it – a fact amply attested by Huph's subsequent hospital stay: neck brace, fractures, and all. Mill won't have it either.

If you want to be a great thinker, you have to love the truth more than you love being popular. You have to refuse to "mesh together" with the other unthinking "cogs" in society's feeling and preference driven "clock." You have to commit to pursuing good *reasons* as the proper basis for your conduct and opinions. And if you do that, you won't dream of silencing those with whom you disagree – or at the very least you'll mightily resist the temptation. For truth "depends on a balance to be struck between two sets of conflicting reasons."[27] That's why a jury has to hear *both* sides of an argument before rendering its verdict. "He who knows only his own side of the case," states Mill, "knows little of that."[28] For if you can't refute the reasons on the other side, or don't even know what they are, then you have "no ground[s] for preferring either opinion."[29] You should "self-silence" and remain agnostic on the matter.

Of course, the politicians may retort that the "Join Us or Go Away" campaign is so important, so beneficial to society that it must be shielded from rational scrutiny. After all, what if the public isn't convinced? They might not support the ban. That's right. In fact, they might even ask you for reasons for thinking it *is* important. That's the risk you run, if you decide to become philosophically engaged. And the same goes for the illustrious members of the "Supers Club" – Gazerbeam, Frionic, and all the rest. They may well be in possession of a good power, but if they don't want their secret identities to be their only identities, if they want to exercise their powers for society's good, they might want to consider adding a Super Philosopher (like John Stuart Mill) to their ranks.[30]

Notes

1. Locke, J. (2003). A letter concerning toleration. In: *Two Treatises of Government and A Letter Concerning Toleration* (ed. I. Shapiro), 250. New Haven: Yale University Press.
2. Ibid.
3. Ibid.
4. Ibid., p. 245.
5. Ibid., p. 246.
6. Ibid.
7. What? You've never heard of this? The Supers Club is mentioned by Mr. Incredible in his eulogy for Gazerbeam in the *Incredibles 2* deleted scene "Return of the Supers." Always watch your deleted scenes!
8. Mill, J. S. (1989). *Autobiography*, 52. London: Penguin Books.
9. Mill, J. S. and Warnock, M (eds.) (2003). *Utilitarianism and On Liberty*, 2e. Malden, MA: Blackwell.
10. Ibid., p. 91.
11. Ibid.
12. Ibid., p. 94.
13. Ibid., p. 91.
14. Ibid., p. 92.
15. Ibid., p. 93.
16. Ibid., p. 93.
17. Ibid., p. 92.
18. Ibid., p. 92.
19. Ibid., p. 97.
20. Ibid.

21. Ibid., p. 94.
22. It is important to add that Mill doesn't hesitate to say that *seemingly* private actions – for example, drunkenness – can also fall under the penalty of law. For the "making himself drunk, in a person whom drunkenness excites to do harm to others, is a crime against others" (ibid., p. 166).
23. Ibid., p. 93.
24. Ibid., p. 100.
25. Ibid., p. 113.
26. Ibid., p. 112.
27. Ibid., p. 115.
28. Ibid.
29. Ibid.
30. Special thanks to my daughter Madelyn Davis for incredible conversations about all things *Incredible*, and for her close and careful comments on a draft of this chapter.

6

Accommodating Dory, but Disempowering Dopey? Dilemmas of Disability from *Snow White* to *Finding Dory*

Kevin Mintz

So often, when Disney tells stories about diversity, those who are non-believers of the "Magic" whine like unruly princes or princesses that these stories are too much like After School Specials. When I began working on this chapter, one of these lovable non-believers told me that watching *Finding Dory* overwhelmed him, with its cast of marine creatures, most of whom have disabilities, all working together to help everyone's favorite forgetful blue tang find her parents.

I certainly saw his point. In case you haven't noticed how disability-friendly the Big Blue World is before reading this, catch a ride with Crush to your favorite video retailer or online streaming service and look closer. Nemo has a deformed fin that his father, Marlin, calls his "lucky fin." Marlin himself lives with forms of post-traumatic stress disorder and obsessive–compulsive disorder, which manifest themselves in his overprotecting of Nemo and Dory. Dory tells us multiple times that she "suffers" from short-term memory loss. Hank is missing one of his tentacles, making him a septopus rather than an octopus. Destiny the whale shark has low vision, and her friend, Bailey the beluga whale, has temporary loss of echolocation due to a concussion. These are just a few examples. Yes, start making your flow charts now!

Disney and Philosophy: Truth, Trust, and a Little Bit of Pixie Dust, First Edition.
Edited by Richard B. Davis.

My friend's point was that in the Finding Nemo Universe, the Pacific Ocean is a disability paradise, where the Pixar animators want you to not-so-subtly realize that disability can become a source of strength, especially when sea creatures work together to accommodate each other's limitations. Those who do not buy into the Disney style of storytelling can rightly point out that the inclusion of people with disabilities in the real world has subtleties that are lost in translation when injected into the Big Blue World. However, in my dual identities of Disney fanatic and philosopher of disability, I was as delighted as a five-year-old on their first trip to the Magic Kingdom to see the progress that Disney had made in *Finding Dory* by depicting what philosophers call the social model of disability.

Brought into maturity by philosophers like Adrienne Asch,[1] Anita Silvers,[2] and Tom Shakespeare,[3] the social model of disability views disability as the result of interactions between impairment and the social environment that should be made accessible to those with disabilities through elimination of barriers. Consider, for example, how Dory's parents, Charlie and Jenny, scatter purple seashells (Pixar's Big Blue World twist on the bread crumbs from *Hansel and Gretel*) to help Dory find her way back to them. Jenny and Charlie want the seashells to serve as a feature of the seafloor that naturally accommodates Dory's memory loss. When Dory has the seashells to guide her, the ocean is no longer a disabling environment. This is one instance in *Finding Dory* where the social model takes center stage. In contrast to the social model of disability, we often see the medical model, in which disability is understood as an individual problem to be remedied through medical treatment or charity.[4]

Not to get too far ahead of ourselves, but Dopey from *Snow White* is a perfect illustration of a character with a disability portrayed in terms of the medical model. Dopey is nonverbal, and his inability to talk is cast as a problem he has all on his own. Recall Happy's observation to Snow White on this subject: "He don't know, he never tried [to talk]." Throughout the film, we see Dopey as the recipient of Snow White's charity (in his defense, who wouldn't want extra kisses on the forehead from a Disney princess?), and the other dwarfs often protect him from danger in a way that casts him as helpless because of his limitations. There's much, much more to say about Dopey, but we're only just starting our journey together.

If you'll let me, I'd like to serve as your philosophical Jiminy Cricket, taking you through the history of Disney animation's depictions of disability. Along the way, we will trace a philosophical evolution from sidekick characters molded by the medical model, to heroes who succeed because they are able to minimize the social obstacles that come their way – not in spite of, but because of their disabilities. Making this philosophical journey even more magical, we'll discover interesting connections between disability and the very nature of humanity itself. What do you say? I promise this will be anything but an After School Special.

Seven Dwarfs, a Mouse, and the Medical Model

As other intellectual tour guides have pointed out, characters with physical and intellectual disabilities have existed in Disney's Magical World tracing back to Walt's first venture into feature-length animation.[5] All seven of Snow White's housemates in *Snow White and the Seven Dwarfs* are short-statured men who act like children. Before meeting them, Snow White even mistakenly believes they *are* children, exclaiming to her flurry of furry and feathery friends from the forest, "Maybe they have no mother. Then they're orphans; that's too bad! We'll clean the house and surprise them. Then maybe they'll let me stay." The seven dwarfs are, with this dialog, placed into a perpetual state of childlike innocence and ignorance, which some proponents of the medical model believe define the day-to-day lives of the disabled.[6]

For our purposes, we'll focus on Dopey, who, unlike the other dwarfs, doesn't mature over the course of the film. This is probably because in addition to his short stature, Dopey also has an intellectual disability. Though we never find out what that disability is, it is safe to assume that Dopey has a form of Down syndrome. His big ears, hard to miss eyes, and larger than life grin are reminiscent of physical features often associated with young children who have Down syndrome. While we cannot know that it was the animators' intention to draw Dopey in this way, a not so uncle-like quote from Walt Disney himself sheds some light on the question. He reportedly believed that the animators drew Dopey like "too much of an imbecile, which was not what we had in mind."[7] Whatever Walt's or anyone else's intentions were, with the depiction of Dopey as intellectually disabled, a disability hierarchy emerges in *Snow White*.

Like most children, the other dwarfs are destined to mature. (Even Grumpy learns to shed a tear and crack a smile). Dopey, however, will always be in need of care from the other dwarfs, even after Snow

White, transient mother that she is, rides off into the sunset with the prince, giving a very emotionally one-dimensional "goodbye."

The portrayal of disability in *Snow White* parallels discussions of intellectual disability in the writings of John Locke (1632–1704) and John Stuart Mill (1806–1873). In his *Second Treatise on Government*, Locke tells us that people with intellectual disabilities will never have full citizenship rights as typically developing (and male) children will, and "so lunatics and idiots are never set free from the government of their parents."[8] Much later, in his treatise *On Liberty*, Mill argues that those who are unable to care for themselves should not have the same freedom of speech expression and thought as others.[9] Applying these limitations to Dopey raises some important questions. If Dopey is never set free from the authority of his parents, who is responsible for him after Snow White rides off, neglecting her assumed maternal responsibility? Maybe the other dwarfs take up the slack, but at what point do they transition out of their perpetual child-like state to take care of Dopey? What will happen to Dopey if the other dwarfs become ill or die before he does? Will Dopey ever have a place for himself that isn't defined by his dependence on the other dwarfs?

These disturbing existential questions are critical for Disney fans with disabilities, who, like me, look for role models in their favorite films. Yet the questions find no answers for reasons that actually have very little to do with disability. Dopey and the other six dwarfs exist for one reason – to serve as sidekicks. Their stories end as soon as Snow White is rescued by the prince.

Dopey in particular, in the context of 1937 Hollywood, seems to be a tribute to the silent, slapstick antics of Charlie Chaplin. He exists strictly for comic relief. Early in the film, when the dwarfs are seen working in the mine, Dopey is made to sweep up diamonds and other gems while the other dwarfs "dig dig dig with a shovel and a pick." When Dopey puts diamonds in his eyes to get Doc's attention, Doc hits him over the head with his hand in a very slapstick way. Yes, this makes most of us laugh, but in the non-Disney world, would we really want Dopey under the authority of someone who slaps him over the head to punish his playful nature? Probably not.

Dopey's disempowered legacy continues thirteen years later in *Cinderella* with the lovable Gus-Gus. From the first time we see Gus-Gus, we understand that he is physically and intellectually slower than the other mice. He scrambles to get as much cheese from Cinderella as he can, and can only echo what Jaq and the other mice say. Lucifer, the ferocious feline, loves going after Gus-Gus even more so than the other mice because he knows Gus-Gus is a much easier catch. Like Snow White with Dopey, Cinderella takes on a motherly role. She comforts and protects Gus-Gus, but never really empowers him to become more than a mostly nonverbal mouse.

How should Disney fans conceptualize why Dopey and Gus-Gus seem to be more comedic devices than characters in their own right? An answer to this question might come from Nancy Hirschmann, who has argued that disability is synonymous with fear for many non-disabled people. On her account, those without disabilities fear those with them (and treat them differently) because they fear their own humanity and vulnerability.[10] On this account, the other characters in *Snow White* and *Cinderella* treat Dopey and Gus-Gus the way they do because they fear that one day they too might be nonverbal.

To be fair to the characters who care for Dopey and Gus-Gus, Disney's magical fairytale landscapes don't provide resources for giving voice to those who are nonverbal. However, for dwarfs or mice inclined to spontaneously burst into a high-spirited "Heigh Ho" or a cheerful "Cinderelly" while performing hard labor, the inability to talk might well induce fear.

Let's not forget that, in their own way, our two heroines also contend with the fear of being silenced. Snow White is terrified of being murdered by the evil queen; so she willingly becomes a young mother to seven strange but lovable dwarfs. Both of Cinderella's stepsisters, Anastasia and Drizella, as well as her stepmother, have systematically bullied her – so much so that singing is the only way she can really be heard. Under these circumstances, wouldn't you fear or pity those who had no voice of their own at all? This is a question that continues to confront us in Disney's more contemporary disability narratives.

Disability as "Part of Your World"?

Thirty-nine years after Cinderella's dreams come true, another Disney heroine must contend with the realities of being – quite literally – silenced. I am referring to the rebellious teenage mermaid, Ariel, who sells her voice to the sea witch, Ursula, to have a chance at true love with Prince Eric. In *The Little Mermaid*, fans observe a trope that matures in *Beauty and the Beast* – in order to be human, one must love and be loved in return. Because disability can be an important part of someone's humanity, it is not all that surprising that both of these films deal with disability.

In *The Little Mermaid*, Ariel must not only try to win Eric while unable to speak, but in her undersea world she fantasizes about being a physically able-bodied woman. In "Part of Your World," she dreams of seeing, jumping, dancing, strolling, walking, running, and standing. This notion of human flourishing – emphasizing physical ability over all other capacities – actually excludes anyone whose disabilities preclude them from being active.[11] As such, Ariel only becomes truly human when King Triton gives her legs. But is having legs and being able to use them what makes someone truly human? *The Little Mermaid*'s answer rings as loud and clear as Cinderella's and Ariel's wedding bells: yes. The implication here is that disability is a negative state.

Beauty and the Beast presents a slightly different take on the same question. While Beast must learn to love in order to be human, Gaston's sidekick, LeFou (French for "the fool"), must decide whether to be his own person or a blind follower of Gaston's vain and evil pursuits. LeFou follows Gaston so blindly that someone who just read our discussion of Dopey and Gus-Gus might get the impression that LeFou has another kind of intellectual disability – one that disempowers him in ways similar to Dopey and Gus-Gus. Just as Doc routinely slaps Dopey over the head, Gaston repeatedly attacks LeFou when he does something wrong. When LeFou mistakenly begins conducting a version of Wagner's "Bridal Chorus" after Gaston fails in his proposal to Belle, Gaston throws LeFou into a pigsty after choking him and proclaims: "I'll have Belle for my wife, make no mistake!" LeFou, like Locke's "lunatics and idiots," is never able to free himself from his abusive, paternalistic relationship with Gaston. After Gaston dies, LeFou is never seen again.

It's ironic. One would hope Gaston's and LeFou's antics would land them in a prison or mental asylum, but it is Belle's father who is temporarily committed because of his alleged fantastical sighting of Beast. This is all just another ploy by Gaston to compel Belle to marry him in exchange for freeing her father. This element of Gaston and LeFou's storyline parallels Michel Foucault's (1926–1984) observation in *The Birth of the Clinic* – that the purpose of medical institutions is to use the body and the idea of illness to assert power and control over someone's life.[12] Despite 54 years between Dopey's antics in *Snow White* and LeFou's antics in *Beauty and the Beast*, not all that much has changed. Disabilities are still seen as pitiable conditions requiring a medical solution.

It will take another cast of sea creatures entirely to teach us what it really means to live independently with a disability. So let's take a deep dive into the Big Blue World of Nemo and Dory to get a clearer view of things!

"You Remembered in Your Own Amazing Dory Way!"

Have you ever noticed how most Disney heroes and heroines begin their journeys believing they can complete their (impossible) quests entirely on their own – only later realizing, thanks to a trusty sidekick – that they really need a little help from their friends?

Consider *Finding Nemo*'s Marlin – a swimming contradiction. He's a clownfish without a sense of humor. Traumatized by the death of his partner Coral and all but one of his unborn children, he becomes obsessed with controlling everything and everyone in Nemo's life. Nemo gets lost in large part because Marlin is so overly controlling. In fact, without the assistance of Dory, Crush, and the other creatures Marlin meets on his undersea quest, he would never have succeeded in finding Nemo. The same goes for Dory in her sequel. Without natural supports in her social environment (recall the seashell discussion at the beginning of our time together), Dory would never be able to liberate her sea friends from the life of segregation in the aquarium to be free in the all-inclusive ocean.

Both Marlin and Dory's stories have embedded within them a philosophical dilemma about what it means to be an autonomous creature in the Big Blue World. In a traditional philosophical sense, where being autonomous means doing things entirely for yourself, the characters in *Finding Nemo* and *Finding Dory* are anything but autonomous.[13] After all, no one in the Big Blue World succeeds by doing anything alone!

In contrast to the traditional view of autonomy, we need to consider what feminist philosophers have called relational autonomy, the idea that only within broader social networks, where people depend on each other, can we achieve true independence.[14] Dopey, Gus-Gus, Ariel, and LeFou are largely defined in terms of their dependence on other characters. By contrast, our Pixar heroes and heroines with disabilities thrive because they are able to use the assistance of others to succeed on their own terms. "Remembering in your own amazing Dory way" involves using your talents and the help of others to reach the point where disability *is* a form of mere difference, a trait as inconsequential as the color of your scales. As Louis Armstrong exclaims toward the end of *Finding Dory*, "What a wonderful world!"

Or is it? Is there something about the experience of people with disabilities that is lost when impairment is framed strictly in terms of the diversity and inclusiveness of the Pacific Ocean? One of the strongest criticisms of the social model of disability is that it denies the reality that disability carries with it a difference that does cause distress.[15] Dory repeatedly tells others that she suffers from short-term memory loss – something for which Pixar has been criticized by some defenders of the social model. The word "suffer," they say, places disability strictly within the individual rather than in social context.[16] Isn't it true, however, that there are moments when Dory is actually frightened by her inability to recognize her surroundings? She is a very young blue tang and the inability to remember from moment to moment does make her more vulnerable to, for example, being misguided by Marlin and stung by jellyfish. These are the kind of philosophical details that get lost in translation when a Disney film tries to take a stand on something as complicated as disability. Then again, when watching a movie, especially one made for children, do we need to be reminded of how complex the world really is? Keep pondering that while we consider a darker side to the *Finding Dory* disability paradise, one that reveals it is only a wonderful world for those who can speak.

Does Dopey's Disempowered Legacy Live On?

While Dory succeeds in her own right, there are two characters in her sequel that still seem defined in terms of their dependency on others: Becky, the Loon (note the verbal similarities between the word loon and lunatic) and Gerald, the sea lion. For those of you who have been following along, can anyone guess what Becky and Gerald have in common with Dopey, Gus-Gus, and Ariel?

If you guessed that they are nonverbal, pat yourself on the back! Both Becky and Gerald have intellectual disabilities and are treated as comic relief like Dopey was in 1937. Becky humorously tries to eat a popcorn bucket and her nonsensical imprinting sound "oo-roo" is particularly funny when echoed repeatedly by the always uptight Marlin (as only Albert Brooks can voice him). Gerald, on the other hand, scurries about trying to take back the rock from the other two sea lions, Fluke and Rudder. In turn, they condescendingly but humorously ask Gerald to give them his bucket and bark "off, off, off!" Thankfully, both sidekicks get more satisfying endings than Dopey and Gus-Gus: Becky saves Marlin and Nemo from the truck going to Cleveland, and Gerald, in a scene after the credits, finally gets his rock, at long last! Nonetheless, we can be critical of the fact that these nonverbal characters in the Big Blue World are still relegated to sidekick status, where their primary function is to be laughed at. To be fair, since they rely on the spoken word as a means of communication, Disney/Pixar animators might reasonably be expected to experience anxiety over the absence of speech in their medium. Why resort to comedy, then? Well, as the saying goes, laughter is often the best medicine.

What might be lost in the conflation of nonverbal disability is an opportunity to use Disney animation as a means to explore the inner-workings of minds that cannot easily express themselves. But maybe this is getting too speculative and philosophical, even for a book called *Disney and Philosophy*. I'll leave that for you to decide.

What We Have Learned, or "Always Let Your Conscience Be Your Guide!"

On this brief philosophical journey, we have discovered an ongoing conflict in the history of Disney animation with respect to how to frame discussions of disability. On one end of the spectrum, our favorite forgetful blue tang, Dory, reflects the progress of philosophers of disability in advocating for acceptance of the social model. Dory becomes the hero of her own story because she has a disability that forces her to view the world differently than everybody else.

On the other end of the spectrum, Dopey is forever the subject of paternal authority, a sidekick molded in the spirit of the medical model. Gus-Gus, LeFou, Becky, and Gerald share Dopey's status as disempowered sidekicks. Each reflects the need for comic relief as a means of reconciling the fear society has toward nonverbal disability. Ariel has her moments with this philosophical quandary herself. In her depiction, physical ability is conflated with what it means to be human. She gets herself into her pickle because Ursula takes away one of her most important physical abilities – the ability to speak.

What should we make of all of this? Well, disability helps us see both the hero and villain in all of us. In enabling people with disabilities to "fight for their own hands", allies and advocates need to support them while giving them the autonomy to write their own stories. How do we decide the right balance between independence and dependence? The answer, to take a leaf out of Jiminy Cricket's book, is to "always let your conscience be your guide!"

Notes

1. Fine, M. and Asch, A. (1988). Disability beyond stigma: social interaction, discrimination, and activism. *Journal of Social Issues* 44: 3–21.
2. Silvers, A. (2009). An essay on modeling: the social model of disability. *Philosophical Reflections on Disability, Philosophy and Medicine* 104: 19–36.
3. Shakespeare, T. and Watson, N. (2001). The social model of disability: an outdated ideology?. In: *Research in Social Science and Disability Exploring Theories and Expanding Methodologies: Where We are and Where We Need to Go* (ed. S. N. Barnartt and B. M. Altman), 9–28. Bingley, UK: Emerald Group Publishing Limited.
4. See Shakespeare, T. (2014). *Disability Rights and Wrongs Revisited.* London: Routledge.
5. Lutfiyya, Z. and Hansen, N. (2003). Dopey's legacy: stereotypical portrayals of intellectual disability in classic animated film, In: *Diversity in Disney Films: Critical Essays on Race, Ethnicity, Gender, Sexuality and Disability* (ed. J. Cheu), 179–194. Jefferson, NC: McFarland Publishing.
6. Mintz, K. T. (2018). "My Blessed Child Does Not Need to Know about That!": how should sexual health educators confront the challenge of religious pluralism in working with individuals who have intellectual disabilities? *Ethics, Medicine and Public Health* 5: 8–17.
7. Lutfiyya and Hansen, "Dopey's Legacy," p. 183.
8. Locke, J. (1980). Of paternal power. *Second Treatise of Government* (ed. C. B. Macpherson), 34. Indianapolis, IN: Hackett.
9. Mill, J. S. (2007). On Liberty. *On Liberty and The Subjection of Women* (ed. A. Ryan), 85–105. London: Penguin Group.
10. Hirschmann, N. J. (2013). Queer/fear: disability, sexuality, and the other. *Journal of Medical Humanities* 34: 139–147.
11. Nussbaum, M. C. (2007). *Frontiers of Justice: Disability, Nationality, Species Membership*. Cambridge, MA: Harvard University Press; Kittay, E. F. (1999). *Love's Labor: Essays on Women, Equality and Dependency*. New York, NY: Routledge.
12. Foucault, M. (2010). *The Birth of the Clinic*. London: Routledge.
13. See Raz, J. (1988). *The Morality of Freedom*. Oxford: Oxford University Press.

14. Nedelsky, J. (2013). *Laws Relations: A Relational Theory of Self, Autonomy, and Law*. New York: Oxford University Press.
15. See Barnes, E. (2016). *The Minority Body: A Theory of Disability*. Oxford: Oxford University Press.
16. Elizabeth Picciuto (2016, June 19). "'Finding Dory,' Disability, and Me." *The Daily Beast*. https://www.thedailybeast.com/finding-dory-disability-and-me.

From Snow White to Moana

Understanding Disney's Feminist Transformation

Edwardo Pérez

MOANA: I am not a princess. I'm the daughter of the chief.
MAUI: Same difference.
MOANA: No.
MAUI: If you wear a dress, and have an animal sidekick, you're a princess.

Is Maui right? Does merely wearing a dress and having an animal sidekick turn a girl into a princess? What about the ability to belt out a show-stopping, goosebump-inducing tune? I know what you're thinking: Maui is just being a sexist. And Moana, like any good feminist, is simply throwing off her princess title. Perhaps so. But why, we might ask, couldn't a Disney princess be a feminist? If we dig beneath the surface a bit, I think we'll see that Disney princesses and feminists both have been tragically misunderstood. Not all Disney princesses are so-called "damsels-in-distress," and not all feminists are man-haters. These negative stereotypes have persisted, of course, but as live-action Disney princess (and self-avowed feminist) Emma Watson laments, "It is not the word ['feminism'] that is important; it's the idea and the ambition behind it."[1]

So what is this idea of feminism and how does it relate to being a Disney princess? Is feminism a one-size-fits-all-princesses philosophy? Or has there been some sort of feminist transformation from Snow White to Moana? In fact, there are four waves of feminist philosophy which can help us understand the progressing role of Disney princesses

Disney and Philosophy: Truth, Trust, and a Little Bit of Pixie Dust, First Edition.
Edited by Richard B. Davis.

since Snow White's debut in 1937. Let's start by catching the first wave and surveying our first trio of princesses.

Someday my Prince Will Come

In America, feminism's first wave officially begins with Elizabeth Cady Stanton's *Declaration of Sentiments*, introduced at the Seneca Falls Convention in 1848. Though more political than philosophical, Stanton's treatise expresses the perspective shared by most first-wave feminists: that women have been oppressed by men and especially by the governments of men, rendering women "civilly dead" and deprived of all inalienable rights. Not until the 19th Amendment was ratified in 1920 was the legal right to vote officially and broadly granted to American women. Of course, despite the progress made a century ago, inequality remains. Otherwise, there would have been no need for three more waves of feminist protests.

In the wake of feminism's first wave, Walt Disney gave us *Snow White* (1937), *Cinderella* (1950), and *Sleeping Beauty* (1959). These films didn't just create the first three Disney princesses (Snow White, Cinderella, and Aurora), they also marked a step backwards in terms of feminist progress. Indeed, all three princesses are essentially treated as property in their respective films – of the old (and not as beautiful) women who ruled over them (which creates another set of issues), and of the men who "saved" them from the old women. So they're not just damsels-in-distress incapable of problem-solving and thinking for themselves; they're also chattel devoid of natural rights and freedom, thereby betraying the advances made by first-wave pioneers. Indeed, Snow White and Cinderella are no better than domestic servants, with Cinderella being degraded and dehumanized by her evil stepmother and stepsisters. Aurora doesn't have it much better. In fact, from a first-wave perspective, Aurora seems to be little more than a piece of property, a prize to be had: passed from parents, to fairies, to Maleficent, and finally Prince Phillip. She has no say in her life because it's all been prearranged (her marriage included). Her rights aren't even acknowledged, much less respected. Does she really want to marry Prince Phillip? Does it matter that she's only 16? As Stanton might observe, the inalienable rights of the original trio of Disney princesses (to life, liberty, and the pursuit of happiness) are trod under foot.

It's worth noting that Disney also gave us *Alice in Wonderland* in 1951, a story about a (beautiful, vulnerable) girl led about by a variety of strange characters, while thankfully being the property of none. Although Alice is portrayed as extremely gullible and naive (more stereotypes for young girls), at least she's resourceful and brave. She doesn't need a prince to save her. Of course, Alice doesn't play the part of a princess on screen (though she does fit Maui's definition). But what's to prevent her from wearing the "Disney princess" label?[2] Is it because she's only "seven and a half exactly" and far too unruly?

Here we might also wonder why no Disney princess films were made during the era of second-wave feminism (1960s–1980s), which challenged stereotypical roles of women at home and in the workplace, arguing not only for a woman's protection against domestic violence (including marital rape) but also for her reproductive rights. Well, there's no need to speculate. Let's take a moment to understand the changes ushered in by second-wave feminism.

Once upon a Dream

Philosophically, feminism's second wave begins with two landmark volumes: *The Second Sex* (1949) by philosopher Simone de Beauvoir (1908–1986), and *The Feminine Mystique* (1963) by writer Betty Friedan (1921–2006). According to Beauvoir, women are defined by society, not their biology. Hence, her famous quote: "One is not born, but rather becomes, woman."[3] Beauvoir thus endorses a form of *social constructionism*: the idea that society creates the roles that women and men are expected to fulfill – even the role of damsel-in-distress princess who needs to be saved by the heroic prince (all too often from evil, older women who transform into dragons). As Beauvoir observes,

> Everything encourages [a girl] to abandon herself in dreams to the arms of men [...] She learns that to be happy, she has to be loved; to be loved, she has to await love. Woman is Sleeping Beauty [...] Cinderella, Snow White, the one who receives and endures.[4]

Indeed, Beauvoir says, "love and suffering are intertwined in a troubling way," since little girls are essentially taught to be martyrs (and little boys heroes) through "a whole cohort of tender heroines beaten, passive, wounded, on their knees, humiliated, [who] teach their younger sisters the fascinating prestige of being martyred, abandoned, and resigned beauty."[5]

For Friedan, the martyrdom and domestication of women noted by Beauvoir is part and parcel of what defines "the feminine mystique" or "the problem that had no name."[6] Women have been kept from achieving their full potential as human beings, at least in part because of their dissatisfaction with marriage, housework, and rearing children. As Friedan notes, "the feminine mystique permits, even encourages, women to ignore the question of their identity. The mystique says they can answer the question 'Who am I?' by saying 'Tom's wife… Mary's mother.'"[7] We might not get to hear a princess say "Mrs. Prince Charming," but Friedan's point is that the feminine mystique is rooted in an identity problem for women, a problem that is ultimately solved when women decide to forge an identity beyond being a wife and mother. "Why should a woman bother to be anything more than a wife and mother," Friedan asks, "if all the forces of her culture tell her she doesn't have to, will be better off not to, grow up?"[8]

The observations of Beauvoir and Friedan resonate with Disney's original princess trio, as the societies depicted in each of their tales (including the women in each princess's life) work to promote patriarchal roles. After all, isn't the goal of a Disney story to save the princess by having her marry a prince? Isn't this what "happily ever after" is all about? Does it matter that Snow White and Aurora are too young to give legal consent?[9] For second-wave feminism, the woods may be enchanted, the songs sentimental, and the fairy-tale – of course set in a faraway, magical land with castles and costume balls – romantic, but in the end these tales suggest that a woman's happiness is measured not by her identity, but by what society says she is able to provide for a man: a home with children. What would have happened if Aurora had woken up, decided to finish high school, go to college, and earn a law degree before marrying Prince Phillip?

Kiss the Girl

Let's see what happens when history enters the third wave of feminism and Disney finally gives us another princess after a thirty-year absence. Feminism's third wave doesn't have a unifying philosophical theme or perspective: no single cause to identify the wave (like the legal freedom of the first wave and domestic freedom of the second). Rather, the third wave presses a variety of issues such as race, social class, gender rights, single parenthood, maternity leave, and the so-called glass ceiling, Let's take a look at three significant perspectives outlined by feminist philosophers, Naomi Wolf (b. 1962), Judith Butler (b. 1956), and Carol Gilligan (b. 1936),[10] applying their insights to the Disney princesses who ride feminism's third wave: Ariel (1989), Belle (1991), Jasmine (1992), Pocahontas (1995), and Mulan (1998).

One of the requirements Maui overlooks in his definition of a princess is beauty, which Naomi Wolf sees as inextricably linked with power.[11] As a woman's social power increases, Wolf argues, so does the pressure for her to conform to certain standards of beauty – socially constructed, unrealistic, and largely due to the influence of mass media. For Wolf, the need to meet such standards adversely affects a woman's ability to function in society to the point that contemporary women "may actually be worse off than [their] unliberated grandmothers."[12] She dubs this unattainable standard of beauty, punitive for all those who fail to meet it, an *iron maiden.*[13] In Disney's world, falling short of this standard is the lot of every princess just by virtue of her being a princess, and indeed every little girl who ever struggled to live up to the image of her favorite Disney princess. Beauty might as well have been a character in the first three Disney princess films. It's certainly the focus with Ariel and Jasmine, both of whom are drawn in revealing ways. They may not be iron maidens, but given the image of a perfect body they convey, they certainly fit Wolf's definition.

For Judith Butler, Ariel and Jasmine can be seen as performing the feminine roles society expects of them, which includes dressing the way they do. Butler agrees with Beauvoir that gender (and sexual) roles are socially constructed, but Butler goes a step further. Men and women play these parts, not because they want to, but because society has conditioned them to do so. It's not a matter of choice; it's a matter of necessity. This is what Butler refers to as her theory of *Gender Performativity*, which offers another explanation for why Disney princesses feel obliged to pair up with a man and seek marriage – patriarchal society expects women and men to be heterosexual. However, this is what also makes Pocahontas and Mulan so different from their predecessors. They choose not to marry their love interests: a choice that becomes more and more common for Disney princesses, but one that doesn't necessarily stem from their being non-heterosexual. In fact, if you think about it, every Disney princess is simply assumed to be heterosexual. When we get to the fourth wave of princesses, however, we'll see how this could very well change.

Of course, there's no denying that Ariel, Belle, and Jasmine choose to marry. Still, it's fair to say that Belle is a young woman who goes against the role society (especially Gaston) has dictated. This is true of

Ariel as well, defying her father (and the natural order of their undersea society) to be with a human male. Likewise, Jasmine falls in love with Aladdin, which requires the Sultan to change the law so that Jasmine can marry him. Yes, Ariel, Belle, and Jasmine end up married. However, in an apparent response to the feminist critique of our original Disney trio, their marriages are depicted as much more of a choice.

It's also fair to point out that both Ariel and Belle display clear examples of Gilligan's *ethics of care*, which observes that men and women reason through moral dilemmas differently.[14] Ariel cares for Eric as much as Belle ends up caring for Beast. More to the point, however, Ariel and Belle make their moral judgments differently from their fathers and the other men in their stories. They end up loving Eric and Beast, but their ethical thought processes, their reasoning through their respective situations, aren't focused on abstract principles or on selfish desires. Rather, they consider the feelings and well-being, not just of Eric and Beast, but of their larger communities too. They transform from passive, receptive, waiting princesses into active, aggressive heroines. They retain the magical fairytale qualities of being a Disney princess (they fit Maui's definition), they end up married (perhaps at too young an age and because society says so), and they remain specimens of physical beauty. Yet they begin to assert themselves in more positive ways, admirably carving out their own identities.

Pocahontas and Mulan take things a step further, showing us that a girl can choose not to marry and still be a princess. In fact, Pocahontas and Mulan seem to be a better fit with the 1990s cultural ethos than Ariel, Belle, and Jasmine – not just in their independence but in their ethnicity and appearance.[15] Indeed, they are not drawn as revealingly as Ariel and Jasmine. Thus, while feminist critiques remain, the second group of Disney princesses offers a more feminist-friendly image of what it means to be a princess than the original trio – so much so that all five could be labeled feminist princesses, given how they each challenges her patriarchal society.

Let's see how the final group of Disney princesses continues this transformation amidst feminism's fourth wave.

Let It Go

What we've seen thus far is that each wave of feminism broadens the debate, moving from legal rights of women, to the recognition of the social construction of gender, to issues of caring, gender performance, beauty, and sexual objectification. While these issues remain, fourth-wave feminism adds a technological focus to the critique, challenging the misogynistic use of technology (especially through social media) while utilizing technology (such as blogs and posts) to mount such challenges.[16] So, the hallmark of feminism's fourth wave is its ability to include a plethora of voices from a variety of backgrounds working in harmony to continue to strive for equality. Let's see how our six remaining Disney Princesses – Tiana (2009), Rapunzel (2010), Merida (2012), Elsa and Anna (2013), and Moana (2016) – illustrate the issue of equality while continuing to transform the definition of a Disney princess.

Perhaps the defining feature of fourth-wave princesses is that none of them needs a man – at all! Men are in their lives, but they're secondary, making this group of princesses more independent than their predecessors. Marriage exists, but it's based on choice, not on a patriarchal compulsion, heterosexual directive, or the imperative to procreate. Tiana and Rapunzel choose marriage and choose their husbands. Merida chooses not to marry (and she grants everyone the right to choose, not only who their spouse will be, but whether to marry at all). Anna hastily gets engaged to Hans, but ends up becoming a couple with Kristoff. Elsa never has a love interest; neither does Moana, though Maui does seem to subtly flirt with her. What does this mean for the issue of equality? Is being independent the same as being equal? Let's consider the status of each fourth-wave princess.

Tiana, at 19, is a business woman whose goal is to own a restaurant. Rapunzel, at 18, is a princess by birth whose power resides in her hair. It has magical properties, and is a really fun weapon and tool to boot! Merida, 16, is a strong-willed, tomboyish Scottish princess who breaks the rules and competes for her own hand. Deciding to change her fate, she ends up changing the rules of marriage and the tradition of her society. Elsa, 21, is crowned queen of Arendelle, while Anna, 18, is a princess who, after Elsa flees, takes charge of Arendelle and embarks on her own to rescue Elsa. Each of these princesses is responsible for solving the dilemma that drives her respective narrative. They have become active rather than passive participants in deciding their own fates – a radical transformation from that original princess trio, and strong development of the second. They're independent, but are they equal? What about the men in the fourth-wave films? Have they, too, transformed?

Indeed, they have. Rather than functioning as stereotypical Prince Charmings, the men who accompany fourth-wave princesses seem to occupy sidekick roles. Naveen in *The Princess and The Frog*, Flynn (Eugene) in *Tangled*, Kristoff in *Frozen*, and Maui in *Moana* are all shown on a far more level playing field with their respective princesses, who are pictured as equally capable (if not more so) than the men. In terms of equality, each of these men is also feminized, in the sense that their masculinity is not absolute. They are allowed to experience emotional pain and show emotional growth. For instance, Naveen learns his lesson so well, he's willing to stay in frog form just to be with Tiana. Later, after they become human again, he helps her open a restaurant. Flynn, who begins as a selfish thief, ends up sacrificing himself in the end to save Rapunzel. Kristoff's sad orphan backstory, which resembles Elsa's and Anna's childhood, makes him sympathetic, softening his otherwise imposing presence as he transforms from an alpha male to a person with a genuine love and respect for Anna. Maui's backstory (he was abandoned by his parents) functions the same way, enabling his transformation from an arrogant Demi-God into a caring mentor and friend for Moana. It's also worth noting that Flynn, Kristoff, and even Maui to some extent, are essentially antiheroes resembling Han Solo: imperfect scoundrels who do the right thing but not always for the right reason.

So while the fourth-wave princesses become more responsible for saving themselves (and the world), the men who accompany them become flawed – just as much in need of saving as the women. There are hints of this transformation in the male characters in the third wave (especially in Aladdin and Beast), yet the fourth-wave men are developed in a way that makes them more vulnerable. But does this really make Disney princes and princesses equal? And what about the host of other issues associated with feminism?

Take the marriage issue. Elsa is arguably the most interesting of the fourth-wave princesses. She's the first to become a queen; she's the oldest (gasp!) at 21; and she's unwed (more gasps!). Some fans have even suggested, Elsa might be a lesbian (even more gasps!). Indeed, the recent strong push for LGBTQ rights and recognition, coupled with taking Elsa's show-stopping tune (and overall narrative) as a metaphor for "coming out," has led to the creation of #GiveElsaAGirlfriend. The hope for some (which includes the desire to see Elsa in a biracial lesbian relationship) is that Disney could use the character of Elsa to fully transform what it means to be a Disney princess, thereby advocating for equality, not just between women and men, but between heterosexuals and non-heterosexuals. After all, can't lesbians be princesses too? Shouldn't lesbian girls be given princess role models, to see that it's okay for a princess to love another woman instead of a man? And what about a transgender princess? Could that be possible?

How Far I'll Go

Disney's three waves of princesses reflect the waves of feminism from which they emerge. In subtle but profound ways, Disney princesses have evolved as each wave of feminism has crashed upon the shores of culture. They shift our focus from reinforcing patriarchy, to challenging it, and finally turning it on its head, redefining our very understanding of what it means to be feminine and masculine.

The implication is that equality isn't based on making women and men equal to one another, but rather on making them balanced within themselves. Going forward, we can only imagine what the next batch of Disney princesses will offer. Will they continue to transform themselves, mirroring the social, political, and cultural concerns of whatever contemporary feminist theories abound? Will feminism itself continue to evolve in its objectives, perspectives, and mission? Will there be a fifth wave? Will Vanellope or Elastigirl or Jessie be added to the list of princesses? To paraphrase Moana, who knows how far it'll go.

Notes

1. Emma Watson (2014, September 22). "Emma Watson at the HeForShe Campaign 2014 – Official UN Video." *YouTube*. https://www.youtube.com/watch?v=p-iFl4qhBsE
2. And why not Mary Poppins, Tinker Bell, Wendy Darling, Esmerelda, Megara, Nala, Jane, Kida Nedakh, Sally, Jessie, Vanellope, or Elastigirl?
3. de Beauvoir, S. (2011). *The Second Sex*, 330. New York: Vintage Books.
4. Ibid., p. 352.
5. Ibid, p. 353.
6. Friedan, B. (1963). *The Feminine Mystique*, 15. New York: W.W. Norton & Company, Inc.
7. Ibid, p. 126.
8. Ibid, p. 204.
9. And though Cinderella may be 19, she nevertheless seems young.
10. Wolf's *The Beauty Myth* and Butler's *Gender Trouble: Feminism and the Subversion of Identity* were both published in 1990. While Gilligan published *In a Different Voice: Psychological Theory and Women's Development* in 1982 – technically, at the end of the second wave – it arguably functioned as a precursor to the third wave.

11. Where de Beauvoir and Friedan seem to hold beauty as both a currency and a solace.
12. Wolf, N. (1991). *The Beauty Myth*, 115. New York: William Morrow & Co.
13. Which would give us an interesting analysis of *Snow White*'s evil queen, Cinderella's stepsisters, and Maleficent – all of whom struggle with falling far short of the beauty of Snow White, Cinderella, and Aurora.
14. For Gilligan, men tend to approach problems as matters of principle, while women often view things contextually, relying on empathy and caring.
15. Of course, Jasmine presents the first example of a non-white princess whose ethnicity and culture are non-American. Yet her narrative aligns more with the narratives of Ariel and Belle than with Pocahontas and Mulan.
16. See, for example, such websites as *The Everyday Sexism Project* hosted by British writer Laura Bates, the *Feminist Frequency* hosted by Canadian-American media critic Anita Sarkeesian. See also movements such as *#MeToo*, *#YesAllWoman*, *#BringBackOurGirls*, and *#LoveWins*, writers in the established media (like *The Guardian*'s Kira Cochrane), and to celebrities such as Emma Watson, whose 2014 United Nations speech launched the *HeForShe* campaign.

"Always a Team, Always United"

Disney's Philosophy of the Family

Kody Cooper

MR. INCREDIBLE: Mommy and I are always a team. Always united against the forces of...

ELASTIGIRL: Pigheadedness.

MR. INCREDIBLE: I was gonna say evil or something.

Disney's animated film canon offers two contrasting visions of marriage and parenthood, which correspond to two rival portrayals of family life. The first vision of the family is what we can call the Irrational Matriarchy and Patriarchy (IMP) model. The second is what we can call the Family Unity Model. Is either superior to the other? Let's see.

Acting IMPishly

Irrational matriarchs and patriarchs abound in Disney animated films. After Ariel disobeys her father by going to the surface, King Triton decides that she needs "constant supervision" and assigns Sebastian to the task. When he discovers that she's gone to the surface again and saved Eric's life, the King refuses to listen to anything she has to say, furiously destroying her collection of human artifacts. This breakdown of the father–daughter relationship leaves Ariel broken, crying, and vulnerable to manipulation by Ursula.

Disney and Philosophy: Truth, Trust, and a Little Bit of Pixie Dust, First Edition.
Edited by Richard B. Davis.

We see this a lot in IMPish households: overbearing and/or abusive parents leave children confused, alienated, and driven to search out some other (often magical) authority figure for wisdom and guidance. Sometimes this magical figure is benevolent. Lady Tremaine slave-drives her stepdaughter Cinderella, who bears the abuse with grace and patience. But she is finally driven to despair when her stepsisters tear apart her ball gown. It is at this point, with the complete break-down of the family, that Cinderella's Fairy Godmother intervenes.

More often than not, however, the magical figure takes advantage of the child for evil purposes as when Ursula seeks to overthrow Triton. Driven away after her mother, Queen Elinor, throws her bow into the fire, Merida happens upon a shady witch who doles out dangerous potions for pay without explaining their properties. This eventually results in Merida's inadvertently transforming her mother into a bear. Whether the auxiliary is benevolent or not, the common denominator is that the parental rule is imbecilic, if not abusive, threatening the freedom, creativity, and happiness of the child.

Locke's Liberty to Leave

Disney's IMP families often recapitulate an old debate in political philosophy – that between Robert Filmer (1588–1653) and John Locke (1632–1704). Filmer was a defender of patriarchy. According to Filmer, the idea that people are born free and equal was a novel but dangerous democratic doctrine. Filmer defended its antitheses: natural subjection and monarchy. For Filmer, fatherhood and regal power were created together, and the latter flowed from the former in the biblical person of Adam and all his posterity. Adam's children were subject to him, and the children of the patriarchs who followed were subject to them, and so on down the line. This was an absolute power because it was a power over life and death. Such a power logically implied plenary powers of parents over children.

Locke disagreed. He defended the idea of natural freedom and equality. According to Locke, the most promising argument for the patriarchist position is that parents give their children life and therefore have a power over their lives. Locke's reply, however, is that parents don't really give existence to their children. *God* does that. According to Locke, children are entrusted to their parents by God to be raised until such time as their powers of reason and will are sufficiently developed that they can live independently. Parents are stewards – obligated to nourish, educate, and rear their children until they leave the nest to pursue happiness.

IMP parents have a tendency to instrumentalize their children to their own happiness. After Frollo kills the gypsy woman, the archdeacon of Notre Dame gives him the penance of raising her orphaned son Quasimodo. Frollo initially feels the pangs of conscience from the "eyes of Notre Dame" – the Holy Virgin and Child, and chorus of saints – but finally agrees when he calculates that this "foul creature" might one day prove useful to him. Frollo then imprisons Quasimodo in the bell tower, feeding him a steady diet of lies about the outside world to keep him in line. This script is replayed between the witch, Lady Gothel, and her "adopted" daughter Rapunzel. What these IMPs fail to recognize is that children are not playthings to satisfy the selfish desires of adults.

Of course, there are parents – for instance, Triton, Elinor, and Chief Powhatan – who genuinely do seek the good of their children. They see the prevention or perhaps necessity of marriage for their daughters as essential to their well-being. In some ways, the youthful rebellion of the daughters is an offense against the proper authority of the parent. Still, their parenting undervalues what Locke would have seen as the legitimate claim of the adolescent to exercise her free will in the most consequential of choices – the choice to marry. This idea did not originate with liberal modernity. Locke traces a person's right to choose a marriage partner to the ancient divine sanction: *to leave one's father and mother and to cleave to one's spouse*. "To leave" suggests a decision to put one's self in motion: away from one party to another. It thus involves a capacity to choose and must be respected.

In the end, however, Disney's most memorable portrayals of marriage are not Lockean. For Locke held the idea that marriage could be a mere temporary contract to stay together until the children were raised – at which point spouses would be at liberty to separate: "there being no necessity in the nature of the thing, nor to the ends of it, that it should always be for life."[1]

Pongo, Perdita, and Procreation

In contrast with the Lockean vision of marriage, consider the marriage vows between Pongo and Perdita (and their "pets" Roger and Anita):

> Wilt thou love her, comfort her, honor and keep her in sickness and in health, and forsaking all others, keep thee only unto her, so long as ye both shall live?

Here marriage is conceived as something more akin to a covenant or sacrament: a permanent conjugal friendship through good times and bad. It is intrinsically lifelong, exclusive, and dyadic. Its dyadic nature is accentuated in that animals promiscuous by nature – once anthropomorphized – are monogamous, as with Mufasa and Sarabi, Simba and Nala.

Further, this concept of marriage doesn't preclude having and nourishing children. Perdita has 15 puppies. Mufasa and Sarabi, as well as Simba and Nala, produce heirs. But this does not mean that a fruitless union isn't a genuine marriage. In *Up!* Carl and Ellie dream of having children – to the point that every cloud they gaze at looks like a newborn baby. Yet Ellie has fertility problems and cannot. Still, they live out a beautiful relationship of mutual self-giving until Ellie's death. And Carl comes to discover the joys of parenthood in an unexpected way, as a sort of surrogate father for Russell.

Marriage is thus portrayed as an essentially fulfilling aspect of human flourishing whose permanent, exclusive, dyadic, and fruitful features are freely chosen. As Pongo puts it, the notion of the bachelor's life as all carefree glamour is "nonsense." Such a life is, rather, "downright dull." Even Mr. Incredible, who enjoys riches and fame as a bachelor Super, remarks "Sometimes I think I'd just like the simple life, you know? Relax a little and raise a family." The conception of marriage as genuinely good is the foundation of the Family Unity Model.

Heaven's Light or Frollo's Song?

After his encounter with the kind and lovely Esmeralda, Quasimodo sings about the beauty of marriage in celestial terms:

> So many times out here
> I've watched a happy pair
> Of lovers walking in the night
> They had a kind of glow around them
> It almost looked like heaven's light.

Quasimodo channels a theme found in the Christian philosophical tradition, eloquently restated and defended by John Paul II (1920–2005) – at once Pontiff and philosopher.

According to John Paul II, a key to unlocking the true meaning of marriage is to be found in the creation narrative in the book of Genesis: "It is not good for man to be alone."[2] It is not that the first man, Adam, was without the company of other beings. There was plenty of other plant and animal life around that he was authorized to *use* for his own purposes. Rather, his original solitude consisted in his experience of aloneness as a person – that is, a rational individual, valuable as an end-in-himself, and not reducible to a mere means to another's end. He wasn't created for that; he was created for a *community of persons*.

Thus according to the narrative, God creates Eve so that the first man and first woman might love one another through making gifts of themselves to one another – a becoming of "one flesh," actualized in physical and spiritual intertwining of persons in a shared life. From this union proceeds new life. This mirrors, says John Paul II, the archetype of love in the Trinity: The Father eternally begets the Son – the Holy Spirit proceeding from the mutual self-giving love of Father and Son. The test of authentic love, then, is whether it truly images God, that is, reflects heaven's light.[3]

Still, one needn't be a religious believer to see this point. We can see – by the light of unaided reason, as a philosopher might say – that "use" and "love" are opposites. To use something is to make an instrument of it, to treat it as a means to one's end. By contrast, love is a conscious and free-willing of a good (an aim, or end) for the sake of another. In a marriage context, this common good has a twofold character: the marital friendship itself and the having-rearing of children. This vision of love sharply contrasts with "using" another to satisfy one's carnal lusts or emotional desires, thereby violating their dignity.[4]

Frollo sings a different song altogether. After his encounter with Esmeralda, he croons:

> Why I see her dancing there
> Why her smoldering eyes still scorch my soul
> I feel her, I see her
> The sun caught in her raven hair
> Is blazing in me out of all control…
> Like fire, hellfire
> This fire in my skin
> This burning desire
> Is turning me to sin.

For Frollo, Esmeralda is not another *person*, an equal with whom he can engage in the mutual sacrifice of marriage. Not one bit. She is an object of his lust, fit only for sexual conquest. The root of his evil behavior is the denial of Esmeralda's equal dignity and personhood.

Gift-love is transformative. Nowhere is this more evident than in the story of the Beauty and the Beast. The Beast is self-seeking and superficial; he sees value only in one's looks and wealth. And for that he is accursed. Meanwhile, Belle has an inner virtue that radiates through her kindness to others, in particular her willingness to sacrifice herself for her father. This takes the Beast by surprise and sparks a desire in him for her – even more importantly, a desire to be virtuous and worthy of her. Through a series of self-denying acts (saving her from the wolves, giving her his whole library, freeing her from the castle), he eventually attains the inner beauty of virtue. The beast becomes a man through the love of a virtuous woman.

"You Can't Grow Up Without a Decent Education, You Know"

Here is another Disney doctrine: what unites a family is its joint action toward a common goal. Groups abound in civil society: clubs, co-ops, charities, and churches. What marks them off as *communities* is their pursuit of a common good together. If Pongo and Perdita are right, procreation is at least part of that good ("That's marvelous! That's fabulous! Why Pongo, you old rascal!"). But there's more; there is also education, household maintenance, and recreation.

Education is essential to proper childrearing. As Merlin, surrogate father to Arthur, declares, "You can't grow up without a decent education you know." Arthur must learn a range of essential subjects: mathematics, history, biology, science, English, Latin, and French. But Merlin also prizes the instillation of practical virtues. Indeed, he values "experiential" learning. For example, he transfigures both himself and his pupils into various animals to teach them the value of prudence among other things. Merlin emphasizes the *usefulness* of knowledge. But Disney also values studies for their own sake – as when Duchess directs the education of her kittens in music and painting and music; or when Bob and Helen let Dash join the track team.

The importance of education is accentuated by the negative effects of its neglect. Jasmine is the future queen of Agrabah, and yet she has never been allowed outside the palace walls. The education of this future ruler has failed because Jasmine doesn't share the common experiences and needs of her people. Indeed, her ignorance of the basics of economics nearly leads to the loss of her hand.

No doubt parents have a right to educate their children, since they have a duty to take care of their own. But Disney's Family Unity Model also knits together wise parental guidance with the good of children. When Pongo's son Patch opines that TV celebrity Thunderbolt is the greatest dog in the world, Penny replies that "no dog is better than dad." And indeed, Pongo wisely creates a plan to locate the stolen puppies and (with Perdita's help) devises various strategies to avoid detection. Mufasa instructs Simba in the ways of the savannah and kingly rule; however, Simba's youthful rebellion leads to disaster, not happiness. Without Elastigirl's maternal leadership and encouragement, Violet and Dash would never have come close to reaching their potential. If you desire a flourishing family life, you'll want to prize a complementarity and unity among parents and children. That's the (educational) gospel according to Disney.

On the flipside, think of Arthur and Cinderella and the disastrous consequences of neglecting their respective educations for the sake of household maintenance. Injustices abound – only underscoring the norm that maintaining the home is a common task of the *whole* family. Here Cinderella's stepmother gives a handy summary of the litany of non-negotiables: in addition to cooking, mending, and ironing, there is the cleaning – of laundry, carpets, windows, tapestries, draperies, garden, terrace, halls, stairs, and chimneys. But wait! There's more, Lucifer, the cat, must be given his bath. The members of the United Family will all have to pitch in to achieve optimal domestic order. Bob and Helen will have to team up: Bob lifting the furniture the furniture with one hand; Helen vacuuming underneath with the other.

And then a family must rest – relaxing and enjoying recreational activities *together*. Whether it is Belle and the Beast cuddled by a fire reading a book, or the Pongo family watching an episode of *The Thunderbolt Adventure Hour*, or Duchess, Thomas O'Malley, and their kittens singing and dancing with Scat Cat and his crew – to achieve optimal levels of happiness, balance, and well-being, a family must repose and recharge after its collective hard work.

"Done Properly, Parenting is Heroic"

But are the nitty-gritty realities of family life really worth it? One of the most prominent twentieth-century critics of the bourgeois family was the French existentialist and feminist philosopher, Simone de

Beauvoir (1908–1986). Beauvoir famously portrayed female embodiment as enslaving and alienating in its reproductive functions.

According to Beauvoir's version of feminism, a woman's reproductive organs express the "tyranny of the species" over the individual because of the arduous biological substratum of motherhood: menstrual cycle, gestation, birth, and breastfeeding. However, biology is not destiny. Human beings are radically free to impart a wide range of meanings to these essentially valueless biological facts. Thus, Beauvoir considers stories housewives might tell themselves to dignify their place in the home. Finding them all wanting, she engages in a broadside against housewifery:

> day after day, one must wash dishes, dust furniture, mend clothes that will be dirty, dusty, and torn again. The housewife wears herself out running on the spot; she does nothing; she only perpetuates the present.[5]

Housework snares the woman in "immanence," a degradation of existence that entraps because it is a repetitive drudgery that produces nothing new. Its opposite, "transcendence," is the experience of an open-ended self-creation through goal-setting and undertaking great projects. Motherhood is a form of servitude and therefore a form of immanence.

Disney's Family Unity Model rejects Beauvoir's brand of feminism outright. We need only consider Elastigirl. In an interview in her prime – during the "Glory Days" – she might well have been channeling Beauvoir when she scoffs at "settling down." Leave the saving of the world to the men? "I don't think so," she retorts. Yet she chooses to marry Mr. Incredible and then has three children. We see her cooking, cleaning, and doing laundry, but we sense no bitterness. She has hung up her Super suit for the joys of domestic housewifery.

Naturally enough, Elastigirl's body has changed since the glory days – the natural effect of pregnancy and childbirth. As most mothers do, she makes this observation with a sigh, but not a sigh of regret. She would not trade Violet, Dash, and Jack-Jack for a younger body and those lost years of crime-fighting. The woman who can bend her body into any shape gladly bends her life in a new direction for the good of her children. This is the heart of femininity and the heroism of motherhood. When Marlin the clownfish loses his son Nemo to a scuba diver's net, he leaves the safety of his reef, traveling hundreds of miles, battling sharks, mines, and jellyfish; riding sea turtles and escaping the clutches of a whale and pelican. All of this (for the good of) and to save his child. This is the heart of masculinity and the heroism of fatherhood.

In the Family Unity Model, having and rearing children is not to be feared as a threat to one's liberty, success, and happiness. Indeed, *The Incredibles* turns Beauvoir's critique of the family on its head in several ways. Child-rearing is the great project that has transcendent meaning. In the words of the inimitable Edna Mode, "Done properly, parenting is heroic." By contrast, *superheroic crime-fighting* is likened to drudgery. As Mr. Incredible says of his experience of constantly saving the world: "I feel like the maid; I just cleaned up this mess!" To be sure, Mr. Incredible later experiences ennui with his 9-to-5, white-collar grind. And admittedly, the family's crime-fighting adventures do have moments of transcendence that make us exclaim: "That was totally wicked!" Nevertheless, Bob Parr's uncontrollable craving to relive the glory days has decidedly negative effects: the near death of his wife and children and the near kidnapping of his son, Jack-Jack. His revelatory moment comes when he finally realizes that he is missing the adventure right in front of him: home life and raising a family.

Even when Helen and Bob switch places in the sequel, Elastigirl is hesitant to leave the home. She sees the ultimate end of their family plan not as reestablishing her primacy as an active superhero, but to return home and give her children the choice to one day become public Supers. Meanwhile, Mr. Incredible discovers the heroic feats necessary to help Dash with his math homework and Violet with her boy problems – all the while keeping baby Jack-Jack from blowing up the house!

The sacrifices of parenthood are not enslavement but salvation. For all their Super powers, neither Elastigirl nor Mr. Incredible is able to defeat the Screenslaver. It is *their children* who ultimately save the day. They fight their way onto the hijacked boat and then it is Jack-Jack – not even a toddler – who finally frees his parents from the Screenslaver's control. The defeat of evil requires the effort of team: an entire family. "You are my greatest adventure," says Mr. Incredible, "and I almost missed it."

Robots and Romance

Radical critics of the family have suggested that it be abolished. The ongoing needs of society and human nature itself have proven to be stubborn obstacles. Could technology, perhaps, replace the family and all the benefits it affords? Imagine a world in which the goods of reproduction, education, household maintenance, and recreation were provided solely by robots. That is precisely the world envisioned in *WALL·E*, where an apocalypse of toxic pollution has devastated the world, forcing a small remnant of humanity to live on board a spaceship for the past 700 years.

In the *WALL·E* world, human beings spend their day flitting from one self-absorbed hedonic pleasure to the next on motorized chairs with a holoscreen constantly before their eyes. Babies are manufactured and raised by robots. Humans are so overweight and their muscles so atrophied that they cannot even stand on two feet. Meanwhile, the robots WALL·E and EVE spark a romance. The constant refrain during their courtship is a song from the musical *Hello, Dolly!*

> It only takes a moment
> For your eyes to meet and then
> Your heart knows in a moment
> You will never be alone again
> I held her for an instant
> But my arms felt sure and strong
> It only takes a moment
> To be loved a whole life long.

The irony is that the technologically pampered humans live a robotic existence where all contact is mediated by screens and machines, while artificial beings see the beauty of genuine love and seek to experience it through the touch of holding hands. WALL·E's and EVE's romance awakens two people, John and Mary, from their technological slumber, and with the barest physical contact, a romance between them buds. It takes the love of two robots to remind humanity of what they have lost – and to warn us what we are at risk of losing.

In the climactic scene of the struggle to return to Earth, the ship tilts, throwing the people into a heap, sending a gaggle of toddlers hurtling downwards. Mary yells: "Hey John, get ready to have some kids," as they join arms to save the toddlers before the ship sets a course to return to Earth. The double-meaning of her words is not lost on us. Rebuilding the world begins with the family.

Notes

1. Locke, J. (1988). *The Two Treatises of Government*, 321. Cambridge: Cambridge University Press.
2. Genesis 2:18.

3. Paul II, J. (2006). *Man and Woman He Created Them: A Theology of the Body* (trans. M. Waldstein), 162–164. Boston: Pauline Books and Media.
4. Wojtyla, K. (1981). *Love and Responsibility* (trans. H.T. Willetts), 21–34. San Francisco: Ignatius Press.
5. de Beauvoir, S. (2011). *The Second Sex* (trans. C. Borde and S. Malovany-Chevallier), 539. New York: Vintage Books.

Part III

"YOUR IDENTITY IS YOUR MOST VALUABLE POSSESSION"

How to Convince Sleeping Beauty She's Not Dreaming

C. A. McIntosh

You know the story: the much-anticipated princess, Aurora, is born to throngs of celebration. It is hoped that she will grow up to marry the prince of a neighboring kingdom, uniting the two into a single royal bloodline. The sun is shining. People are smiling. The future seems bright … until Maleficent shows up and casts her dreadful curse: that before the sun sets on Aurora's 16th birthday, she will prick her finger on the spindle of a spinning wheel and die. Fortunately, one of the good fairies is able to mitigate the curse so that Aurora will not die but merely sleep, and sleep she will until true love's kiss breaks the spell.

And so it comes to pass, despite the king and queen's destruction of all spinning wheels in the kingdom, and the three good fairies' best efforts to hide Aurora away in the forest. The princess is brought back to the palace (perhaps a little prematurely) on the evening of her 16th birthday, lured into a secret room containing a spinning wheel, pricks her finger, and falls into a deep slumber. Luckily, Prince Phillip is able to thwart Maleficent's evil scheme and awaken his Sleeping Beauty with a kiss, so that they can live happily ever after.

A fairytale, quite literally. We don't blink an eye at how exotic the whole thing is. But put yourself in Aurora's shoes for a moment. The whole ending scene probably feels a bit surreal to this young lady, who was raised in the woods by three old women. Until the day before, she didn't know that she was a princess, much less anything about the existence of good fairies and evil sorceresses. Now all of a

Disney and Philosophy: Truth, Trust, and a Little Bit of Pixie Dust, First Edition.
Edited by Richard B. Davis.

sudden, she finds herself saved from a terrible curse, dancing with a handsome prince in the middle of a palace ballroom! Would we blame her for questioning whether any of the events of the last 24 hours were real, speculating that perhaps it was all just a dream? Indeed, the whole situation gets even more complicated when we remember that Aurora had a dream about Prince Phillip before she ever met him in real life. She sings in the woods:

> I know you, I walked with you once upon a dream
> I know you, that look in your eyes is so familiar a gleam
> And I know it's true that visions are seldom all they seem
> But if I know you, I know what you'll do
> You'll love me at once, the way you did once upon a dream

What if her dream had started before she pricked her finger, and even before her encounter with Prince Phillip in the woods? Or what if, instead of walking and singing freely with the birds for the past 16 years, Aurora had actually been caught by Maleficent much earlier, and has been lying asleep in a dungeon the whole time? Perhaps her whole life up to this point has only been an elaborate illusion foisted upon her by Maleficent to keep the princess in her power. In short, Aurora might ask, "How do I know I'm not dreaming? How do I know any of this real?"

Maleficent, the Evil Genius

But you don't need to be living in a fairytale to ask yourself such questions. The philosopher René Descartes (1596–1650) is famous for showing that these questions are just as pressing for us in real life. In his search for certainty, Descartes found that there is precious little that cannot be doubted, including whether he is in fact awake and not dreaming:

> For example, there is the fact that I am here, seated by the fire attired in a dressing gown, having this paper in my hands and other similar matters. And how could I deny that these hands and this body are mine…? …At the same time I must remember that…I am in the habit of sleeping, and in my dreams representing to myself the same things… [I]n dwelling on this reflection I see so manifestly that there are no certain indications by which we may clearly distinguish wakefulness from sleep that I am lost in astonishment. And my astonishment is such that it is almost capable of persuading me that I now dream.[1]

And just in case you think you do have some way of distinguishing wakefulness from sleep, Descartes has another card to play. What if there were some god-like evil genius who "has employed his whole energies in deceiving me"? He writes:

> I shall consider that the heavens, the earth, colors, figures, sound, and all other external things are nought but the illusions and dreams of which this genius has availed himself in order to lay traps for my credulity; I shall consider myself having no hands, no eyes, no flesh, no blood, nor any senses, yet falsely believing myself to possess all these things.[2]

Sure, we don't believe we are being deceived this way by an evil genius. But isn't it at least possible? And if possible, how can we say we know for sure we aren't? The problem is even worse for Aurora. It's not merely possible that there could be an evil genius in the story; there is one in Maleficent! This kind of observation leads Descartes to doubt whether he can be sure that any of his experiences are of real things beyond his own mind.

But how so? Let's see if we can outline his reasoning step-by-step. The first step is:

> I don't know I'm not dreaming.

Remember, Descartes is thinking that it's at least possible all my experiences are a mere dream induced by a Maleficent-like evil genius. Why think that's possible? Possibilities come cheap. Philosophers tell us that to see if something is possible we just have to conceive of a scenario – any scenario – where it happens, and isn't strictly illogical or contradictory. Nearly all Disney movies represent to us mere possibilities. I can conceive of scenarios with genies, wooden puppets coming to life, flying elephants, and mermaids. I can conceive of scenarios with talking animals, insects, toys, robots, and even household objects like clocks and candlesticks. And there certainly seems to be no special problem in conceiving of a scenario where all my experiences are a mere dream induced by a Maleficent-like evil genius. But now the question is: if that's possible, how do I know it's not *really* the case? The question doesn't arise with respect to the other possibilities, because they differ so radically from our everyday experience of the real world. But in the case of being deceived by a Maleficent-like evil genius into dreaming what I think is real, all my experiences would be exactly the same! And if I have no way of telling whether I'm dreaming or not, how can I say I know I'm not dreaming? I guess I can't.

This leads to us to the second step in Descartes' reasoning:

> If I don't know I'm not dreaming, I don't know there is a real world beyond my own mind.

The connection between the first and second steps should be obvious enough. If I don't know I'm not dreaming, how do I know if *any* of my experiences correspond to anything real outside of my own mind? A dream is more than "a wish your heart makes," as Cinderella says. Dreams are mental phenomena, akin to memories or what you might see in your "mind's eye" as you imagine something with your eyes closed, that occurs while you sleep.[3] Some dreams are as bizarre as the stuff of the most exotic fairytales – just think of the White Rabbit, Caterpillar, Mad Hatter, and Queen of Hearts from *Alice's Adventures in Wonderland*. So many nonsensical, bizarre scene changes occur that we aren't really surprised when Alice wakes up under a tree and discovers that it was all a dream. But other dreams are more mundane, such as Dumbo's elephants on parade, Lightning McQueen's dream of racing, and Bruno the dog's dream of chasing Lucifer the cat. And from such dreams we groggily wake up in confusion and come to our senses moments later.Yet sometimes we have dreams more mundane still – ones that are easy to confuse with what's real. Probably most of us have sometimes paused and thought, "Wait, did I dream that, or…?" I'm convinced that my wife dreams of tasking me with certain daily chores and errands, which later, to her disappointment, I do not recall in the slightest (her theory – that I just wasn't listening – is less exotic). In such cases, we find ourselves unsure of what's real and what's not. And if you don't know if something was a dream or not, you don't know if it is something real, beyond your own mind. Now finally we can complete the reasoning. Given the first two steps in Descartes' thinking, his conclusion follows:

> So, I don't know that there is a real world beyond my own mind.

There you have it. What is Aurora to make of this argument? Is she doomed to being skeptical of there being a real world for the rest of her life? And for that matter, what are *we* to make of it?

Epistemology's Prince Charming

As you can imagine, epistemologists (philosophers who think about the nature of knowledge) have tried to slay this skeptical dragon for millennia. Perhaps the most infamous knight in philosophical armor to do so is the Englishman G. E. Moore (1873–1958). Moore's response, which he humbly dubs a *proof*, is disarmingly simple. How can Aurora know there is a real world beyond her own mind? All she has to do is pass what we might call *the Pinocchio test*. The test is easy. When Pinocchio wakes up to find that he has turned into a real boy, he looks at his hands in astonishment and exclaims, "I'm real! I'm a real boy!" The proof was right there before him. His own two hands! So, to pass the Pinocchio test to see if you're real and not just dreaming, Moore would tell Aurora and us to do the same: just take a look at your hands. There is one. And there's another. Voilà! There's the proof that there are at least two real things that exist beyond our mind. Moore's proof goes like this: Here is a hand and here is another; If that's right, then there is a real world beyond my own mind; So, there is a real world beyond my own mind.

Unimpressed? Well, what did you expect? Moore insists that his argument meets the technical standards of a proof. First, the steps or premises are different than the conclusion; so we aren't reasoning in a circle. Second, the conclusion follows logically from the premises. And finally, the main premise – that therereally are two hands before me – is not just a mere opinion, but something I can be said to know. That's just a matter of common sense.

This last aspect of Moore's proof is what makes it so memorable, but also hated among philosophers. Philosophers have a well-earned reputation for being abstract and aloof from the ordinary and mundane, finding delight instead in the inner citadel of the mind. The ancient philosopher Thales (c. 625–c. 545 BCE), preoccupied philosophizing about the heavens, allegedly wandered straight into a well. Immanuel Kant (1724–1804) wrote thousands of mind-numbing pages exploring what we can know by reason alone apart from experience. And legend has it that Descartes locked himself in a Dutch oven until he could think of at least one thing he could be absolutely certain of. Indeed, some of the intellectual castle-building efforts of philosophers wind up resembling the imaginary worlds of Disney more than our own. But Moore, while not incapable of esoteric theorizing himself, nonetheless kept his theorizing grounded in common sense.

But what, exactly, is common sense anyway? Philosophically speaking, it is more than commonly held beliefs that are sensible. The belief that the Earth is round is commonly held and sensible, but it's not a common-sense belief by Moore's lights. Common sense beliefs are beliefs so obvious and self-evident that we simply find ourselves with them, often without even realizing it. In "A Defense of Common

Sense,"[4] Moore lists a host of examples by no means limited to the following:

- I exist and have a body
- Other people like me exist
- Material objects exist
- Space and time are real.
- I (and others) know these things.

Of course, Moore is well aware that certain philosophers have denied such beliefs. Leibniz (1646–1716), for instance, denied that space is real. Idealists deny the existence of material objects. Moore's teacher John McTaggart (1866–1925) famously denied the reality of time. Contemporary philosopher Peter Unger has denied that people exist, including himself! And of course a radical skeptic would deny that we know all of the above. Moore won't have any of this. Moore allows that the correct analysis of what these statements ultimately mean may be subject to debate, but to one who straightforwardly denies that we know them, Moore has "nothing better to say than that it seems to me that I do know them, with certainty."[5] They are proper starting points of *what* we know, even if we don't know *how* we know them.

The Flight of Phillip's Sword

Moore's emphasis on common sense isn't a cop out; it is part of a strategy for handling pesky philosophical arguments for bizarre, counterintuitive conclusions like "I don't know there is a real world beyond my own mind." It's easy to confuse not knowing how to answer such arguments with being irrational for resisting the conclusion. But that is a mistake.

Let me illustrate with a different example. Maleficent, in the form of a fire-breathing dragon, has Prince Phillip balancing on the edge of a fiery precipice. A good fairy comes to his aid, telling him to hurl the sword. "Oh sword of truth, fly swift and sure, that evil die and good endure!" Just as Phillip readies himself for the throw, suppose Maleficent interrupts with one last attempt at deception:

MALEFICENT: You fool! It's impossible to kill me that way!
PRINCE PHILLIP: Impossible? Whatever do you mean?
MALEFICENT: Well, it is impossible to traverse an infinite. No matter how far you get, there's always infinity to go. But if it is impossible traverse an infinite, then motion is impossible! For between any two points A and B there are infinitely many

> intervals: before your sword can reach $^1/_2$ way between you and me, it must reach $^1/_4$ of the way. But before it can reach ¼ of the way, it must reach $^1/_8$ of the way. And before $^1/_8$, $^1/_{16}$. And so on, *to infinity*. But since it's impossible to traverse the infinite, and there are infinitely many intervals between you and me, your sword can never reach me!

Maleficent, being the evil genius she is, is using the ancient philosopher Zeno's (c. 490–c. 430 BCE) argument against the possibility of motion:

> It is impossible to traverse an infinite.
> If it is impossible to traverse an infinite, then motion is impossible.
> So, motion is impossible.

Now, even supposing Prince Phillip doesn't know how to answer Maleficent's argument, would he be unreasonable in continuing to believe that motion is possible – that his sword could "fly swift and sure" to hit its mark? No! The reasonable thing to do would be to simply reject the main premise of her argument (namely, that it is impossible to traverse an infinite) even if he doesn't know what's wrong with it. But why so? Because he can be more certain that motion is possible than its being impossible to traverse an infinite. So he reasons as follows:

> Motion *is* possible.
> If it is impossible to traverse the infinite, then motion is impossible.
> So, it is not impossible to traverse the infinite.

And the deciding factor between Maleficent's argument and his own is...common sense. Moore writes: "The only way...of deciding between my opponent's argument and mine, as to which is better, is by deciding which premise is known to be true."[6] And clearly we know to be true that motion is possible. That is a common sense belief if anything is. Moore continues:

> I think we may safely challenge any philosopher to bring forward any argument in favor either of the proposition that we do not know [some proposition of common sense], or of the proposition that it is not true, which does not at some point, rest upon some premise which is, beyond comparison, less certain than is the proposition which it is designed to attack.[7]

In other words, if you're confronted with an argument against something as commonsensical as "there is a real world beyond my own mind," or "motion is possible," the main premises in those arguments will invariably be less certain than the commonsense beliefs themselves. Because I am more certain that there is a real world beyond my own mind than I am that I don't know I'm not dreaming, the Moorean shift (as it is sometimes called) in response to the radical skeptic would be:

> I *do* know there is a real world beyond my own mind
> If I don't know I'm not dreaming, I don't know there is a real world beyond my own mind.

And how do I know that there is a real world beyond my own mind? Passing the Pinocchio test. "Here is a hand, and here is another." Common sense. We can thus conclude:

> So, I do know I'm not dreaming.

If nothing else, the Moorean shift is a way to keep us safe from falling victim to what I call *the madman fallacy*, inspired by G. K. Chesterton's (1874–1936) observation that "if you argue with a madman, it is extremely probable that you will get the worst of it; for in many ways his mind moves all the quicker for not being delayed by the things that go with good judgment."[8] The madman fallacy, then, is dumbfounding an interlocutor by saying something that goes against basic good sense. When an annoyed Simba asks the crazy Rafiki the meaning of his seemingly nonsensical chant "Asante sana squash banana, wewe nugu mimi hapana" and is told "It means you're a baboon, and I'm not!", we might say Rafiki stumped poor Simba with the madman fallacy. And we can definitely say you've been duped by the madman fallacy, if you have nothing to say to someone who insists you don't know you're not dreaming. Just hold up your two hands and say, "Look, I'm more certain that there's a real world beyond my mind than that I don't know I'm not dreaming."

Visions Are *Often* all they Seem

If you're still unsatisfied with Moore's common sense response to the problem of skepticism, maybe we can push it a bit further by directly attacking the first step in the argument for skepticism, that I don't know I'm not dreaming. Recall that in response to someone who denies that we *know* common sense beliefs, Moore has "nothing better to say than that it seems to me that I do know them, with certainty."[9] Moore's use of the word "seems" here is important. Contrary to Aurora's lyric "visions are seldom all they seem," how things seem or appear to us is good reason to believe that's how things in fact are. Of course, it's *possible* I'm merely dreaming what I think is real, but until I have reason to think I *am* dreaming, I can continue believing I'm not. There appear to be two hands before me; so, there probably are two hands before me, because if there weren't, how things appear would likely be different.

The problem in the present context is that the possibility of a dream-inducing Maleficent-like evil genius guarantees that how things appear would be no different, whether I'm dreaming or not. But maybe there *is* a difference: does it not appear to me that there is a difference between dreaming and wakefulness? The very fact that I am aware of such a distinction at all suggests the distinction is real. If our whole lives were merely a dream, how could we even be aware of such a distinction as that between dreaming and wakefulness? To say I merely dreamed of the distinction does nothing to discredit its legitimacy: I have the idea of a mental state called "dreaming," and I also have the idea of a different mental state, one that is not dreaming. The distinction is as conceptually solid as any other between two distinct things. But then how do I get the idea of wakefulness in the first place other than from a state of wakefulness? It would be like having the idea of a color without ever having seen that color.

So the fact that it appears to me that there is a distinction between dreaming and wakefulness justifies my belief that there is something that induces non-dreaming states – that is, a world beyond my own mind. But does it justify the belief that I am not dreaming *now*? Well, I don't see how it could *seem* to me that there is a distinction between two mental states without having actually experienced those different states, because "seemings" just are mental states. I must know what it's like to dream, and know what it's like to be awake. So, contrary to what Descartes says, I must be able to tell the difference *somehow*, even if I can't articulate *exactly* how.[10] Indeed, when I am awake, it never seems to me that I'm dreaming; but it does sometimes seem to me that I'm dreaming when I'm dreaming![11] So I have good reason to believe that it is false that if I were dreaming, things wouldn't seem different to me. And since it seems to me *now* that I am awake and not dreaming, I am justified in believing I am awake and not dreaming.

Happily Ever After

Okay, maybe that last point was a bit trippy. You might be wondering here, "Why should Aurora care so much about knowing she's not dreaming? She marries her prince, the two kingdoms are united, and they dance the night away. Dream or not, what difference does it make, as long as she lives happily ever after?" This is a good question. And we should ask it of ourselves. Suppose you could have nothing but pleasurable experiences for the rest of your life, only you had the choice between it all being a dream or it being real. Would you choose that? Most of us, I expect, would choose real life, even if our experiences would be no different. In fact, I suspect many of us would choose real life even if that meant experiencing pleasure *and pain*. Why is that?

We'd prefer a real life over an experientially identical dream life, or even a more pleasurable dream life, because there's more to life than just experience. We want pleasurable experience, yes; but we also want *authenticity*. To paraphrase the philosopher Robert Nozick (1938–2002), I don't want to just experience myself as a good person – courageous, kind, intelligent, witty, and loving – I want to *be* a good person.[12] Think of Bolt, the dog who believes he's got superpowers because he was raised on a Hollywood special effects set designed to make it look like he does. There's something pathetic about that. He's not *really* a superdog. We wouldn't want to be Bolt. Each of us wants to be a person whose experiences are backed by reality. That is why Aurora should care. And that is why we should, too. A true "happily ever after" ending will be one where we know our experiences are authentic. Thankfully, to know that, all we need are our own two hands and a little common sense. Of course, a romantic kiss from a significant other will do, too.[13]

Notes

1. Descartes, R. (1970). Meditations on first philosophy. In: *The Philosophical Works of Descartes*, vol. I (trans. E. S. Haldane and G. R. T. Ross), 145–146. Cambridge: Cambridge University Press.
2. Ibid., p. 148.
3. *Pace* Norman Malcolm, who denies that dreams are experiences (insofar as all experience is conscious experience). See his "Dreaming and Skepticism," *The Philosophical Review* 65 (1956), pp. 14–37.
4. Moore, G. E. (1962). *Philosophical Papers*, 32–59. New York: Collier Books.
5. Ibid., p. 43.

6. Ibid., pp. 121–122.
7. Moore, G. E. (1959). *Philosophical Studies*, 227–228. Paterson, NJ: Littlefield, Adams & Co.
8. Chesterton, G.K. (1986). *Orthodoxy*, in *The Collected Works of G. K. Chesterton* Vol. I, ed. David Dooley, 221. San Francisco: Ignatius.
9. Moore, *Philosophical Papers*, p. 43.
10. Here I take no stance on how exactly we might distinguish dreams from reality, which is the subject of an important paper by Macdonald, M. (1953). Sleeping and waking. Mind 72: 202–215. One of her observations is that there is no continuity of experience between dreaming and waking, whereas there is always continuity of experience while awake. Descartes himself makes a similar observation in *Meditation VI,* pp. 198–199.
11. As happens in so-called lucid dreams. I had an amusing lucid dream in May 2015. I dreamt that I was a secret agent, and was close to finishing a mission. But then, in the dream, I started thinking about the dream I was having. I was stealthily climbing a stairwell in hot pursuit, but before reaching the top, I paused and thought something like this: "I am enjoying this dream, and the climax is almost here. But it is about time to get up. Should I continue dreaming and finish the mission, or wake up and not finish? I should probably get up, because I already know how it ends." While I was thinking about the dream and whether to end it, (i) the feeling of being in total control of my decision was palpable, and (ii) I was vaguely aware, though in an inarticulable way, of what was happening (that I was thinking about my dream while still dreaming) and I thought *that* was interesting. Well, I didn't in fact get up, and the dream continued exactly as I thought it would. And, of course, I remembered all this when I finally got up.
12. Nozick, R. (1974). *Anarchy, State, and Utopia*, 43. New York: Basic Books.
13. Many thanks to Elizabeth McIntosh for her help and feedback on this chapter. I could not have written it without consulting her extensive knowledge of Disney films.

Knowing Who you Are

Existence Precedes Essence in *Moana*

William J. Devlin

Disney's computer-animated musical film, *Moana* (2016) tells the tale of Moana, the daughter of Tui, the chief of a Polynesian island, Motunui. Bound by the legendary tradition of her ancestors, Moana is expected to follow her lineage and take over as chief when she grows up. Her father and mother, Sina, equally bound to this tradition, prepare Moana for this leadership role. But ever since she was a toddler, Moana has wanted to sail beyond the reef and voyage across the seas – a calling reinforced by her free-spirited grandmother, Tala, who encourages Moana to "know who you are." Despite her father's misgivings and prohibitions, Moana learns that she was chosen by the ocean to restore the heart of Te Fiti, which was stolen by Maui, the shapeshifting demigod who seeks the love and praise of human beings. Upon completing her adventures, Moana successfully restores the heart, thereby saving the people of Motunui.

As we dig beneath the surface level of the story, we find a metaphorical and philosophical level to Moana's journey. Moana must choose between sailing beyond the reef or obeying her parents, resulting in an existential crisis. In effect, Moana faces a choice that everyone faces, between independently creating one's own identity or merely following the crowd. To explore this crisis, and gain a better understanding of her decisions, let's join Moana on her wayfinding adventures, using the philosophy of existentialism as our navigator.

Disney and Philosophy: Truth, Trust, and a Little Bit of Pixie Dust, First Edition.
Edited by Richard B. Davis.

"This Suits You"

From the opening scene, we learn that Moana yearns to become a voyager. Her grandmother tells the frightful tale of the demon, Te Kā, who seeks the heart of Te Fiti after Maui steals it. Tala cautions that, unless someone restores the heart, darkness will spread "until every one of us is devoured by the bloodthirsty jaws of inescapable death!" While all the other children run and cry in fear from this story, little Moana listens intently, eager to be the one to restore the heart. But her father forbids her from having such seafaring aspirations. Chief Tui offers two reasons against sailing away. First, he persistently cautions Moana that she'd be violating a Motunui rule, "No one goes beyond the reef." Second, advising her that she "must learn where you're meant to be," he argues that everything in Motunui has a role. From the people, such as the dancers and the fishermen, to the natural elements on the islands, such as the coconuts and leaves – everything on Motunui serves a purpose. As he explains to Moana, she too has a purpose: to become the "next chief of our great people." The people of Motunui will need a chief and "there you are."

Tui's worldview echoes the philosopher Aristotle (384–322 BCE) in some ways. Aristotle maintains that everything has a function and with it, a specific role. This function and role is the thing's essence – the definition of that thing. The fisherman, for example, has a function to catch fish with the purpose of feeding one's tribe. So the essence of the fisherman is to catch fish. Meanwhile, a thing's worth or value is measured by how well it performs its function. A fisherman is only good as a fisherman insofar as he is able to successfully catch fish. The excellent fisherman is the one who is skilled and successful at catching fish. At the same time, Aristotle contends that human beings generally have a specific function: to reason excellently. The human being is the rational animal. We are therefore already born with a purpose or role – to reason. So we are measured by how well we perform the function of reasoning.

For Tui, everything on Motunui has a specific purpose. In his view, tradition commands that Moana's role is specifically to serve as chief. Here we can also say that each person or thing has an essence that precedes its existence. That is, Moana's role as chief was determined even before she was born. Her family lineage dictates that the child of Chief Tui will necessarily become the next chief. Thus, Moana's essence is defined prior to her birth. Her father explains this to her in a private moment at "the place of chiefs," the island's highest mountaintop where each new chief adds a stone to a column to raise the island higher. He tells Moana that there will "come a time when you will stand on this peak and place a stone on this mountain." For Tui, the role of chief is Moana's essence, and so "it's time to be" who the people "need you to be."

After years of coaxing and training (and singing "Where You Are"), Tui and Sina convince Moana to take her role as the next chief. As a teenager, she shadows her father as chief, demonstrating the idea that one's essence precedes one's existence – that she was always meant to become Motunui's leader. Likewise, Moana echoes Aristotle's concept of being excellent in one's function, as she excels in her leadership role. In response to a leaking roof, she discovers that the issue was not because of the fronds but because the wind shifted the post. In response to diseased coconuts, she directs the harvesters to clear the diseased trees and start a new grove elsewhere. Moana thus not only adopts the role of chief, she performs above and beyond expectations. So much so that her father, seeing her excellence, proudly tells her, "This suits you."

"But the Voice Inside Sings a Different Song"

Though Moana excels in her leadership role, she soon finds that she does not want to become chief. In response to the issue of having no fish in the lagoon, she insists (to her father's anger) that the solution is to fish beyond the reef, arguing that the rule of not sailing beyond the reef is antiquated given these new circumstances. Though her public reasoning is attached to her role as chief, Moana privately laments that the ocean is "calling out to me." While she wants to "be the perfect daughter" and fulfill her parents' wishes that she become chief, she comes "back to the water" because it is the place she longs to be. She admits that her father's Aristotelian views make sense – everything on the island is "by design" so that everybody "has a role on this island." Still, she doubts that the role of chief is the role she wants. Instead, Moana yearns to become a wayfinder who travels across the seas to restore the heart of Te Fiti to save her people.

Moana thus faces a dilemma: become chief or sail beyond the reef. As such, she is torn between the dictates of perceived tradition as presented by her father and her introspective yearning toward defining herself through different actions. This dilemma strikes at the heart of the philosophy of existentialism. For existentialists, human beings are unique in the sense that "who you are and who you will become" is always up for reevaluation and reconsideration. A human being is a *being-in-question*, meaning that we can always reflect upon how we define ourselves and freely determine who we want to become. As Moana agonizes over whether to be a chief or voyager, she demonstrates that her own being is in question. On the one hand, she accepts that she could "lead with pride" and help strengthen the village. On the other hand, she knows "the voice inside sings a different song." In her heart, she wants to sail beyond the reef. Thus, Moana faces an existential crisis.

Moana's questioning her role as chief exemplifies another important existentialist idea, one that counters Aristotle's view that humans have a fixed essence. The existentialist philosopher Jean-Paul Sartre (1905–1980) argues that humans are the kind of being whose "existence precedes essence." The human being is born without a fixed, unchanging essence. She first "exists, turns up, appears on the scene, and only afterwards, defines" herself through her decisions, choices, and actions. As such, the first principle of existentialism is that the human being "is nothing else but what he makes of himself."[1] Because we don't have a pre-determined essence, we have the freedom to determine who we are and who we will become.

In contrast, Sartre suggests that for other nonhuman things "essence precedes existence."[2] Take Moana's sidekick chicken, Heihei, for example. Heihei acts in a fixed and unchanging manner. As a chicken, he is constantly pecking to eat food. But, peculiar to Heihei, he also pecks at anything – from chicken feed to rocks to nothing at all! He even eats the heart of Te Fiti! But, as peculiar as Heihei is, we don't expect him to ever change his behavior. His behavior remains exactly the same throughout the movie. He cannot and will not change. This is why we find that many characters – from Moana to Maui to the ocean – often have to protect him from his own quirky behavior. Following Sartre, we might say that Heihei cannot change his behavior because his essence precedes his existence. He has no capacity to choose to be anything but what he already is: an eccentric, bizarre chicken.

Heihei's essence is fixed, but Moana recognizes that her existence precedes her essence, and so she is free to create herself in the way she sees fits. This freedom makes her dilemma more challenging. As the existentialists see it, many people ignore their individual freedom and instead find solace in denying such liberties. Rather than fully acknowledge and embrace one's capacity to legislate one's own essence, a person may instead let others define them – telling them what to do, who they are, and what they should become. In so doing, a person relinquishes their freedom and their individuality, becoming a nameless, faceless, member of the group that defines them. The existentialists refer to this group as "the crowd" or, more negatively, "the herd," suggesting the vapid and unreflective commonality of such an identity. In Moana's case, her father and the people of Motunui serve as the crowd. They compel her to conform to their social rules and norms, to give up her passion to become a wayfinder, and to accept a predetermined essence as chief.

It's easy to lose one's individuality and slip into the crowd mentality. Often reinforced through social norms, rules, and guidelines, the crowd absorbs the individual, so that she might not even be aware she's losing her freedom. Take Tui, for example. As Sila recounts, Tui was once like Moana when he was younger. Though compelled by an individual passion toward voyaging, he is forbidden by social rules to act on his calling. Nevertheless, he sneaks out with a friend to set sail. But he encountered an "unforgiving sea" which capsized his canoe and led to his friend drowning. Letting his fears and regrets get the best of him, Tui relinquishes his yearning to sail and accepts his role as chief, becoming part of the crowd. Sartre refers to this status – the state of rejecting one's individual freedom and responsibilities – as *bad faith*. Tui demonstrates bad faith in at least two ways. First, as suggested, he denies his own freedom to continue sailing and winds up conforming to the crowd. Second, he attempts to pull Moana into the crowd mentality, arguing that she really has no choice in the matter because she must conform to the rules. The rules dictate that she cannot sail beyond the reef; so she should relinquish her freedom and become absorbed in the crowd. Moana thus struggles with losing her individual freedom and passion, running the risk of living in bad faith and becoming a member of the crowd.

"That Voice Inside is Who You Are"

Existentialism holds that, despite the dangers of losing one's identity to the crowd, we have the ability to embrace our freedom and preserve our individuality. Sartre refers to this state as *authenticity*. The authentic individual not only acknowledges her freedom, but also assumes full responsibility for her actions and decisions. By doing so, she doesn't ignore her choices and simply follow the command of others. Likewise, she doesn't excuse her behavior on account of social rules, traditional norms, or religious commands.

Moana's grandmother, Tala, exemplifies living with authenticity. Rather than conform to the crowd, she lives by her own standards. She sings to Moana that she likes the water because it doesn't conform to common norms: "it is mischievous" and "misbehaves." Tala stands apart from the crowd, even flouting the leadership of her son, the chief. When Moana worries that she'll inform her dad about the failed trip beyond the reef, Tala responds, "I'm his mom. I don't have to tell him anything." Similarly, from the viewpoint of the crowd, Tala appears like "the village crazy lady" because they "say I drift too far" from the ordinary. Nevertheless, she embraces her individuality and uniqueness, freely defining herself. As she explains to Moana, "once you know what you like, well, there you are," even if it is outside of what is commonly expected and accepted.

Tala not only models authenticity, but she also teaches Moana to live the authentic life. Aware of Moana's dilemma, Tala advises that though she should generally mind what her father says, there will come a time when she'll have to follow her own heart and define herself in her own fashion. Tala sings, "You may hear a voice inside / And if the voice starts to whisper / To follow the farthest star / Moana, that voice inside is who you are." This advice echoes Sartre's own existentialist advice, "You're free, choose, that is, invent."[3] Tala thus guides Moana toward answering the question of "who you were meant to be," by revealing that while the people of Motunui are currently homebound villagers, they were originally voyagers. On the one hand, this revelation suggests that Tui's appeal to tradition is misplaced. If one examines the deeper traditions of Motunui, the rule forbidding sailing is invalid. On the other hand, it encourages Moana to follow "that voice inside," which is telling her to become a wayfinder.

Moana is motivated by her ancestors and inspired by her grandmother's dying wish that Moana find Maui and demand that he help restore the heart of Te Fiti. Unlike her father, Moana overcomes her fears from her first disastrous seafaring outing, and she commits to sailing beyond the reef. In a touching moment, when she passes away, Tala reincarnates as a stingray, and guides Moana's canoe across the reef. Moana sings, "See her light up the night in the sea, she calls me / And yes, I know, that I can go." She thus resolves her dilemma so that "All the time wondering where I need to be is behind me." Her choice is to live the authentic life, free from the crowd, so that "I'm on my own, to worlds unknown / Every turn I take, every trail I track / Is a choice I make...From the great unknown, where I go alone, where I long to be." In short, at this point, Moana journeys to authenticity.

"Do You Know Who You Are?"

Moana's adventures across the sea embody the authentic life, in terms of both the richness and trappings of independence. Friedrich Nietzsche (1844–1900), a forefather of existentialism, held that "You shall become the person you are," meaning we're in a constant state of becoming.[4] We're always changing, growing, and redefining ourselves through our actions and decisions. This is part of the richness of authenticity. Moana embodies this as she continues to grow throughout her expedition. She matures in her firmness with Maui, even pulling the demigod's ear to get him to listen to her demands for help. She develops an expertise as a voyager, growing from a helpless traveler who needs the ocean to guide her, to a devoted student who learns under Maui's tutelage, and finally to an independent wayfinder. She exudes courage as she retrieves the heart of Te Fiti from Kakamura, the dangerous, blow-dart shooting, pirates. Even when Maui attempts to flee in fear, she boldly boards their ship, dismissing them as just coconuts. Similarly, she bravely enters the Realm of Monsters and assists Maui in retrieving his hook from the menacing crab, Tamatoa. She wisely notices that Tamatoa is immersed in a herd mentality, whereby he rejects a voice inside since he'd "rather be shiny." Playing on his superficiality, Moana displays her cleverness as she outwits Tamatoa and tricks him into continuously talking about himself and distracts him with shiny objects. In this way, she adheres to Sartre's existential dictum that the human being is only what she wills herself to be after she is born.

But, as Moana quickly learns, living the authentic life has its challenges. Sartre explains that an individual who escapes the crowd to truly embrace freedom will inevitably encounter three states of being. First, one lives in *anguish* insofar as each choice does not simply involve oneself; rather, it involves all humanity. When the authentic individual acts, she is aware that her action is a statement to humanity that this is the right action. Each decision thus carries a heavy weight.[5] Moana undergoes anguish as she becomes aware that her adventure literally involves humanity – the people of Motunui and beyond – as she needs to prevent Te Kā's darkness from spreading. She becomes so anxious from this weight that she's haunted by their "inescapable death" in her nightmares.

Second, Sartre contends that the authentic individual lives with *forlornness* as she must accept that she, and no one else, is responsible for her decisions and actions. Here the weight of responsibility is all the more pressing, since there are no excuses for one's actions. All praise, all blame, all accountability rests with the individual. Sartre emphasizes this point, arguing that the human being "is condemned to be free."[6] Moana thus acts with forlornness as she nearly succumbs to the weight of responsibility for her voyage. She cannot blame her parents, her grandmother, Maui, or even the ocean for anything she does. She must own her actions.

Finally, the authentic individual lives in *despair* as she must confine herself to acting within the collection of probabilities that make her action possible.[7] For example, when Moana plans to leave Motunui to restore the heart, she can only act within the possibilities available to her. Sure, she could pray to the gods, hoping they'll promptly transport her to Te Fiti so that she can restore the heart without Te Kā's knowledge. But Sartre would suggest this is outside of the realm of realistic possibilities. The authentic individual must focus only on those possibilities that involve one's direct actions.

These three states of being collide for Moana after she and Maui are summarily defeated by Te Kā in their first attempt to restore the heart. With his hook severely damaged, Maui refuses to make a second attempt, yelling to Moana, "We're here because the ocean told you you're special and you believed it. I'm not killing myself so you can prove you're something you're not." Overwhelmed by these hardships, Moana shifts away from authentic living, blaming both Maui and the ocean. She's angry that Maui "stole the heart in the first place." She's frustrated with the ocean, exclaiming "Why did you bring me here? I'm not the right person." Feeling helpless and hopeless, she returns the heart to a reluctant ocean, and considers returning home. Moana thus becomes enveloped in the dark aspects of authenticity and borders on bad faith.

Tala – Moana's inspiration and model of the authentic life – returns to her during this low point, offering existential advice. Moana should find resiliency in her authenticity, since she "stands apart from the crowd." And though these hardships can be debilitating since "the world seems against you" and they "leave a scar," Tala argues that such scars can "heal and reveal where [and who] you are." Tala echoes Nietzsche's famous existential idea, "what does not destroy me makes me stronger."[8] The authentic individual is not only able to endure suffering, hardships, and failures in life, she is also able to learn, grow, and be strengthened by them. Here Tala reminds Moana of the passions that define her: "she loves the sea and her people." These passions and the lessons she learned through her adventures will guide her in self-overcoming. So no matter what hardships Moana faces, the voice inside will always show "who you are."

Tala's advice motivates Moana to fight through, and overcome, her anguish, forlornness, and despair. Moana sings that she, herself, has "delivered us to where we are." Living the authentic life through her adventures, she has defined herself as a wise leader of Motunui and a skilled wayfinder who has journeyed farther than ever before. She announces that, even after her hardships, she still hears the call to restore the heart. But this call is not from the ocean; it's her inner voice. With this revelation, she emphasizes her commitment to authenticity as she proudly announces, "I am Moana!"

"I Am Moana!"

The story of *Moana* has layers. First, it is literally a tale of Moana's voyage *outside* beyond the reef so that she can restore the heart of Te Fiti and save the people of Motunui. She closes this tale with a happy ending as she simultaneously lives the life that she freely chooses, becomes the leader of her people (by saving them) as her parents wanted, and honors her tradition insofar as she restores her ancestors' tradition of wayfinding. Moana's abilities as a wayfinder become so obvious that even her father overcomes his own bad faith, proudly telling Moana upon her return, "It suits you." Second, metaphorically and philosophically, *Moana* is an inner journey of self-discovery. Moana embodies the existential philosophy of living an authentic life. She shows us what it means to be free in terms of following one's passions, choosing for oneself, and taking full responsibility for one's actions.

Like her grandmother, Moana is able to help guide others to authenticity and to become who they are. Maui lives in bad faith before he meets Moana. Utterly dependent upon the idea that he is a "hero to all" people, he believes that his essence precedes his existence in that he only became "Maui" upon receiving his hook. Maui repeatedly tells Moana, "I am nothing without my hook!" But Moana teaches him that he can be who he is without this divine gift. He overcomes bad faith so that, after his hook is destroyed, he tells Moana, "Hook. No hook. I'm Maui."

Moana is able to see beyond the superficial appearance of Te Kā and realize that this demon is really Te Fiti without her heart. With such insight, Moana restores the heart and teaches Te Fiti that her existence precedes her essence, since "this [stolen heart] does not define you." She also teaches her people of Motunui to no longer feel bound by their current social routines and norms, as she guides the sedentary villagers – including her parents – to become voyagers and learn the skills of wayfinding.

Most importantly, perhaps, Moana teaches *us* about authenticity. Embodying Nietzsche's idea that the best educators are those who teach as outward examples, Moana models how to live authentically by doing so herself.[9] Her actions and decisions demonstrate that we can define ourselves freely and take responsibility for who we are. Even Maui learns that his preconceived notions about her were inaccurate. Maui had already formed notions about the crowd mentality of human beings, stereotyping every person based on their functions. Because she is a "mortal," she will be too frightened to enter the Realm of Monsters. Even worse, since she wears a dress and has an animal sidekick, Moana is dismissed as a "princess": weak, demure, and dependent on others. Thus Maui acts with bad faith and refuses (at first) to teach her to sail, believing she simply cannot become a wayfinder.

By the story's end, however, Maui realizes his mistake as Moana becomes etched on his mural of tattoos – not as a passive and superficial member of the crowd, but as a self-overcoming and independent wayfinder. Ultimately, then, Moana shatters the concept of "princess" both for Maui and us, the viewers. No longer bound by archaic labels – even those of earlier "Disney princesses" – Moana defines herself as a free, authentic individual. Rather than let herself become defined by the label "princess," she defines herself as a strong and independent young woman – capable of living life on her own terms. By overcoming antiquated and inaccurate stereotypes, Moana demonstrates that if you listen to the voice inside, you too can (and should) avoid the social pressures of the herd mentality to discover who you truly are.[10]

Notes

1. Sartre, J.-P. (1995). The humanism of existentialism. In: *Essays in Existentialism* (ed. W. Baskin), 36. New York: Citadel Press.
2. See Sartre, pp.34–35.
3. Sartre, p. 45.

4. Nietzsche, F. (1974). In: *The Gay Science*, vol. 3 (ed. W. Kaufman), 219–270. New York: Vintage Books.
5. See Sartre, pp. 38–40.
6. Sartre, p. 41.
7. See Sartre, pp. 45–46.
8. Nietzsche, F. (1968). Twilight of the idols. In: *The Portable Nietzsche* (ed. W. Kaufmann), 467. New York: Penguin Books.
9. See Nietzsche, F. (1997). Schopenhauer as educator. In: *Untimely Meditations* (ed. and trans. D. Breazeale and D. Breazeale), 136–137. New York: Cambridge University Press.
10. I dedicate this chapter to my daughter, Meggie. May you always listen to the voice inside that sings the song of who you are.

Saving Mr. Banks

Reclaiming Our Childhood, Remembering Who We Are

Mark D. Linville and Shawn White

When *Mary Poppins* blew into the theaters in 1964, I[1] was seven and in the second grade. Our teachers evidently saw the film as a great teaching opportunity because one day they lined us up and marched us several blocks across a neighborhood to the local theater. For days afterwards they talked about the film, explaining the scenes and teaching us the songs. We even learned to say the biggest word you ever heard – and to say it backwards! *Dociousaliexpilisticfragicalirupus.*

With my child's eyes I saw *Mary Poppins* as a child's film. And so it is. But it also carries a more mature theme that quite escaped me then. *Mary Poppins* is a magical film, but it is also a story of redemption that might be placed alongside the Parable of the Prodigal Son or *A Christmas Carol.* Mary may be the star of the film, but George Banks is its subject. Though he may not have realized it, Mr. Banks needed salvation, and this is because he had quite forgotten who he was.

Unexamined is the Life I Lead

George Banks had become an ambitious man of business, and as such he had no time for childish nonsense. Nor did he have a great deal of time for children, including his own. As his theme song, *The Life I Lead*, has it,

Disney and Philosophy: Truth, Trust, and a Little Bit of Pixie Dust, First Edition.
Edited by Richard B. Davis.

It's 6:03 and the heirs to my dominion
Are scrubbed and tubbed and adequately fed
And so I'll pat them on the head
And send them off to bed
Ah! Lordly is the life I lead!

His rigorous schedule affords approximately two minutes between his "marching through the door" at 6:01 and – after a paternalistic pat on their heads – sending the children upstairs to the nursery, out of the way, and in the care of a hired nanny. One of the prospective nannies observes to the others, "I've known this family for years, father works all of the time, takes his job at the bank very seriously. He never spends time with his children, and most nights they are in bed before he gets home." Banks *is* serious – not to mention practical, responsible, disciplined, and respectable – and there is little time in a life filled with such concerns for bedtime stories or making kites or an afternoon in the park. Such things amount to dawdling on that straight and narrow path to respectability. And the *very idea* of squandering tuppence on "a lot of ragamuffin birds" borders on blasphemy.

When the family seeks a new nanny, the children write their own advertisement and share it with their father. They hope for someone who will "take them on outings," "sing songs, bring sweets." Mr. Banks replies, "Thank you! Most interesting! And now I think we've had quite enough of this nonsense. Please return to the nursery." Winifred urges, "They were only trying to help. They're just children." Banks replies, "I'm quite aware they're just children, Winifred. Play games, sing songs, eat treats…Ridiculous!" He has more solid qualifications in mind, and so he shreds the childish advertisement and tosses it into the fire.

After Mary Poppins has, by some magic, received the shredded advertisement and effectively maneuvered Banks into giving her the position, we find him complaining to Winifred. It seems the entire household has fallen under Mary Poppins' spell – "even the cook and the maid are singing!" he laments. Why, everything was higgledy-piggledy! Later, after their outing that included a tea party on Uncle Albert's ceiling, the children are excited to tell their father of their day. "We had the most wonderful afternoon with Mary Poppins!" Jane says to a distracted and impatient father. When Michael attempts to share the clever joke about "A man with a wooden leg named Smith," Banks is flustered, humorless: "Smith? We don't know anyone called Smith?" He shuts them down with, "Oh children, please be quiet," adding his signature refrain – "Please return to your room."

George Banks is a man who dreams of "walking with giants" – such as the senior Mr. Dawes, "a giant in the world of finance" – and carving one's "niche on the edifice of time," according to his song *A Man Has Dreams*. If the world ever seemed wonderful and filled with surprises for George Banks as a child, it has since been supplanted by a world that is mechanical, predictable, and subject to the demands of business and of propriety. When the children ask him if he can see the woman feeding the birds, he barks, "Well, *of course* I can see her! Do you think I can't see past the end of my nose?" Actually, this is *precisely* what we think. Like many – perhaps most – of us, he has grown jaded as he has grown older and thus fails to see things as they really are.

They say that philosophy begins in wonder. If that is so, then George Banks is decidedly not a philosopher. He is an instance of the person who leads what Socrates called the "unexamined life" – a life that the philosopher declared not to be worth living. Banks has forgotten the wonder of childhood. Having forgotten that, he is blind to the wonders of the world and, like Scrooge, to the needs of those around him. This is why he needs saving; this is why Mary Poppins has come. As Walt Disney comes to realize in the film *Saving Mr. Banks*, "It's not the children she comes to save. It's their father." Jenny Koralek, a friend of the late *Mary Poppins* author P. L. Travers, confirms that, according to Travers, "Mary Poppins has come to remind Mr. Banks that he was a child once, and some of the most powerful things in the book are moments when he sort of remembers."[2]

The Man Who Forgot Who He Was

Disney's *Mary Poppins* is set in London in 1910. It is thus easy to imagine that George Banks, on his walk to and from the bank each day, might have passed "a Falstaffian figure in a brigand's hat and cloak" – G.K. Chesterton, a contemporary and fellow Londoner – on his way to or from the newspaper or, more likely, a favorite pub. Unless Banks had the good fortune of striking up a conversation with the jocund journalist he could never have guessed that Chesterton held the very key to his salvation. (Mary Poppins might have been saved considerable trouble!) Chesterton had the cure to what ailed Banks because he had the correct diagnosis: "Every man has forgotten who he is."[3]

Among the things that we forget is the wonder and astonishment that characterizes the child – an astonishment even over the things that most adults have come to see as mundane. Chesterton kept before his mind what, for most of us, is submerged "at the back of our brains," namely, a "blaze or burst of astonishment at our own existence."[4] For the child, "The earth, and every common sight" still seems "Appareled in celestial light," as Wordsworth said.[5] But the poet lamented that "The things which I have seen I can now see no more" and thus, "There hath past away a glory from the earth."[6] It is the child who sees things as they are because "we see things fairly when we see them first."[7] "If we saw the sun for the first time it would be the most fearful and beautiful of meteors." The man who grows "weary of wonders"[8] and thus ceases to wonder, sees instead the mere "light of common day"[9] – taking no notice while taking it all for granted. We are not told whether George Banks kept bankers' hours, but if he rose early it was more likely for business than for the joy of seeing the sunrise or to hear the birds sing. The small child is much as you and I would be were we suddenly to awaken in one of Bert's chalk drawings and encounter for the first time those strange surroundings. She is thus more likely than we to see things *as they really are*. What is needed, perhaps, is the child's imagination – "a wild and soaring sort of imagination…the imagination that can see what is there."[10]

On a first visit to Yellowstone National Park, finding herself surrounded by steaming mountains that whistled like tea kettles, boiling mud pots, geysers, and other geothermal features, a woman[11] remarked, "For the first time in my life I realize that we live on a *planet*." A dullard (such as our banker) might reply, "Well, *of course* you live on a planet! Where else could you have been all this time?" But with rekindled imagination she was seeing for the first time the shocking nature of our actual situation, namely, that all this time we have dined and danced and slept and had babies and raised families and engaged in commerce while floating about on a thin crust – rather like the cooled skin on the top of a cup of hot cocoa – over the very fires of Mordor. And so she realized that Earth is as startling and strange as Elfland, only we have grown accustomed to it. "The function of imagination is not to make strange things settled, so much as to make settled things strange; not so much to make wonders facts as to make facts wonders."[12] Perhaps what is most startling about seeing what is really there is the realization both that there is really something there to be seen and that there is someone to see it.

Gottfried Leibniz (1646–1716) said that the most fundamental philosophical question is "Why is there something rather than nothing?"[13] And Bertrand Russell (1872–1970) reflected that it is a "strange mystery" that nature has "brought forth at last a child…gifted with sight, with knowledge of good and evil, with the capacity of judging all the works of his unthinking mother."[14] For Chesterton, "mere existence" itself is "extraordinary enough to be exciting."[15]

"Please Return to the Nursery"

George Banks sends the children back to the nursery when their childish nonsense distracts from important adult concerns. Chesterton might counter that the frivolous concerns of the parlor distract from the serious business of the nursery. He insisted, "My first and last philosophy, that which I believe in with unbroken certainty, I learnt in the nursery."[16] He confesses that those things he has always believed most – throughout life – have their origin in fairy-tales.[17]

Chesterton learned of *our* world and how to live in it through stories from another world – Fairyland – that "sunny country of common sense."[18] Such tales teach the primary and permanent things. From *Jack the Giant Killer* we learn that when pride has grown to gigantic proportions it ought to be killed; *Cinderella* teaches that the humble are exalted; *Beauty and the Beast* demonstrates the principle that loving the unlovable may result in the transformation from the beastly to the beautiful; and *Mary Poppins* reminds us that "There's no greater joy than that seen through the eyes of a child," as Walt Disney observes in *Saving Mr. Banks*.

Fairy-tales usher us into an enchanted world in which anything can happen – pumpkins become carriages, mice morph into horses, and princes into frogs; there are palaces of crystal and apples of gold; a kiss can break a spell or a magic word slay a dragon. Such astonishing tales "touch the nerve of the ancient instinct of astonishment."[19] The instinct is "ancient" in that it harkens back to the antiquity of early childhood. The child in the nursery need not be presented with *golden* apples in order to be astonished. A green apple from the local grocer will have that effect. The entrance of a dog is as good as the appearance of a dragon. This is as it should be, for dogs, rightly seen, are every bit as fantastic as dragons. Of course, the baby may grow up as yet another man weary of wonders and bored with dogs; there are possible worlds in which dull grownups are bored with dragons. The small child just coming to consciousness of the world about her experiences "a new universe…a new system of stars, new grass, new cities, a new sea."[20] And so "mere life is interesting enough."[21]

The imagination of the nursery helps us to see things as they are. Tales of talking animals may remind us of the remarkable fact that we are animals that talk. Stories of monsters with monstrous features may lead us to reflect that each person we meet is, in fact, "a monster with mysterious eyes and miraculous thumbs, with strange dreams in his skull, and a queer tenderness for this place or that baby."[22] From tales that include toys or teapots that have become sentient, we might reflect on the wonder that *anything* is conscious and realize that "every instant of conscious life is an unimaginable prodigy."[23] Fantasies of what *might* have been may be the occasion for my considering what is but might *not* have been – and that this includes me, personally. It is astonishing that there is something rather than nothing. It is a strange mystery that creatures such as ourselves should be a part of what there is. For each of us individually there is the inexplicable mystery that, of all of the possible creatures that *might* have existed, this thing that each of us refers to as "I" made the cut and came to be.

Sadly, Mr. Banks is far too practical and ambitious for all this. These are mere children's stories that it would be best to grow out of so that one can get on with the serious business of life. He has forgotten the lessons of the nursery, and he has allowed his ambition and pride to drain the romance out of the world and his relationships. A monomaniacal concern for a balance sheet has left his life out of balance. A monocular focus on such things as wealth has blinded him to the rich world around him and left him impoverished concerning things of the greatest value. He cannot see past the end of his nose, as Mary Poppins suggests. Nor does he realize that, like Jacob Marley, who was chained to his cash-boxes and ledgers, he has become a prisoner in a "bank-shaped cage," as Bert observes. Marley learned too late that mankind was his business. Banks, too, neglected his business, as he passed the poor bird woman each day without so much as noticing her. But Scrooge was saved in the nick of time, and our story has a similar happy ending.

Let's Go Fly a Kite!

The story of George Banks and his family is book-ended with a kite. We are first introduced to the household when "storm signals are up at number 17," as Admiral Boom warns Bert. Katie Nanna, the children's nanny, is storming out, resigning her position, because "Those little beasts have run away from me for the last time." But we soon learn that they disappeared not out of mischief but in order to retrieve their runaway kite. As the Constable who returned Mr. Banks' "valuables" (that is, his children) explains, "In a manner of speaking, sir, it was the kite that ran away, not the children." The children, their dilapidated kite in hand, explain, "It was not a very good kite. We made it ourselves." They appeal to their father: "Perhaps if you helped us to make one…." The Constable supports the idea – "Kites are skittish things" – but Banks abruptly dismisses both the idea and the Constable. We sense early on that George Banks has little time for such trifling pursuits as kite-making or affectionate fatherhood.

Much like the kite, the Banks family itself seems to display a kind of brokenness. Both parents have their preoccupations that pull them away from one another and from their children. George places priority on his business ambitions; Winifred breezes in and out, either heading to another suffragette rally or returning from one. The children are farmed out to hired servants and are left to make their own kites – and make their way through childhood without the affectionate involvement of their parents. This is the condition of the family throughout the film until George comes to a crisis moment that transforms his outlook.

The crisis comes for Banks when, on the occasion of their visit to the bank, Jane and Michael refuse to hand over their tuppence for investment, preferring instead to feed the birds. They inadvertently cause a run on the bank, angering the Senior Dawes. It is clear that Banks is to be terminated. Bert helps Banks to see that while he is "grinding at that grindstone" the childhood of Jane and Michael is slipping away "like sand through a sieve." We see the change come over Banks at that moment. "The way to love anything is to realise that it might be lost,"[24] and the fleeting moments of childhood – as of our lives – are too precious to be squandered. How ironic that the man who would dismiss nursery tales of giants as a distraction from the serious business of adult life had allowed his "dreams of walking with giants" to distract him from the more serious business of the nursery. Chesterton observed that "It is only the grown man who lives a life of make-believe and pretending; and it is he who has his head in a cloud."[25] Banks sees this, perhaps, when in the process of being sacked he exclaims to the senior Mr. Dawes – that giant of finance – "Do you know what there's no such thing as? It turns out, with due respect, when all is said and done, that there's no such thing as you!"

When next we see him, George Banks is a mended man holding a mended kite. Winifred adds her suffragette banner ("A proper kite needs a proper tail, don't you think?") and as George, Winifred, Jane, and Michael skip out the door together with the kite, to which all four have now contributed, we see a mended family. This is Mary Poppins' cue to leave, as her mission is accomplished. She is carried away on the same wind that carries the mended family's mended kite.

As Walt Disney promises P. L. Travers in *Saving Mr. Banks*, "I swear that every time a person goes into a movie house – from Leicester to St. Louis – they will see George Banks being saved. They will love him and his kids, they will weep for his cares, and wring their hands when he loses his job. And when he flies that kite, oh! They will rejoice, they will sing." The song they sing tells us,

> With your feet on the ground you're a bird in flight
> With your fist holding tight to the string of your kite

In the end, the bank's directors – who, under the influence of Banks, his children, and a man with a wooden leg named Smith, are seen flying kites of their own – not only reinstate Banks but give him a promotion, which Banks happily accepts. We may infer that it was not George's practicality that was the issue; it was his practicality *to the exclusion of all else*, including the things of the nursery. But the things of the nursery are not meant to run wild and loose without any kind of anchoring. Indeed, a kite can soar on the winds only when its string is held tight in the fist of a grounded kite flyer. The message, then, is not that we should all cease being responsible adults to play hopscotch or make mud pies. It is possible to keep the heart of a child while also maintaining the mind of an adult. It is possible to be a bird in flight while keeping your feet on the ground.

We thus leave a rejuvenated George Banks with the same sort of assurance with which we left Scrooge, knowing that "His own heart laughed: and that was quite enough for him."[26]

Notes

1. Mark D. Linville.
2. *The Real Mary Poppins*. Online streaming video, Amazon Prime. Directed by Lisa Matthews. Los Angeles: Essential Media, 2014.
3. Chesterton, G.K. (1986). Orthodoxy. In: *G.K. Chesterton Collected Works: Volume I* (ed. D. Dooley), 257. San Francisco, CA: Ignatius Press.

4. Chesterton, G.K. (1988). The autobiography. In: *G.K. Chesterton Collected Works: Volume XVI* (ed. G. J. Marlin, R. P. Rabatin and J. L. Swan), 97. San Francisco, CA: Ignatius Press.
5. Wordsworth, W. (2008). *Ode: Intimations of Immortality from Recollections of Early Childhood*. In: *William Wordsworth: The Major Works* (ed. S. Gill), 297. Oxford: Oxford University Press.
6. Ibid.
7. Chesterton, G.K. (1986). The everlasting man. In: *G.K. Chesterton Collected Works: Volume II* (ed. G. J. Marlin, R. P. Rabatin and J. L. Swan), 148. San Francisco: Ignatius Press.
8. G.K. Chesterton, "Heretics," in *G.K. Chesterton Collected Works: Volume I*, 128.
9. Wordsworth, *Ode*, 297.
10. G.K. Chesterton, "The Everlasting Man," in *G.K. Chesterton Collected Works: Volume I*, 148.
11. Mark's wife, Lynn.
12. Chesterton, G.K. (2012). A defence of China shepherdesses. In: *The Defendant* (ed. D. Ahlquist), 36. Mineola, NY: Dover Publications.
13. Leibniz, G.W. (1989). Principles of Nature and Grace, Based on Reason. In: *Philosophical Essays* (ed. R. Ariew and D. Garber), 210. Indianapolis: Hackett Publishing.
14. Russell, B. (1957). *Why I Am Not a Christian And Other Essays on Religion and Related Subjects*, 107. New York: Simon and Schuster.
15. Chesterton, G.K. (1988). The autobiography. In: *G.K. Chesterton Collected Works: Volume XVI* (ed. G. J. Marlin, R. P. Rabatin and J. L. Swan), 96. San Francisco: Ignatius Press.
16. G.K. Chesterton, "Orthodoxy," 252.
17. Ibid.
18. Ibid.
19. Ibid., 257.
20. G.K. Chesterton, "A Defence of Baby Worship," 70.
21. G.K. Chesterton, "Orthodoxy," 257.
22. G.K. Chesterton, "Heretics," 68.
23. Ibid.
24. Chesterton, G.K. (2016). The advantages of having one leg. In: *Tremendous Trifles*, 49. Baton Rouge, LA: Mud House Art and Literature.
25. G.K. Chesterton, "The Autobiography," 58.
26. Dickens, C. (2003). A Christmas Carol. In: *A Christmas Carol and Other Christmas Writings*, 27–118. London: Penguin Books.

WALL·E and EVE

Disney's Intelligent Machines

Timothy Brown

In 2007 I went to see a film that had recently been released. When the trailers began to play, one stood out as different from all the others. It featured a narrator telling the story of a lunch meeting in the summer of 1994 that led to the production of four Pixar films. By 2007, three of these films had been released: *A Bug's Life*, *Monsters, Inc.*, and *Finding Nemo*. The trailer was promoting the fourth film – *WALL·E* – and the narrator was Andrew Stanton, *WALL·E*'s director, co-writer, and screenplay co-author.

From the trailer it was obvious that *WALL·E* would be everything a Pixar film had previously been: original, a little bit daring, and beautifully animated. It was also obvious that *WALL·E* would be significantly different from previous Pixar feature-films, in at least one important way.

WALL·E: a Significantly Different Pixar Film

WALL·E was significantly different from previous Pixar films in that its central characters – the intelligent machines WALL·E and EVE – were depicted as potentially real, given enough time and technology. To be sure, previous Pixar films presented us with intelligent characters: intelligent toys, intelligent animals, and even anthropomorphized intelligent automobiles. But it never so much as crossed

Disney and Philosophy: Truth, Trust, and a Little Bit of Pixie Dust, First Edition.
Edited by Richard B. Davis.

the viewer's mind to think of, say, *Toy Story*'s Woody or Bo-Peep, or *Finding Nemo*'s Marlin or Coral, as possible future realities – even less so Lightning McQueen and Sally of *Cars* fame. Why, then, are WALL·E and EVE significantly different in our minds?

In a film-viewing experience, there are real things all around us: the screen and seats, the butter and salt on our popcorn, and that person next to us who rudely insists on texting during the show. Even the light and sound inside the theater are real. It's just that the spaceship on the screen isn't making that light or those sounds: the projector and speakers are. We all get that; none of us is confused on that score.

But due to a directorial decision from Andrew Stanton, however, *WALL·E* was intentionally animated to lull viewers into the belief that WALL·E and EVE themselves are the actual causes of our sensory experiences inside the theater. According to Jeremy Lasky, *WALL·E*'s director of photography: camera, "Andrew came into the movie wanting a very photographed look, he had been always looking at live-action films as his inspiration...and he wanted the audience to understand WALL·E as a real thing."[1] And in fact, Pixar went to extraordinary lengths to accomplish a sense of realism in *WALL·E*. They brought in a live-action cinematographer (to replicate live-action lighting and staging), a live-action director of photography, and ARRI camera bodies with Panavision lenses to imitate live-action focus and depth of field qualities. All of this was done for the purpose of leaving viewers with the unquestioned belief that WALL·E and EVE weren't animated on-screen characters, but rather spatiotemporally real, intelligent machines that have simply been captured on film.

Is WALL·E Artificially Intelligent?

Naturally, this raises the all-important philosophical question: Can there really be intelligent machines like WALL·E and EVE? There is though an even more fundamental question: Is artificial intelligence (AI) even a possibility? Today we are inundated by claims that AI is not only possible, but actually present in the latest TVs and phones. Is this just marketing propaganda, or can there be artificially intelligent machines and devices? To answer this question, we must look into the meaning of the words "artificial" and "intelligence." This may sound like a simple task, but given that much ancient ink was spilled on the meaning of such words such as "virtue," "justice," and "courage," sometimes the simplest tasks – getting clear about the meaning of words that carry philosophical freight – can prove the most difficult.

Analyzing "Artificial"

Normally, it isn't difficult to distinguish between natural and artificial things. In *WALL·E*, supposing its characters to be real, the human captain is quite obviously natural while AUTO is clearly artificial. We don't have to be told this; it is perfectly obvious. However, it is by no means easy to say just *why* the human captain is natural and *why* AUTO is artificial. At first glance, we are inclined to equate the natural with what is "real" or "not-man-made", and the artificial with what is "unreal" or "man-made." In truth, neither of these conceptions is correct. Fortunately, the Aristotelian philosophy of Thomas Aquinas (1225–1274 CE) can help us to get clear about the distinction. On Aquinas's view, natural things have an intrinsic principle that accounts for both their change and their stability. Artificial things, by contrast, lack such a principle.[2]

Change is evident all around us at every moment. In fact, it is so prevalent that some ancient philosophers conjectured that all reality was change. *WALL·E* is itself full of instances of change: human beings changing their location (from Earth to the Axiom and back), their activity levels (from active to virtually inactive), and even their bodies as they experienced what Shelby Forthright describes as some "slight bone loss."

But what is change? Change is what occurs when a thing becomes actually, what it was once only potentially. The humans in *WALL·E* were able to change their location, since they first had the potential to be in a different location. They were able to change their activity level, since they first had the potential to have a different activity level. And they were able to experience bone loss, since they first had the potential to have different bone densities. In each case, they changed when they became actually what (previously) they were only potentially.

Stability, too, is ever-present in our experience of the world. Indeed, it is so prevalent that some ancient philosophers conjectured all reality was stability. Stability is the opposite of change; stability is when a thing does not have the potential to be other than it is, and thus remains what it actually is. While change points to what a thing may potentially be, stability points to what a thing actually is.

With the notions of *change* and *stability* in hand, we can say that natural things have an intrinsic principle which accounts for (that is, causes) their being potentially or actually what they are. In artificial things, there is no such principle. Just think of all the cases of causation in *WALL·E.* Human beings cause the Earth to become polluted, and they cause the Axiom to leave the Earth and then return. Shelby Forthright causes the override directive A113 to be implemented. But when we speak of a principle that causes a thing to be what it potentially and actually is, we are speaking of a different sort of cause then these altogether.

As Aristotle and Aquinas see things, there are four kinds of causes. The *formal* cause of a thing is that which makes it to be what it is as opposed to something else. The formal cause of the Axiom was the idea of the Axiom in the mind of the *Buy n Large* engineers. The *efficient* cause of the Axiom – that which acts most directly to produce or bring a thing about – was the direct efforts of the hard-working *Buy n Large* ship-builders. The *material* cause of the Axiom consists of the many futuristic materials out of which it was constructed. And then finally – pun intended – its *final* cause is that for the sake of which it was brought about: to transport thousands of people into outer space in order to save their lives.

So the Axiom – an artificial thing – has four causes, including a formal cause. But the important thing to see is that its formal cause (what makes it what it is as opposed to something else) lies *outside* of it and in the mind of the *Buy n Large* engineers. And that is precisely what makes it an artificial thing. If it were a natural thing, its formal cause would reside *inside* it. What can we say is natural in the film WALL·E? Certainly, the human captain is natural, as are the cockroach WALL·E befriends and the last living green plant he finds. All of these, like the water in the pool on the Axiom, have an intrinsic formal cause and are therefore natural things. They are all natural for one and the same reason: what makes them what they are, as opposed to something else, is intrinsic to them; this cause isn't imposed from outside.

Are WALL·E and EVE natural things? The answer is no; they are artificial. Like the Axiom, WALL·E and EVE are artificial because their formal causes are not intrinsic. Like the Axiom, their formal causes are imposed from outside. WALL·E and EVE are artificial.

Interpreting "Intelligence"

Fair enough. But couldn't they also be intelligent? Well, it depends on what we mean by "intelligent." Some think of intelligence as a "thing" that can be quantified in some way – something people can have more or less of. Aquinas, however, tells us that "'intelligence' properly signifies the intellect's very act, which is to understand,"[3] indicating that intelligence is not a thing at all, but an act, and specifically the very act of the intellect to understand.[4] But what does it mean to understand?

There are various acceptable ways the word "understand" may be used, but we are using it to indicate the formation of a concept: apprehending the general essence of something (such as triangularity or humanity), as opposed to one merely encountering individual concrete things (such as triangles or humans). Thus Edward Feser tells us: "through hearing, seeing, tasting, touching, and smelling, we can perceive individual, particular things; this triangle, cat, and so forth. But the intellect can grasp triangularity in general, 'catness' in general, and other universals."[5] Now consider this fact. WALL·E is presented to us as a machine with the ability to understand. He can sort spoons and forks because he understands *spoon-ness* and *fork-ness*, and he knows to place the "spork" he encounters mid-way between the spoons and forks because he understands *spork-ness* relative to *spoon-ness* and *fork-ness*. Mentally grasping the "what-ness" of something is just what it means to understand it, and intelligence is the act of the intellect to understand. Why think, though, that an artificial thing like WALL·E, EVE, or the Axiom could actually be intelligent?

Aquinas tells us that "the intellect is a power of the soul."[6] Ultimately then, if we are looking for the cause of intelligence, and if we take Aquinas as our guide, our search turns to the soul. The intellect is one power of the soul, and the act (or action) of the intellect to understand is intelligence. If Aquinas is right, the soul is the formal cause of a living thing: "the first principle of life of those things which live."[7] Feser clarifies:

> The soul is neither a ghost…nor some spooky kind of "stuff" non-physical, quasi-physical, or otherwise. Nor are they [meaning those who are describing the soul as the formal cause of a living thing] presenting a pseudo-scientific empirical hypothesis on which the existence of the soul is "postulated," as the best way of "explaining" how matter can have the form of a living thing. Again, by "soul" they just *mean* the form of a living thing, so that anything with such a form has a soul by definition.[8]

To be sure, not every formal cause is the same. "Soul" is the technical name given to the formal cause of a living thing, but clearly it is very different than the formal cause of a non-living thing. After all, being the formal cause of a living thing, the soul is the difference between a human and a corpse. It is the difference between an animal and a carcass, between a plant and vegetative remains. In each instance the former has a soul, while the latter does not. Moreover, not every soul is the same. Humans on the Axiom have souls, as do the cockroach and Earth's last green plant; each has a formal cause. But they're not all the same. As Aquinas notes, some souls are intellectual, some sensitive, and others vegetative – each with distinct powers.

If artificial things are to have intelligence, we need to know whether they can have intellectual souls. Here we should note that while animals and plants have souls, they do not have intellectual souls. Peter Kreeft explains: "Animals apparently cannot perform [the] act of understanding; if they can they do not express it in words. Computers certainly cannot do this; a computer no more *understands* what you program into it than a library building understands the information in the books you put into it."[9] According to Kreeft, then, animals (and plants) cannot be intelligent. Animals – and some plants – may be able to encounter what is around them, but they cannot *understand* what is around them. In the same way, says Kreeft, computers cannot be intelligent. Computers – and artificial things in general – do not *understand*. For only things with an intellectual soul are intelligent. And according to Aquinas, humans have intellectual souls, whereas animals and plants do not. Humans have an intellect that can act to understand, and humans can understand things such as triangularity and humanity, as well as virtue, justice, and courage. Animals, plants, and computers cannot understand or grasp these.

So what things count as intelligent in *WALL·E*? The humans on the Axiom are intelligent; they have an intellectual soul, the chief power of which is the intellect. Sadly however, neither WALL·E's insect friend, nor his living green friend are intelligent. For quite clearly, neither has an intellectual soul.

One question remains: Are WALL·E and EVE intelligent things? If Aristotle and Aquinas are right, the answer must be a most painful "no." They are certainly (and delightfully) depicted in the film as being intelligent and wise – even more so than some humans of our acquaintance. But lacking an intellectual soul, they merely mimic intelligence without being intelligent.

Where Do We Go from Here?

We have considered the question of whether intelligent machines like WALL·E and EVE could potentially be real. We've also considered the more fundamental question of whether AI is a possibility. *Is* it possible? If we accept the meanings of "artificial" and "intelligence" from Aquinas, the answer is no. Of course, if we do not agree with Aquinas, a different answer might follow. But that is a debate for another time and place.

Given enough time and technology, will there ever be a point at which WALL·E and EVE could be considered *intelligent* machines? If we follow Aquinas, our answer must be no; they are artificial and unintelligent machines. Artificial intelligence isn't possible, regardless of the time and technology devoted to its development. This is because intelligence itself can only be found in natural, living, intellectual things. It cannot be replicated (but only mimicked) in an artificial, non-living, non-intellectual thing. The barrier to AI isn't simply quantitative (we need *more* research and development), it is qualitative (intelligence can't be found in an artificial thing). But what about all the claims that AI is not only real, but also that it is part of the newest phones and televisions? Here we cannot ascribe intelligence to even our most cherished devices without redefining the meaning of "intelligence." We can do that, of course, but it won't thereby change our phones and televisions.

Returning to *WALL·E*: should we no longer enjoy the film because of what we have concluded about WALL·E and EVE's inner life and intelligence? There is absolutely no reason to think so – just as there is no reason we shouldn't enjoy *Toy Story* because Woody and Bo Peep are purely artificial and wholly unintelligent. Would anyone boycott *Finding Nemo* on the grounds that Marlin and Coral – being mere fish – aren't intelligent, or that since Lightning McQueen and Sally (as mere cars) could at best count as artificial, unintelligent artifacts be downcast at the movie's end. I should think not! Indeed, quite the opposite. That WALL·E and EVE can't be *intelligent* machines, but are portrayed as though they are, is precisely why *WALL·E* captures our imagination and unfailingly holds our attention.

Notes

1. See the extras that appeared on the 2008 Blu-ray release of *WALL·E* titled "The Imperfect Lens: Creating the Look of WALL·E."
2. Feser, E. (2014). Scholastic Metaphysics: A Contemporary Introduction, 160, 164. Neunkirchen-Seelscheid, Germany: Editions Scholasticae.
3. Aquinas, *Summa Theologica* 1, 79, 10. New Advent Online Edition. http://www.newadvent.org/summa.

4. Ibid.
5. Feser, E. (2009). Aquinas, 143–144. Oxford: Oneworld Publications.
6. Aquinas, *Summa Theologica*, 1, 79, 1.
7. Ibid., 1, 75, 1.
8. Feser, *Aquinas*, pp. 133–134.
9. Kreeft, P. (2010). *Socratic Logic: A Logic Text Using Socratic Method, Platonic Questions, and Aristotelian Principles*, 3e, 28. South Bend: St. Augustine's Press.

Inside Disney's *Inside Out*

Ellen Miller

Inside Out takes us on a journey into terrain not often explored in animated films – the inner workings of the developing 11-year-old self. No superheroes, no princesses, no cute anthropomorphized animal characters. Our affable protagonist is Riley, a pre-teen, loving, goofy, and talented hockey player from Minnesota. The other main characters are Riley's parents along with all their core emotions who come to life as separate animated characters.

As I watched the film for the first time with a group of eight kids (a mix of genders and ages) who were a few years younger than Riley's character, I kept wondering whether they were enjoying the film as much as I was. To my great delight, they were laughing and engaged throughout the entire film. I'm not sure any of them cried as much as I did at the end, but this highlights the film's main theme of childhood loss. We do not experience childhood as childhood until we have moved beyond this phase of existence.

When I turned to examine the philosopher side of my philosopher-mom insights, I was transported back to my first philosophy class. Here was a film that put the workings of the mind-emotions, control central, personality islands, daydreams, REM sleep, short-term and long-term memories on full display.

Disney and Philosophy: Truth, Trust, and a Little Bit of Pixie Dust, First Edition.
Edited by Richard B. Davis.

I Feel, Therefore I Am

Inside Out takes a girl's emotional development as important, primary, and worthy of attention. Along the way, audiences come to appreciate that even though emotions often feel singular, solitary, and intense, some aspects of emotions are universal and cut across age, gender, and culture. The movie also highlights the social dimension of emotional expressiveness. The directors were originally going to include many more emotions than the five core emotions they depict: Joy, Sadness, Anger, Disgust, and Fear. The choice to focus on five primary emotions allows us to better appreciate how emotions are central to selfhood and how our emotions influence our memories and self-understanding.

The film focuses on Riley's individual feelings and emotions. Yet, it also teaches us about emotions more broadly, and how they aren't just private events that cannot be accessed or understood by others. Riley's parents possess emotions that are depicted as grown-up versions of Riley's own. Her dad's core emotion – anger – looks just like Riley's version of anger except for the fact that he has a brown mustache. As we are in the process of living through childhood and adulthood, it is often difficult to articulate what we are experiencing at any given moment. We can step back from the flux of everyday life while we are living it, but we might lose our actual experience of what is happening. *Inside Out* shows the dynamic nature of the self at work in the world, takes emotions seriously, and doesn't portray Riley's emotions as merely a result of her gender. Her emotions are gendered both male and female which further highlights this fluidity.

Inside Out gives audiences a complex depiction of the self at work and helps us live though Riley's emotional development along with her. Even though this must be conveyed to us through on-screen representations, the film moves beyond these representationalist views of the self, which hold that our immediate sense perceptions (this or that particular taste, sound, or visual sensation) are actually objects in our minds. For a representationalist philosopher like René Descartes (1596–1650), there can be no perception without accompanying mental ideas. Emotions are accompanied by mental representations, that is, miniature virtual-reality images in the mind. A popular contemporary version of this way of thinking holds that the brain resembles a computer with our feelings, perceptions, and thoughts being made up of brain computations and their relationship to mental imagery.

When we are introduced to the anthropomorphic renderings of Riley's five core emotions, we witness a film version of the famous homuncular understanding of the self. Homunculus arguments state that we have little people inside us that are responsible for our feelings, thoughts, and brain activity. These arguments are meant to explain how the mind works, but unfortunately they get us into an infinite regress. How do the minds of these miniature people work? Ah, they must also have *homunculi*! This fallacy arises because we are trying to understand our whole self, but we end up imagining that an individual part of our body can do the work of the whole body. As scientists have discovered more and more about the brain, they have often left the impression that the self can be reduced to the brain without remainder. This is evidenced in the way we have come to talk about ourselves. "My brain is fried," we say. Even though it might be tempting to explain complicated perceptions, thoughts, and feelings by imagining there is a person inside our heads that receives stimuli, this only leads to more questions. We still don't understand how these homunculi see, think, feel, and perceive.

Riley's seemingly independent core emotions give every impression of being homunculi. So, is *Inside Out* endorsing a problematic view of the self? I don't think so. Riley's core emotions are mutually dependent; they can't function without each other even though Joy's narcissism leads her to think she can fly solo. Ultimately, the movie advances a rather sophisticated understanding of the self as holistic and also proposes that our emotions remain central throughout our lives and help guide our decisions. The movie shows that we cannot understand ourselves in purely intellectual ways with the mind manuals that Sadness reads in detail, nor can we understand ourselves as purely physical beings.

Inside Out turns traditional philosophy's emphasis on reason inside out. We witness Riley's first emotions in early infancy, and her emotions always arise alongside other people and in particular situations. Her emotions even impact her understating of past events as we see Joy – Riley's central emotion – develop throughout the film. After her family moves, her previous happy memories of Minnesota are saturated with the blue hue of Sadness. Also, if Riley doesn't care about a memory, it fades. Memories are fluid and dynamic rather than fixed and static. Riley's affective states always arise in situations. We cannot understand joy, sadness, fear, disgust, or anger in isolation from the world or other people. This is Joy's biggest revelation at the film's end when she realizes that emotional complexity involves combining multiple emotions and sharing the spotlight with Riley's other emotions.

"Riley, Just Be Okay. Okay?"

Even though we learn that Riley's mom's primary emotion is sadness, she still keeps urging her daughter to just be her same smiling, happy girl. This familiar refrain reminds us that most parents don't care if their kids are famous or rich; they just want them to be happy. Of course, we all know we can't be happy every moment of our lives. However, it's really easy to forget this as we attempt to live with someone who is sad. Sometimes it's hard for parents to get through even one meal with a sad child, especially when they know circumstances are not going to change anytime soon. Joy admits that we all have our off days, but she also keeps pushing Riley to look on the bright side and remain optimistic even when pizza in the new town is ruined by a broccoli invasion.

Inside Out demonstrates the futility of striving for constant happiness. Joy's narcissistic attempts to block other emotions from gaining dominance highlights that even if our sadness does not reach the level of depression, we sometimes need to stop moving forward and accept where we are. Joy keeps pushing through, exclaiming, "We've been through worse," in order to maintain control and centrality in Riley's life. Joy has been this way since Riley was a baby, and she continuously pushes Sadness aside so she can maintain primacy.

Riley's mom's requests parallel Joy's demands. Mom asks Riley to at least remain okay if not joyful. However, okay doesn't leave room for sadness, anger, or fear. When Joy and Sadness leave the control center to save Riley's core memories from sadness, her parents don't have a clue how to deal with other emotions being at the head of Riley's control center.

Riley's journey teaches us that growing up involves periods where joy and happiness do not dominate. In the film, this gives us a chance to appreciate the other emotions that have been blocked by Joy's dominance. We learn that Sadness is necessary and must be accepted. Even so, if we're not careful, we can slip into the grayness of depression the way Riley does when she moves from feeling too many emotions to the flatness of depression. We (the viewers) come to see that sadness and depression are not the same thing; we also come to realize that we can't simply will our sadness and pain away. Joy does everything she can to prevent any tinge of sadness from entering Riley's being, but this comes only at the expense of repressing her other feelings.

I Think, Therefore I Am?

There is something else you need to know about Descartes. He endorsed a stoic attitude toward the body, even if that body was in a state of illness. In his correspondence with Princess Elisabeth,[1] Descartes urges her to use her mind to control her body and overcome bodily illness. Descartes' attitude mirrors Nike's message to "Just do it." You might be ready to pass out, but just will yourself through and overcome bodily pains and limitations. It's freeing to imagine we can control our bodies and do anything if our wills are strong enough. Mind over matter! It's liberating and fear-reducing to think that our minds can overcome the physicality of the body. Sometimes we can do this: childbirth, firefighters saving multiple lives, ordinary people lifting incredible weights to save a child. Yet, what does this model say to those suffering from illness, those who try to push through but can't will themselves out of a fever? When we emphasize the mind/brain's abilities, we sometimes lose sight of our real living bodies at work in the world.

One of Descartes' main tasks in the *Meditations on First Philosophy*[2] was to explain human nature, the relationship between mind and body. Even though he admits we need our bodies to provide the sensory information that helps us discover scientific laws, at our core we are thinking beings. Mind over matter! What we truly are is *really distinct* from our bodies. Descartes doesn't think the emotions should be eliminated, but he does think they need training and guidance, in order to imagine new states of affairs when emotions overwhelm us. Descartes identifies six (not five!) core "primitive" passions: wonder, love, hatred, desire, joy, and sadness. He takes a very stoic attitude toward these passions, making it all too easy to blame someone for not being smart enough or strong enough to master their emotions.

Inside the Lived Body

Whereas Descartes thinks we can only have knowledge of the outside world through the ideas we have inside our minds, French philosopher Maurice Merleau-Ponty (1908–1961) rejects this brand of mind–body dualism and its mechanical understanding of the body. For Merleau-Ponty, emotions don't exist in our heads. Rather, we live through our emotions as we move through the world and the world moves through us: "The world is not what I think but what I live through."[3] Our minds and bodies are connected – so much so that Merleau-Ponty understands humans as body-subjects. We are primarily embodied beings, holistic entities that are always connected to the world and others. Merleau-Ponty doesn't think we can understand the mind or brain separately from the entire person; nor can we understand human beings apart from their surroundings and other people. They cannot be understood without looking at how they are connected to the world in families and other settings. Our thinking is embodied and emotional. We are not merely thinking beings. Rather, we are perceiving, emoting, moving, and thinking beings. These various dimensions are related and constantly at play, with some coming forward as more important depending on the situation.[4] So, when Riley plays hockey, the tactile dimension comes into focus and other dimensions recede but do not disappear, as her emotional connections with her teammates on the ice make clear. Her body moves skillfully after years of practice on the ice. Merleau-Ponty thinks our emotions are always connected with our sense perception. Our selves extend into the world and overlap to such an extent that we can't understand one without the other. We are not isolated beings; we are essentially embodied, worldly, social beings connected with others. Our minds and bodies are inseparable.

Inside Out drives home the point that we are always in relationship with others, even if those others are other parts of our selves. Riley's memories come from her engaged encounters with friends and family. Her core memories power five islands of personality: Family, Friendship, Hockey, Goofball, and Honesty. Each demonstrates the importance of connection and love in Riley's life. A single emotional experience can be given to more than one subject at a time. For Merleau-Ponty, there is no inner person, and the world doesn't exist as a mere object for human subjects. Our feelings, emotions, and perceptions can only be understood as situated and indeterminate. I can only feel and think because I am in the world. Merleau-Ponty's views differ sharply from those of mainstream cognitive science. He doesn't think our feelings and perceptions need to be explained away as virtual-reality replicas in the mind or brain.

Descartes sought certainty and clarity, but Merleau-Ponty embraced ambiguity and fluidity. Children are probably better able to deal with this openness and fluidity than most adults. The world is full of ebbs and flows, uncertainties, and changes. This is one of the main reasons I cried toward the end of the film, as I felt the loss of my childlike ways of opening up to the world. Even though philosophy and art help retrieve some of this openness, we never re-enter childhood completely and directly. This explains why Riley's parents are torn between wanting her to just be okay and understanding that Riley has to live through the feelings she is experiencing. Artworks – especially those like *Inside Out* that focus on experiences – hold experiences before us so that we can feel them instead of pushing past them.

The living body, according to Merleau-Ponty, is not reducible to brain states. As we live through our ordinary experiences, the world makes its way through us and leaves its marks on us. Gestures, pauses, unspoken bodily cures, silent spaces between actions, leave their marks on us. Our bodily knowledge, our grasp of the world is primary to who we are becoming. The world shows up as we become more skilled at dealing with the situations which present themselves to us. Thus, when Riley first starts playing hockey, the stick is *separate* from her body and she must think about her every move. As she becomes more skilled, the stick becomes an *extension* of her body. Her hands (not just her mind or brain) possess knowledge.[5]

Similarly, the beginning piano player who looks at the keys must also think about reading the notes, rhythms, sitting straight, hitting the correct keys, and curling her wrists. As her skill and competency increase, she becomes more emotionally engaged in the musical encounter; eventually it becomes difficult to remember what it was like to be an emotionally less-involved novice. Joy instructs Sadness to "read some mind manuals." Joy tries to get Sadness to focus on these manuals (which are stored in headquarters) to prevent her from taking the lead on Riley's first day at her new school. Sadness is the one who has been reading the manuals. And while Joy and Sadness glean helpful information from them, it can only be applied as Riley makes her way through new schools, new friends, new hockey teams, new pizzas, and new boy bands. Manuals will only get Riley so far. In order for Riley to fully understand *in the world*, the content of the manuals must be accompanied by skilled engagement with other people.

Even though *Inside Out* depicts separate aspects of Riley's self, each is embodied, rich, and complex. The film shows that our emotions are not entirely private and incomprehensible to others (as homuncular views would have it). Childhood and adulthood are not completely different, as we see in the depiction of Riley's parents' emotions. For the movie (and Merleau-Ponty!), without our emotions we couldn't engage in the world at all; we couldn't understand ourselves or others.

Our childhoods differ in part due to economics, gender, ethnicity, culture, and parental personalities. And yet they all share a common way of experiencing temporality – an emphasis on the lived present. Riley's journey captures childhood's ongoing focus on the present as we are living through it. *Inside Out* reminds us that in order to maintain the awe and wonder of childhood, we must remain mindful and attentive to all aspects of our selves, especially our emotions and the connections they sustain with those around us.

Notes

1. See Shapiro, L. (ed.) (2007). *The Correspondence between Princess Elisabeth of Bohemia and René Descartes*. Chicago: University of Chicago Press.
2. Descartes, R. (1993). *Meditations on First Philosophy*, 3e, (trans. D. A. Cress). Indianapolis, IN: Hackett.
3. See Merleau-Ponty, M. (2002). *Phenomenology of Perception*, xviii. New York: Routledge.
4. Samuel B. Mallin identifies these dimensions of the self in his book *Merleau-Ponty's Philosophy* (New Haven, CT: Yale University Press, 1980).
5. Merleau-Ponty uses the example of a blind man's stick that becomes an extension of his body and is no longer just an object separate from his body. See Merleau-Ponty, *Phenomenology of Perception*, pp. 165–166.

Part IV

"YOU CAN BE ANYONE YOU WANT TO BE"

To Be or Not to Be ... the Lion King

Existentialism in Disney and Shakespeare

Megan S. Lloyd

Picture this – a darling newborn, with wide-eyed expression, held high above for all to see by an elder statesman. Cue tribal music and sunbeams – you have the opening to *The Lion King*. It's an iconic moment, copied and parodied throughout popular culture since the 1994 movie hit the big screen.

Picture this – a young man, dressed in black, sitting hunched over, peering at something in his hand, ... could it be a skull? This, too, is an iconic image copied and parodied throughout culture since the 1600 premiere of *Hamlet*.

It's not just coincidence that the scene of the cute, cuddly newborn lion cub, Simba, being raised high above Rafiki's head on Pride Rock, is as iconic and familiar as the dark-shrouded Hamlet, contemplating Yorick's skull. It's not just coincidence that *hakuna matata* may be as familiar an expression as is "to be or not to be." *The Lion King* is a Disney version of Shakespeare's most famous play, *Hamlet*. But it didn't start off that way. Simba's story began as something very different when it was conceived in 1988. *The Lion King* was going to be the first Disney animated feature film based on an original concept – no source material. The executives had their doubts, and the script went through a number of rewrites until a story with a series of kings started to take shape. Disney CEO Michael Eisner suggested that the film could be made into *King Lear*. That's when a producer named

Disney and Philosophy: Truth, Trust, and a Little Bit of Pixie Dust, First Edition.
Edited by Richard B. Davis.

Maureen Donley realized that the archetype of the story they wanted to tell was *Hamlet*. The rest is movie history.[1]

In case you hadn't realized it before, consider the similarities. In *Hamlet* and in *The Lion King*, a younger brother murders his older brother for control of the kingdom. In both, ghostly fathers appear to their sons and motivate them to act. Both sons are connected with killing the king – Simba is told that he is responsible for his father's death, and thus indirectly, is his murderer, while Hamlet must decide to *be* a murderer.

The question of *being* that both *Hamlet* and *The Lion King* grapple with is the question of "Who am I, and what am I to become?" This question is particularly relevant in existentialism: a philosophy that reacts to an apparently absurd or meaningless world by urging the individual to overcome alienation, oppression, and despair through freedom and self-creation in order to become a genuine person[2] (or lion, as the case may be).

The savannah of *The Lion King* is not a trouble-free paradise. Forget about the feel-good message of the circle of life. Nature is absurd, "red in tooth and claw," even though much of the killing is Disneyfied in the Pride Lands. Scar's opening scene is an exception to the lack of cruelty, however, and depicts a familiar philosophical stance. As he holds a mouse by the tail, he says, "Life's not fair, is it?" before eating the little guy.[3] Likewise, Hamlet's famous "to be or not to be" soliloquy rings with existential absurdity, and his morbid brooding reflects a sense of meaninglessness.

But existentialism is not about being stuck in a morass of self-pity and despair. Rather, as Jean-Paul Sartre (1905–1980) says, it is a philosophy of optimistic toughness; it is a philosophy of action.[4] As Sartre sees it, we are completely free, and we are completely responsible. It is up to us to make the most of our circumstances to define ourselves. Such is the challenge for both Hamlet and Simba.

The Courage to Be and to Become

The existential question of being permeates both play and film. Shakespeare presents us with a son full grown, mature, and dealing with grief, who waits, broods, and as many believe, talks too much. Hamlet contemplates the question "Who am I?" even before he hears about the ghost. Simba, too, wrestles with the question "Who am I?" – with how to be – albeit in a cheery, Disney sort of way. There's a selfishness of youth and arrogance in Simba, but we see him grow up on film, a truant son, throwing off the watchful eye of Zazu, Mufasa's right-hand bird, and bopping to the sunny tune of "I Just Can't Wait to Be King," a cheerful reinforcement of epicurean indulgence. His song explores a more positive way of being, compared with Hamlet's own gloomy thoughts, but Simba thinks "a king can do whatever he wants." Good ruler and father, Mufasa, who resembles Hamlet's own father, a monument of greatness, quickly instructs Simba that "there's more to being king than ... getting your way all the time." Simba has not yet learned to be.

Quickly, both Simba and Hamlet are confronted with awful circumstances and urgent decisions concerning what they will become. The ghost of Hamlet's father, already haunting the battlements of Elsinore, appears to Hamlet and reveals that Hamlet's uncle murdered him, and that it is Hamlet's duty to take revenge. The melancholy Dane struggles to be and to do as his father instructs. Simba's dilemma is similar. His uncle Scar lures him to a gorge where he has told Simba that his father has planned a "marvelous surprise." The surprise is a deadly one for Mufasa and Simba – Scar has set up a wildebeest stampede meant to kill them both. Mufasa jumps into the gorge, saves Simba, and claws his way up the cliff, only to encounter Scar guarding the ledge. The evil younger brother digs his claws into the struggling Mufasa and pushes him back into the canyon where he falls to his death. Scar's actions are blocked from Simba's view, and so the young cub believes Scar's lie that he is responsible for his father's death. Thus, Simba must confront his guilt and take responsibility for the reality he assumes is true.

In less than an hour and a half on screen, Simba covers the same emotional territory as Hamlet, who takes four plus hours to understand himself on stage. Although Simba's journey is shorter, both heroes must work through their grief before they are able to become what they choose to be. Each works through hardships, runs away, and learns lessons to take charge of yourself and be your own person. In other words, each discovers "the courage to be."[5]

Hamlet's Circle of Death

The paramount philosophical notion found in the film is pounded into the viewers through the Oscar and Grammy award winning song (1995) by Elton John and Tim Rice, "The Circle of Life," and reinforced through lines of dialogue as well as the film's structure, with the Pride Rock ceremony of Rafiki holding the new cub up high for all to see, acting as bookends for the story. On the edge of Pride Rock, Mufasa tells his son, "A king's time as ruler rises and falls like the sun. One day, Simba, the sun will set on my time here, and will rise with you as the new king [...] Everything you see exists together in a delicate balance. As king, you need to understand that balance and respect all the creatures, from the crawling ant to the leaping antelope." Simba replies with confusion, "But, Dad, don't we eat the antelope?" Mufasa gently puts his son's confusion to rest, explaining, "When we die, our bodies become the grass. And the antelope eat the grass. And so we are all connected in the great Circle of Life."

Shakespeare's play gives father and son no warm and fuzzy edifying moments. Instead, we are introduced to Hamlet in the midst of grief. He has just lost his father and his world has been turned upside down. Thus, the circle of life is explained in less rosy terms aside a grave, "A man may fish with the worm that hath eat of a king and eat of the fish that hath fed of that worm."[6] Indeed, *Hamlet* gives us more a circle of death. The body count is high – Polonius, Rosencrantz and Guildenstern, Ophelia, Laertes, Gertrude, Claudius, Hamlet, not to mention Old Hamlet himself, whose murder begins this circle of death. The circle resumes in both plots, but much more positively in *The Lion King*. In both, the murderous brothers assume their nephews are long dead, Hamlet "to't" in England, and Simba presumed killed by Scar's hench-hyenas. The little cub is faced with a dreadful scenario. He mistakenly believes that if he returns to the Pride Lands he will be seen as his father's murderer and his own life will be in jeopardy. Hamlet's scenario is no less foreboding. When he comes back to Denmark from England, he returns as murderer of Polonius and as potential murderer of his uncle. Hamlet's own life is threatened by Laertes, whose father Hamlet has killed. Likewise, in both plots, the murderous uncles meet their own demise. In the Pride Lands' circle of life, Simba is not the instrument of death; the mature yet huggable Simba makes a point of refusing to kill Scar when he has the chance, ordering him to "run, run away, Scar, and never return." Scar ultimately succumbs to his own hyenas. By contrast, Hamlet chooses to be the "scourge and minister"[7] of justice; taking responsibility, he kills his uncle, completing the circle of life but dooming himself with this action.

From Aesthetic to Ethical

The Lion King transfers Hamlet's contemplative question about life and death to not one but two delightful characters, perfect for manufacture and distribution as stuffed animals, plastic action figures, plates, cups, stickers, you name it. After he leaves the Pride Lands, Simba runs into Timon the meerkat and Pumbaa the warthog who offer him an answer to Hamlet's question. Unlike the fair-weather Rosencrantz and Guildenstern, invited to distract and spy on Hamlet, Timon and Pumbaa are stalwart friends. "*Hakuna matata* / It means no worries / For the rest of your days. / It's our problem-free / Philosophy," sing Timon and Pumbaa, in a gleeful, lively, catchy tune. They live within what the existentialist philosopher Søren Kierkegaard (1813–1855) called the aesthetic stage of existence. A Dane even more melancholy than Hamlet, Kierkegaard depicted the aesthetic stage as characterized by seeking pleasure, varying activity, and lacking commitment, or in Swahili, *hakuna matata*, "There are no problems here." Despite the happy appearance of the aesthetic stage, there is an underlying despair, according to Kierkegaard. If one allows oneself to become bored the despair will manifest and rise to the surface.[8] Hence the constant activity and pleasure-seeking.

Hakuna matata may be construed as the Disney alternative for "To be or not to be." Timon, Pumbaa, and Hamlet all share in a version of Kierkegaard's aesthetic stage, but Hamlet contemplates escaping his problems totally. Hamlet famously muses: "To be or not to be – that is the question: / Whether 'tis nobler in the mind to suffer / The slings and arrows of outrageous fortune, / Or to take arms against a sea of troubles."[9]

As Hamlet recognizes, this philosophy has its drawbacks, especially "the dread of something after death, / The undiscover'd country from whose bourn / No traveller returns."[10] For Hamlet, this escape is not merely outside the circle but beyond life itself. Timon and Pumbaa, two creatures whose own outcast habits have forced them into believing in *hakuna matata*, run away from their problems, though their problems still exist. They still fear lions, live on grubs, and keep on the move. What Timon and Pumbaa lack in living this "problem-free philosophy" is community and a sense of commitment. In their aesthetic existence, they are not a part of the circle of life. By joining Timon and Pumbaa, Simba retreats and lives apart from his former circle of life, in the outcast world of meerkats and warthogs. If Simba is to progress, he must choose and commit himself to something larger than his own momentary pleasure. He must enter what Kierkegaard calls the ethical stage. As Kierkegaard says, "the [a]esthetic in a person is that by which he spontaneously and immediately is what he is; the ethical is that by which he becomes what he becomes."[11]

Rafiki Holds the Mirror Up to Nature

Several encounters, first with Nala, then Rafiki, and finally with the ghost of his father, catalyze Simba's commitment to return to Pride Rock and become the king he was meant to become. First, his best friend, Nala, comes across Pumbaa, Timon, and Simba. Although Nala wants Simba to return with her, Simba refuses, quoting Timon's words, *hakuna matata*. For Simba, "sometimes bad things happen and there's nothing you can do about it. So why worry?" Opposing the escapist, carefree lifestyle she sees them living, Nala challenges Simba, reminding him that returning is his responsibility. Hamlet is of the same mind as Simba:

> Thus conscience does make cowards of us all;
> And thus the native hue of resolution
> Is sicklied o'er with the pale cast of thought,
> And enterprises of great pith and moment
> With this regard their currents turn awry
> And lose the name of action.[12]

Not keen on accepting the responsibility to avenge his father, Hamlet takes four acts to *act*. Simba is a little quicker, but it takes a ghostly encounter to set him in motion as well.

Simba walks off, distraught, and mulls over what Nala has said to him: "She's wrong. I can't go back. What would it prove, anyway? It won't change anything. You can't change the past," he ponders. Looking up into the heavens where his father said the great kings of the past would watch over him, he continues, this time talking to Mufasa: "You said you'd always be there for me! But you're not. And it's because of *me*. It's my fault. It's my fault." Admitting his culpability in his father's death, Simba recognizes his freedom and responsibility, even though he's mistaken about his blame.

"Become who you are." Thus spoke Nietzsche (1844–1900).[13] As if hearing Nietzsche's gnomic imperative, Rafiki leaves his meditative lotus position to guide Simba in seizing control of his life. But Rafiki's appearance occurs only after Simba himself has accepted responsibility for his actions. Once Simba accepts his role, Rafiki leads him along, using the Socratic method to ask the existential question that Hamlet himself poses.

SIMBA: Creepy little monkey. Will you stop *following me?* Who *are* you?
RAFIKI: The question is *Whooo* are *you?*
SIMBA: I thought I knew. Now I'm not so sure.
RAFIKI: Well, *I* know who you are. ....

As if luring Simba to see a ghost, Rafiki takes him to a pool of water to see his father. Disappointed by seeing his own image, Simba complains, "That's not my father, that's just my reflection," to which Rafiki responds by waving his hands over the water. As the image transforms from Simba's face to Mufasa's, Rafiki says, "You see, he lives in *you.*" Rafiki holds the mirror up to nature, showing Simba "virtue her own feature, scorn her own image, and the very age and body of the time his form and pressure."[14] The son is now the father, Simba no longer has to be but is, and the circle of life moves on.

The winds start up, and a ghostly figure of Mufasa appears in the skies, reminiscent of the ghostly sightings of Old Hamlet. Both ghostly fathers instruct their sons on how to be. Hamlet's father tells him to revenge his death, taint not his own mind, and leave his mother alone, actions Hamlet has difficulty with. The ghost concludes his demands with, "Adieu, adieu, adieu. Remember me."[15] Mufasa guides Simba in a more positive, Disney sort of way. "Look inside yourself, Simba. You are more than what you have *become*. You must take your place in the Circle of Life. ... *Remember who you are.*" And if Simba still doesn't quite understand his identity, Mufasa reminds him, "You are my son, and the one true king." Mufasa might as well say it: "Become who you are."

In response, Simba claims, "I know what I have to do. But, going back means I'll have to face my past. I've been running from it for so long." Rafiki knows that all of life isn't fair and gives Simba a bonk on the head with his stick rather than an answer to his situation. In pain, Simba cries out, "Ow! Jeez ... What was that for?" surprised that Rafiki would strike him for no reason. Laughingly, Rafiki responds, "It doesn't matter; it's in the past." Simba agrees, but answers, "Yeah, but it still *hurts.*" Rafiki the teacher, responds, "Oh yes, the past *can* hurt. But the way I see it, you can either run from it or *learn* from it." And immediately, Simba does. Rafiki attempts to strike him again, but this time, Simba ducks.

In this simple lesson, Rafiki revises the *hakuna matata* philosophy showing that "no worries" doesn't always mean escape, but a moving forward not back, not dwelling – the pain may still be there, but past is past and we can learn from it. Simba realizes he must rejoin the circle of life and take his proper place in it. Running from his problems and not facing what he thinks he has done is no longer an option. Sent away from Denmark, Hamlet, too, realizes what he must do.

While away, Hamlet has learned responsibility and selfhood. When he returns to Denmark, crashing Ophelia's funeral, Hamlet publicly claims his role as heir; he says, "This is I, / Hamlet the Dane."[16] Similarly, Simba returns to Pride Rock to reign as the son of Mufasa should. To do so he must depose Scar and take responsibility for what he thinks he has done. Scar urges Simba to tell the assembled Pride Land creatures who is responsible for Mufasa's death. Quickly, simply, and without equivocation, Simba answers, "I am." His triumphant "I am" echoes Hamlet's bold statement of identity. For both heroes, this statement of being answers the existential question, "To be or not to be?" In the end both Hamlet and Simba face up to the existential absurdity of life. And through acts of freedom and self-creation they become a genuine person and a genuine lion. *The Lion King* ends with song and the celebration of Simba's own son – the circle of life continues. *Hamlet*'s ending is not so cheery, as the circle of death encloses the tragic hero and nearly everyone else.

Given this ending, with the hero killed and most of the cast dead, Shakespeare gave himself really no chance for a sequel. Disney's superb ability to market, manufacture, and sell its brand, its merchandise, its ideas is something of which William Shakespeare would have been proud. Shakespeare, if anything, was an entrepreneur who knew how to tell a story and make a pound, just like Walt, himself, and had Shakespeare access to media outlets, he, too, would have capitalized on *Hamlet's* popularity, just like Disney, with sequels, *The Lion King II* (1998) and *The Lion King 1½* (2004), the television shows, *Timon and Pumbaa* (1995) and *The Lion Guard* (2015), and *The Lion King*, the stage play, running strong since its 1997 Broadway premiere. Perhaps not surprisingly, many of these sequels continue to borrow from the bard. *The Lion King II* retells the story of *Romeo and Juliet* in the Pride Lands, where Simba and Nala's daughter, Kiara, fancies Kovu, a lion outcast primed to replace Scar in the Outlands. *The Lion King 1 ½* provides the back story of Timon and Pumbaa, à la Tom Stoppard's *Rosencrantz and Guildenstern are Dead* (1966), itself a modern sequel to *Hamlet*. In *The Lion King 1 ½* we learn how Timon and Pumbaa's lives have interacted with Simba's. For instance, the two witness Scar conspiring with the hyenas, and they are caught in the wildebeest stampede.

With *The Lion King* live action movie reboot in 2019, the circle of life certainly continues, and with it, so does its message, *hakuna matata*, to be or not to be. Fuzzy or dark and brooding, cuddly, romping or gloomy, through Shakespeare and Disney, we continue to be shown how to be.

Notes

1. For more of the story of how *The Lion King* became *Hamlet*, see Grant, A. (2016). *Originals: How Non-Conformists Move the World*, 134–138. New York: Penguin.
2. Irwin, W. (2015). *The Free Market Existentialist: Capitalism without Consumerism*, 12. Oxford: Wiley-Blackwell.
3. Allers, R. and Mikoff, R. (dirs.) (1994). *The Lion King*. Burbank, CA: Warner Home Video. All references to *The Lion King* come from this edition.
4. Sartre, J. P. (1947). *Existentialism* (trans. B. Frechtman), 40. New York: Philosophical Library.
5. To echo the title of the existentialist theologian Paul Tillich's magnum opus, *The Courage to Be* 3rd Edition (New Haven: Yale University Press, 2014).
6. William Shakespeare, *Hamlet*, Barbara A. M. Mowat and Paul Werstine, eds. (Folger Shakespeare Library). www.folgerdigitaltexts.org, (4.3.30-31). All subsequent references to *Hamlet* come from this text.
7. *Hamlet*, 3.4.196.
8. Kierkegaard, S. (1959). *Either/Or*, vol I (trans. D. F. Swenson and L. M. Swenson), 287–294. Princeton: Princeton University Press.
9. *Hamlet*, 3.1.64–67.
10. *Hamlet*, 3.1.86–88.
11. Kierkegaard, S. (1987). *Either/Or*, vol II (trans. H. V. Hong and E. Hong), 178. Princeton: Princeton University Press.
12. *Hamlet*, 3.1.91–96.
13. Actually, Friedrich Nietzsche's character Zarathustra says it, echoing the Greek poet Pindar (518–438 BCE), in *Thus Spoke Zarathustra* trans. Walter Kaufmann (New York: Viking, 1954), 239.
14. *Hamlet*, 3.2.24–26.
15. *Hamlet*, 1.5.98.
16. *Hamlet*, 5.1.270–271.

15

True Freedom in *Toy Story*, or You Are a Child's Plaything!

Armond Boudreaux

The captivating premise of the *Toy Story* movies is that toys have secret lives of which we are completely unaware. We can learn a lot from toys, as it turns out, including what it means to be free. On the one hand, being a toy means being subject to the will and whim of one's human owner. On the other, it means choosing between living with an identity you were given and creating a new identity for yourself in response to other toys facing similar choices. Each of the first three movies explores a different way of thinking about freedom, and together they help us learn that, paradoxically, freedom is choosing the good of another over one's own good.

Stay Out of My Room!

One way of defining *freedom* is in terms of stability and control. To be *free* means to have control over one's life and environment. Children like Andy and his sister Molly can exercise their freedom precisely because their mother has provided a predictable and stable environment for them – a place where they can act freely without fear. To be sure, there are some restrictions. Children must obey when they're told to do their chores, but the restrictions are part of an environment in which children learn what it's like to exercise control over their world. When we first meet him in *Toy Story*, for example, Andy has already decorated his room with posters and drawings, and he has

Disney and Philosophy: Truth, Trust, and a Little Bit of Pixie Dust, First Edition.
Edited by Richard B. Davis.

probably been given some say in how his room and toys are organized. As Andy grows older, the measure of control his mother extends to him will no doubt become even greater. If all goes well, this kind of freedom will help Andy become a mature adult who can freely control his environment in ways that benefit himself and other people.

That's No Happy Child

But there is also a dark side to understanding freedom merely as stability and control. Sid Phillips – the spoiled and violent kid who lives next door to Andy – has tremendous control over his tiny world. His room is decorated with all sorts of ugly and horrific images to match his personality, and he has absolute control over the toys that are unfortunate enough to belong to him. He is free because he gets to make the world what he wants it to be: a place no less ugly than his personality.

One of the dangers, then, of promoting *freedom as control* is that it tends to produce folks like Sid – people who get their fulfillment from mistreating others. But there is another problem – a problem that affects even those who aren't despotic monsters. If *freedom* means our ability to control the world around us, then whatever we can't control becomes a threat to our freedom. Any change in our world that we don't consciously choose is then interpreted as a threat not just to our personal happiness, contentment, or safety, but to our very freedom. Nowhere is this problem better illustrated than in *Toy Story*.

There's Been a Bit of a Mix-Up: This Is My Spot

Before it gets interrupted by a major change in the toys' social order, Woody's life as Andy's favorite toy is perfect. In the world of Andy's room, Woody is surrounded by reminders of himself – in pictures that Andy has drawn, and in Andy's cowboy bed comforter, for example. Woody's designated "spot" is at the head of Andy's bed. He is the center of every game that Andy plays, every adventure that Andy has, and every imaginary scenario that Andy dreams up. These are things Woody can count on, that he can take as the stable (even *given*) elements of his life. The order of it all makes him feel happy and in control – *free*, in other words.

Moreover, Woody's special role extends to his relationship with the other toys in the room when Andy isn't around, when the toys are allowed to "come to life." The community of toys is far from a dictatorship, but Woody is clearly the leader. More importantly, however, we can see as Woody moves among the other toys that he has qualities of leadership that are far more important than his ability to command. He has amiable relationships with the other toys (even the brash Mr. Potato Head and the sarcastic Hamm); and most of the others look to Woody for approbation. They respect his opinion and value his approval.

The status quo of Andy's room changes in a flash, however, with Andy's birthday party. The *pièce de résistance* (said in my best Chicken Guy voice) of Andy's gifts is a Buzz Lightyear. Buzz not only excites Andy, but he also displaces Woody as the most important toy in Andy's room. When the other toys ask if Woody has been replaced, Woody insists that "no one is getting replaced." In other words, *nothing is going to change.*

Strange Things Are Happenin'

It very quickly becomes clear, however, that things are about to change (a *lot*) for Woody and the rest of the gang. Woody remains in denial for a while – "Oh, in a couple of days, everything'll be just the way it was" – but in the montage that follows, we see Woody's world being turned upside down. Instead of protecting and rescuing the other toys in Andy's games, he becomes laser fodder for Buzz, and Andy hangs up his cowboy hat for a homemade space suit. Cowboy posters on the walls and drawings on the bulletin board become images of Buzz. Even Andy's cowboy bed comforter gets replaced with a Buzz comforter. It isn't just Woody's environment that changes; even his relationship with the other toys is disrupted. Instead of looking to Woody for leadership, approval, and help, they now look to Buzz.

Because of his inability to handle change, Woody behaves – let us say – somewhat less than gallantly. He becomes sullen and irritable toward the other toys, and when Andy goes to Pizza Planet, he schemes to trap Buzz behind a desk so that Andy can't take him along. Until now, Woody has thought of his place and his world as stable and unchanging, and it's easy to feel free when you can always predict what the day holds. But what Woody has to learn from Buzz's arrival is that our freedom isn't measured only by our ability to control the world around us. It's also measured by our ability to respond with integrity to changes we may not like.

Not Sid's Room! Not there...

But the disruption Buzz causes in Woody's life is only the beginning. As a result of his bad reaction to Buzz's arrival, Woody and Buzz get accidentally taken to Sid's house of horrors. Now they're both being held prisoner in the room of a sadistic toy-torturer. How could anyone be less free?

What saves Woody is his willingness to give himself up for the good of another. It begins with Woody's efforts to return Buzz to Andy's house. Yes, of course he realizes that he can't go home without Andy (because the other toys think that he tried to murder Buzz), but his self-serving motivations quickly develop into a willingness to risk and even sacrifice his own life to save Buzz's. He enacts an elaborate and dangerous plan to keep Sid from launching Buzz into the air with an explosive rocket. Later, he passes up the chance to escape on the back of Andy's mom's car when he sees that Buzz is trapped in Sid's fence. Most importantly, when Sid's dog is about to pull him off the back of the moving truck and tear him to shreds, Woody looks up at Buzz and says, "Take care of Andy for me." This isn't just Woody resigning himself to his fate. He's acknowledging that both Buzz's good and Andy's good are more important than his own. There can be no freer act than this: to think of others as more important than yourself.

Who Am I ... To Break Up the Roundup Gang?

So maybe "freedom" has to mean something other (or more) than just "control." We might say that it has to include living a life of "authenticity," being faithful to one's "true self." Freedom consists in our ability to live up to our *identity*.

Indeed, the idea of *identity* is crucial to the meaning of freedom. In fact, recent political debates about racial, national, religious, and sexual identities have brought to the fore the notion that one's identity has a tremendous influence over one's choices and behavior. To many people, political freedom means getting to fully express and live out their identities both in public and in private.

So it shouldn't be surprising that the *Toy Story* series highlights the role identity plays in how people act and how they make their day-to-day decisions. Consider, for example, the fact that each of the primary characters is a toy. As toys, much of their identity is simply fixed and given before they ever begin to make meaningful choices.

This means that there are lots of choices toys don't get to make. Toys don't get to choose who their owners are. They don't get to decide how their owners treat them. They don't get to decide what games their owners play. And they don't get to decide when or whether their owners cast them aside.

Human experience is similar. Even though many of us like to believe that old canard, "You can do anything you want to as long as you believe in yourself," in our honest moments we know that this really isn't true. When I was a kid, I wanted to be a fighter pilot or an astronaut, but as I got older I found out that my eyesight would never allow me to fly anything (luckily, my interests had changed, anyways). And try as I might, I'll never be a basketball player, a math teacher, a rapper, or a lifeguard. For various reasons – mostly having to do with talent – those options aren't available to me. Limitations are part of what makes us human. This doesn't mean that I'm less free than someone who *can* be a basketball player, a math teacher, a rapper, or a lifeguard. It just means that I don't get to choose which options are available to me; I only get to choose what I *do* with those options.

But we can describe it in a more positive way too. For example, toys exist for the entertainment and delight of others. That's what they *do*, what they're *good at*, and what they're *made for*. The job of the tougher toys might be to entertain rough and rambunctious toddlers, while the stuffed animals are designed to be cuddled by sleeping children. A toy's job might be to play the role of a hero on horseback in a little boy's games. It might be to portray the Scary Witch of a little girl's imagination. It might also be to sit on a display shelf in the office of a nostalgic adult (or, less pleasantly, to hang on the radiator grille of a garbage truck!).

Many of us bristle at the idea that we're born with an identity, a role to play in life – and understandably so. It seems like a tremendous limitation on our freedom to say that *who we are* is chosen for us from the beginning – that God, genetics, nature, or our environment shapes our identities before we are even aware that we *have* identities. But it is true that at least part of our identity is determined for us by forces beyond our control.

You Don't Know Who You Are, Do You?

In *Toy Story 2* we make a fresh discovery about freedom: its connection with our sense of our own identity. Poor Woody is first stolen by Al, the Chicken Guy from Al's Toy Barn, and then added to a collection of toys that includes Stinky Pete, Jessie, and Bullseye. He learns that he is the star of a show called *Woody's Roundup*, a black and white marionette show that got canceled at the dawn of the space race and the sudden public interest in "space toys." Woody is excited by this discovery. He finds himself surrounded by toys and memorabilia featuring his name and face, and he feels a strong connection with Jessie, Bullseye, and Pete – the other three members of the Roundup Gang. Having spent most of his life surrounded by more contemporary toys, he quickly begins to feel at home around Jessie, Bullseye, and Pete, who are old-fashioned dolls just like Woody.

However, when he learns that the toys are being sold to the Konichi Toy Museum in Japan, Woody feels torn between two identities. On the one hand, he feels completed by discovering the truth about his past and learning that he is a member of a group of toys who all come from the same television show. But Woody also looks at the word "Andy" written on the bottom of his boot and remembers that the only home he has ever known is Andy's room. The obligations that he feels to both families creates a real problem for Woody. Should he choose the family and the owner that he has always known? Or should he join the Roundup Gang so that they can go to the museum?

Stinky Pete tries to exploit Woody's conflicted feelings by reminding him that one day, Andy will outgrow toys. Moreover, he argues that Woody's "true" identity is as a member of the Roundup Gang. After all, *Woody's Roundup* is the very reason that Woody exists, and he was created as part of a set that included Jessie, Bullseye, and Stinky Pete. This line of reasoning works, and for a time Woody becomes convinced that the only future he can have is behind glass in a museum.

I'm Still Andy's Toy

The choice Woody faces doesn't necessarily fit the most popular understanding of freedom. Woody isn't choosing between two different life paths, each of which has its own pros and cons. Instead, he's choosing between two conflicting obligations – one to Andy and to the family that he has known all his life; the other to what we might call his "biological" or "genetic" family.

Three times Woody has to choose between these two options. His first choice is instinctual. He chooses what is familiar: the home he already knows and to which he feels the most powerful sense of obligation. This isn't really a decision about what will bring him the greatest happiness; it's a decision for what he believes he *ought* to do, morally speaking.

But as he is getting ready to make his escape and leave Jessie, Bullseye, and Pete behind, Jessie tells Woody her story. She once belonged to Emily, a "real special kid" just like Andy. But Emily grew up, forgot Jessie, and finally discarded her. Jessie's story tugs at his heart strings and finally changes Woody's mind. He decides to join the other three in the museum. But again, even in deciding to abandon Andy for the other toys from *Woody's Roundup*, Woody isn't deciding primarily for his own happiness. He *does* fear one day suffering Jessie's fate; but ultimately, Woody decides to go to the museum because he believes that he must embrace his "true" identity and the obligations it brings. "Who am I to break up the Roundup Gang?" he tells them.

What brings Woody to his senses is a reminder from Buzz: "Somewhere in that pad of stuffing is a toy who taught me that life's only worth living if you're being loved by a kid." Woody remembers Andy's name written on the bottom of his boot, and he realizes that he doesn't have to choose between his two families. Jessie and the others can come home with him, and together, they can all do what they're truly made for and what makes them really *free:* delighting and being loved by a child. The choice isn't an easy one, though. In order to make it home, Woody and his friends have to fight off Sneaky Pete, who is determined to take the entire Roundup Gang to Tokyo. And yet that is often what the freest choices are like: those most difficult to make and to carry out.

He Can't Hurt You No More

Toy Story 3 embraces a further dimension of freedom: freedom from loss and pain. In so many ways, the human narrative is a story of people desperately trying to escape suffering. We are predisposed to seek comfort and pleasure and to avoid pain. For most people, this is obvious and commonsensical. Pain means unhappiness or a threat to our well-being; pleasure and comfort mean happiness and health. So we pursue pleasure and do our level best to avoid suffering.

Still, there are dangers with seeking freedom from pain. The first is that if we always seek pleasure and avoid pain, we will end up being miserable and unhealthy. This is true both physically and morally, but it also extends to the societal and political. History is full of people who believed that they could create a perfect society in which everyone would be happy and no one would suffer. Without fail, however, those who have sought power in order to realize their idea of a perfect society have created misery for the people they tried to benefit.

First Thing You Gotta' Know About Me: I'm a Hugger

There are few better examples of this phenomenon than Lots-O′-Huggin′-Bear: the antagonist of *Toy Story 3*. When Andy prepares to leave for college, his toys find themselves accidentally donated to Sunnyside Daycare, a "place of ruin and despair" where the toys are ruled by Lotso, a cast-off and bitter teddy bear.

All of Andy's toys except for Woody are initially thrilled to find themselves at Sunnyside. Andy is now grown up, and they believe that their obligation to him is fulfilled. At Sunnyside, they hope to be able to live freely and never again have to suffer the heartbreak of belonging to an owner who forgets them. It doesn't take them long to learn the truth about Lotso and his utopian society. While Lotso acts the part of a kindly old bear, he turns out to be an embittered nihilist who treats those closest to him with contempt, using others to shield himself from suffering and loss. Lotso's promise that Sunnyside is a place where "no owners means no heartbreak" turns out to be a familiar utopian lie. Lotso and his cronies live a comfortable life at Sunnyside, but only at the expense of the other toys.

Lotso wasn't always a tyrant, though. What drove him to tyranny was personal loss and pain. He started out belonging to Daisy, who loved him dearly. He was a "good toy" and "a friend" to her other toys. But one day Daisy accidentally left Lotso in a field. When Lotso walked for miles to find her, he discovered that he had been replaced with a new bear.

Lotso's devastation over this loss ultimately colored his view of all toys and all relationships. Because the most important relationship in his life turned out so unfortunately, Lotso concludes that there is nothing worthwhile in the world except control. For him, happiness can come only through the use of power to ensure that he never has to hurt again.

He'll Be There For You, No Matter What

What saves the toys from Lotso's tyranny is Woody's stubborn insistence that they must all escape and go back to Andy's house: "I have a kid. *You* have a kid: Andy!" In other words, their only shot at freedom and happiness is to be there for Andy.

Now this is a hard pill to swallow. Their true freedom lies in freely giving themselves to another person. But doesn't that fly in the face of common sense? To most people, freedom can't include anything like duty. What Lotso's life teaches us, however, is what freedom looks like when we treat it as merely a means to our own happiness and fulfillment.

And let's not forget what happens at the end of *Toy Story 3*. When Andy is leaving for college, he decides (with a little help from Woody) that it would be better to let someone else benefit from his toys. So he takes the toys to Bonnie, a little girl who lives around the corner from his house. But Andy isn't merely discarding (in the most convenient way possible) items he doesn't need anymore. Even as a young man on his way to college, he is reluctant to give up these particular toys – especially Woody. Like his beloved cowboy, Andy realizes that it is better to choose the good of another person over his own good.

In the end, then, Woody's determination and faithfulness to Andy proves not only to be for Andy's good; it is for the good of all the other toys as well. Instead of being resigned to the attic or having to live in misery at Sunnyside, the toys begin a new life with a little girl who will delight in them in the same way as Andy once did.

"Our Fate Lives Within Us"

Character and Choice in *Brave*

Louis Colombo and Steve Jones

> There are those who say fate is something beyond our command. That destiny is not our own, but I know better. Our fate lives within us, you only have to be brave enough to see it.
>
> Princess Merida

Merida puts a lot of stock in the ancient notion of fate, the idea that "whatever happens *must* happen."[1] Unlike fate, fortune involves irregularity, unfairness, or indeterminacy: the property of accident rather than order.[2] Aristotle (384–322 BCE) describes a farmer who digs a hole only to find (quite unexpectedly) that he has unearthed a pot of gold. Neither the farmer who did the digging, nor the individual who hid his wealth by burying it, intended that it be found.[3] That's fortune.

An individual can be affected by both fate and fortune.[4] In Disney's *Brave*, Merida is clearly a child of good fortune. She is born a princess, free to run and play without economic worry. She is healthy and talented. She bears the hallmarks of one especially favored by fortune – obviously, with that big red hair! But Merida also has a fate.

What Is a Queen?

Merida's bow, given to her by her father, is symbolic of a recurring argument between Merida and the Queen. That argument concerns one central question: "What is a queen?" On the one hand, a queen is

Disney and Philosophy: Truth, Trust, and a Little Bit of Pixie Dust, First Edition.
Edited by Richard B. Davis.

simply "a woman who rules a country because she has been born into a royal family, or a woman who is married to a king."[5] In this sense, to be a queen is to occupy a position, with no regard for *how* one occupies that position. One can be a good queen or a bad queen, an elegant queen or a rude queen, a queen who is fit for the position, or one who is not. For Elinor, being a queen certainly implies specific obligations, not just of position, but of character. That is, being a queen doesn't just mean occupying a position, but occupying it in a definite manner. One must behave *as a queen behaves*. Likewise, to be a princess is to be a queen in waiting, that is, to occupy a position in the social hierarchy. It equally requires that one behave *appropriately, as a princess*. A princess is therefore elegant, graceful, and speaks clearly. Knowledgeable about her kingdom, she is practiced in the refined arts, modest, compassionate, patient, cautious, clean, and last but not least (as Queen Elinor admonishes): "a princess strives for, well, perfection." That these virtues clash with Merida's temperament is given a striking visual representation when Elinor attempts to dress Merida in a formal gown to appear before the suitors who will compete for her hand in marriage. Although Elinor does her best to stuff her into the dress, Merida is visibly uncomfortable: "I can't breathe!" she says, defiantly pulling a lock of red hair from beneath her tight headdress.

What, then, is a queen? On the surface at least, a queen must be poised, elegant, graceful, modest, and in all ways perfect. But this should not be mistaken for weakness; for the beautiful surface conceals a great power. Fergus may be all brawn and bluster, and lucky as well, but Elinor's power issues from a different source: from the moral authority of one who has mastered who – or what – she is. If Fergus occupies his position as king through bravery and luck, Elinor occupies her position as queen, not just because she is Fergus's wife, but through her skillful embodiment of being what a queen should be. More problematically, the "perfection" that a queen embodies is not simply the perfection of a queen, but of a "lady," which is to say that Elinor is presented as deriving her moral authority from skillfully embodying quaint notions of the feminine ideal.

Here we need to say a bit about the odd-sounding notion of "being what one is." One might well ask, "Insofar as Elinor is married to Fergus, isn't she the queen? Isn't she the queen simply by marriage? If she's married to Fergus, how could she fail to be queen? How could she not be 'what she is'"? Let's turn to Aristotle for help.

Become Who You Are

In the Western philosophical tradition, Aristotle gets credit for introducing "virtue ethics," even though the word "virtue" does not appear in his writings.[6] "Virtue" is the Latin translation for the word that Aristotle does use, *arête*, which is better translated as "excellence." To plumb the meaning of "virtue," we also need another Greek word, *ergon*, which we can translate as "function." It is the specific excellences of a thing, says Aristotle, that allow it to carry out its function. Put another way, a thing lacking in specific excellences, and thus unable to carry out its function, is that thing in name only. The function of a chair, for example, is to enable someone to sit comfortably. To achieve its purpose, a chair needs specific excellences – a seat, back support, and a sturdy base. Now imagine a chair lacking these excellences; perhaps the back is broken, the seat has a big hole in it, and the base is wobbly. We might *call* it a chair, but it no longer functions as a chair. We certainly can't use it; it is a chair in name only. As it stands (no pun intended!) no one would reach for it, if asked to "pull up a chair."

Returning to Queen Elinor and her daughter: what Elinor and Aristotle recognize is that what one *is* places specific demands on how one *ought to be*. The flip side of this truth is that insofar as Merida fails to live up to her ethical commitments, she isn't truly what she claims to be: a princess. Chairs are what they are. Once they're made, they needn't bother much about remaining chairs. Likewise for plants and animals. A fern doesn't struggle with its "fernness"; a lion doesn't have to decide to live up to its "lionness." Things are different for human beings. Merida will one day become queen. And thus Elinor, who must oversee Merida's proper acculturation to the throne, is very much concerned with *how* Merida will fulfill her role. By developing our character, says Aristotle – through practice and habit – we become what we should be. Well, Merida, as seen through Elinor's eyes, simply lacks the proper habits and character befitting a queen.

In her rejection of her mother's values, Merida is either rejecting who she is ("I'm not really a princess") or what it means to be a princess ("Yes, I am a princess, but I'll be a princess on my own terms!"). Here Merida is wrestling with profound philosophical questions. Does my *is* determine my *ought*? Can an accident of birth (fortune) determine my future? Is my freedom limited to accepting the fate I've been given? Am I free to fashion my fate and my future in any way I can imagine? Or is Queen Elinor right: we "cannot run from who we are?"

Being Led

When Merida storms out of the castle after arguing with her mother, she wants nothing more than to change her mother's mind. Her mother is a threat to the freedom she enjoys and wants to prolong. In Merida's mind, fate consists of a string of freedom-negating obligations. In an act that is neither brave nor self-reflective, Merida chooses to flee to the forest rather than reasoning with her mother. And then the Will O′ the Wisps appear to her for a second time.

In her early childhood, a Wisp first appeared to Merida as she ran to retrieve an arrow in the forest. In her attempt to catch the Wisp, she declares – full of excitement – "They are real." Her mother tells her, "Some say that Will O′ the Wisps lead you to your fate." And yet Mor'du, the "demon bear," appears, takes Fergus's leg, and then vanishes into the forest. "Mor'du has never been seen since. And he's roaming the wild, awaiting his chance for revenge." Ever since early childhood, Merida has been linked to the chaos, violence, and vengeance of Mor'du. And she is led to the encounter with him by the Wisps.

Years later, the Wisps, again linked with fate, appear as Merida angrily flees her mother. But Merida's concept of fate is still very limited. As she tells the witch, "I want a spell to change my mom. That will change my fate." After her mother's catastrophic transformation, however, Merida confesses: "I didn't ask her to change you into a bear. I just wanted her to change … you." Rash and hot tempered, Merida chooses to alter the circumstances given her by fortune without knowing the consequences of those choices. She feels that she can achieve what she wants – her own uncompromised freedom – by altering things around her. She wants to alter her fate, but she ends up altering her fortune.

The woodcarving witch is polite, but nevertheless overbearing. Everything she touches turns to bears. All she sells are images of bears. And now, for the second time, Merida is linked to Mor'du. The witch alludes to the prince who had wanted the strength of 10 men, and who acquired the strength of Mor'du. Did he foresee the nature of his transformation, or did he choose a wretched fate through reckless ignorance? And why doesn't Merida recognize that she is drawing near to Mor'du? She sees the witch for who she is, but can't see consequences of the request she is about to make. She places herself in the hands of fortune.

Twice the Wisps lead Merida into peril: first costing her father a leg; and second causing her to lose the loving (if disagreeable) guidance of her mother. Is there some higher purpose, a fate connected with the intersection of Merida and Mor'du? And how does this pertain to Merida's character?

Perhaps the clearest indication of Merida's choice to embrace the Wisps is found in her second encounter with the witch's power. Lost in the woods with her transformed mother, she comes upon the circle of standing stones where the Wisps had once appeared. She despairs when they don't offer their guidance. Here she must choose to guide herself; she must embrace her own fate. When she suddenly recognizes the location, the cottage appears in the forest, and Merida is given the means to repair what she has done by surrendering to the unpredictable consequences of fortune. The witch presents her with a riddle: "Fate be changed, look inside. Mend the bond torn by pride." Musing on the witch's meaning, Merida begins the process of coming to terms with her mother, her role as princess, and her larger role as an agent of fate. As Merida and her mother wander in the woods, the Wisps again appear, guiding them to a site of instruction, the ruined castle. Merida initially asks, "Why did the wisps bring us here?" Gazing upon the ruined statues of the four princes of the fallen kingdom, she finally comprehends her connection with Mor'du: "The spell! It's happened before! ... Fate be changed. Changed with fate." Through the guidance of the Wisps, she realizes that her own willingness and strength in acting are necessary if she is to fulfill her fate, and be released from the uncertainties of fortune.

As long as Mor'du roams the woods, Fergus's kingdom can never be safe. Neither Fergus nor Elinor is capable of ending the potential for strife. Rather, it is Merida's fate to do so. When she returns to mend the tapestry, she finds the clans fighting. She resolves the conflict not by agreeing to the traditional marriage contest, but by altering its rules, getting all parties to agree that she and her suitors all have the right to choose whom they marry. Young Macintosh applauds her: "A grand idea! Give us our own say in choosing our fates." In the end, however, it is custom and circumstance, not fate, that she has changed. When she has mended the tapestry, and thus the bond with her mother, family, and society, Merida at last understands the significance of her actions for the kingdom and its future. Moreover, through her transformed mother's bear strength, she now has the force necessary for confronting Mor'du.

On Being and Not Being Bears

In *Brave*, bears symbolically represent the antisocial part of our character – that which is selfish, greedy, and hungry for power. The prince was mastered by these antisocial tendencies and was transformed outwardly, via the witch's potion, into the bear that he already was on the inside. In the prince's case, the witch's spell seems only to have highlighted his true character. But the spell cast on Merida transforms her mother (not her) into a bear. Why so? It is Merida who is bound to Mor'du, not Elinor.

Although Elinor presents herself as the model of civility – a standard for Merida to attain – we shouldn't think that her character has been forged by accident. We see her cultivating virtue in Merida; presumably, these same traits must have been cultivated in the young Elinor. Characters aren't simply given; they are achieved through practice and habit. The character we see in Elinor isn't a biological accident; it is an earned "second nature," much in the way that an athlete (a baseball player, say) must work to perfect her swing. The swing looks effortless, but a batter's making contact with the ball is the result of countless hours of practice, with many of the practice swings looking far more awkward than effortless. Some aspects of character are no doubt given through the lottery of birth; others must be attained with great effort. In Elinor's case, this results in the character of the stately queen who greets us in the film. In the prince's case, sadly, his failure to change his antisocial character ends with his becoming who (at least in part) he already was.

This is the moral choice we all have to make: accept the character we are given, with its positive traits and flaws; or work to change our character into what we would like it to be. Elinor's susceptibility to taking on the form of the bear suggests just how fragile our character formation really is. A failure to work earnestly at upholding our "second nature" can easily result in our falling back into old patterns of behavior. For all her poise and grace, it is Elinor, who in the film's opening scene, jokes with the young Merida, "I'm going to gobble you up." And it is also Elinor, later in the film, who taps into some of her natural "bearishness" to quiet the warring clans and restore order. Are we all potentially bears in need of the civilizing grace of education? *Brave* suggests that we are.

Practically speaking, Elinor's turning into a bear serves yet another purpose. For in seeing her mother become more and more "You're a bear on the inside!" Merida recognizes the danger of her own antisocial behavior, as she works to prevent her mother from becoming "a real bear." Confronting her mother's transformation into a bear allows Merida to confront her own bearishness, facing the unpleasant truths about her own character displaced into another. As she learns how to "tame" her mother, she simultaneously learns how to "tame" herself: a life lesson far more effective than the rote lessons provided by her mother. As Aristotle himself would say, lectures on ethics should be accompanied by practical experience. In the woods dealing with Elinor the bear, Merida undergoes the experience that will ultimately make her mother's lessons, particularly about the legend of the clans, meaningful. It is this experience that will allow Merida to undo what her surrender to fortune has done.

The riddle of the witch and woodcarver runs: "Fate be changed, look inside, mend the bond torn by pride." Understood and applied, such a change will allow Merida not only to reverse the spell, but to change her fate. She is directed to "Look inside." That is, instead of looking to an external solution, like a magic potion, Merida must "look inside" and change herself, her own character. By changing her character, and mending the bond with her mother, the spell can be reversed and fate changed. The witch is perceptive enough to point to Merida's character flaw, the one that she shares with the prince and Elinor: *pride*. To change her fate, Merida must correct her stubborn pride. If pride is the hardness of heart that prevents us from looking at things from the point of view of another, the hardness of heart that stands in the way of empathy, then the witch is calling for the breaking of Merida's hard heart. This is what the prince failed to achieve, and it tore him, and the kingdom, apart. Merida has been given the chance to repair all of this, but doing so requires not simply that she sew up the tapestry that she cut in anger – a mere mending of external symbols – but that she change her character, replacing pride with empathy. As Heraclitus (535–475 BCE) once cryptically wrote, "character is fate." Only after Merida, truly sorry for what she has done, weeps over her mother, is the spell lifted. The bond was mended; fate was changed. Or was it?

Changing Fate or Being Changed by Fate?

The final battle with Mor'du raises questions about the relationship of fate, fortune, and character. It seems clear that Merida is fated to confront Mor'du. The Wisps, who act as her guides, appear on occasions when she is helpless, when she is selfish, when she is confused, and finally when she is determined to save her mother, who has been driven from the castle and attacked by her own husband. Guided by the Wisps, Merida defends her mother from her father, reversing her familial allegiances, until Mor'du intervenes. In the ensuing struggle, it is clear that the human forces are helpless against the beast, and that without the protective maternal strength of the transformed bear, Mor'du would prevail. Merida's thoughtless and selfish wish to transform her mother ultimately has a constructive purpose. As it is, Mor'du appears at the point of triumph when a chance collision with a stone of the henge causes it to topple on Mor'du, whose death releases the soul of the prince. Encased in the glowing blue halo of the Wisps, the liberated spirit of the prince nods his gratitude to Merida and her mother. Ultimately, fortune seems as responsible as courage, strength, or determination for the defeat of Mor'du. But without the external transformation of Elinor, and the inner transformation of Merida, there is no overcoming Mor'du. It is as though the Wisps were preparing Merida for this moment all along. Have fate, fortune, and character coalesced at this moment?

Merida herself recognizes that she has changed, but it is not quite as clear that she has changed her fate. The world presented by *Brave* is one in which problems can be solved. Relationships can be mended, bad customs altered, and the chaos and destructive energies released by self-seeking and pride directed by constructive purposes. As Merida tells us, the accidents of fortune can be overcome by looking within and being brave. But she must also solve the riddle and follow the Wisps. In ancient Greek, Heraclitus's statement that "character is fate" can also be read as "fate is character." And the Greek word for "fate" is *daimon*, which can mean a "personal divine guide," as well as the fate to which the guide steers the individual. So in the end we must wonder: Did bravery allow Merida to change her fate, or did fate allow Merida to become truly brave?

Notes

1. See Solomon, R. (2003). On fate and fatalism. *Philosophy East and West* 53:435–454.
2. Ibid.
3. Cioffari, V. (1935). *Fortune and Fate from Democritus to St. Thomas Aquinas*, 16–17. New York: Columbia University Press. Aristotle's

example of finding a buried treasure is found in Aristotle's *Metaphysics*, trans. Richard Hope (Ann Arbor, MI: University of Michigan Press, 1960), 1025a, p. 121.

4. Eidinow, *Luck, Fate, and Fortune*, pp. 56–57. In Sophocles's play, the term *moira* is used six times, suggesting Oedipus's personal destiny and that which enforces it. *Tyche* is used 12 times, and in a general sense traces the movement from favorable outcomes, such as solving the riddle of the sphinx, to the final recognition that he is guilty of his father's despite Oedipus's great efforts to avoid the fate Apollo had revealed to him.

   In Aristotle, *tyche* controls only external goods: noble birth, wealth, power, social relationships, and the like. See Aristotle. (1975). *Aristotle Nichomachean Ethics* (trans. H.G. Apostle), 11. Grinnell, IA: The Peripatetic Press, 1098b12.
5. Queen. (n.d.) In *Cambridge Dictionary* online. Retrieved from https://dictionary.cambridge.org/us/dictionary/english/queen.
6. Aristotle's ethical writings (*ta ethika*, or "writings about character") are collected in two main sources, the *Nichomachean Ethics*, a collection of Aristotle's lecture notes edited by his son, Nichomachus, and the *Eudemian Ethics*, another collection of notes edited by Aristotle's friend Eudemus.

Breaking the Spell

Beauty and the Beast and Plato's Prisoner

Nathan Mueller and Leilani Mueller

"But don't you see, this is the girl we have been waiting for! This is the one who will break the spell!" exclaims Lumière, the candlestick, to Cogsworth, the grumpy clock. And why shouldn't Cogsworth be grumpy? Cogsworth, Lumière, and all the occupants of the Prince's castle have been reduced to mere items of furniture under a wide-ranging spell that has also transformed their master into a fearsome beast. For "there was no love in his heart," explains the enchantress. By the time we are introduced to Cogsworth and Lumière in Disney's *Beauty and the Beast*, they are already in danger of becoming permanent household fixtures: the footmen to articles of royal furniture, and the kitchen staff to pots, pans, and more. Hope is very nearly lost, for (as the voice-over intones) "Who could learn to love a beast?" How in the world is a terrible spell like this to be broken – if ever?

The Enchanting Trap

With the Beast and his staff thus confined, we wonder whether they are destined to live out their days in this shadowy existence. Is this really their fate? After all, they're still alive. They can still talk. Lumière, the Spoons, and Forks, can cancan with the best of them. Moreover, the Beast's strength is positively overwhelming; as is demonstrated when the Beast single-handedly drives off a pack of wolves in just a few moments. And yet the existence of these characters is

Disney and Philosophy: Truth, Trust, and a Little Bit of Pixie Dust, First Edition.
Edited by Richard B. Davis.

shadowy at best. Early in the film, Belle finds her way to the forbidden West Wing of the castle. The muted colors and deteriorating décor depict for us what life is really like for the cursed ones who live in the castle. Everything is decaying towards death. The glass-encased, enchanted red rose, loses one petal at a time, heralding the dire straits of those who live in the castle. They are trapped – trapped because of a lack of love.

Naturally, of course, there are different ways of being trapped. The Beast and his attendants are still largely able to move at will about the castle. So they are not trapped in a straightforward sense. Rather, the Beast and his attendants are imprisoned in a deeper, more fundamental way. Trapped in the form of a candelabra, clock, teacup, teapot, and feather duster, Lumière, Cogsworth, Chip, Mrs. Potts, and Plumette are not simply confined to their household forms (loosely corresponding to their prior roles when working for the Beast), they undergo and experience a significant diminishing of their personal capacities. Bounded by their new external constraints, the members of the Beast's household can no longer fully express their capacities as persons. Lumière longs to kiss his love Plumette. Not surprisingly, the embrace between candlestick and feather duster is cold, feathery, and barren – far, far short of what it would have been had they been in full possession of their human capacities.

Freeing Plato's Prisoner

In another world far, far removed (in time, place, and imagination) from the Beast and his castle, Plato (428–348 BCE) was telling the tale of another prisoner – shackled and trapped inside a cave, accompanied by scores of his fellow human beings in the same predicament. "Imagine," he says, the state of these prisoners: "human beings living in an underground, cave-like dwelling, with an entrance a long way up."[1] Unlike the Beast and his servants, however, these prisoners have "been here since childhood, fixed in the same place, with their necks and legs fettered, able to only see in front of them because their bonds prevent them from turning their heads around."[2]

While light shines in from the entrance above, the prisoners reside in the depths of the cave away from the light. Behind the prisoners is a fire, which casts shadows on the wall, creating a shadow show of people holding various artifacts, "made out of stone, wood, and every material."[3] All the prisoners know of hammers, chairs, and other artifacts are the shadows cast by these objects on the stone wall in front of them. All they know of light is the fire's flickering shadow. They are trapped believing "that the truth is nothing other than the shadows of those artifacts."[4] Like the Beast and his servants, these prisoners are shackled in a state that doesn't allow them to be what humans were meant to be – people who encounter a real world and thereby possess knowledge instead of ignorance.

To be a prisoner either in Plato's cave or in the Beast's castle is a form of existence no one would desire. And yet the story of *Beauty and the Beast* – in particular, the spell that imprisoned the Beast and his servants – is a tale as old as time. It is our common human experience: our recognition that we are shackled by ignorance and unfulfilled potential, and our desperate desire to escape. Unfortunately, however, breaking the chains and ending the spell is no easy feat.

"What If She's the One?"

"What if?" is the all-important first question in breaking a spell. Recall that moment Belle first walks into the castle. Slowly, the large door to the castle creaks open. "Hello," she calls into the seemingly empty corridor. In the shadows, the furniture servants observe and whisper hopefully, "What if she's the one? The one to break the spell?" They remember the conditions of the enchantress's curse. The curse can only be broken when the Beast learns to love another and be loved in return. This particular "What if" becomes a real spell-breaking possibility. For just as the Beast and his household companions represent a cave-like imprisonment, Belle represents in her person the two ideals necessary to break the spell: *love* (which drew her to the castle to find her father) and *beauty* (which can compel the love of another). The towns people sing: "It's no wonder that her name means beauty. Her looks have got no parallel." Thus, viewing Belle as representative of beauty is indeed an intended consequence of her name.

In the Allegory of the Cave, Plato imagines a moment in which one of the prisoners is set free from his chains and is "suddenly compelled to stand up."[5] However, Plato never tells us what breaks the chains and compels the prisoner to stand. Plato's silence here is noteworthy. What is it that breaks the chains? The answer lies in the context. The story of the cave and its prisoners appears in a conversation between Socrates (470–399 BCE) – Plato's teacher and the lead character in many of his dialogues – and various discussion partners. Socrates tells the allegory to teach this lesson: due to a lack of a proper education, people neither desire the truth nor do they understand reality as it truly is. All they ever experience are the fleeting and flickering shadows of reality: imitations and copies of eternal realities. Because they can't conceive of anything apart from their sensory world of shadows, they have no desire to move out of the cave. But how is that desire to be awakened? The answer lies in another of Plato's dialogues, and provides the clue for how the Beast, who has "no love in his heart," can love and be loved.

Beauty and Love's Pursuit

In Plato's *Symposium*, a handful of Greek gentlemen gather to celebrate the recent victory of Agathon (a playwright) in a prestigious competition the night before. As they recline and drink in celebration, they decide to have each member of the party give a speech in honor of Eros, the god of love.

When it is his turn to speak, Socrates recounts a story told him by the priestess Diotima. According to the story, Eros, the god of love, was the son of Porus and Penia – the god of plenty and the goddess of poverty. Eros was conceived on the day Aphrodite was born and, as a result, Eros always follows beautiful Aphrodite.[6] As Plato puts it, Eros "always lives with need," (an inheritance from his mother) and always "[schemes] after the beautiful and the good" (an inheritance from his father).[7]

One way to understand the nature of love, then, is to see it as existing between two realms. Eros exists as a daemon, standing midway between the realm of the gods and the realm of men – halfway between lack and plenty, between ignorance and knowledge. As the son of poverty, he recognizes his need. As the son of resource, he strives toward what is lacking. However, his status as a daemon makes him unable to completely attain that which he pursues. Eros, then, has the power to draw us ever upward and onwards, closer to the object of our love. But what is the proper object of Eros?

Diotima insists that what motivates Eros is beauty. Eros was conceived on the day that incomparably beautiful Aphrodite was born. Eros must therefore pursue beauty. Therefore, since Eros seeks beauty and Eros is love, it follows that love seeks after beauty as well. But then, given that Eros can never fully attain that which he pursues, his pursuit of beauty is never complete. Nevertheless, love's pursuit of beauty (Diotima tells us) is characterized by ever more fully realized stages, allowing us to ascend a ladder from the realm of the physical and transient to that of the immaterial and eternal.

Love begins, says Socrates, by aiding us to love beauty as it is found in one body. It then teaches us to love that same beauty in all bodies, and (by a process of abstraction) as it's found in other minds, discourse, laws, truth, and knowledge. And thus we learn to love beauty itself – that is, beauty apart from its being found in the world. The final step is our seeing the Beautiful in itself. Assisting us in this climb, this pursuit of Beauty, is the work of Eros. However, given his origins, this pursuit is fated to remain incomplete – a lifelong pursuit that brings riches at every turn, yet never fully reaches its goal.

But what has all of this to do with the Beast – cursed because he "had no love in his heart"? How does someone who has no love become a person who loves? The answer is Beauty. Eros, by its very nature and origin, follows Beauty whenever it is perceived. We can even say that Beauty *causes* Eros – a fact reinforced by Eros's conception on the day beautiful Aphrodite was born. Beauty compels love, because love is only felt or experienced when there is an encounter with something beautiful.

There is a sense, then, in which the enchantress's curse simply turns the Beast into what he had already become: a brute animal with no need for beauty and no feelings of love. His transformation symbolizes the fact that he is indifferent to beauty and its upward pull to goodness, the very desire that separates human beings from other animals. Living apart from the appropriate desire and need for love, the Beast in effect gave up his full humanity. Indeed, we wouldn't be too far wrong if we thought of him as having cursed himself, and the enchantress as merely having revealed to him the consequence of his choice to ignore beauty, goodness, and love.

To become human again, something must compel the Beast's love – something beautiful. Love never happens without an encounter with beauty.

Encountering Beauty

"There must be something there that wasn't there before," sing Lumière, Cogsworth, and Mrs. Potts as they watch the progressively enamored interactions between Belle and the Beast. In one such encounter, the two are feeding birds and Belle looks over to see little birds perching on the Beast's ungainly frame. She smiles and looks away. "There must be something there that wasn't there before."

"What's there, mamma?" asks Chip while Mrs. Potts looks down at him with the knowingness of a teapot who has experienced love. "Shh. I'll tell you when you are older," she responds. At this point, the servants are hopeful and expectant. They can finally see a way for the spell to break. What they see, and what Chip is too young to understand, is that the Beauty and the Beast are each beginning to recognize and experience the beauty they each find in the other.

There are multiple aspects to Beauty. The iconic scene when Belle and the Beast meet at the top of the stairs to dance reveals the outward aspect of beauty – the first of Diotima's stages of ascent. Belle shimmers in gold and the Beast is ennobled in his blue tailored suit. The music swells as they sweep down the stairs. The high ceilings and the lighting radiate outward beauty. Then the Beast walks Belle outside and we are shown the inward aspect of beauty: its second stage.

Belle wants to know how her father is doing, and the Beast presents her with a magical mirror that allows her to see him. But when Belle sees the danger her father is in, the Beast releases her. Belle's loving care for her father and the Beast's willingness to set her free are vivid displays of inward beauty: the beauty of the soul. In Belle's relationship with the Beast we the rungs of Diotima's ladder of love.

Shortly thereafter, as the Beast leans over the enchanted rose, he says to Cogsworth: "I let her go." Cogsworth exclaims, "You what? How could you do that?" The Beast replies, "I had to." "Yes, but why?" asks Cogsworth. The curse is on the brink of permanency and Cogsworth droops and his hope fades. "Because … I love her," says the Beast. Having ascended ever higher on Diotima's ladder, he might just as well have said, "I find her beautiful – both inside and out."

Love Sets Things Free

The questions "Who could learn to love a beast?" and "What breaks the chains and compels the prisoner to stand?" are two ways of asking the very same question: "How can human beings become who they are intended to be?"

After the fight with the villagers and Gaston, the Beast lies seemingly defeated and close to death. Belle caresses his head, tears in her eyes. The surrounding atmosphere is gray and rainy, mirroring the loss of something beautiful that approaches Belle and the Beast. "At least I got to see you one last time," the Beast gasps before what seems to be his death.

When the Beast turns to Belle in order to "see" her, he shows how much he has grown in his capacity to desire beauty. It shows that he has been changed by her, and with his death fast approaching, he recognizes the experience of beauty he has had while in her presence. She has led him upwards. And when love rightly pursues beauty with spell-breaking, chains-releasing, compelling power, the story does not end with death.

"Please don't leave me. I love you," Belle calls out, leaning over the Beast's body. Something profound has taken place. If he hadn't learned to love and be loved in return, the Beast would have remained a beast – forever. If he hadn't desired beauty enough to allow himself to be loved, he would have remained a beast. If Belle hadn't found the Beast's soul beautiful, there would have been no release from his prison.

With Belle's declaration of love, light pierces the darkness of the scene and sparkles all around. It reminds us of Plato's prisoner when he finds his chains broken, and stands to face the source of the previously hidden light. Belle sits back and watches the Beast change before her eyes. He is a prisoner freed. With light emanating out of him from within, the radiance of his beauty slowly frees the castle from its curse. Belle can only watch as the spell breaks before her eyes. The Beast, like Plato's prisoner, has been released.

Happily Ever After?

"Are they going to live happily ever after?" Chip asks his mother. Belle and the Beast, now turned into a handsome prince, twirl across the ballroom. In the background, the chorus rings out, "Certain as the sun." When beauty is experienced, love is provoked, and spells break.

Chip's mother looks at him and giggles, "Of course my dear," she sighs with a look of happy contentment. "Of course."

Notes

1. Plato. (1997). Republic. In: *Plato: Complete Works* (ed. J. M. Cooper), 1132 (514a–b). Indianapolis, IN: Hackett Publishing Co.
2. Ibid., p. 1132 (514a).
3. Ibid. (514b–c).
4. Ibid., p. 1133 (515c).
5. Ibid. (515c–d).
6. Plato, *Symposium*, in *Plato: Complete Works*, p. 486 (203d).
7. Ibid.

18

True Love in *Frozen*

Jamey Heit

Imagine a love that is deep and fulfilling with an intimacy that binds you to the other person. Next, imagine that your beloved is beyond your reach, behind a door that cannot be opened. All you can do is call out to this person knowing that you will not receive the answer you desire. You sing with a mix of sadness and hope: "Let me see your face, let me hear your voice."[1]

This is the love story that defines Anna and Elsa's relationship in *Frozen*. What do we learn about love while watching Anna and Elsa? At first, it appears that their relationship is a kind of warning. The very desire for intimacy will disappoint, because desire creates distance. But in the end, the tie that binds Anna and Elsa teaches us that true love overcomes fear.

"Please, I Know You're in There": The Absence of the Other

Jean-Luc Marion, a leading French philosopher, cautions us about a simplified understanding of love. If we do not understand love but still speak of it, then "we say nothing."[2] This nothingness, in turn, can easily damage the relationships that we speak of when we say we love another.

Too often, we define love in terms of our own ego.[3] In other words, love is not really about the other person, but rather about our own

Disney and Philosophy: Truth, Trust, and a Little Bit of Pixie Dust, First Edition.
Edited by Richard B. Davis.

interests. At first, self-interest is apparent in Anna's love for Elsa. She is lonely and longs for company – lonely because she can't play with her sister and because her parents are dead. However, Anna's cheerful tone cannot mask her fragility. She is at a breaking point, and her desire for companionship is so strong that she's talking to pictures on the wall.

Marion argues that love is about our desire to know the answer to the question "Can someone else love me?" We long for the certainty that confirmation brings. There is a big difference between someone saying, "Yes, I do love you" rather than "No, I don't," or, even worse, saying nothing at all. Love is a very human desire to know and be certain, which is why the simple statement "I love you" has such weight in our culture. But the statement is deceptive, because to say "I love you" is to affirm our own egos. In Marion's language, this statement "certifies" ourselves.[4]

At its core, the story of *Frozen* is about two sisters who love one another but cannot be together. As children, then as adults, a heavy door keeps Anna and Elsa apart. In the early days of their childhood, Anna jumps into Elsa's bed and asks, "Do you want to build a snowman?" There is a wonderful mix of excitement and intimacy, but unfortunately their joyous intimacy does not last. While building the snowman together, Elsa inadvertently shoots ice magic and hits Anna. The trolls heal Anna and remove all memory of Elsa's powers. Fearful, their parents decide to shelter Elsa behind closed gates. But they also separate the sisters by a locked door, rupturing their relationship.

The door between the sisters is both a reminder of how close they used to be, and a barrier keeping them apart from one another. Anna expresses hope that the door will open despite knowing it will stay closed, when she repeatedly asks "Do you want to build a snowman?" Elsa, her voice sad, says distantly, "Go away Anna." As long as fear rules, they must remain apart.

"Let It Go": The Psychology of True Love

The girls' physical separation carries significant psychological and emotional weight. Elsa internalizes the accident in a way that defines her character. As she and Anna sing in anticipation of Coronation Day, Elsa steels herself to face the public (including her sister): "Conceal, don't feel, put on a show. Make one wrong move and everyone will know." Elsa fears that she will be unmasked as one who harmed the sister she loves and, by extension, she fears that her feelings make her dangerous to everyone she loves. The reason for the coronation makes this point implicitly. Elsa's parents are dead as the result of another accident. Elsa's closest relationships as a child and young woman are defined by significant trauma. Her isolation is a precaution against her ability to harm the ones she loves.

Anna has also internalized the accident and subsequent separation from her sister as being her own fault. This is why Anna struggles to make small talk with her sister at the coronation. In the same song where Elsa reminds herself not to feel, Anna expresses a fear directly tied to that childhood accident. She longs for the intimacy she knew before she was separated from Elsa: "For the first time in forever, I could be noticed by someone." Although she may desire a romantic partner, her wish for recognition reaches back to the intimacy she knew with Elsa. Her isolation while growing up, coupled with the death of her parents, makes her desperate for love, so much so that she becomes engaged to Hans on the same day that they first meet.

Thus, the sisters share a mindset grounded in fear, rooted in their separation and the love that binds them together. The point is made clearly when the sisters' separate verses converge in "For the First Time in Forever." Just before Elsa sings to let the gates open, Anna and Elsa sing the same line: "It's agony to wait." Expectations differ, but their shared feelings grow out of their experience of intimacy followed by separation.

To fully understand the love that defines Anna and Elsa's relationship, we have to appreciate the driving force of their shared fear. Anna is afraid she'll be rejected because Elsa is continually absent. But why is that? It's because of Elsa's own fears. "Listen to me, Elsa," the ever-wise Grand Pabbie says, "your power will only grow. There is beauty in your magic … But also great danger. You must learn to control it. Fear will be your enemy." Elsa replies, "No, I belong here – alone, where I can be who I am without hurting anybody." So, it's not just that Elsa is afraid she'll hurt Anna one more time. She dreads Anna's rejection – of *who she is* and cannot help being.

Only true love can overcome fear, and ultimately, it is an act of true love that saves the sisters. The notion of true love that unfolds in *Frozen* is not your typical two-dimensional story, where the prince saves the princess. It's far more complex and empowering. Again, a brief turn to Marion's philosophy of love can help us clarify what love *is* and what our culture frequently *takes it to be*, namely, the feeling that our needs are being met by others.

Love Is an Open Door: The Deception of the Typical Romance Narrative

For most of the movie, Hans seems like a good match for Anna. They are both lost in the long shadows cast by older siblings. To all appearances it is love at first sight when they meet. But by the end we learn that Hans had other plans all along. His desire to be king and his manipulation of others reveal how a self-driven love is precisely the opposite of real love. Hans's declaration of "love" is, in Marion's words, merely "vanity" and thus not love at all.[5] His actions cast him as the very antithesis of his "loving" words to Anna as they dance through the night. Vanity and love are oil and water.

Hans's "love" for Anna reveals his selfish intent. There is no love in him beyond what he wants for himself. Just imagine Hans asking: "Could anyone *really* love me for who I am?" The question answers itself. For as we come to see, Hans is actually a terrible person; so "no." Hans is the very embodiment of the point Marion is making. Love in the service of one's own interests isn't the kind of love that defines meaningful relationships.

To recover the richness and elusiveness of love, Marion tells us that statements of love must be reframed in the form of a question "Does anyone out there love me?"[6] Here, of course, we run the risk that the answer is "no." We must confront the possibility that our advance toward another will be rejected. It is in running this risk that we glimpse the transformative nature of the true love binding Anna and Elsa together. Anna's love is expressed in a simple question ("Do you want to build a snowman?"), but also one that risks (and at least in the short term ends in) rejection. Behind her bedroom door, Elsa's answer is "no."

Stronger than One, Stronger than Ten: Defining an Act of True Love

A willingness to be loved exists alongside the possibility of being rejected, but this does not deter the love that drives Anna to knock on Elsa's door. For Marion, the asking is the act that defines true love. Think of Anna's knocking as she breaks into song for her beloved sister. It is a love that risks rejection. In her willingness to speak despite their separation, Anna reveals a hint of the true love that will later save both Elsa's life and her own.

Now of course we can read Anna's struggle against her own disappointment as a drift toward selfishness. We may even hear in Anna's voice a demand that her own desires be satisfied. "Please," she says, "I know you're in there." However, let's remember that these words are spoken only after Anna's hopeful request to build a snowman with her sister. They are an aftershock of the love that pulls Anna closer to Elsa. They're not a sign of Hans-like self-centeredness. Instead, they are an attempt to reopen a loving relationship. As St. Paul says, "Love is patient, love is kind. It does not envy, it does not boast, it is not proud. It does not dishonor others, it is not self-seeking, it is not easily angered, it keeps no record of wrongs. Love does not delight in evil but rejoices with the truth. It always protects, always trusts, always hopes, always perseveres."[7] These words lay bare Hans's lack of love, and they set a standard for love that is rare in our world.

"For the First Time in Forever"

Anna's love really is remarkable in its commitment to Elsa. Anna's patience, kindness, trust, hope, and perseverance in pursuit of Elsa meet with the constant refrain: "Go away Anna." In the face of this dismissal, Anna nonetheless clings to the hope of future joy and relationship with her sister. And it is what motivates her to pursue Elsa after the great freeze on Coronation Day. The possibility of regaining her relationship with her sister, however remote, is the crux of the matter in loving the way St. Paul outlines. Loving fully is a divine concept that carries us past life and death. As St. Paul explains, "For now we see only a reflection as in a mirror; then we shall see face to face. Now I know in part; then I shall know fully, even as I am fully known."[8] The answer does not arrive when we ask the question. It is the asking of the question that reveals partially what is possible when love is fully known.

Now it's certainly true that Elsa's answer doesn't quite map to Anna's initial question. Anna asks if Elsa *wants* to build a snowman, but Elsa's answer is only whether she *will*. Having grown up calling to Elsa through a closed door, Anna knows her request will be rebuffed. But in one way, it doesn't matter. For the act of asking *is* the sign of the love that binds the sisters together. The willingness to ask, despite outward rejection, is the mark of a deep and abiding love. Anna's risk-taking love for her sister, despite rejection, plays itself out later when Anna immediately and without hesitation declares she will go after her "sorcerous" sister to make things right and bring back summer. Yet again, Anna thinks that the Coronation Day fiasco was all her fault, but Anna's quick response to follow Elsa and her almost offhand reply to those in fear of Anna's own safety – that "She's my sister; she would never hurt me" – underscore Anna's longstanding, patient, trust and commitment to Elsa. She loves Elsa.

Ultimately, only an act of true love will save Anna. The audience is set up to think that it will be true love's kiss from Hans, and when Hans is revealed as a villain, we are led to think that Kristoff will save Anna. The way things play out is very different and far more empowering.

Our culture has a clear storyline for thinking about love, and Disney has certainly capitalized on it: the man wins over the woman. In the process, the woman must typically be saved from distressing events she can't handle on her own. The man's success in saving the woman almost always stems from his culturally masculine virtues: strength, courage, a healthy sense of self, the jawline to match, and, often, a weapon to seal the deal. Hans not only embodies a self-interested conception of love, he also projects how the ego-driven understanding of love in our culture denies the openness and intimacy that characterizes true love.

With an understanding of true love based on opening ourselves up to another, we can see the impotency of the unidirectional love that our culture so often privileges. Hans rages as he fails to get what he wants – just what we'd expect from a prince based on our cultural stereotypes. It's not Hans but rather Kristoff who embodies true love. The snowman, Olaf, is correct when he says to Anna,

> Love is ... putting someone else's needs before yours, like, you know, how Kristoff brought you back here to Hans and left you forever. There's your act of true love, right there, riding across the fjords like a valiant, pungent reindeer king! Come on!

When Anna is most in need of true love, it is Kristoff who bursts forth to give her the kiss everyone assumes will save her. For a Disney movie, this is how the love story is supposed to end.

What happens next undermines those expectations. Anna turns away from Kristoff to protect Elsa from Hans. As Hans swings his sword, which condenses all of the masculine-defined tropes in anger, to kill Elsa. When Anna shatters Han's sword, we finally realize the power of true love. Anna overcomes fear and puts her sister's safety before her own. The act of true love that saves Anna is her own loving act for her sister.

We Can Fix this Hand in Hand

While Anna defies expectation in her loving gesture, it is important not to frame her action as self-sacrifice. Yes, it is done *for* someone else, but the decision to save Elsa is no different than her willingness to stand outside her sister's door. Anna expects the answer will continue to be "no." In the same way, Anna saves Elsa expecting that her act will make their separation permanent in death. For a moment, that is how it looks, but then a single breath breaks through Anna's apparent death. Her passion for her sister, her act of true love, is fiercer than the grave.

Developing a frozen heart (and living a life devoid of true love) is an ever-present danger in a culture that rewards those who pursue pleasure and self-interest. If *Frozen* teaches us anything, it's that there are no quick fixes. Like Anna, we need to heed Grand Pabbie's words: "your life is in danger. There is ice in your heart ... If not removed, to solid ice will you freeze, forever." Like Kristoff, we may prefer the quick fix: "So remove it, Grand Pabbie." But even the magic of the trolls has its limits. "I can't," he says; for it's not a matter of the head, but of the heart: "Only an act of true love can thaw a frozen heart."

Notes

1. Song of Solomon 2:14. All biblical quotations are from the New Revised Standard Version. Attridge, H.W. and Meeks, W.A. (ed.) (2006). *HarperCollins Study Bible New Revised Standard Version*. New York: Harper One.
2. Marion, J.-L. (2008). *The Erotic Phenomenon* (trans. S.E. Lewis), 4. Chicago: University of Chicago Press.
3. Ibid., p. 6.
4. Ibid., p. 12.
5. Marion, p. 19.
6. Ibid., p. 24.
7. 1 Corinthians 13:4–7.
8. 1 Corinthians 13:12.

Part V

"ALWAYS LET YOUR CONSCIENCE BE YOUR GUIDE"

Mencius Spins *The Emperor's New Groove*

Dean A. Kowalski

Young Emperor Kuzco – "the hippest cat in creation" – has been groomed to be the sovereign of Mesoamerica (where that includes Peru in this fictional yarn). Living a life of privilege, he has become pretty selfish. On the other side of the real world, Mencius (372–289 BCE), the "Second Sage" of Confucianism, taught that human nature is inherently good. As we'll see, interpreting Kuzco's character arc in *The Emperor's New Groove* through Mencius's ideas about human nature sheds light on Kuzco's move away from selfishness and toward compassion.

Kuzcotopia, Ox Mountain, and Family

Mencius's position on human nature is open to one immediate and glaring objection: If everyone is inherently good, then how do we explain the fact that so many people do morally objectionable things? For example, recall that Kuzco summons Pacha to the palace only to ask him which part of his hillside village receives the best sun. Kuzco thereupon announces that this spot will house his new pool. Pacha is confused: "What pool?" The emperor explains that Pacha's village will become the ultimate summer getaway – "Kuzcotopia" – complete with waterslide. Kuzco can't contain his excitement any longer: "It's my birthday present to me! Ha! I'm so happy!" Kuzco expounds, "Tomorrow at my birthday celebration, I give the word and your

Disney and Philosophy: Truth, Trust, and a Little Bit of Pixie Dust, First Edition.
Edited by Richard B. Davis.

town will be destroyed." To which Pacha asks, "But where will we live?" Kuzco mindlessly responds, "Hmm … don't know, don't care. How's that?" This is a fictional example, obviously, but it is indicative of the selfish and heartless things people do every day. If Mencius is correct that human nature is innately good, then we would not expect people to act in cruel or selfish ways. But they do.

Like most worthy philosophers, Mencius anticipated this sort of objection. Mencius's position is first and foremost about human *nature*. Even though each of us has the same nature, it does not follow that each of us behaves exactly the same way. Consider that even though it is the nature of pear trees to bear fruit, some pear trees do not, due to specific circumstances. Perhaps the ground is not sufficiently fertile. Perhaps the tree was planted in a location without proper sun (or shade). Perhaps it was planted in an unsuitable climate. Any of these possibilities would explain why this or that pear tree does not bear fruit even though it is the nature of pear trees to do so.

Mencius's parable of Ox Mountain is intended to capture his insight about human nature and particular humans. Mencius writes:

> The trees of Ox Mountain were once beautiful. But because it bordered on a large state, hatchets and axes besieged it. Could it remain verdant? Due to the respite it got during the day or night, and the moisture of rain and dew, there were sprouts and shoots growing there. But oxen and sheep came and grazed on them. Hence it was as if it were barren. Seeing it barren, people believed that there had never been any timber there. But could this be the nature of a mountain?[1]

Many of Mencius's views are conveyed via parables and implicit arguments. Philosophical messages conveyed this way often operate at different levels, and this example is no different.

Initially, Mencius's message seems fairly clear: There are various circumstances that impede the foliage on Ox Mountain from being as lush as one would otherwise expect. However, at another level, Mencius cautions that individual persons are unlike mountains in that those who suffer impediments are not merely passive recipients. He likens hatchets and axes to the way that individuals "discard their genuine hearts of benevolence and righteousness" during the day, and despite any healing or rejuvenation that may take place in the evening, these unfortunate individuals only "fetter and destroy it" in the morning. If this process occurs repeatedly, then such persons are "not far from animals" and people come to believe that such individuals "never had any natural capacity" for goodness.[2] Thus, Mencius believes that although human nature is good, it can be impeded in the way that a flower garden can be overgrown with weeds. If each of us is not a constant gardener regarding the goodness that springs naturally from us, then we will not act in beautiful ways.

Mencius notes that a lack of financial stability is an external circumstance that often impedes one's natural moral development. He compares financial stability and the lack of it to seeds planted in nutrient rich soil and seeds planted in dry dirt.[3] *The Emperor's New Groove* reminds us that too much wealth can also be detrimental to one's proper moral growth. The early scenes of the film depict a very pampered Kuzco. When, as an infant, he squeezes the head off his favorite stuffed animal, his wails are immediately quelled by *eight* hands offering him an identical replacement. This sort of pampering continues into his teenage years. A young girl drops rose petals on the path he walks. Masons quickly appear to create a new royal entryway for him so he doesn't have to turn the corner in his palace. He has various personal attendants: a litter-bearer who carries him up the steep steps of his throne, a butler, five chefs, six maidens who feed him as he reclines, a valet who finds him potential brides, and a theme song guy who sounds like Tom Jones. (How cool would that be?!) It's clear that Kuzco has not had to work at anything. He is not mindful of anyone or anything outside of his immediate personal desires. Kuzco "fetters" every morning only to "hatchet" his natural goodness throughout his days.

To Mencius's credit, he was aware of the potential for emperors and kings to turn out this way. In fact, this was one of the reasons why he endeavored to become a royal advisor (and indeed became the high minister of the state of Qi for a time). Mencius explains: "Don't be surprised at the king's failure to be wise. Even though it may be the easiest growing thing in the world, if it gets one day of warmth and ten days of frost, there has never been anything capable of growing. It is seldom that I have an audience with the king, and when I withdraw those who 'freeze' him come. What can I do with the sprouts that are there?"[4] The king, as does young Emperor Kuzco, possesses the sprouts of natural goodness all persons possess. If such sovereigns were more regularly attuned to them, their sprouts would flourish. However, for many sovereigns, there are too many hampering influences that "freeze" out the sprouts, making them less than virtuous rulers.

Presumably, Kuzco's lavish lifestyle, with its multitudinous servants and personal armed guards, is full of such "freezing" influences. But, arguably, Yzma is more responsible than anyone for "freezing" Kuzco's moral sprouts. We meet Yzma as she hears the plea of a peasant. She yawns, "It is no concern of mine that your family has … What was it again?" "Food," a small man humbly answers. To which Yzma crassly declares, "Ha! You really should have thought of that before you became peasants. Take him away." Kuzco interrupts her, and complains that she is not the emperor – she is the emperor's advisor.

It seems clear that Kuzco, an only child, was orphaned as a young boy. Yzma was deemed his regent; she would help the young emperor rule until Kuzco came of age. On the eve of his 18th birthday, Kuzco unceremoniously fires her. Yzma is furious. With the help of her personal manservant Kronk, she vents her frustrations by repeatedly smashing stone busts of Kuzco with a sledgehammer. She laments, "Who does that ungrateful little worm think he is? … Why, I practically raised him." And, in a way only Patrick Warburton can, Kronk replies, "Yeah, you think he would've turned out better." But there is more than just a bit of sarcasm in Kronk's words (to Warburton's credit). Yzma did not raise Kuzco in any real sense of the term. No one raised him, and this is the main reason for Kuzco's stunted moral development. Confucian scholar Bryan Van Norden puts the point this way: "It is loving and being loved in the family that first germinates our capacity for compassion."[5]

"Give-Aways" and Thought-Experiments

Mencius believes that because of financial, familial, or social factors some people do not develop their natural goodness as they otherwise would. But why does he believe that human nature is innately good in the first place? Mencius has two basic sorts of arguments for his view: empirically based examples and thought-experiments.

Mencius's arguments from empirical examples carefully assess how people actually behave. Mencius's clearest example of this describes one of his interactions with King Xuan of Qi. When Xuan witnessed an ox that was about to be sacrificed for a blood ritual, he said to his attendant, "Spare it. I cannot bear its frightened appearance, like an innocent going to the execution ground."[6] The king ordered that a sheep be used instead. Mencius considered Xuan's action carefully, and explained to the king, "This heart is sufficient to become King. The commoners thought Your Majesty was being stingy. But I knew that Your Majesty simply could not bear the suffering of the ox. … What you did was just a technique for (cultivating your) benevolence. You saw the ox but had not seen the sheep. Gentlemen cannot bear to see animals die if they have seen them living."[7] Mencius recognized something that others, perhaps including the king, did not. The king's innate sprouts of compassion led him to spare the ox. This sort of example makes Mencius believe that anyone – regardless of how heartless they tend to behave and even if they are not (fully) aware of the true motivations of their actions – will (sometimes) act from compassion.[8] When a wise person points this out in one of our actions (as Mencius did for the king), we can better recognize our compassionate nature and act accordingly.

Confucian scholar Philip Ivanhoe labels these sorts of unexpected behaviors "give-away" actions. Consider how a person will sometimes act for motivations that he either doesn't fully realize or simply denies. For example, consider a young man who refuses to admit to his friends that he loves a particular girl, even though he regularly goes nine blocks out of his way to walk by her house and often visits her at her job. His actions give him away, despite his protestations to the contrary.[9] Analogously, it would be easy for King Xuan to believe that he was being financially prudent in substituting the sheep for the ox. However, Mencius believes that this would be little more than self-deception because the king would act similarly if he saw a sheep about to be sacrificed.

Mencius's arguments from thought-experiments are the best-known parts of his book. Imagine you are out for a walk in the country some afternoon, and you happen to see a small child playing alone near a well. How would you react? Mencius thinks he knows: "The reason why I say that all humans have hearts that are not unfeeling toward others is this. Suppose someone suddenly saw a child about to fall into a well: anyone in such a situation would have a feeling of alarm and compassion. … From this we can see that if one is without the feeling of compassion, one is not human."[10] Mencius believes that one would be immediately, and without reflection, moved to help the child. This is a natural reaction, and one not motivated by self-interest – not for fame or reward. Perhaps not everyone would actually rescue the child, but everyone would have a feeling of alarm and concern, and this innate feeling would motivate many to rescue the child.

Drama Llamas and Compassion Sprouts

In *The Emperor's New Groove*, both sorts of argument conveniently converge in Kuzco rescuing Pacha at the gorge. To set this up, recall that Yzma plots her revenge against Kuzco by inviting him to dinner, only to poison him. She would subsequently seize the throne. But Kronk administers the wrong vial, and Kuzco is turned into a llama. Yzma orders Kronk to "finish the job," but Kuzco, now knocked unconscious and stuffed in a sack, winds up on Pacha's cart. Once back at his hillside village, Pacha discovers his stowaway, and Kuzco discovers he's been turned into a llama. Kuzco is mortified (and one wonders whether *The Emperor's New Groove* singlehandedly created the "drama llama" meme). Kuzco orders Pacha to take him back to the palace. Pacha agrees but only on the condition that Kuzco build Kuzcotopia somewhere else. Kuzco refuses and sets out on his own. Pacha attempts to dissuade Kuzco, informing him how dangerous the journey is, but then attempts to rationalize that all of his problems are solved: "No Kuzco, no 'Kuzcotopia'; takes care of my problem." Alas, Pacha's moral fiber won't allow him to sit idly by. He winds up rescuing Kuzco from a prowl of jaguars.

Pacha again attempts to change Kuzco's mind about Kuzcotopia. He reasons, "I just think if you really thought about it, you'd decide to build your summer home on a different hilltop." To which Kuzco queries, "And why would I do that?" Pacha expounds, "Because, deep down, I think you'll realize that you're forcing an entire village out of their homes just for you." Kuzco clarifies, "And that's … bad?" Pacha concurs, "Well, yeah, nobody's that heartless." To which Kuzco retorts, "Hmmm … Now take me back!" But Kuzco sleeps on it, and returning the cloak Pacha provided him, promises that if Pacha takes him back, he will select a different hilltop. Pacha remains suspicious, and requests that they shake on it. On their journey, Pacha falls through a rope bridge and hangs precariously over a rushing river. Kuzco seizes the opportunity and refuses to help, explaining, "Well, I was going to have you imprisoned for life, but I kind of like this better." Pacha rhetorically asks, "So, it was all a lie?" And Kuczo answers, "It was all a lie. Toodles!" Kuzco takes a step and falls through the bridge (of course); he is in the same treacherous position as Pacha. They begin to argue again (of course). Pacha yells, "Why did I risk my life for a selfish brat like you?! I was always taught that there was some good in everybody, but, ooh, you proved me wrong." Kuzco immediately retorts, "Oh, boohoo, Now I feel really bad. Bad llama!"

When both plummet toward the river, they are forced to have each other's back – literally. Backs pressed firmly together, they attempt to walk up the gorge. Alligators await them if they fail. Just as the gorge widens to a point where they cannot any longer place footholds on the cliff walls, Pacha desperately grabs a dangling rope. After a quick series of unlikely events too dizzying to describe (seriously, you'll have to rewatch it yourself), Pacha and Kuzco (somehow) land on the grassy edge of the cliff. But Pacha's weight is too much, and the earth begins to give way beneath his feet. As fast as Pacha begins to fall, Kuzco instantaneously pulls his comrade to safety. Kuzco recognizes his heroism. He begins strutting, at least as much as llamas can strut, and declares, "Whoo-hoo! Yeah! Ooh, look at me and my bad self! I snatched you right out of the air." Pacha stares in amazement. He finally utters, "You just saved my life," and Kuzco stammers, "Huh? So?"

At this point, the conversation becomes rather reminiscent of the exchange between Mencius and King Xuan. Just as Mencius did with Xuan, Pacha has a better grasp of what transpired than does Kuzco. Pacha shares, "I knew it." Puzzled, Kuzco asks, "Knew what?" To which Pacha answers, "That there is some good in you after all." "Oh, no." "Admit it." "Wrong." Recall Xuan was somewhat receptive to Mencius's analysis of why he spared the ox, but Kuzco is adamant that Pacha is mistaken. So, Pacha reiterates, "Hey, you could have let me fall." Kuzco admits, "Come on, what's the big deal? Nobody's that heartless." Kuzco gasps. Is Pacha correct? Kuzco quickly regroups, saying, "Don't read too much into it. It was a one-time thing." Sarcastically, Pacha replies, "Sure. Right." Pacha clearly believes that Kuzco's heroic act was not for self-aggrandizement; such an explanation is little more than self-deception. Pacha would agree that it was a "give-away" action. Mencius would argue that Kuzco's rescuing Pacha, despite the fact that Kuzco is a selfish brat, is evidence of his sprouts of compassion coming unexpectedly to the surface.

Kuzco's rescuing Pacha also has obvious affinities to Mencius's thought-experiment about seeing a child about to fall into a well. Indeed, Pacha was much like an innocent child (albeit a very large child) about to fall into a deep well – chasm, really – from which there is no return. Kuzco, just as Mencius argues, showed obvious signs of alarm and concern about Pacha's dire situation – so much so that his natural feelings of compassion moved him to "snatch Pacha right out of the air" and take him to safety. Thus, Kuzco's heroic deed conveys elements of each of Mencius's arguments: It was a thought-experiment that the filmmakers brought to life via Kuzco's give-away compassionate action. In this way, the film (implicitly) reaffirms Mencius's position that Kuzco demonstrates his humaneness – his human nature – by naturally expressing his compassion toward others in need.

Kuzco's Two Journeys

Mencius is clear that our naturally existing sprouts of moral goodness must be nurtured. All by themselves, and without proper care, individual persons will not develop virtuous moral characters. Mencius puts the point this way:

> The feeling of compassion is the sprout of benevolence. The feeling of disdain [or shame] is the sprout of righteousness. The feeling of deference is the sprout of propriety. The feelings of approval and disapproval is the sprout of wisdom. ... Having these four sprouts is like having four limbs. ... Having these four sprouts within oneself, if one knows to fill them all out, it will be like a fire starting up, a spring breaking through! If one can merely fill them out, they will be sufficient to care for all in the Four Seas.[11]

Thus each of us can become benevolent, righteous, proper, and wise, but we do so only by reflecting on our naturally existing moral feelings. This leads many commentators to stress the importance Mencius places on the "heart-mind." Ivanhoe explains, "Of critical importance is the role that our *xin* or 'heart' plays. For the early Chinese, the xin contained cognitive (i.e., rational) faculties, affective (i.e., emotional) faculties – including the four moral 'sprouts' – as well as volitional abilities. ... Mengzi argued that unlike our other parts, our *xin* [heart] is able to consider, weigh, and judge between competing courses of action. ... It is the natural governor of the self."[12] Our eyes and ears are not able to reflect on what we see or hear; thus, they can be easily led astray from what is important and good. But the heart-mind, when functioning properly, keeps us on the proper path. Just as judgment must be used in how we nourish and exercise our bodies to bring about proper physical development, the moral sprouts must be tended to so that we develop into virtuous moral persons. But neither happens overnight. Each takes a great deal of consistent effort. But once accomplished, you become energized and able to do a great many things that once may have seemed impossible for you.

The fact that moral development is a process probably explains why Pacha agrees to help Kuzco find an alternative route back to the palace after the bridge collapses. He does this even though Kuzco made a lying promise to him about relocating Kuzcotopia. Pacha realizes, as did Mencius with Xuan, that he needs more time with the young emperor. He must continue as Kuzco's advisor. If he doesn't, then his royal attendants and palatial lifestyle will probably freeze out the sprouts that Kuzco is only now recognizing. His rescuing Pacha the peasant would indeed be a one-time thing.

On the circuitous route back to the palace, Pacha and Kuzco encounter Yzma and Kronk at a roadside diner. Pacha overhears their plot to kill Kuzco, and he attempts to whisk Kuzco away undetected. But Kuzco is incredulous: "Kill me? Their whole world revolves around me." Pacha is adamant, and Kuczo becomes suspicious and angry. He blurts out, "Oh, I get it … This has all been an act, and I almost fell for it. All you care about is your stupid hilltop!" Kuzco's moral development is very much a work in process, and he stumbles backward here. Feeling unappreciated, Pacha storms away. Kuzco seeks out Yzma and Kronk, but he (also) overhears their plan to kill him. To make matters worse, he hears Kronk claim that nobody seems to care that he's gone. Kuzco realizes his mistake and looks for Pacha, but he is nowhere to be found. Not surprisingly, Pacha finds him – in a herd of llamas – and unflappably asks, "So, you tired of being a llama?" Pacha knows that Kuzco is bound to make a few missteps on his difficult journey of moral development. Everyone needs a knowing guide.

In preparation for the last part of their journey back to the palace, Pacha takes Kuzco to his hilltop village for supplies. Introducing Kuzco to his family suggests that Pacha has become a father-figure to the young emperor. Perhaps if Pacha quasi-adopts Kuzco, this will correct for what he missed in his childhood, namely the moral stability that a loving family provides. However, Yzma, and Kronk anticipate Pacha's choice, and Yzma poses as Pacha's great-aunt while the two wait for Pacha and Kuzco to arrive. Pacha's wife is on to the two strangers immediately, and she plays along until Pacha arrives. Husband and wife hatch a plan that will put Yzma and Kronk in their place, and allow Pacha and Kuzco to escape undetected. The fact that Pacha's family is willing to aid the young emperor bolsters the idea that they have adopted him. Consequently, Pacha attempts to strengthen Kuzco's sprouts by replanting them in richer family soil, which can only aid him on his journey of moral development.

Pacha and Kuzco escape, but Yzma and Kronk somehow inexplicably meet them at the palace (again, you'll have to rewatch this for yourself). A struggle for Yzma's potions ensues. Kuzco is faced with a choice: he can drink the potion that will turn him back into a human, or he can save Pacha's life. As Pacha is about to lose his grip on a high palace ledge, we see a llama paw reach out and pull him to safety. This is evidence that Kuzco is making further progress on his journey.

Indeed, in Hollywood-type fashion, and in a way that Mencius would probably disapprove, the audience is led to believe that Kuzco's moral journey is now complete and that he returns to the palace as a changed man. This is reinforced by the closing scenes of the film. First, Kuzco apologizes to the elderly man who "threw off his groove" in the beginning of the film. The man kindly accepts the emperor's apology, and claims that it was not the first time he was thrown out a window. This demonstrates Kuzco's righteousness and wisdom. Second, Kuzco chooses to build his summer home on the smaller hill next to Pacha's village, and it is a far cry from the outlandish and gaudy structure he originally intended. The two – along with the rest of Pacha's family – enjoy the warm summer day splashing in the water. Demonstrating Kuzco's propriety and the importance of familial relationships, the family hugs Kuzco as the theme-song guy belts out, "You'd be the coolest dude in the nation. Or the hippest cat in creation. But if you ain't got friends, then nothing's worth the fuss. … A perfect world begins and ends with us." At least Mencius would agree with this sentiment.

The Rhythm by Which We Live Our Lives

Like most of us, Kuzco had a rhythm, or pattern of behavior, by which he lived his life – his "groove." By interpreting *The Emperor's New Groove* through Mencius, it seems clear that it is not always a bad thing that we change our groove. Mencius would no doubt concur that the film serves as a kind of extended thought-experiment with a moral: It might seem like you have everything, but if you have not cultivated your inherent goodness properly, you have nothing truly worth having. The film implicitly encourages us to reconsider our own efforts at moral self-cultivation. Haven't we all experienced pangs of compassion or shame? When this happens, do we properly recognize our moral sprouts? Do we sufficiently tend to them with careful reflection of the heart-mind? Are we the constant gardener, or do we fret idly by as our incipient moral goodness withers? Ivanhoe would recognize the value of interpreting the film in this way. He writes, "A fascinating aspect to such moral thought experiments is that if Mengzi is right, all of us, in contemplating this hypothetical scenario and reflecting upon it, will imaginatively experience *our own* moral sprouts. … We too will feel a 'stirring in our hearts' that testifies to our own standing disposition to feel sympathetic concern for our fellow human beings."[13]

If we come to recognize that we would do good – become good – by adopting a "new groove," that cannot be a bad thing. Indeed, each of us would then participate in the human condition in a deeper and more meaningful way. And if we have someone like Mencius – or even Pacha – to guide us, imagine how far we could go. Just ask Kuzco. Boom baby!

Notes

1. Mengzi. (2009). *The Essential Mengzi: Selected Passages with Traditional Commentary* (trans. and ed. B.W. Van Norden). Indianapolis: Hackett, 73. Future citations of Mencius will be from this source and will appear by standard margin reference number; this passage appears at 6A8. "Mencius" is the Latinized version of Mengzi; although "Mengzi" better represents the philosopher's name and title, this essay keeps with the more familiar usage.
2. Mengzi, 6A8.2.
3. Ibid., 6A7.
4. Ibid., 6A9.
5. *The Essential Mengzi*, xxviii. Van Norden cites Confucius's *Analects* (1.2) in support of his interpretation. See also *Mencius,* 7A15 (recalling that the book is named after the philosopher).
6. Mengzi, 1A7.4.
7. Ibid., 1A7.5–8.
8. For another example of this sort in the *Mencius*, see 3A5.
9. Ivanhoe, P.J. (2000). *Confucian Moral Self Cultivation.* Indianapolis: Hackett, 18.
10. Mengzi, 2A6.3.
11. Ibid., 2A6.4–7.
12. Ivanhoe, *Confucian Moral Self Cultivation*, 19–20.
13. Ibid., 19 (emphasis in original).

"Handed Down from Goof to Goof"

What Goofy Can Teach Us About Becoming Good

Robert M. Mentyka

Goofy is one of the most beloved and enduring members of the Disney family. Although not always in the spotlight, his presence always brings a light-hearted, joyful tone to the proceedings and a level of physical comedy unmatched by his more dexterous companions. His impact on popular culture is undeniable, even if most of his appearances end with the infamous Goofy holler of, "Yaaah-hoo-hoo-hoo-hooey!"

In one of his better known series of cartoons, Goofy stars in humorous takes on the genre of instructional videos. Known as the "How to…" series, these cartoons lampoon the ease with which the actors in such tutorials typically go about accomplishing the tasks set out for them. Instead of leading Goofy to success, the narrator of these animated shorts causes nothing but stress for poor Goofy, often leaving both him and the audience in stiches (albeit of a decidedly different nature).

The general format for these cartoons was laid out in the early 1940s with shorts like "The Art of Skiing" and "The Olympic Champ." In 1942, "How to Play Baseball" gave the series its name as Goofy entered one of his most prolific periods starring in standalone cartoon shorts. The same general plot would be reused numerous times in the years to come, arguably influencing the direction that his animated series *Goof Troop* took in the 1990s and seen most recently in the animated short "How to Hook Up Your Home Theater" (2011) and the live-action sequence "The Art of Vacationing" (2012).[1]

Disney and Philosophy: Truth, Trust, and a Little Bit of Pixie Dust, First Edition. Edited by Richard B. Davis.

With these classic cartoons in mind, perhaps Goofy can help us tackle one of philosophy's most fundamental issues. Throughout its history, philosophy has struggled with the question of "How to be a Good Person." In many ways, finding the answer to this question is the ultimate goal of all philosophy. Although entire libraries have been written about this topic and countless hours have been dedicated to discussing it, precious little consensus has been reached. As we shall see, even though philosophers tend to speak and act like the narrator in these cartoon shorts, they more often mimic Goofy in their clumsy attempts to illustrate "How to be a Good Person."

The Art of Narration

Ah, philosophy. That most noble of the humanities and pillar of any worthwhile liberal arts education. For centuries, this dynamic discipline has inspired countless thinkers to probe deeper into their lives in order to discover the hidden mysteries of wisdom that inform our day-to-day experiences. At the core of philosophy stands the all-encompassing question of the so-called "Summum Bonum" and its practical application to moral living. What kind of life must I live in order to achieve ultimate fulfillment? In other words, how can I be a good person?

Alright, enough of that! The "How to…" series prominently featured a rather overbearing narrator who would approach the cartoon's subject matter with an off-putting level of *gravitas* and arrogant erudition. While it's certainly fine to take pride in things that we are passionate about, the narrator's haughty focus on the "finer" aspects of the topic perfectly encapsulates the obnoxious elitism that can sometimes infect any skill-based activity. In the cartoons, the narrator's emphasis on excellence is played for laughs against the bumbling antics of Goofy as he attempts to replicate the instructions given to him.

Unfortunately, while the narrator's domineering demeanor is part of the comedy in these cartoons, a similar method of approaching the subject matter all too often hamstrings the efforts of philosophers. While it may not require the physical prowess or technical know-how behind other activities, philosophy is itself a very skill-intensive field of study. Learning how to philosophize can take many years of dedicated study, during which the student must review over 2000 years of philosophical history as she enters a conversation held between thinkers from every culture and era. In our own day and age, the majority of this training is done at colleges and universities, which have their own particular hurdles and distractions to navigate in order to achieve success (as Goofy learned the hard way when going back to school in 2000's *An Extremely Goofy Movie*).

It shouldn't surprise us, then, that philosophers can sometimes struggle with presenting their ideas in an approachable way. For instance, philosophy relies heavily on jargon and nuanced ways of speaking that simply aren't that common outside of scholarly circles. The *Summum Bonum* mentioned above is Latin for "the highest good," and is used to signify the end goal of human life, the thing that all of our actions are, ultimately, directed toward. Regarding the issue at hand, it serves as the reason why one would want to become a good person at all. Naturally, we assume that living the best possible human life is the surest guarantee of reaching a person's *Summum Bonum*.

It's common to rely on such linguistic shortcuts when discussing philosophy in order to cut through to the real content of an argument more quickly. After all, if philosophers had to explain each and every term they employ every time they use them, philosophical writings would be even longer and more tedious than they often already are. Mix this in with varied vocabulary and an exacting grasp of grammar, and you've got the perfect recipe for a piece of writing that alienates the very people it's meant to educate.

The first lesson we can take from Goofy's exploration of "How to be a Good Person" is one for philosophers themselves. In puzzling over the more difficult conundrums of philosophical thought, we must try our hardest to keep the discussion simple and open for everyone. While it can be tempting to dress up our arguments with layers of scholarly acumen, this doesn't guarantee the presence of real wisdom in what we say and can unnecessarily gate off the dialog from those who lack a formal education in philosophy. Just as Goofy's catastrophe-ridden attempts at various disciplines in the "How to…" cartoons can show us a more accurate portrayal of what it's like to actually engage in those skill-based activities, so too can a more grounded approach to philosophy lead to some real inspiration and insight into these time-honored ideas.

"Could You Back Up a Bit, Mr. Foot, Uh, You're Out of Focus"

I begin this section with a quote from *A Goofy Movie (*1995)[2] – while hopefully insightful, our discussion thus far has gotten a little off-track. It has helped to lay a groundwork for our investigation and clear up some confusion regarding the manner of our inquiry, but our exploration has focused on a bit more of a "meta-concern" for our investigation than the actual issue itself. The prefix "meta" is used in philosophy to denote the fundamental concerns behind a given topic. For instance, "physics" deals with the core forces and relations that determine movement in reality, so "metaphysics," a branch of philosophy, looks at the foundational existence of things that can or cannot move. One would use physics to study the arc of Goofy's ski jump in "The Art of Skiing," whereas one would use metaphysics to argue about whether or not Goofy actually exists and can feel the pain brought about by his return to earth at the end of that cartoon.[3]

So, putting aside the style with which we approach the topic, just what can Goofy teach us about being good? To start, the good-natured Disney character can help us understand just why we ask this question in the first place. With so many day-to-day concerns pressing in for our attention, why should men and women spend precious time pondering how to live a good life?

Over the years, Goofy has found himself in all manner of roles and situations. He's fought ghosts alongside Mickey and Donald in 1937s "Lonesome Ghosts," been "A Knight for a Day" in 1946, and tried to cure the common cold in "Cold War" (1951). After struggling as a single, working father in *Goof Troop* during the early 1990s, Goofy became an AI-controlled party member in the successful *Kingdom Hearts* video game franchise (2002–present) and even began moonlighting as Darth Vader for *Star Wars*-themed events at Disney amusement parks. In every iteration of the character, Goofy enthusiastically tries his best and approaches the tasks set out for him with an endearing (some might say naive) optimism.

Whatever his role, Goofy gives his all and tackles the job to the best of his ability, regardless of the obstacles he encounters or the mistakes he makes along the way. For instance, his Darth Vader costume at Disney parks is pretty screen-accurate from the waist up. Unfortunately, in his haste to get dressed, Goofy forgot Vader's matching black trousers and must instead greet guests in naught but his Mickey Mouse brand boxers. Many of us can relate to Goofy, in that the things we are passionate about (such as family, friends, work, and hobbies) are things in which we try our very best. We often fall short of our expectations for ourselves in these matters, however, and must confess that, while our intentions are good, our actions frequently fail to measure up.

Goofy's clumsiness and bumbling nature are often contrasted with other characters' relative skill at the tasks they set for themselves.

Perhaps the best and most frequent example of this is Goofy's antagonistic neighbor Pete from *Goof Troop*. Whereas Goofy thinks the best of everyone and is quick to give his all to a task, Pete always assumes the worst and is constantly on the lookout for ways to weasel his way to success. Although it's revealed over the course of *Goof Troop*'s run that Pete does have a softer, more caring side to him, the show hinges on the contrast between these two characters and their respective approaches to life. While conventional wisdom might suggest that Pete is better suited to achieve his goals, all too often it is Goofy who wins out in the end.

At this point, we're left with several, seemingly inconsistent observations. On the one hand, we see in Goofy an awkward, ineffective mess of a character whose attempts in any given field appear doomed to failure. This is not due to any lack of conviction on Goofy's part, as he always gives his all to any task assigned him and is nothing if not earnest in his endeavors. On the other hand, we have characters like Pete, who understand how the world works and are quick to always put their own interests first. In many ways, we should prefer the character of Pete and look up to him, but few people express this preference.

It becomes clear from these comparisons that there is something more to our actions than mere success or failure. We can admire Goofy despite his proclivity for accidents. It's in the desire to emulate the praiseworthy aspects of characters like Goofy, while avoiding the mistakes made by those like Pete, that we first begin to ponder how to be a good person.

"There's Nothin' Can Upset Me Cause Now We're on Our Way. Our Trusty Map Will Guide Us Straight and True"

Philosophy, much to its students' chagrin, is rife with possible answers to the question of how to be a good person. Socrates and Plato, two of philosophy's founding fathers, were among the first to voice an opinion on this matter. Teaching in Ancient Greece during the fourth century BC, they advocated that education was the key to living a moral life. By their understanding, doing good was, quite naturally, good for the person. Since no man or woman ever knowingly seeks to do themselves harm, the only real reason why people would commit evil actions would be because they do not know any better.

Right off the bat, Goofy's example throws a curveball for this way of thinking, in that he is traditionally portrayed as rather uneducated. Several of Goofy's defining features were directly designed to suggest a lack of learning on the character's part, and, as previously mentioned, he did not get the chance to attend college until *An Extremely Goofy Movie*, nearly 70 years after his initial introduction.[4] Are we to believe that any good in Goofy's actions is purely random, rendering his decisions inconsequential in the face of blind cosmic chance?

Beyond that, this view of things seems to take a lot for granted, as most of us can point to decisions in our lives that we knew were not in our best interests. Sure, we all act out of ignorance sometimes, but there are occasions when we allow our stubbornness and pride to overrule sound judgment. We don't have a problem with Goofy's usual absent-mindedness, but his stubborn refusal to believe that Max is anything but trustworthy in *A Goofy Movie* leads to real heartache on their trip together during the film.

As time went on, philosophers began to tie their thinking about morality in with their religion, marrying the logic of reason with the mysticism of faith. There's a lot of good discussion to be had here, but, for the purposes of our investigation, it's an issue we will have to save for another day. The religious beliefs of Disney characters are hardly, if ever, discussed, and so it would be difficult to talk about just how Goofy might apply the Muslim thought of Ibn Sina (980–1037), the Catholic ideals of Thomas Aquinas (1225–1274), or the Jewish influences of Baruch Spinoza (1632–1677).

The desire for a universal moral compass, applicable to thinkers of any background, led to the development of two great schools of thought. The first of these is known as *deontology*, and it answers the question of "How to be a Good Person" with the relatively simple response of, "Do your duty." Deontology posits that there are universally applicable moral laws that can point to our duties and guide us in our decision-making. These laws are not based in any religion or cultural background, but can be accessed solely by reason and are, therefore, binding for everyone.

The most famous proponent of deontology was Immanuel Kant (1774–1804). He proposed a "Categorical Imperative," a single, relatively simple rule that can be applied to every decision in our lives in order to ensure that we do good and avoid evil. It ran thus, "Act only according to that maxim by which you can at the same time will that it should become a universal law."[5] In simpler terms, always act the way you think other people should act in any given set of circumstances.

On the surface, this kind of morality seems like a godsend for Goofy, who can barely keep his thoughts together on the best of days. Having just one rule to follow no matter the situation would certainly make for a clear-cut system of ethics. Unfortunately, it's in the very act of applying this imperative to every situation that its flaws begin to manifest. In the course of *A Goofy Movie*, Goofy passes on to his son, Max, a fishing pole that's "been handed down from Goof to Goof to Goof." Obviously, this pole is one of Goofy's prized possessions and he takes great pride in gifting it to Max. Unfortunately, in doing so, he violates Kant's categorical imperative, since the handing on of this pole isn't something that Goofy could mandate be done by everyone. He wouldn't want Pete handing this rod to his son, PJ, since it's a Goof family heirloom.

Problems like this one led to the development of another great school of thought known as *utilitarianism*. Championed by thinkers like John Stuart Mill (1806–1873), this viewpoint seeks to circumvent some of the problems of deontology by focusing on the results of our actions rather than our duties. Utilitarianism advises us to focus on creating the greatest amount of happiness for the greatest number of people. By doing so, we create a world that has a quantifiably greater amount of good in it and thus become better people ourselves.

The problem of the fishing pole discussed above is less of an issue for this school of thought, because it takes into account the differing degrees of happiness this gift brings to different people. PJ might derive some utility from Pete's gift of the Goof family fishing pole, but it would pale in comparison to the joy Goofy takes in handing it on to his son, not to mention the extreme amount of distress it would cause poor Goofy knowing that such a prized possession was no longer his. Because doing so makes the world a happier place, Goofy is justified in handing the pole on to Max.

Max's response to the gift, however, raises new issues, as the younger Goof is nowhere near as excited about this present as his father is. Goofy acted with the expectation that this gift would bring great joy to his son, but Max's reception of the pole is lukewarm, at best, and the entire fishing trip that follows is one that brings young Max no small amount of pain and frustration. Contrary to the utilitarian goal, Goofy's actions resulted in less happiness for his son. Despite Goofy's good intentions his action fails for factors mostly outside of his control.

The problems only intensify with more recent developments in philosophy, such as those championed by contemporary philosopher

Peter Singer. Singer claims that the utilitarian method needs to be extended to all creatures, not just rational human persons. According to Singer, Goofy needs to consider the interests of Mickey's dog Pluto and Minnie's cat Figaro as well as the happiness of Max, Pete, PJ, and the rest of the Disney family whenever making a moral decision. Given the vague distinctions between Pluto, a dog, and Goofy, a dog who is nonetheless treated as a person, this addendum to the argument opens a whole new can of worms for the issue. What started off as a simple question about the gift of a fishing pole has now brought the very societal structure of Mickey's Toontown into question. For all of our efforts, the answer to our initial question of "How to be a Good Person" seems further away than ever.

"You Know, It's Funny, But None of Your Techniques Worked for Me. The Harder I Tried the Worse it Got. Once I Eased Up, Things Just Clicked"

By now it should be clear that philosophers do not have a definitive answer to the question under investigation. However, if we go back in our discussion a little bit, we might be able to find some hints about where we, as moral decision-makers, should go from here. It's by no means a knock-down, drag-out victory, but it does point us in the direction of an authentic answer.

In considering why ordinary men and women start to wonder about ethical living, we used Goofy's example of humble but accident-prone dedication to examine what constitutes success in moral decision-making. Throughout that discussion, we constantly referred back to Goofy as a character who, despite his flaws, is considered by many to be morally good. Now, in some ways, that discussion fell to a classic error, as we assumed Goofy to be a good character without first having defined what "good" itself meant.

If we step back and look at our own experiences, however, we find that this sort of situation is fairly common. Without having studied any ethical treatises about right and wrong, we encounter people and their actions that we consider "good" or "evil." It is through the example of other people that we first experience the underlying ideas of morality and begin to ask these questions in the first place.

The German philosopher Max Scheler (1874–1928) was similarly dissatisfied with the prevailing ethical theories of his day. For Scheler, all the discussion of universal rules and intentional consequences seemed secondary, because our primary ethical experience came from other people and the values they represented. When we choose good or evil, we don't focus on the laws we're possibly breaking or the quantity of happiness being produced. Rather, we experience such moral actions as movements toward or away from the things we value. If Max betrays PJ, he doesn't feel bad because he broke their parents' rules or made their hometown a sadder place. He feels bad because he hurt his best friend and violated the trust that once existed between them.

For Scheler, ethics is the movement toward or away from values, and the way we learn about those values is through the example of other people. "Moral exemplars" are people who instantiate specific values, opening us up to their goodness or showing us the poverty of a world without them. They can be actual people we know or fictional entities, such as Goofy and the rest of the Disney family. This is how Goofy, a clumsy, good-natured cartoon dog, can teach us about what it means to be a good person and how, despite its comedic focus, the "How to…" series can help us to learn something about the disciplines it's parodying.

"It's Been Handed Down from Goof to Goof to Goof, and Now, It's Yours, Son"

While it's only just a start, Goofy's look into "How to be a Good Person" has yielded some fruitful insights. In the first place, we were reminded about the humility needed in approaching such an important topic. We may like to pretend that we've got all the answers, much like the narrator in the "How to…" series, but, more often than not, we find ourselves in Goofy's shoes, struggling to apply the things we've learned and making numerous mistakes in the process.

It may be a difficult question to tackle, but "How to be a Good Person" is an issue that simply needs to be addressed. Far from an esoteric study of abstract concepts, it's vital in our day-to-day interactions with others. Whether we like it or not, we find ourselves thrust into a world of competing values vying for our attention, and it's up to us to decide how to prioritize them. There are many ethical theories out there that can help or hinder us, but, ultimately, the examples of the people in our lives, both real and fictional, awaken us to the things that truly matter.

It's a daunting project, but one that we can handle given the proper awe and reverence for the subject matter. Again Goofy can guide us here, as sometimes the best response to the challenge of ethics is a well-placed, awe-filled "Gawrsh!"

Notes

1. The dates and information regarding these shorts are widely available online, and there are numerous outlets for viewing them. As of this writing, the most recent additions, as well as a few of the classic cartoons, can be watched for free at Disney's official site: https://video.disney.com.
2. Quoted section titles are all taken from *A Goofy Movie* (1995).
3. See Merriam-Webster's definition of the prefix at https://www.merriam-webster.com/dictionary/meta-.
4. For a rather unflattering description of the character as initially conceived, see Art Babbit's discussion of the character in O'Brien, F. (1986). *Walt Disney's Goofy: The Good Sport.* Tucson, AZ: HPBooks, 18.
5. Kant, I. (1997). *Foundations of the Metaphysics of Morals and What Is Enlightenment?*, The Library of Liberal Arts Series, (trans. L. Beck) 2e, revised Upper Saddle River, NJ: Prentice-Hall, Inc., 38.

"Let Slip the (Donald) Ducks of War!"

Ethical Considerations About Disney's War Propaganda

Tuomas W. Manninen

Mention the classic 1930s and 1940s Disney cartoons to someone, and they'll very likely think of the antics of Mickey, Donald, and Goofy. They probably won't think of propaganda for the Allied forces during the Second World War. But according to John Baxter's comprehensive history *Disney During World War II*, the Disney studios' overall output during the war years of 1942 through 1945 was more than 90% war materials.[1]

Granted, some of these materials included training films commissioned by the military – films featuring generic characters rather than Mickey, Donald, and other better-known Disney figures – as well as sundry artwork ranging from patriotic posters to unit insignias.[2] But in addition to these training materials, the Disney studios produced propaganda films – such as *Donald Gets Drafted*, *Donald's Decision*, *Commando Duck*, and *Der Fuehrer's Face* – all of which featured Donald Duck. A whirlwind tour of these forgotten films teaches us something important about the nature of propaganda: it's not just the bad guys who make propaganda, nor is it always wrong to make it.

What Are the Disney Propaganda Films?

The World War II Disney propaganda films – the propaganda and entertainment shorts – are included in the *Walt Disney in the Front Lines* boxed set, which was released as part of the third wave of the

Disney and Philosophy: Truth, Trust, and a Little Bit of Pixie Dust, First Edition.
Edited by Richard B. Davis.

Walt Disney Treasures collection in 2004. The shorts, which are available in public domain, have their URLs included in the notes at the end of this chapter. Let's get acquainted with a few.

Donald's Decision (1942)

In this three and a half minute short,[3] Donald is listening to a radio ad urging him to invest in war savings bonds. Inspired by the ad, Donald agrees to do so – tomorrow. During his nap, his better and worse sides fight it out as an imaginary angel and devil. The devil (whose first appearance is associated with the mailbox handle spinning to form a swastika) urges Donald to spend his savings on himself. The angel prevails in the fight and leads the now saintly-looking Donald to the post office to use his savings on war bonds instead. The closing message: "Invest in victory."

The New Spirit (1942)

Much like its sequel *The Spirit of '43*, this short film[4] focuses the viewer's attention on individual income and how it should be spent. Donald is shown listening a radio announcement about how everyone should do their part now that the country has entered World War II. Donald's initial enthusiasm quickly fades though, when he learns that he can contribute to the war effort by promptly paying his income tax. The film manages to revive Donald's spirits by stressing the message that making financial contributions to the war effort on the home front helps defeat the enemy.

Der Fuehrer's Face (1942)

Originally titled *Donald Duck in Nutzi Land*, *Der Fuehrer's Face* focuses on Donald's nightmare living under the Nazi rule. He is awoken by a brass band composed of Nazi soldiers (crude caricatures of Axis leaders), forced to read *Mein Kampf* over a breakfast consisting of wooden bread and coffee brewed from a single bean, and then escorted at bayonet point to his work at a munitions factory. After toiling all day long and being forced to salute even the picture of the Fuehrer, Donald is chosen to work overtime, which results in his mental breakdown. Donald finally wakes up from his nightmare to the realization: "Am I glad to be a citizen of the United States of America."[5]

The Spirit of '43 (1943)

While *Donald's Decision* was produced by the National Film Board of Canada, the *Spirit of '43*[6] was distributed "under the auspices of the War Activities Committee, Motion Picture Industry." The voiceover makes the message patently clear: American workers receive millions of dollars each payday, and they fight two conflicting urges over what to do with their money. The Thrifty figure urges Donald to save up to pay his taxes. ("This year, thanks to Hitler and Hirohito, taxes are higher than ever before," says the voiceover.) By contrast, the Spendthrift urges Donald to "spend it – it's your dough." Leaving subtlety aside, the subsequent tussle results in the Spendthrift entering a lounge through a swastika-shaped swinging door, while Thrifty, having been knocked down, is shown against a wall with a stars-and-stripes motif. After a montage of the different sorts of weapons that could be manufactured using tax dollars (along with some borrowed footage from *The New Spirit*), the concluding message is, "Taxes – to bury the Axis." Donald finally knocks down Spendthrift, who crashes through the bar door, with the pieces landing in the shape of "V" – for victory (with the accompanying opening bars from Beethoven's Fifth playing in the background).

Commando Duck (1944)

Of all the wartime short movies, the closest Donald Duck gets to experiencing combat occurs in *Commando Duck*. Donald is tasked with traversing a treacherous terrain carrying not just a rifle but also a machine gun – not to mention a full kit. Before he parachutes from the plane, his orders are explained to him: he is to contact the enemy's large airbase, surround the enemy, and wipe them out. Although most of Donald's mission in *Commando Duck* (generally not counted among the propaganda pieces) is carried out in his reckless, pre-war slapstick style, this short is best classified as a propaganda piece, if only for its description of the enemy.[7] As the enemy snipers position Donald in their crosshairs and prepare to fire, one of the voices is heard saying, "time for shooting now please, I hope." Another voice responds: "No, no. No, wait, please. Japanese custom says, always shoot the man in the back, please." Donald completes his mission without firing a shot, as he inadvertently causes a duck-made tsunami that wipes out the airbase, leaving Donald happily chuckling as he writes his report to his CO: "Contacted the enemy. Washed out the same."

What Is Propaganda?

The World War II Disney films raise two important questions: What is propaganda? And is propaganda good or bad? If asked to define *propaganda*, someone might answer like Justice Potter Stewart when he was asked to define *pornography*: "I know it when I see it."[8] Over the years, many philosophers have offered definitions of propaganda. In his book *Media, Persuasion and Propaganda*, Marshall Soules discusses the various forms propaganda can take.[9] It can be political or sociological. It can be agitation propaganda (which stirs up the target audience) or integration propaganda (which unifies the target audience). It can be vertical (originating from an authority and imposed top-down on the masses) or horizontal (traveling among grassroots groups).[10] Philosopher Douglas Walton identifies no fewer than 10 characteristic features of propaganda.[11] Part of Walton's motivation in constructing such an extensive list is to avoid drawing negative conclusions about all propaganda films. It is a mistake, he argues, to dismiss something out of hand simply because it is propaganda.

Rather than address all the nuances here, let's take a neutral definition of propaganda – one that doesn't foreclose on the question of its moral acceptability. For this purpose, Randal Marlin's definition will serve nicely. According to Marlin, propaganda is "the organized attempt through communication to affect belief or action or inculcate attitudes in a large audience in ways that circumvent or suppress an individual's adequately informed, rational, reflective judgment."[12] This definition allows us to talk about the WWII Disney shorts as pieces of propaganda, but without making sweeping statements about their rightness or wrongness.

Dispelling the misconception that only the bad guys employ propaganda is crucial for an objective and fair analysis. Disney itself was ambivalent about the use of the label in classifying its wartime productions, and we still face questions about the peculiar character of Disney's propaganda shorts.[13] Thus according to Baxter,

> Disney made a number of shorts and features during World War II that fell into the general category of propaganda, though most were more educational or entertaining than propagandistic. But the line between educating and influencing opinion is often blurred.[14]

There is nothing wrong with that. After all, educating and influencing opinion are not mutually exclusive. Indeed, don't we educate people – at least in part – to influence their opinions in the right direction?

The Point of Propaganda

Each of the Disney propaganda shorts comes with a specific message, though the common purpose was "intended to help the war effort, whether by encouraging thrift and sacrifice, [or] demoralizing the enemy."[15] If we look at a specific piece, we can fill in the blanks with greater detail. Take, for instance, *The Spirit of '43*. We can represent its message in the following argument:

1. On payday, every worker faces the choice of being thrifty with their paycheck, or being spendthrift and squandering it on personal indulgences.
2. Being spendthrift takes money away from the government, which reduces the revenue needed for war efforts, and thus helps the Axis.
3. Everyone should want to defeat the Axis (implied).
4. Thus, everyone should be thrifty with their money, thereby assisting the war effort.

Although this is a faithful rendition of the film's message, it is likely that such reconstructions can occur only after the fact – not at the moment of first viewing. The message isn't conveyed through reason, but through popular appeal and emotion. At this juncture – as Walton points out – many logicians and critical thinkers cry "foul." Appeals to the popularity of a view or its emotional appeal are textbook cases of informal logical fallacies.[16] But here Walton would bid us to consider the function that propaganda serves. In keeping with *The Spirit of '43*, it seems obvious that the goal of the film was *not just* to have the audience agree with the message "You should save your money and contribute to the war effort." The goal was *also* to prompt the audience to act on the message. So while propaganda may employ seemingly fallacious reasoning, that doesn't mean that propaganda is inherently fallacious. An appeal is fallacious to the extent that it supplants logically relevant reasons with merely emotional reasons. However, if the message of the film is "save your money so you can contribute to the war efforts against the Axis," watching Donald Duck punch out Spendthrift (shown as a Nazi colluder) *is* logically relevant to the conclusion.[17]

We can put this even more pointedly: "the goal of propaganda is to change the respondents' beliefs or to persuade the respondents to accept some proposition as true (or false). But these goals, although they are typically part of propaganda, are secondary to the ultimate goal, which is always ... to get the respondents to do (or abstain from doing) something."[18] Here Walton's analysis aligns with the views of the Scottish philosopher David Hume (1711–1776).

In his book *A Treatise on Human Nature*, Hume argues that reason is subservient – a slave even – to the passions. Hume argues that philosophers (among others) often take reason and passion to be opposed to one another, and many claim that virtue can be found in following the former over the latter.[19] Hume's aim is to show that this view is wrong because "reason alone can never be a motive to any action of the will."[20] But if so, he says, then reason is equally incapable of having any influence on passions needed for action – hope, fear, grief, joy, and the like. Thus, the only point of conflict between reason and passion occurs when a passion is unreasonable or based on a false judgment.[21] And thus, Hume concludes, reason is "and only ought to be the slave of the passions, and can never pretend to any other office than to serve and obey them."[22]

We can easily see how this line of thinking applies to a propaganda piece like *The Spirit of '43*. The passions of security (against the Axis) and fear (of being attacked by the Axis) are on full and powerful display, not the step-by-step construction of the argument. To the audience, the visual depiction of these sentiments is more forceful and persuasive than simply hearing the same message delivered by means of an emotionless premise-to-conclusion – argument. And the same point can be generalized across the other propaganda shorts. Whether it is the pareidolic depictions of Nazi submarines in *The Spirit of '43*, or the caricatures of the German leaders in *Der Fuehrer's Face*, or the portraits of the Japanese troops in *Commando Duck*: the point is that these all rouse the passions in a way that purely verbal descriptions of the Axis soldiers never could.

Is Propaganda Permissible?

Now that we have a basic grasp of what propaganda is, the question arises: should we allow it to be disseminated? In answering this question, we can do no better than turning to John Stuart Mill's (1806–1873) classic argument for freedom of expression in *On Liberty*. According to Mill, suppressing any viewpoint in public discourse (even if it's false) is far more detrimental to the liberties of an individual than allowing that viewpoint to be heard.

Mill's argument for freedom of expression is rather lengthy and involved. Fortunately, Francis Gill is has provided a brilliantly succinct summary. Mill's argument, says Gill, comes to the following:

1. Humans are fallible. Fallibility means that they are always subject to error in their beliefs.
2. Humans are corrigible. Corrigibility means that humans have a rational capacity to correct their errors by discussion and experience.
3. Thus, knowledge requires not only possession of true beliefs, but also an environment in which they are subject to questioning.
4. For a true belief to be questioned, someone must hold or at least entertain the plausibility of its contradictory, a false belief.
5. Thus, false beliefs have value and should be freely expressed because the expression of false beliefs contributes to human knowledge.[23]

In light of Gill's reconstruction of Mill's argument, we can say that propaganda materials – including the Disney shorts – should at least be allowed a seat at the table of public discourse. If, for example, the message of *The Spirit of '43* is correct, then of course it ought to be heard. And even if it is false, allowing public discussion of its message is still valuable; for it can serve as a counterpoint to the truth.

Even though, at first glance, Mill's views seem to allow for the inclusion of propaganda in public discourse across the board, this initial appearance is somewhat misleading. For one thing, problems can arise with respect to the temperance of the discourse. We must exercise caution, says Mill, to steer clear of "what is commonly meant by intemperate discussion, namely invective, sarcasm, personality, and the like."[24] But surely this isn't sufficient for excluding a viewpoint from public discourse. Just because *Der Fuehrer's Face* relies on mocking the Axis leaders in making its point, that doesn't mean it is automatically out of bounds. The same goes for the other propaganda shorts.

But there is a second problem with uncritically using Mill's argument to defend propaganda pieces – and it is one that Mill himself notes. He writes:

> No one pretends that actions should be as free as opinions. On the contrary, even expressions lose their immunity when the circumstances in which they are expressed are such as to constitute their expression a positive instigation to some mischievous act.[25]

Mill's point here apparently cautions against what Walton called the "ultimate goal" of propaganda – enticing someone to act in an inappropriate way. If a propaganda piece incites someone to act in a manner that harms others, then it is rightfully prohibited. Is this the case with the Disney propaganda shorts? Not obviously. How does being thrifty, paying one's taxes, and donating money to the war effort qualify as harmful and mischievous? The clear and evident goal of the Disney propaganda shorts, as Baxter puts it, was to help the war effort.

Consider the following thought-experiment. Imagine that there's a cartoon studio – call it the Yensid studio – similar to Disney in its capabilities, but that makes propaganda films supporting the Axis war efforts. Its messaging is precisely the opposite of Disney's. So for Disney's *Der Fuehrer's Face*, Yensid releases *Uncle Sam's Posture*; for *Commando Duck*, they give us *Der Kommando Donald*, and so on for all the other shorts. The question now becomes: if we allow the Disney propaganda shorts to be propagated, why not the Yensid propaganda as well?

A full and complete answer to this question would no doubt take up a book in itself. It's worth noting, however, that another eminent and noteworthy World War II propagandist, Theodore Geisel (better known by his pen name, Dr. Seuss) purposely distanced himself from his previous propaganda work. His classic *Horton Hears a Who* – with the message "A person is a person, no matter how small" – was intended to make personal amends (a penance of sorts) for Geisel's dehumanizing depictions of the enemy. Nevertheless, it is undeniable that there is a significant and real distinction between the Disney and fictional Yensid propaganda shorts:

> From the beginning, the Axis regimes had forfeited the moral high ground of international opinion through their unprovoked attacks on

> other nations and their subsequent treatment of occupied civilian populations. There was no acceptable justification for such behavior, so their propaganda had to consist almost entirely of barefaced lies about themselves and scurrilous innuendo about anyone opposing them. Conversely, the Allied propagandist's job was a simple matter of holding a mirror up to the enemy and reciting his résumé in order to depict him as a menace to civilization.[26]

Just so.[27]

Notes

1. Baxter, J. (2014). *Disney During World War II: How the Walt Disney Studio Contributed to Victory in the War*, 1. Los Angeles: Disney Editions.
2. Ibid., pp. 3–6.
3. "Donald's Decision" by Walt Disney Studios (1941). http://Archive.org. Available in the public domain: https://archive.org/details/DonaldsDecision.
4. "The New Spirit" by Walt Disney Studios (1942). http://Archive.org. Available in the public domain: https://archive.org/details/TheNewSpirit.
5. Baxter, *Disney During World War II*, pp. 60–63.
6. "The Spirit of '43" by Walt Disney Studios (1943). http://Archive.org. Available in the public domain: https://archive.org/details/TheSpiritOf43_56.
7. Baxter notes that this was standard fare in all wartime Hollywood productions. See *Disney During World War II*, p. 116.
8. *Jacobellis v. Ohio*, 378 U.S. 184 (1964): 197.
9. Soules, M. (2015). *Media, Persuasion and Propaganda*. Edinburgh: Edinburgh University Press.
10. Ibid., pp. 6–8.
11. Walton, D. (1997). What is propaganda, and what exactly is wrong with it? *Public Affairs Quarterly* 11: 383–413.
12. Marlin, R. (2013). *Propaganda and the Ethics of Persuasion*, 2e, 12. Peterborough, Ontario: Broadview Press.
13. Baxter, *Disney During World War II*, pp. 36–37.
14. Ibid., p. 37.
15. Ibid.
16. Walton, "What is Propaganda," pp. 386–388.
17. Ibid., pp. 390–391.
18. Ibid., p. 394.
19. Hume, D. (2000). Of the influencing motives of the will. In: *A Treatise on Human Nature* (ed. D.F. Norton and M. Norton), 265. New York: Oxford University Press.

20. Ibid.
21. Ibid., pp. 266–267.
22. Ibid., p. 266.
23. Gill, F. (1999). Mill on censorship. *Philosophy in Contemporary World* 6: 33–37.
24. Mill, J.S. (1978[1859]). *On Liberty* (ed. E. Rapaport), 51. Indianapolis: Hackett Publishing Company.
25. Ibid., p. 53.
26. Baxter, *Disney During World War II*, p. 37.
27. I would like to express my gratitude to Mr. Ryan Ehrfurth for providing most helpful suggestions with some of the source materials on Disney, and to Dr. Bertha Manninen for her help in improving this essay.

WALL·E, the Environment, and Our Duties to Future Generations

J. Edward Hackett

"WALL·E" stands for Waste Allocated Load Lifter Earth-class. The last robot on planet Earth, WALL·E is programmed by the Buy n Large (BnL) Corporation to clean up the environment. Fittingly, in the first moments of the movie the robot acts on a moral reason to care for a part of nature. As he is going about his official duties, WALL·E finds a plant. Instead of leaving the plant, he brings it back to his lair and gives it sunlight. With this depiction of a world in which only a single green plant survives, *WALL·E* offers a brilliant look at environmental devastation. Beyond that, *WALL·E* raises important questions. Since the environment isn't a human person, do we have a duty to treat it in certain ways? Is our duty instead to future generations? If we have violated our duty, how can we move forward?

The Problem of Future Generations

Imagine that you find a wallet in the food court at the local shopping mall. What would you do? Morality is meant for these occasions. If you keep the wallet your action will have a negative effect on someone else *in the present*. Maybe that fact would be enough to motivate you to return the wallet.

But what about an action that will affect a future generation, people who have not even been born yet? What can we say about our duties beyond present intrapersonal relationships?[1] What can we say

Disney and Philosophy: Truth, Trust, and a Little Bit of Pixie Dust, First Edition.
Edited by Richard B. Davis.

about our use property and land? What can we say about consuming resources that others may need in the future but that we have abundantly in the here and now? These questions depend on our understanding of what it means to have intrapersonal relationships and the very limits of our Western thinking when it comes to morality.

Here's a thought-experiment independent of the movie. Suppose we find a plant in the woods of the Pacific Northwest. We cannot farm this plant in fields or grow it artificially. The plant would, if harvested, eradicate brain tumors. Morally speaking, it might be our duty to allocate this resource among those in the present who we know are suffering from brain tumors. However, we may use it up and consequently deprive future people of this resource. It's easier to conceive of a moral duty to alleviate suffering of those around us now who have brain tumors than to entertain the conditions of those so far away from us temporally.

The Problem of Valuing Nature Like Persons

One way to overcome the tendency to shortchange future generations is to focus on the intrinsic value of nature. If we can show that nature-as-a-whole is a person or has the same intrinsic value as a person, then we can argue that morality should also take into consideration nature-as-a-whole. When WALL·E finds a plant jutting up from the ground, he assumes a level of care that someone might exhibit if they found that nature-as-a-whole was in danger.

At first it may sound strange to conceive of nature-as-a-whole as a person, but we need to give it due consideration. Some non-Western religions emphasize interdependency and interconnectedness with nature, but Western individualism – in terms of how we organize ourselves socially, economically, and politically – gets in the way of learning from those religions.

To be a "person" might be too human-centric, considering some major elements of Western thought: the Judeo-Christian God, the Greco-Roman rational soul, and certain interpretations of Darwinian evolution. Each conception is entirely human-centric. Moreover, some primacy of the individual is valued in each of them. Individuals are thought to be rational, self-sufficient, and more-or-less associated with consciousness. The Greco-Roman and Judeo-Christian conceptions often associate the most real elements of the person with an immaterial consciousness devoid of a physical body. But in the late nineteenth century, Darwinian evolution was sometimes interpreted in materialist and individualist terms in the form of social Darwinism. The rich evolved to be rich, and nature sorted out losers and winners. The freedom of the individual was rooted in the liberty to be a property-owning male, and in this economic system (very much favored by conservatives and free-market enthusiasts) freedom does not entail any obligations to people beyond those with whom you enter into contractual agreements.

To be clear, though, we are not considering the obviously false idea that nature is a person in the sense of being human. Rather, we are considering the possibility that nature might be a "person" in the sense that means a bearer of rights. Along these lines, James Hutton (1726–1797) proposed the idea that the earth is a superorganism, inspiring the later work of James Lovelock, whose *Gaia: A New Look at Life on Earth* argued that the planet Earth (named Gaia) is a sentient being and that many aspects of this being regulate the environment.[2] The take away from this all-too-brief summary is that an environmental ethics that attempts to move past our human-centricity must posit a metaphysical reason for why it is the case that we have obligations beyond the immediate necessity (whether it is the Gaia hypothesis, deep ecology, process theology, nature spirituality or some other alternative not listed here). In *Wall·E*, the animators attempt to overcome the defects of our own self-interest by illustrating the love and care for the plant. We can see this depiction of love of the environment as an effort to prompt us to think more about the environment as if nature is a person.

Capitalist Greed Gets in the Way of Valuing Nature and Persons

As demonstrated by the BnL Corporation in *WALL·E*, the value judgments of corporations may be the biggest obstacle to accepting the rights of nature as a person. From the capitalist perspective, nature does not have rights of its own. Quite the contrary, nature is something owned and harnessed. It is simply instrumental to acquiring wealth and property. If the corporations were the only ones who thought this way, we would have a good chance of opposing them, but most of us tend to see the world through the same capitalist, individualist lenses. The antagonists in *WALL·E* work for BnL, taglined throughout the movie as "your very best friend." The robots are like us, programmed to serve the interests of corporate overlords. The BnL Corporation and the starliner Axiom, have a vested interest in keeping the human beings on the ship obese, lazy, and distracted from the possibility of a new society and home.

Insofar as corporations are profiting, they would like to keep us blind to the devastating effect they are having on the very possibilities for our world. Recall the scene when WALL·E finds himself on the Axiom before he meets John. Human beings are in huge recliners with their heads fixed before screens, as huge gulping drinks simply float to them. They need not have any concerns apart from what products and interests the BnL Corporation provides on the ship. In effect, the Axiom is one giant super mall; it is the perfect metaphor for capitalist greed writ large.

Corporate interests dominate in our world as well. Tobacco companies resisted putting warning labels on cigarettes despite decades of verifiable science, much as the petroleum industry refused to acknowledge the verifiability of dangers posed by leaded gasoline. In light of corporate greed, we should not be surprised when AUTO reveals to the Captain that his orders included never returning to Earth. The Axiom had received the order in 2110, and so the BnL Corporation has kept the human beings floating in space for seven centuries. Whenever you challenge prevailing corporate interests and the status quo, the powerful will fight back, as AUTO does against the protagonists EVE and WALL·E.

An intriguing element in the story of *WALL·E* is that in order for capitalist greed to go unchecked, BnL had to remove people from Earth while the Earth healed. The BnL Corporation knew that its days were numbered because the mass consumption of the planet was unsustainable. Thus, *WALL·E* satirizes capitalism. The way corporations were going had already damaged Earth beyond repair – so much so that BnL put people in intergenerational ships where the activities of BnL would cause no damage. Only when the Captain starts watching videos about Earth does he even conceive that there might be a better way to exist beyond living out the isolationist capitalist prison of his ship. If the humans aboard the Axiom were educated, then they could move beyond the capitalist prison BnL created.

Intergenerational Ships and Sustainable Duties

In science fiction, the idea of the intergenerational ship has its root in the reality that we may never be able to reach beyond the speed of light. What's more, we might not even have the ability to cryogenically freeze ourselves for trips that might take centuries. Given this reality, one might speculate that we'll move to other parts of our galaxy in "real-time." This type of travel would require that whole human communities persist from generation to generation.

The intergenerational ship also captures the conditions under which BnL could thrive. They need people to be blind to the effects that their consumption and resource allocation have on the planet. The fact is that present-day people can exercise control over the conditions that future persons will inherit, and we might have to think long and hard if our current generational aims and projects are coming at the cost of future persons. Rather than profits, we need to consider justice, value, and morality.

In *Wall·E*, humans on the intergenerational ship have lived so long under BnL rule that they cannot conceive of a place like Earth. Thus we find the Captain researching all the aspects of life on Earth, and even things like a "hoedown" are wildly unfamiliar to him. The Captain, WALL·E, and EVE are agents of change, persons (not all human) who see a new horizon of possibility and fight to make change happen. In effect, their efforts raise some alarming questions about intergenerational justice: Why should we continue as we have been going? How might we learn to change our ways given a new redemptive chance at a new and healed Earth, as opposed to the one we are currently ruining? Even more urgently, how do we design our society to have less impact – or none at all – on the very world we all share with others?

There are no easy answers to these questions, but we do have sustainable duties to future persons. Our science can calculate rates of pollution, and we have a deep understanding of how technologies impact the natural world beyond our human borders. So, allow me to offer a principle of environmental ethics that addresses the minimal threshold of what our actions require:

Principle of Sustainable Duties: All persons should act in ways that minimize or do not contribute to the overall net damage to our current environment and should envision the long-term impact of how we organize our material needs along the same lines.

In effect, our human world includes the world of future generations (and while I haven't argued for it here, animals who live in and around us). The ending of *WALL·E* is suggestive along the lines of sustainability, but it does not come out and directly advocate for solutions.

Instead, we find people learning to be more human once again and connecting to the environment, with the Captain, for example, telling a young boy that they will learn farming again. The movie ends by suggesting that humans might adopt something like the *Principle of Sustainable Duties*, but we are less than certain that the humans will make it. With the brilliance of a Platonic dialog, *WALL·E* leaves us with an *aporia,* an impasse, an unresolved ending requiring us to think more about it.

Personally, I don't know if we can get there. I say this not as a pessimist, but as a realist – the damage to the Earth might be too far gone for any utopian change to occur. At this point, the *Principle of Sustainable Duties* becomes, as it were, justification to engage in consequential reasoning to maximize any course of action that will lessen the damage currently underway.

If we're feeling pessimistic, we might understand *WALL·E* as a dystopian story. The movie presents itself in classic Disney fashion. Love will solve our problems, or at least transform our harsh realities. But consider that only the love of robots can survive those harsh realities. Perhaps this means we may need to change our own physical realities to cope with the damage that we organic human beings did to the environment. In addition, corporate interests are so recalcitrant that they have put up effective barriers to changes needed worldwide, at least as far as global warming is concerned. Even now, you've bought a book made of paper. Trees were cut down to read this book. If you're reading it on a tablet or computer in electronic form, then a coal plant may be burning fuel right now so that your device may be powered. In this way, you have consumed and are consuming a good that might have been better off had it not been written. We might be screwed beyond all recognition, given the price we pay both for the materiality of human existence and the impact that materiality has on the environment. Consequently, we may need to transform ourselves into something more than human to survive the very destruction we've caused in what scholars are now calling the *anthropocene*.

Notes

1. A similar concern exists in Aldo Leopold's land ethic when he mentions the principle of expanding our conception of moral community to the biotic community at large. The ambiguity of the principle doesn't lend itself to clarity in the same way that morality does as I am explaining here.

2. Lovelock, J. (1979). *Gaia: A New Look at Life on Earth*. Clarendon: Oxford University Press. Lovelock expressed these ideas earlier in two notable journal articles, and I'd like to mention them here for the reader. First, Lovelock, J.E. (1972). Gaia as seen through the atmosphere. *Atmospheric Environment* 6 (8): 579–580. And with Lynn Marguilis he published Atmospheric Homeostasis by and for the Biosphere: the Gaia Hypothesis. *Tellus* Series A 26(1–2). (Stockholm: International Meteorological Institute, 1974): 2–10.

23

Is There Any Utopia in Zootopia?

Frauke Albersmeier and Alexander Christian

Disney's *Zootopia* (2016) is a crime story about the involuntary partnership between Judy Hopps, the first rabbit police officer in the city of Zootopia, and Nick Wilde, a red fox making his living as a con artist. Together they uncover a conspiracy that threatens to shake the foundation of the mammalian metropolis: the peaceful coexistence of animals who used to be predators and prey. Strikingly, peace between the species is not even Zootopia's claim to fame. What makes Zootopia a utopia and the city of Judy's dreams is that it appears to be "where anyone can be anything." However, Judy learns that reality doesn't always live up to this promise. She faces discrimination, is taken in by stereotypes herself, and has to acknowledge: "we all have limitations." But in a final speech, marked by Disney-brand optimism, she remains fiercely attached to her ideals, urging her fellow creatures: "I implore you: Try! Try to make the world a better place."

Utopias feed such aspirations by depicting ideal states of affairs. They spell out in detail what the perfect world would look like, but they run up against factual barriers in the attempt to translate ideals into reality. *Zootopia* confronts us with three utopian ideals: of security and social order, of individual self-determination and fulfillment, and of a just multispecies society. As we shall see, the line between realistic expectation and far-out fantasy is always moving. Indeed, Judy's reluctance to accept cultural and biological barriers to social progress pushes the boundaries of our thinking.

Disney and Philosophy: Truth, Trust, and a Little Bit of Pixie Dust, First Edition.
Edited by Richard B. Davis.

Man Is a Wolf to Man

The term "utopia" – originally coined by Thomas More in his sociopolitical satire *Utopia* – comes from the Greek *ou-topos* (literally: "no place"), undoubtedly a pun for *eu-topos* which simply means "good place."[1] A utopian society exists in no actual place; it is an idealized fiction. While striking us as unreal (or perhaps even unrealizable), utopias nevertheless depict society at its civil best: the absence of war, ample opportunities for intellectual growth and development, and lives consistently lived by the highest moral standards. *Zootopia* has "political ideal" literally written all over it. But what kind of utopia is Zootopia?

Zootopia begins with the founding myth that tells the story of how the animals overcame an anything-but-ideal natural state, in which prey animals lived in constant fear of predators. Thomas Hobbes (1588–1679), whose political theory was birthed in the midst of civil unrest and war in England, based his reflections on a pre-civilized human existence strikingly similar to that of primitive Zootopia.

According to Hobbes, all of us are motivated by self-preservation and the pursuit of pleasure. In sharp contrast to the views of such political philosophers as Aristotle and Jean-Jacques Rousseau, who envisioned human beings as naturally social, Hobbes took a rather bleak outlook on human life outside political structures. Describing existence in a state of nature where everyone pursues self-interest without restraint, Hobbes famously says that life would be "solitary, poor, nasty, brutish, and short." Without a strong government, human beings must live in a state of "war of each against all,"[2] in which they are simultaneously both predators and prey – with each posing a grave threat to the others. No one is exempt because even the strongest individuals can't watch out for danger 24/7. Hobbes writes that without a strong government, "Man is a wolf to Man."[3] Despite his grim view of human nature, Hobbes doesn't think we're bound to live in this state of nature. Instead, humans can forge a social contract, transferring their natural rights to a political authority – whether it be a king or a committee – whose role is to secure the safety and freedom of the citizens by upholding law and order. Of course contemporary political philosophy holds democratic values in higher regard, but maintaining a social order is still a rather uncontroversial responsibility of the state.

In Zootopia, animals have achieved a seemingly stable social order. Carnivores and herbivores live together in peace. Still, this accomplishment might be too little to qualify the Zootopian society as utopian. In most parts of the world, establishing social order and protecting individual rights is no longer deemed utopian. Rather, it is regarded as a basic and primary function of any state. And the movie, too, takes this function as a given fact. For Zootopia's forefathers (depicted in the school play) and Hobbes's contemporaries (not to mention the many individuals – animal and human – in crisis-shaken parts of the world today), securing a social order may be a far-out ideal. The fact is: contemporary Zootopian animals and human moviegoers are looking for a lot more than simply not living in a state of nature.

"You Can Only Be What You Are"

Life in the city of Zootopia promises more than just law and order. Zootopia is committed to ensuring *individual self-determination and self-fulfillment*. At least this is the promise of the city's slogan: "Where anyone can be anything." This claim seems to have two connotations: on the one hand, everyone can overcome individual biological traits (nature); on the other, social upbringing (nurture) doesn't determine your future way of life. This is why Judy – though raised in the countryside as one of the many children of rabbit vegetable farmers – moves to Zootopia to fulfill her dream and become the first rabbit police officer.

The realization of such ideals is often an indicator of upward social mobility: where individuals are free to determine their own life goals, experiencing the self-fulfillment that comes with that, and even acquiring a new social status (apart from the one they were born into). To be sure, you can't become just anything. If you're blind, we can't allow you to pursue your dream of becoming a commercial airline pilot. That's out of the question and for good reason. What matters is that restrictions are put in place that ensure fairness, that every citizen is entitled to a fair chance, unhindered by illegitimate interference on the part of the government or even other citizens.

Frustration with how society falls short of this ideal is the driving force behind *Zootopia*'s plot. In a conversation with Judy, standing knee-deep in wet concrete, Nick expresses his disillusionment on the painful lack of social mobility: "Everyone comes to Zootopia, thinking they could be anything they want. But you can't. You can only be what you are. Sly fox. Dumb bunny." On another occasion, while walking into the department of motor vehicles (DMV) in order to figure out some details of their case, Nick teases Judy about her naive belief in the Zootopian promise: "Are you saying that because he's a sloth he can't be fast? I thought in Zootopia, anyone could be anything."

Nick's sarcastic comment points to the important distinction between justified (biologically shaped) boundaries to social mobility and misconceptions about one's biological limitations. A sloth can't move quickly (except if he's in a sports car speeding through the streets of Zootopia). Flash can work at the DMV, but he wouldn't be our first choice for a paramedic. Judy can hop the wall in the police academy obstacle course, but it's physically impossible for her to climb it. There's a difference, though, between what prevents Flash from becoming a professional first responder, and the troubles Judy faces in becoming a police officer. In her case, the limitation isn't so much biological as it is the misconceptions of others. She faces artificial and arbitrary barriers to entering the police force that confuse apparent incapacities and real biological limitations. That's the kind of thing that frustrates Nick, and it's the main reason Zootopia doesn't live up to its bumper sticker slogan.

Both Judy and Nick – as well as their antagonist, Dawn Bellwether – are the subjects of stereotyping that prevents them from pursuing their chosen paths in life. When she announces her plans to become a police officer, Judy is laughed at and mocked by the audience at her school play. When young Nick wants to become a boy scout, he is tricked by the other children to think he can, only to be lured into a dark basement, where he is muzzled and held against his will. And then there's the power imbalance between Dawn Bellwether and Mayor Leodore Lionheart. In a revealing speech, the Assistant Mayor attributes her marginalization at the workplace to her membership in the group of prey animals. As a petite sheep, she is naturally much weaker compared to members of the predator species, and she insinuates that this is the real cause for social inequalities. The fact that her evil plan works so well reveals what a fragile society Zootopia really is. It rather quickly loses hold of its ideals, when speculations arise that predators suffer from an infection that causes them to lose self-control and give in to their hunting instinct. A truly free and fair society, where "anyone can be anything," would be far more sensitive in restricting the freedoms of its citizens. Thus Zootopia doesn't appear to *be* a utopia. As the movie draws to a close, however, the *anyone-anything* ideal is held up as a standard – one that might even be within reach.

"Deep Down, We're Animals"

Still, there is a sense in which life in Zootopia rises to utopian heights. For it paints a picture of a rather peaceful coexistence between animals who used to be *predators* and *prey*, but now live together in harmony. Civil *interspecies* coexistence seems like a much more ambitious project than building a society around the interests and needs of just one species (say, humans). In fact, a just multispecies society *is* the latest ideal in political philosophy.

In Zootopia, this ideal has been approximated by luck – through the sheer forces of evolution. In her school play, young Judy explains that "over time, we evolved and moved beyond our primitive savage ways," and later, when Mr. Big discusses the case of Mr. Otterton, one of the animals who have "gone savage," he offers this interpretation of Otterton's behavior: "We may be evolved, but deep down, we are still animals." In other words, the evolutionary account of the sociality of Zootopia's animals also implies that what's "animal" about them is that part of their nature which isn't conducive to peaceful coexistence. Mr. Big's assessment is very much in line with the picture that political philosophy has traditionally drawn of the supposedly unique human capacity for sociality. Hobbes didn't choose the image of man being a "wolf to man" by accident. The Zootopians rightly fear they are reverting back into a Hobbesian state of nature, where life is "poor, nasty, brutish, and short." Judy wants to say the change is a relapse, as she speculates: "It may have something to do with biology … A biological component, you know, something in their DNA." In an explanation that Darwin himself would approve, she concludes: "What I mean is: thousands of years ago, predators survived through their aggressive hunting instincts. For whatever reason, they seem to be reverting back to their primitive, savage ways."

"Even Though You're a Fox?"

No doubt Disney intends this depiction, in part, as a metaphor for how we human beings tend to see each other – as natural threats. But it also says something about our attitudes toward nonhuman animals. In the same way as the all-prey boy scouts are hostile to Nick, the fox, joining their ranks, humans have long kept animals at bay: squarely outside the realm of its political theories and moral demands. The animals won't let Nick join because he's deemed "shifty and untrustworthy." But that at least credits him with a certain intelligence. Until recently, we humans haven't been willing to say even that much about nonhuman animals. At any rate, that's the diagnosis given by Sue Donaldson and Will Kymlicka in their 2011 book *Zoopolis*, in which they develop a "political theory of animal rights."[4] They disagree with the prevailing opinion that animals can't be part of political communities – partly because they already are. Humans have brought domesticated animals like cats, dogs, horses, and cows into their communities, while other animals, like raccoons, pigeons, and mice have made their own homes within human settlements. So multispecies societies are *already* a reality.

Moreover, Donaldson and Kymlicka point out that it was precisely animals' abilities to communicate and cooperate that led us to select them for domestication in the first place. That's why we want them in our lives and homes.

Three capacities are crucial for animals' laying claim to being recognized members of our society:

1. That they know and show what they want and like; they have and communicate "a subjective good";
2. That they are empathetic, understand and internalize rules, and are capable of restraining themselves in interaction with each other and with us (just think of what it takes to engage in play and not let it turn into a fight);
3. That they can take part in shaping rules of interaction, and that it's possible to take their preferences and needs into account in our political decision-making (they can be "co-authors" of the law).[5]

The reason animals have been kept outside of political theory for so long is an over-intellectualized picture of all of these capacities – which doesn't, however, fit the human case either (just think of young children and some people with disabilities). So the mistakes we've made with respect to animals are the same as those that that cause Judy and Nick so much frustration. Like Nick, animals are being *denied the capacity* to sociality that they actually possess; like Judy, they are *held to irrelevant standards* (e.g., standards of rationality we don't even expect from other humans).

Where Humans *Did* Happen

In Zootopia, "humans never happened."[6] Lucky Zootopians, we might say. Because being a nonhuman animal in a world where humans did happen can mean your life will be *made* "solitary, poor, nasty, brutish, and short." The kind of discrimination Judy faces when she is assigned to parking duty, and that Nick experiences as a predatory animal who is often met with distrust, is nothing compared to the treatment nonhuman animals receive in a world ruled by humans who treat them as commodities. Domestication isn't just the process in which animals were selected for having socially valuable traits. But it is the one in which they were bred to fulfill human needs and become dependent on their exploiters. This is the way Donaldson and Kymlicka see it. Unlike other animal rights theorists, however, they don't think the way to undo the injustice that's been done to nonhuman animals is to stop having them around altogether. Instead, domesticated animals need to be recognized as our co-citizens. Animals in Zootopia have become adapted to life in a multispecies metropolis, and similarly domesticated animals in our world have become very unlike their wild ancestors in many ways. They can't, at this point, just be left to live in the wild. The important thing to see is that their social capacities are what *makes it possible* to serve animals' interests by giving them citizenship. However, it *isn't how they earn* the privilege to become co-citizens. Citizenship isn't given out as a trophy for intellectual excellence. Rather, citizenship is a form of protection that gives individuals a place and a community to which they belong, where they share the goods the community provides, and have their interests represented in the political process that shapes their shared lives.

Even though Zootopia is designed to mirror human-specific ways of life, it has some features that might illustrate how drastic the change in our human-centered world would be if nonhuman animals were indeed respected as full-fledged co-citizens. Zootopia's different districts are built to fit different animals' sizes and ways of life, and it even accommodates different climate zones to meet the needs of their respective inhabitants. Judy chasing Weaselton through Little Rodentia graphically shows that public space is not a one-size-fits-all kind of matter for individuals of different species. Similarly, a world built to suit humans is often an inapt and hostile environment for nonhuman animals. If human beings were to respect other animals' claims to space, we would have to build a more Zootopian civilization.

"Real Life Is Messy"

Humans have "happened" not only to the animals that have become domesticated or come to populate human territories, but to wild animals as well. In many ways, human activities pose grave dangers to animals in nature. This is why Zoopolis asks us to respect their need for and claim to their territory, and to cut back our harmful interference with them. But should we perhaps do more than that?

Unlike the animals in Zootopia, many animals in real life have not evolved beyond predation. They eat one another. And even though this can make one miss the fact that empathy, cooperation, and care are just as much parts of many animals' nature as their striving for survival,[7] there's just no denying that the predator–prey-relationship that takes center stage in Zootopia is shaped by fear, suffering, and death. Whether humans might have a duty to interfere in this relationship has been a topic for debate in animal rights theory. It is not clear whether ending predation even qualifies as utopian or rather is a *dystopian* prospect (from Greek *dys*, meaning "bad"). Political and moral philosopher Martha Nussbaum has toyed with the idea of "the gradual supplanting of the natural by the just,"[8] hinting at the possibility of human intervention in predation. In *Zoopolis*, Kymlicka and Donaldson refrain from such a suggestion, claiming that predation is just part of the parameters within which animals in nature can exercise their autonomy. A crucial worry about systematic interference in predation is that it would result in turning the world into a giant zoo – or Disney theme park – thus failing to secure the rights and freedoms of animals.[9]

From this perspective, the most utopian element in Zootopia seems to be what is presented as old news from the start: the end of predation to – seemingly – no one's disadvantage. But the extent of peace that has been achieved in Zootopia occurred thanks to an evolutionary lucky strike, and covers only a small group of animals. After all, Judy passes the fish market on her way into the city, and it is left unclear how the other non-mammalian animals are dealt with by Zootopians.

Zootopia is too much of a metaphor for human ways of life to be a utopian human-animal society, and too "messy" to count as a metaphoric utopia for humans. As Judy puts it: "Turns out, real life is a little bit more complicated than a slogan on a bumper sticker." But in the next few lines of her police academy commencement speech, she also emphatically promotes the way toward improvement. Because utopias are utopian relative to a certain status quo and because an important kind of hindrance on the way toward a better state of affairs is the confusion of biological necessity and contingent cultural barriers, self-scrutiny and individual responsibility are essential to bringing ideals into reach. In the words of Judy Hopps, "Look inside yourself and recognize that change starts with you. It starts with me. It starts with all of us."

Notes

1. See More, T. (1995). *Utopia*. Cambridge: Cambridge University Press. See also Baker-Smith, D. (Spring 2014). Thomas More. In *The Stanford Encyclopedia of Philosophy* (ed. Edward N.Zalta). Stanford, CA: Center for the Study of Language and Information (CSLI), Stanford University. https://plato.stanford.edu/archives/spr2014/entries/thomas-more.
2. Hobbes, Thomas. (2010). In: *Leviathan, Revised Edition* (ed. A.P. Martinich and B. Battiste), 14. Peterborough, ON: Broadview Press.
3. Hobbes, T. (1998). In: *On the Citizen* (ed. R. Tuck and M. Silverthorne), 3. Cambridge: Cambridge University Press.
4. Donaldson, S. and Kymlicka W. (2011). *Zoopolis: A Political Theory of Animal Rights*. Oxford: Oxford University Press.
5. Ibid., p. 103.
6. Zootopia (2016). Official Teaser Trailer #1.
7. See Bekoff, M. and Pierce, J. (2009). *Wild Justice: The Moral Lives of Animals*. Chicago: University of Chicago Press.
8. Nussbaum M. (2006). *Frontiers of Justice: Disability, Nationality, Species Membership*, 400. Cambridge, MA: Harvard University Press.
9. But there are other things from which animals in the wild suffer (for example, starvation and diseases), and in which human beings *could* intervene. See Horta, O. (2010).Debunking the idyllic view of natural processes: population dynamics and suffering in the wild. *Telos*17: 73–90.

Part VI

THE WONDERFUL WORLDVIEW OF DISNEY

How I Learned to Stop Worrying and Love Disney

Marx and Marcuse at Disney World

Elizabeth Butterfield

"You've just won the Super Bowl. What are you going to do next?"
"I'm going to Disney World!"[1]

The Disney vacation[2] is iconic in American culture. Advertising promises us that a trip to Disney will bring adventure, family togetherness, and even happiness itself. But for many, "doing Disney" has also become something to be achieved – something every good American family is *expected* to do. When we post on social media, are we just sharing memories with Grandma back home, or are we also showing off our trip as a status symbol? Maybe those posts are letting everyone know that "We've made it! We are living the American dream! We went to Disney!" What could be a better example of conspicuous consumption?

Many critics scoff at the idea of a Disney vacation. They see it as just another trap of consumer culture, one that makes false promises of happiness as a pretext to get us to spend more money, and that turns precious vacation time into just another opportunity to shop. Other critics take issue with the desire to escape to an artificial Fantasyland while ignoring real-world problems. To these critics, Disney is just a cog in the capitalist machine, and the values it embodies encourage us to accept our own alienation.

While I care deeply about the pitfalls of consumer culture, and I see where these critics are coming from … I love Disney! I always have. I grew up with reruns of *The Mickey Mouse Club* and *The Wonderful*

Disney and Philosophy: Truth, Trust, and a Little Bit of Pixie Dust, First Edition.
Edited by Richard B. Davis.

World of Disney in the 1970s, the Disney channel in the 1980s, and the renaissance of Disney film animation in the 1990s. My working-class parents scraped together enough money to take us on two road trips to Disney World, and as an adult taking my own kids, I fell in love all over again.

Now, my cultural critic friends might read this and conclude that I've been brainwashed by my own upbringing. After all, I have more than 40 years' worth of exposure to media telling me that Disney stands for happiness. But I am optimistic enough about my own free will and self-awareness to suspect there is more to my love of Disney than indoctrination. While these critics might have a point, isn't it also possible that a Disney vacation could play a really positive role in our lives too?

Heigh-ho, Heigh-ho, It's Off to Work We Go

To understand why someone might see Disney as "the ultimate embodiment of consumer society,"[3] we can start with Karl Marx (1818–1883).[4] It might be helpful to temporarily forget everything you've heard about Marx, because what counts as "Marxism" in mainstream culture is often just a caricature of an interesting and wide-ranging philosophy.

In the nineteenth century, Marx was trying to understand the suffering he saw among the working classes in industrial capitalist states. These nations had great wealth, resources, and infrastructure, as well as democratic value systems that claimed each member of society was entitled to "life, liberty, and the pursuit of happiness." So it seemed absurd to Marx that a majority of citizens were living in conditions of poverty, exhaustion, and exploitation, while a wealthy few profited. He believed a better future was possible.

But Marx was not just writing about economics and politics. He was also a philosopher, and he developed a fascinating theory of our human potential. When he described the obstacles that he believed stood in the way of leading meaningful lives, the flip side of this was that he also explored the idea of what is possible for us, and what it might be like to develop our potential, or to fully "flourish."[5]

Marx explained that when the workers went to their dehumanizing and underpaid jobs, they were alienated from both their work and the products they were making. Like the Seven Dwarfs, "we dig up diamonds by the score … but we don't know what we dig them for … we dig, dig, dig."[6] Marx recognized that this alienation occurs because we actually have a true human need for *fulfilling* work. The right kind of work, in which we see ourselves reflected, could be part of our flourishing.

Marx also saw workers as alienated in their relationships, because in a capitalist economy relationships come to be dominated by competition and money. This implies that we have a true human need for relationships of respect and care, and that a positive social life could be another part of flourishing.

Finally, Marx argued that the workers were alienated from their own "species-being," by which he meant their own humanity, or human potential. We are amazing, intelligent, talented, creative beings with so many possibilities. But in oppressive living conditions, the nineteenth century industrial workers were so exhausted, and had so little leisure time, that they didn't actually have the freedom to explore other parts of themselves. Their identities were reduced to their alienated work.

This is where the importance of leisure comes in. To really explore one's human potential, Marx believed, a person needs to have some time that is not dominated by work or the drive to meet basic survival needs. In true "free" time, we could step out of our everyday pigeonholed work identities, and we could experience what it means to be *free*, exploring our interests, our thoughts, and our creativity.

Now Is the Best Time of Your Life! (Isn't It?)

Fast forward to mid-twentieth century America. In the post-war economic boom, it was the age of automobiles, housing construction, and new suburbs. Glossy magazines, radios, and televisions appeared in every home. With a spirit of innovation, new time-saving gadgets came onto the market every day, along with new forms of entertainment. People were experiencing an abundance like never before, only this time, it was not just for an elite few, but for the average Joe.[7] As long as you ignore the occasional atomic bomb drill, you could say that the period was dominated by an optimism about technology and the future.

We can see this in the 1964 World's Fair, where Disney debuted the *Carousel of Progress*, sponsored by General Electric. This performance of ground-breaking audio-animatronics, which you can still experience today in Walt Disney World's Magic Kingdom, shows how through the decades technology keeps making life better and better. As the song goes, "Now is the time / Now is the best time / Now is the best time of your life."[8]

In this context, Marx's concern for the suffering of the masses seems out of place. Surely humans must be able to meet their needs, and to fulfill their potential and fully flourish as never before? But according to a group of philosophers known as the Frankfurt School Critical Theorists, Marx's analysis continues to be relevant. They argue that even in advanced industrial society, we continue to experience alienation from the work itself, from others, and from our own potential for fulfillment. Herbert Marcuse (1898–1979), in his book *One-Dimensional Man*,[9] describes this in American culture in the 1960s. What really worried Marcuse was an innovative new form of social control in which political protest is stifled, not by threat of violence, but by *pleasure*.

According to Marcuse, we continue to be unable to meet our true human needs, and we experience this as a deep dissatisfaction. But to distract us from this suffering, our culture presents us with artificially designed "false needs." We are told that what we *really need* is just the most recent smartphone, the latest video game, or this season's fashions. "Most of the prevailing needs to relax, to have fun, to behave and consume in accordance with the advertisements, to love and hate what others love and hate, belong to this category of false needs."[10]

We are promised that if we just buy these products, we will be beautiful, loved, successful, and happy. Of course this isn't true. Tomorrow we will wake up hungry again, our phones will be outdated, and there will be new fashions to buy. We find ourselves in a cycle of work-shop-work. But in the meantime, Marcuse says, the pleasures of immediate gratification lead us to experience "euphoria in unhappiness."[11]

This euphoria is dangerous because it prevents us from seeing what is truly missing in our lives. In light of our rising standard of living, it appears irrational to challenge the system. After all, we wouldn't want to endanger the system that makes life so good. Consumption "becomes a way of life. It is a good way of life – much better than before – and as a good way of life, it militates against qualitative change."[12]

As our real political freedoms and freedom of thought are gradually eroded, we mistakenly believe that we have more freedom than ever before. This is because true freedom has come to be replaced by the idea of freedom of choice among a range of products. We may be losing the freedom to recognize or question the system that oppresses us, but at least we have the freedom to choose from more varieties of HDTVs than ever before. For this reason Marcuse writes, "a comfortable, smooth, reasonable, democratic unfreedom prevails."[13]

#EuphoricExhaustedBroke

From Marcuse's perspective, we could say that the American culture industry tells us via media and advertising that we *need* to take our families to Disney so that we can be *happy*. And what do we associate with Disney more than the idea of happiness?[14] Of course, this is not true happiness; it is a temporary experience of artificially stimulated pleasures. The parks are designed to create experiences of pleasure and reassurance via the architecture, the staging, the cleanliness, the background music, the piped-in smells. It all works together to stimulate an artificially induced euphoria.

The critic might also argue that going to Disney is a terrible way to spend our precious leisure time. We have a true need for free time. We need it in order to understand how we are doing, to explore our interests, and to think for ourselves. But when we spend our vacation at Disney, free time can easily turn into just another high-pressure checklist of things to be accomplished. While some might waltz into the parks midday with no plan and still enjoy themselves, for many others, a Disney vacation means *Go! Go! Go!* After months of planning, many true parks fans show up with a schedule and a strategy for maximizing experiences while navigating crowds, from rope drop to close. Does this sound familiar? "Hurry! We've got to make it to our next FastPass!" "A bathroom break is not in the schedule!" "No, you can't stop to look at the ducklings; you can see ducks at home!" The constant entertainment and hectic pace of the park experience leaves little time for self-reflection, and we return home exhausted, needing a vacation to recover from vacation.

If "happiness" is the first word we associate with a Disney vacation, surely the second is "expensive." Disney is in business to make money. At the parks, it is unfortunately common to hear a parent yelling at a crying child, "Do you know how much I paid for this? You're supposed to be happy!" We pay for travel, hotel, park tickets, food, and special events and tours. Then once we are in the parks, we are constantly exposed to theming from Disney's IP (intellectual property). You could say that the entire stay is really just an experience of advertising. Then there is the old joke that every attraction exits into a gift shop. For many, shopping is part of the fun, and when we buy Disney products to take home with us, we participate in the advertising ourselves. Our critic would point out that a Disney vacation takes our scarce leisure time, which could be an opportunity to step out of the hamster wheel of servitude to the economy, and "magically" transforms it into just another mode of consumption.

So, we return home exhausted and broke. But hey, at least we got to go, right? And now we get to brag about it, publicly displaying wealth and social power! Our culture tells us that taking our children to Disney is something every parent should aspire to, like a rite of passage in American childhood and a sign of good parenting. We may not be able to meet our true needs, but at least for a little while we get to feel like we did something important because we were finally able to go to Disney like we're supposed to, like everyone else.

Escaping to the Disney Bubble

For true Disney parks fans, however, there is more to the story. If you ask why they continue to return, some of the most common reasons you'll hear are: "It is my happy place," and "it is my escape from real life." From the beginning, Walt Disney intended for his theme park to be a "happy place" where you could "leave today, and enter the world of yesterday, tomorrow, and fantasy."[15] At Walt Disney World in Florida, the man-made Seven Seas Lagoon was constructed with this in mind, so that in crossing a mile of water, guests could literally leave the daily reality behind in order to arrive at the Magic Kingdom. Fantasyland in particular has been described as "a perfect world beckoning, where the killjoy of the clock doesn't exist," and "an immersive land where you are reassured that no matter how chaotic and confusing the outside world gets, this land will remain as it always was."[16]

What could be wrong with the desire to escape from Realityland? Life can be stressful! Even Marx recognized the importance of getting away. But from the perspective of our critic, the spirit of escapism that draws us to a Disney vacation can be dangerous. We are drawn to the "Disney bubble" because it reassures us – but could this be part of the problem?

The critic would argue that Disney presents us with a false reassurance about our history, whether in the idealized *Main Street USA* which never really existed, or in a light-hearted *Jungle Cruise* sailing past "natives" of various sorts, oblivious to any real history of racism or colonialism. Disney also gives us a false reassurance about the state of the world today. Spending time at Epcot would lead you to believe that there is no need to worry about politics or global affairs – we've got it all taken care of. While *Living with the Land* acknowledges environmental concerns, it also reassures us that we're already developing new technologies that will save the day. *Spaceship Earth* tells us that technology is our hope for the future. And the nightly *Illuminations* show reassures us that we can all live together in peace.

The problem with this optimism is that it plays right into the false consciousness of our culture that tells us, yes, "now is the best time!" Yes, if you simply continue to spend (to fulfill your false needs), you can be happy. "No matter how your heart is grieving, if you keep on believing, the dreams that you wish will come true."[17] All you have to do is to "wish upon a star."[18]

There's one Disney sentiment our critic might actually agree with: the placard in the *Splash Mountain* queue that reads "You can't run away from trouble ... ain't no place that far." Escapism is not the answer. This false reassurance works like a drug, blurring our awareness of the true dissatisfaction of our lives in Realityland, and preventing political resistance from taking root. After the vacation ends, we will return to work and continue to support the status quo, when instead we should be challenging the system of alienation itself.

But Everybody Needs a Laughin' Place

Obviously a trip to Disney is not the same thing as true happiness. And yes, the whole experience may be geared toward earning profits. The perfection of the parks is fiction, and sometimes a Disney vacation becomes conspicuous consumption. All of this may be true. But it's also true that a Disney trip could play multiple roles and could mean different things to different people.

As I mentioned at the beginning of the chapter, critics might say that I have just been brainwashed by my own upbringing. As another Frankfurt School philosopher, Theodor Adorno (1903–1969), wrote, "The triumph of advertising ... is that consumers feel compelled to buy and use its products even though they see through them."[19] Maybe my love for Disney is a predictable response to conditioning that encouraged me to accept my own alienation. But I am ever the optimist about my own powers of free thought and self-reflection. I am willing to go so far as to argue that enjoying some time at Disney could actually *challenge* our alienation, and play a positive role in human flourishing.

Part of the alienation we experience in our daily lives is the loss of ourselves to our work identities. Going to Disney can't bring you true happiness, but when it is done right, it can give you a real break. Getting away can help us to remember that, hey, there are other parts of myself, other things I enjoy, other things I am interested in and want to learn about. This can take the form of rebellion and can be a reclaiming of our humanity. Of course you don't have to go to Disney to experience this – with some genuine free time you can experience this anywhere and without paying a dime. But "escaping" to Disney World can open up this opportunity.

Another common reason true Disney parks fans give for why they continue to return is that "when I am there, I feel like a kid again!" Our critic might say that's ridiculous, but I see this very differently. Another element of our alienation in Realityland is the expectation that adults are meant to be serious, and that "fun is only for children or for Saturday nights."[20] But Disney parks provide a space where anyone can embrace childlike joy and playfulness. And though you definitely don't have to go to Disney to experience this, Disney does provide a unique setting where adults can fly with Peter Pan to Neverland, and where we are welcome to wear silly hats, dance in the streets, and go on imaginative adventures.

Frankfurt School philosophers worried that the entertainment industry was causing the death of real imagination, and they saw Disney as a major player in that. But this doesn't have to be the case. Away from the limitations of daily life, we are freed up to explore other aspects of ourselves and our interests, to have fun and to see the world with childlike wonder, and to *imagine*. Though the reassuring messages of the Disney parks might stifle reflection for some, for many others the images of the world they encounter – real and imagined – surely stimulate curiosity and creativity. For many Americans who have little exposure to other cultures, visiting the pavilions of World Showcase in Epcot can nurture a desire to learn more. And in attractions like the *Land Pavilion*, *Spaceship Earth*, and *The Living Seas*, curious children and adults come away excited and wanting more.

Finally, another common reason parks fans give for their love of Disney is that it is something they can enjoy together as a family. We know that the reality of "family togetherness" is not always as rosy as the advertising promises. Especially in the huge crowds and hot temperatures of summer peak season, being in a Disney park can be a recipe for family disasters. But there is still something uniquely welcoming for families at Disney.

We can trace this back to Walt Disney himself. The story goes that Walt was first inspired to build a theme park when he was with his own young daughters, watching a carousel. He was struck with the inspiration that there should be more places in the world where adults and children could have fun *together*.[21] You can see this reflected in the Disney parks today, where most attractions and experiences are designed to be enjoyed together. Disney is also one of the few places where people of diverse abilities can easily vacation and feel welcomed. This can be a big relief for families who deal with obstacles back home on a daily basis.

Disney's emphasis on including everyone and experiencing things together as a family challenges the alienation in relationships we so often encounter. But I also see Walt Disney's concern to include parents in the fun as a rebellion against alienating expectations for adults, and in particular, for the 1950s "serious" working father. Again, you don't have to go to Disney to have quality time with your family. But Disney can provide an opportunity for exploring our relationships outside of our everyday alienations.

Things Worth Believing

Joe Rohde, a Disney executive with an impressive career in Imagineering, recently wrote:

> I'm spending the night at the Disneyland Resort, which gives me an opportunity to meditate upon the nature of our work, because it is nowhere more clear than it is here. Disneyland was created as a place where the young and the old could share experiences and stories equally enchanting to both. But that enchantment is chiefly conveyed through the eyes of children… Our storytelling skills and art design abilities can be appreciated by an adult, but to a child, they are invisible. Invisible because they create an entire captivating reality which a child simply believes. And when we, who are old and weary with knowledge, see the belief in the eyes of a child, especially a child we love, we are revived and reminded that there are things worth believing. I don't necessarily mean the fairies and talking animals, but the deeper things…. the things those imaginary creatures represent…like ideas that good will prevail, that magic can occur, that the lost will be found, that justice will prevail, that someone small and insignificant may be the source of something great. There's no denying that these parks are real places, with all the opportunities and inconveniences that real places

> sometimes present. But they are also transcendent places, where, for a second, all the world and all of time and the secret meaning of everything can be encapsulated in the wonder of a child.[22]

Much of what Rohde articulates rings true for me. As places where young and old can share experiences together, Disney parks really give us "old folks" a chance to see through the eyes of a child again and to feel revived.

But beyond that, Rohde points out that being in a Disney park can remind us that there are values worth believing in – values like goodness, justice, and hope. Disney World is a place where we can feel in touch with something greater. Disney's Fantasyland is "a place of belief amidst a world of doubt, it's a place for renewed perspective, reflection, and of gentle reminders that, in time, happily ever afters and fairy-tales endure more than all hardships."[23]

Our critic might say this talk about values is just marketing. But surely it could also be more. If there were no truth to optimism, or in the hope that it really is possible to do good in the world or to make the world a better place, then really, what is it all for? Yes, the Disney brand emphasizes kindness, friendliness, and trying to do good. This goodness is the heart of Mickey's appeal. But it is also a reality that many people who love Disney, as well as those who choose to work for Disney, are drawn to this because they really do care about kindness, friendliness, and doing good in the world. Some of these values really are worth believing in. In the words of Disney fan and podcaster, Harrison Ownbey,

> For me, Fantasyland is the land for the broken-hearted, because things outside aren't the way they're supposed to be … Fantasyland says that if you keep believing … no matter what kind of trouble you're against, you, yes, you, have a happily ever after waiting for you. And on the way there, be sure to touch the stones of the castle, and breathe in the sweet aroma of the popcorn. The heartbreak, the happiness, the terror, and the triumph, together weave your unforgettable story.[24]

So, dear critic, I would argue that it doesn't have to be an all-or-nothing choice. We can be politically engaged, actively trying to be responsible world citizens who help others, while also having some fun at Disney. In fact, in the right circumstances, a trip to Disney can even challenge our alienations, giving us a chance to explore other sides of ourselves and our relationships. A Disney excursion can open us up to imagining a better future. In reminding us that some values really are worth believing in, Disney can inspire us to bring the magic home, and to make the world more as it should be.

Notes

1. From Disney's "What's Next?" advertising campaign, which first aired in 1987.
2. I use "Disney" to refer to parks at both Disneyland and Walt Disney World.
3. Book description for *Designing Disney's Theme Parks: The Architecture of Reassurance*, ed. Karal Ann Marling. New York: Flammarion, 1997.
4. Marx, Karl. *Economic and Philosophic Manuscripts of 1844* (trans. M. Milligan). Minneola, NY: Dover Publishing, 2007.
5. "Flourishing" is a term from the Ancient Greek philosopher Aristotle, meaning to actualize our potential.
6. "Heigh-ho," Frank Churchill and Larry Morey. *Snow White and the Seven Dwarfs*. Disney, 1937.
7. Despite this abundance, far too many people continue to live in extreme poverty. Frankfurt School philosophers criticized our economic system for pouring so much money into mass entertainment while refusing to use those same resources to end hunger. See Adorno and Horkheimer. *Dialectic of Enlightenment*. New York: Continuum, 1993.
8. "The Best Time of Your Life." Robert Sherman and Richard Sherman. Disney, 1974.
9. Marcuse, Herbert. *One-Dimensional Man*. Boston: Beacon Press, 1991.
10. Ibid., p. 5.
11. Ibid.
12. Ibid., p. 12.
13. Ibid., p. 1.
14. Disneyland is "The Happiest Place on Earth," whereas Walt Disney World's Magic Kingdom is "The Most Magical Place on Earth."
15. This quotation from Walt Disney appears on a sign as you enter the Magic Kingdom at Walt Disney World.
16. Alex Stewart and Harrison Ownbey (2018, February 2). "Fantasyland" episode. *The Back Side of Water Podcast*. https://www.podomatic.com/podcasts/thebacksideofwater/episodes/2018-02-01T21_58_42-08_00. 6:05 and 6:25.
17. "A Dream is a Wish Your Heart Makes." Mack David, Al Hoffman and Jerry Livingston. *Cinderella*. Disney, 1950.
18. "When You Wish Upon a Star." Leigh Harline and Ned Washington. *Pinocchio*. Disney, 1940.
19. Adorno and Horkheimer, *Dialectic of Enlightenment*, p. 24.
20. Lucy AitkenRead (2018, June 27). "Ten Ways to Be Happy." *YouTube*. https://www.youtube.com/watch?v=k6kOwnQ4yNY.
21. Stewart and Ownbey, "Fantasyland" episode, *The Back Side of Water Podcast*. 5:00.

22. Joe Rohde. Instagram post. March 30, 2018. https://www.instagram.com/p/Bg7sogInIjR
23. Stewart and Ownbey, "Fantasyland" episode, *The Back Side of Water Podcast*. 6:30.
24. Stewart and Ownbey, "Fantasyland" episode, *The Back Side of Water Podcast*. 53:30.

Colonizing the Geography of the Imagination

Media, Mind, and the Magic Kingdom

Read Mercer Schuchardt

> All media exists to invest our lives with artificial perception and arbitrary values.
>
> — Marshall McLuhan, *Understanding Media*

> The world of the human will and imagination is the world of mirages. It is common to man and the fallen angels, and imagination is, therefore, often a conductor of demonic energy.
>
> —St. Silouan the Athonite, *The Imagination and the Ascetic Struggle against Its Various Aspects*

When my second daughter Genevieve was three years old I found myself once again re-reading to her *Winnie The Pooh*, by A.A. Milne which was at the time her very favorite book. Her baby brother had just had his Mickey-Mouse-branded Huggies "Snug-N-Dry" Newborn-Size diaper changed, and was fast asleep on the couch next to us. Curled up in a ball of coziness on my chest, with the small-format book in front of us, she actually pulled her legs up and tried to push her delicate feet into the pages of E.H. Shephard's decorations of the Hundred Acre Wood, and whispered to me in all earnestness: "Daddy ... *get me in there!*"

If you understand that feeling, sympathize with that sentiment, and remember having that same desire at some point in your life, then you

Disney and Philosophy: Truth, Trust, and a Little Bit of Pixie Dust, First Edition.
Edited by Richard B. Davis.

already know the secret to the astonishing global success of the Walt Disney Corporation. What they do, amazingly well, consistently, impressively, and with a refinement that staggers the imagination, is *get you in there*. Is there anything more beautiful than the elderly couple's romantic trajectory in the first five minutes of Pixar's *UP*? Is there anything more genius and perfect than making the department of motor vehicles officers all super-slo-mo moving and talking sloths in *Zootopia*? It doesn't matter if *there* is literal or fictitious, historically real or mythically imagined, what Disney is able to do is transport you into the world of the imagination in such a way that will, in all likelihood, make you both enjoy the journey and not want to leave. And it is right there in the middle, between the literal and fictitious, between enjoying the journey and not wanting to leave, that Disney creates a tension that can only be resolved by *not letting you leave a world they have entirely fictionalized*. Because when you leave, you'll hardly ever notice that the *geography of your imagination* – a phrase used by writers from Aldous Huxley to Guy Davenport – no longer has any unexplored territory: no Australias, Timbuktus, or Antarcticas. For Disney is, has been, and forever will be, not only the first and last colonizer of that geography, but also the creator of all mythologies of all possible future visits to that geography. And that is what we need to talk about. So sit down for an hour; this is going to be one of those TLDR (Too Long Didn't Read) articles you're really, *really* going to wish you had finished. The internet can wait.

Johnny Depp Is Channeling Keith Richards as a Permanent Peter Pan Disguised as Captain Hook Doing a *Pepe Le Pew*

By the end of the twentieth century, the Walt Disney Company seemed all out of story. Disney had achieved this fatigued-to-cultural death status by exhausting every narrative option available to them:

- remaking old favorites (*Herbie The Love Bug, Cheaper by the Dozen*).
- buying new properties for cheap (such as the *Winnie the Pooh* franchise from Sears).
- discovering they had no ear or talent for new material (*Pocahontas. Mulan. Hercules*?).

- recycling their animated properties into live action films (*The Jungle Book, 101 Dalmatians, Beauty and the Beast*).
- making sequels, prequels, and "meh"-quels enough to kill the most avid fan (*Long John Silver, 102 Dalmatians, Hercules: From Zero to Hero*).
- remaking a live-action film into an animated film, but with a twist!

Nobody believed this last one could be done, but by 2002, when *Treasure Planet* came out (oh, you missed that one?), the wailing and gnashing of teeth for the glory that was Disney became audible. As if it couldn't get any worse, the company then turned pathetically to a technique that exactly no one had considered before in the quest for novel storylines: deriving a plot from one of their own theme park rides.

This tactic is roughly analogous to recycling toilet paper to make tableware. I mean, how desperate do you have to be when you turn to theme park rides for inspiration for a movie? At least the Tea Cup ride is based on *Alice's Adventures in Wonderland*, and makes you feel small again. But what do you do when …

First *The Country Bears* came out in 2002, based on the Country Bears Jamboree show, with one bear channeling Jerry Garcia and the rest of them channeling The Eagles. Then, in what looked like a final act of desperation, 2003 saw the release of *Pirates of the Caribbean*, a ride most people remembered as being not terribly fun even when they were 11 years old. *Wait a minute. Just a sec.*

Did you just say, *Pirates of the Caribbean*?

I love that movie!

Hang on … Oh, now I remember: EVERYONE loved that movie:

- Gross Worldwide Receipts for *Treasure Planet*: $109 million (on a budget of, ahem, $140 million)
- Gross Worldwide Receipts for Pirates of the Caribbean: $654 million
- Gross Worldwide Receipts for the entire Pirates franchise (5 films thus far, with #6 coming soon): $4.5 billion
- Amount Disney Paid George Lucas for the entire Star Wars franchise: $4.06 billion.

How'd they do this? Well, the first thing is that it is not what it looks like. Just as the 2001 *Planet of the Apes* was not a remake of the 1968 Charlton Heston original but rather a remake of the 1956 Charlton Heston film *The Ten Commandments* (Moses = Semos, Crossing the river to freedom), so too is *Pirates of the Caribbean* hiding in plain sight with its startling premise: it's not a narrativized makeover of a Disney ride. It's a remake of the ride of your life in the capitalists-gone-global-empire story starting from the Dutch East India Trading Company (the world's first multinational corporation) in the seventeenth century to the Disney empire itself in the twenty-first. Executed so beautifully, so stylishly, and so accurately, *Pirates of the Caribbean* has yet to have a film critic recognize it as an allegory of the political economy called globalization ever since America (and then the whole world) went off the gold standard in 1933. It is only in a world where value is an absolutely relative thing that you can create entirely new and entirely arbitrary values (cue the McLuhan epigraph) for a culture to embrace.

We Have Found the Lemmings, and They Are Us

What you see in a movie can affect your perception of reality for the rest of your life. One thing Walt Disney was committed to was the theory of evolution, and he made great and creative use of the medium of animation to demonstrate the plausibility of the theory with his 1940 film *Fantasia*. While Charles Darwin never actually found any evidence of transmutation from one species to the next – the proverbial "missing links" he thought the fossil record would show outnumbering the extant species – the medium of animation can, and does, quite beautifully, demonstrate all the in-between "states" just as compellingly as the ILM film-technology of morphing can demonstrate from 1988s *Willow* to every *Terminator* movie and beyond. So what is visually perceivable by special-effects technology becomes a sort of default retroactive "proof" for a theory that never actually found anything close to the substantive proof it went looking for in the fossil record.[1]

Then, in 1958, Disney actually came up with a misperception that we still cling to today: that lemmings will naturally "select" themselves for annihilation when their breeding population becomes too large. The Disney nature documentary *White Wilderness* actually shows lemmings jumping down a steeply inclined cliff, only at the end, to have them jump headlong into the ocean and swim out to sea where a number of them, the narrator tells us, will drown.[2] What the film doesn't show is the tight angle of production, the importing of these lemmings from a different part of Canada, and the actual corralling of the poor beasts into a funnel so that the film crew can actually force them to their deaths. In other words, Disney wanted this element of natural selection to include group suicide, and so he "made it so" by documenting it in film. To this day, popular culture speaks of lemmings and lemming-like behavior as though it is as true and obvious as the ostrich burying its head in the sand, another natural phenomenon that never once in the history of the universe has actually happened.[3]

So if Watching a Disney Product is Good, and Going to Disney World is Better, How Do I Achieve my Best: By *Being* in, Of, and About Disney ... *Permanently*

Like Playboy, McDonalds, and Coca-Cola, the Disney brand is also an epistemology, a philosophy, a metaphysics, a worldview, and a way of life. It teaches you – implicitly and explicitly – how to live, what to believe is real, what to believe is important, and what to value as you journey through this veil of tears.

Ultimately, then, one of the reasons the Walt Disney Company's products and theme parks and movies and toys are so popular is that it is such good fun, such escapist fantasy, such a permanent joyride of nostalgia, that if we are completely honest, we love it so much because it finally represents the death of true religion which everyone (religious or not) secretly hates. Even an old Christian hymn acknowledges this tendency: "Prone to wander, Lord I feel it, prone to leave the God I love." Whether it's their theme parks, movies, events, TV shows, pop stars, princesses, toys, or parades, you know that you never have to live by "the rules" of your ordinary life, your culture, or your religion when you are in a Disney environment. Just drop your garbage right there on Main Street, and an army of Cast Members will dutifully sweep up after you, making the place as clean as Singapore but without all the repressive rules for achieving that effect. You know you are in a Magical Kingdom when the experience actually permits, condones, and even encourages magical thinking of this sort: your actions do not have to have consequences, because we are here to just make it fun for you.

Give Me That Old Time Mythology

What props up all this on the structural subconscious level is that Disney Corp has carefully studied Carl Jung, carefully read Joseph Campbell, and carefully attended, since at least the late 1980s to the company's core internal mantra: "We Create the Mythology of the Future."

If you need a brief primer on this, read up on how Carl Jung dismissed his father's Swiss Reformed Heritage and opted instead for four universal human archetypes – sensation, intuition, feeling, and thinking – which led a Swarthmore College graduate and her mother to develop the Myers-Briggs Type Indicator (MBTI), which is why nowadays you know the four-letter combo that unlocks your personality almost before you learn your own Social Security number. Jung's universalizing was then refined and perfected by comparative religion expert and Sarah Lawrence literature professor Joseph Campbell in *The Hero With a Thousand Faces* which inspired George Lucas to rewrite his *Star Wars* saga into a final draft that had Luke Skywalker taking all 12 steps of the Hero's Journey, a pattern that just about every blockbuster film (and most Disney films, including the aforementioned *Star Wars* franchise which Disney now owns) have subsequently patterned themselves after.

The Myth Made Real ... Must Be Made Mythic Again to Be Tolerable

Campbell's secret project attempted to "remythologize" Christianity away from historical fact by blurring the lines between its claims and the numerous other "messiah figures" that had preceded it. This was a tricky dance in a culture that claimed Christianity as the dominant belief system of its citizens. So what Disney has done, and done really, *really* well, and carefully, and subtly, and sometimes not-so-subtly, has been to "universally mythologize" what was once a "universal religion." So where C. S. Lewis would describe Christianity as "the myth made real" by the historical appearance of the God-man Jesus Christ, Disney has gone to great pains to both appease a Christian culture by purchasing such properties as *The Chronicles of Narnia*, and then to have its actors pronounce in the media that it is not in fact, a Christian story. Here is Liam Neeson 'splaining it to you dummies without the PhDs in comparative mythology:

> "Aslan symbolizes a Christlike figure," Neeson said, "but he also symbolizes for me Muhammad, Buddha and all the great spiritual leaders and prophets over the centuries." Producer Mark Johnson is siding with Neeson, telling the Hollywood Reporter that "resurrection exists in so many different religions in one form or another, so it's hardly exclusively Christian.[4]

What neither Neeson nor Johnson will acknowledge, is that Christianity (like it or not, believe it or not) is the only religion to not claim a "Christ-like figure" but to claim that God actually chose, of His own free will and love, to incarnate as a Palestinian carpenter named Yeshua and then "took pity on your ridiculous plight and entered the space and time of your insignificant planet to tell you something."[5] The Walt Disney Corporation has neither condoned nor approved Neeson's remarks – but neither has it prevented them.[6] Where Christians believe that the incarnation of God in Christ offers the user a means of bearing up under life in a fallen Reality, Disney counteroffers with the illusion of a return to life in a pre-fallen Reality, albeit one that is technologically aided and abetted to produce this very illusion. As Umberto Eco puts it, "Disneyland tells us that technology can give us more reality than nature can."[7] Both worldviews have their believers. You get to choose which is which, and then you get to choose only one, because you can't have both.

And here's the rub: Disney represents a mythology that is universal because they are rapidly acquiring every possible alternate reality that one cares to enter, except for – so far – the sexual realm and the Christian religion realm. Winnie The Pooh? Check. Marvel Universe? Check. Star Wars? Check. About the only alternative universe media franchise bigger than Star Wars is *Pokemon*, which as of this writing Disney has not (yet) acquired. When Disney owns all possible significant alternate universes, then only Disney can colonize your imagination, and only Disney will give you the lens through which to perceive any competing claim on understanding your ultimate Reality. A phrase applied to Steve Jobs and his Apple products was the Reality Distortion Field, referring to Jobs ability to convince himself and others to believe almost anything with a mix of charm, charisma, bravado, hyperbole, marketing, appeasement, and persistence. This is perhaps the most exquisitely perfect description of what life inside the Disney World is like. When you can *Exit Through the Gift Shop*,[8] but not through the *Psychic Structure of* Disbelief,[9] then you actually do have a uniquely metaphysical problem. It's what Walker Percy meant when he said, "It is this monstrous bifurcation of man into angelic and bestial components against which the old theologies must be weighed before new theologies are erected. Such a man could not take account of God, the devil, and the angels if they were standing before him, *because he has already peopled the universe with his own hierarchies.*[10]

What are the Marvel, the Star Wars, and the Disney franchises but a competing series of man-made hierarchies with which to people the universe?[11] As long as I can conceive of Christianity as just another old mythology whose primary value is simply in intertextual homage from which to borrow an occasional "Christ-like figure" or "Judas figure" then I am safe from any existential threat bigger than the question of which is cooler, *Star Wars* or *Star Trek*? To put it another way, there are two ways of creating a plausible incarnation: (i) The Myth Made Real (come to life) via the Incarnation of God in Christ – the downside here is that it requires (a) a lot of faith, (b) a lot of time, and concomitantly, (c) a lot of patience – Christianity is nothing if not the religion of deferred gratification. The other way to do it, is of course, (ii) the Disney Way,[12] or the Myth Manufactured as Playground for those Willing to Suspend their Disbelief. (The only downside here is that it requires a lot of money, but the gratifications are instant, ongoing, and very, very fun.)

In 1983, media watchdog Ben Bagdikian raised the alarm by pointing out that only 50 media companies controlled 90% of what Americans read, watched, listened do, and did for fun. By 2018, that number has been reduced to six major corporations. In order of 2017 revenues, they are as follows[13]:

1. Comcast ($85bn): NBC, MSNBC, Universal Pictures, Telemundo, Dreamworks, Focus Features.
2. Walt Disney ($55bn): Theme Parks, Pixar, ABC, Touchstone, ABC, ESPN, Pixar, A&E, Lifetime, Marvel, Star Wars.
3. AT&T/Warner Media ($31 bn, formerly Time/Warner): HBO, Cinemax, Turner Entertainment Networks, CNN, Time Magazine, Cartoon Network, Adult Swim, DC Comics, New Line Cinema, Fandango, MySpace.
4. 21st Century Fox ($29 bn, formerly News Corp): Fox News, 20th Century Fox, Wall Street Journal, New York Post, FX, Barrons, HarperCollins Publishing, Sky TV, The Sun, The Times, Realtor.com, numerous Australian media holdings.
5. CBS ($14bn): CBS, Simon & Schuster, CNET, Metacritic, ZDNet
6. Viacom ($13bn): Paramount Pictures (Star Trek), Comedy Central, MTV, VH1, TV Land, Nickelodeon, BET.

Right now, in the six-corporation mediasphere you inhabit, the conservative view is held primarily by one company: Rupert Murdoch's 21st Century Fox, formerly News Corp. Like it or not, agree with it or not, or even watch it or not, it does represent a sociocultural point of view not held by the other five major media companies.

So when Disney announced on July 27, 2018 that it would be acquiring 21st Century Fox for 71.3 billion, it means that the ~~metaphysical warfare just hit your wi-fi signal~~ shit just got real: your six-corporation mediasphere will be going down to five.[14] Further, it means that the one conservative media outlet is about to be swallowed by one of the more liberal media outlets. This, by the way, is the entire subtextual message of Disney's 2016 animated film *Zootopia*, in which Judy Hopp (reprising Oswald The Lucky Rabbit, Disney's original cartoon character) has to drag, kicking and screaming, the conservative fox Nick Wilde over to her worldview, and why the "elephant in the room" is the Republican party, the primary customer base of Fox News and other 21st Century Fox media products.[15] What it really means, of course, is that control of the Overton Window – the range of ideas tolerated in public discourse – just got a little smaller, that its opening range just got narrower, and that the whole thing just got harder to budge. Or, as Judy Hopp says in the film, "You can't call me cute unless you're another rabbit."

The Visual Containment of Metaphysical Values

Perhaps one of the best and most effective psychological tricks deployed by Disney to not just *get you in there*, but "keep you in there," is the visual rules of engagement for their theme parks. Next time you visit, notice your environmental surroundings while in the parking lot. Look at the tallest buildings, corporate office towers, and hotels all around you. Then enter the park. Notice that wherever you are, in whatever section of the park you're in, you can't see those buildings anymore because, by clever design of the Imagineers, *you've been visually contained in the fantasy world*. This is part and parcel of the same employee rule that requires each Disney character to keep his or her headpiece on even if they pass out or vomit inside the mask, as one of the Chip and Dale characters famously did on a Disney Parade float years ago. Well, visual containment helps the psyche stay in the mode and the mood for the various psychic propaganda programs being run, and allows you to enjoy and prolong the fantasy, as well as empty your wallet of all possible contents since the only way to experience "more" Disney is to hand them exactly all of your cash.[16] Thus, in short order, Disney has successfully colonized an awful lot of the global imagination, from young to old, male to female, from history to fantasy, and now from right to left.

Hey Goofy! Somebody Just Slipped My Culture a Mickey...

The ONLY place left to go is Pornography and the Bible – the sexual imagination and the Christian imagination. The pornographic imagination is a fairly literal embrace of the limitless possibilities of the animation imagination. Porn Star Lolo Ferrari, before she died at age 37 from complications from multiple plastic surgeries said, “I hate reality; I want to be completely artificial.” Jessica Rabbit, another Disney product, puts it this way: “I’m not bad; *I’m just drawn that way*.” Which is why it’s slightly unsettling to learn that Disney is going to be purchasing 21st Century Fox. If you Google Search “Who owns the copyright to the NIV Bible?” this 2008 answer comes up:

> Zondervan is a subsidiary of HarperCollins, which is owned by News Corp, which is owned by Rupert Murdoch. He is one of the biggest producers of worldwide pornography on the planet. And his company, Zondervan, holds the exclusive publishing rights to the New International Version Bible.[17]

Under these conditions, Disney will go from controlling one-sixth to controlling one-third of the media, or roughly 33% of everything you see, hear, watch, listen to, and do in the mediasphere. In a 12-hours of media per day universe, this means a Disney park, product, character, idea, or belief will be in your head roughly 4 hours per day, which is, after all, *only about one-fourth of your waking life*.

It really is going to be a small world, after all...

Stand up straight, throw your shoulders back, and step right this way, kiddies: you’ll need to be a lot metaphysically taller to take this ride.

Notes

1. For the best, most recent take-down of Darwin’s original theory from a non-religious point of view, see the last testament of Tom Wolfe’s writing career, *The Kingdom of Speech*, a book so loudly ignored that *The New York Times* failed to acknowledge its existence in an obituary that otherwise mentioned by name every other book he wrote.
2. You can see this film, or just this clip, like most everything these days, by doing a simple YouTube search.

3. Ostriches lay their heads and necks flat and show only their bodies when under predation, providing the visual illusion (at a distance) that they have buried their head in the sand. The actual effect is to produce a clump of feathers that at a distance looks somewhat innocuously like a bush or shrub rather than a source of meat.
4. Brittany Mahaney (2010, December 9). "Is Aslan a metaphor for Jesus? Liam Neeson's not so sure." *National Post.* https://nationalpost.com/entertainment/movies/is-aslan-a-metaphor-for-jesus-liam-neesons-not-so-sure.
5. This is Walker Percy's phrasing, not my own. See his 1983 non-fiction work, *Lost in The Cosmos.*
6. And prevent it they would, or could, if they wanted. See Disney's micromanaging of C-3PO's Anthony Daniels over a tweet in which he said he was delighted to have met an actor who was playing a role in *The Force Awakens.* Disney actually required him to remove the Tweet. See James Rainey (2015, September 4). "'Star Wars': Anthony Daniels Slams Disney's 'Kremlin Attitude' Over 'Force Awakens'." *Variety.* https://variety.com/2015/film/news/star-wars-anthony-daniels-slams-disney-force-awakens-secrecy-1201586167/.
7. *Travels in Hyperreality*, Umberto Eco.
8. This is Banksy's memorable phrasing.
9. This is me riffing off Jordan Peterson's phrasing.
10. Emphasis added at the end of the quote; Walker Percy, *The Message In The Bottle*, p. 113.
11. Indeed, if you look at the pages of these alternate universe character's names on Wikipedia, you will see that in several instances they outnumber all the Biblical characters – from historical figures to angelic/demonic characters – from all 66 books of Old and New Testaments.
12. "The Disney Way" is the corporate name of the Disney employee program to understand the "inside" of the system and peek behind the curtains of all seven Disney divisions. It typically has a two-year waiting list to get in, even once you've been employed. By contrast, early disciples of Christ called themselves followers of "The Way."
13. "Media cross-ownership in the United States," *Wikipedia*, last modified September 21, 2018, https://en.wikipedia.org/wiki/Media_cross-ownership_in_the_United_States#Top_Five*.
14. This is a complicated and multilayered deal, as always; so much so that it has its own Wikipedia page if you want to keep up with the origin, evolution, details, and backstory: https://en.wikipedia.org/wiki/Proposed_acquisition_of_21st_Century_Fox_by_Disney
15. Disney hasn't made an animated movie for children in at least three decades, one reason why watching their movies with grown-up eyes is so much fun. Like *The Family Guy* or *South Park*, the trick is to deploy the medium of a children's cartoon in order to carry the message of a

very serious adult conversation – one that you could never get away with on prime-time TV or in a G-to-PG-rated film.

16. The secret reason for Disney dollars is no secret at all: with a one-to-one conversion rate of American dollars to Disney dollars, it would appear that Disney makes no profit on the transaction. Dumbo: the profit is in the *huge percentage* of tourists who want to keep a Disney dollar, a 10, or even a 20, as a memento to put into their scrapbook for memories of their epic vacation.
17. This answer seems dated to 2008, when News Corp had to divest its BSkyB holdings because they were major holders of pornographic film studios and content. But as of this writing, HarperCollins still does own Zondervan which holds copyright on the NIV translation.

"We're All Gonna Die"

Death and the Cycle of Life in Disney

Jessica Miller

My doctor likes to joke that all humans have a sexually transmitted fatal disease: mortality. Funny guy. But he has a point: all living creatures eventually die. Unlike most nonhuman animals, humans can reflect on death as a concept, experience death through personal relationships, and express feelings and beliefs about death through art, traditions, and rituals. Death, for self-conscious beings like us, is much more than an unavoidable future event. We cannot help but have a relationship to our own death, even if we try to ignore it. Death, paradoxically, is an omnipresent feature of life.

Death has always interested philosophers. In 399 BCE, Socrates, addressing an Athenian jury, responded to his death sentence by reflecting on whether life's end might be actually be a blessing. Philosophers wonder when exactly human life ceases, and what our answer to this question tells us about our concept of personhood. They ask whether our deaths harm us, or just the people who might miss us. Does being mortal make our lives more significant or less? Are there virtuous ways of dying or facing death? Would the existence of an afterlife change any of our answers to these questions?

Disney films don't shy away from death, as anyone who has shed a tear over Bambi's mom surely knows. In fact, a recent study of 57 Disney and Pixar animated films found 71 character deaths – more than one per movie![1] Some deaths are implicit (Elsa and Anna's parents in *Frozen*), and some more explicit (Clayton in *Tarzan*). Some

Disney and Philosophy: Truth, Trust, and a Little Bit of Pixie Dust, First Edition.
Edited by Richard B. Davis.

deaths elicit strong emotional reactions (Hiro's brother in *Big Hero 6*), while others are met with sad acceptance (Moana's grandmother).

From *Snow White*'s elaborate glass coffin in 1937, to *Coco* in 2017, a film centered on Día de los Muertos, Disney films draw from multiple cultural traditions which align with Western, Indigenous, Latino, and Eastern philosophies. The movies are thus a rich source of material for introducing the subject of death from a philosophical perspective.[2]

"Hey, I know a joke! A squirrel walks up to a tree and says, 'I forgot to store acorns for the winter and now I am dead.' Ha! It is funny because the squirrel gets dead." —Dug, in *Up*

If death marks the end of human life, we need to know what a human life *is*. From a biological perspective, a living human being is a unified individual, with the capacity to develop and maintain itself via processes like metabolism, growth, and response to stimuli. Humans develop secondary characteristics of self-awareness, rationality, and capacity for language that, together, distinguish them from other living organisms. From this biological perspective, death occurs when all of these vital processes have stopped.

So, poison apple and spindle notwithstanding, Snow White and Sleeping Beauty don't actually die. Rather, they endure the "sleeping death," a spell that sends them into unconsciousness, until, of course, they are revived by love's first kiss. In real-life terms, they are sort of like patients in a persistent vegetative state, who are non-responsive, and whose vital processes are maintained by external means. On the other hand, if we define human life as essentially the physical processes that support our existence as *minds*, then a person who has permanently lost the ability to think, remember, and feel, would no longer be alive, even if other vital processes, such as heart rhythm, breathing, and sleep–wake cycles, persist.

Many philosophers believe that our higher mental functions define what it is to be alive. In addition, many philosophers believe that what makes you *you* is a kind of psychological continuity: memories, intentions, beliefs, goals, and desires creating overlapping chains of identity. After WALL·E is crushed underneath the holo-detector on the ship, the Axiom, EVE rushes him back to his trailer on Earth and fixes him up: new wheels, new binocular eyes, and a new chip. But after being charged back up, WALL·E fails to recognize EVE, ignoring her as he scoops garbage and compresses it into cubes. Although he is a functioning organism, WALL·E the person has disappeared. Luckily, EVE's farewell kiss, assisted by a jolt of electricity, restores his memory and personality. Once that psychological continuity is restored, WALL·E is back.

Frozen's Anna, Beast, and Eugene in *Tangled* all die, but they are quickly reanimated by a loving kiss – or tear. The closest thing to this in real life is the person who experiences a near drowning or near fatal heart attack, someone who not only loses consciousness, but whose heart and lungs stop working. So, as long as we are thinking of human beings in terms of physical processes, it looks like we need to add "permanent" cessation of vital life processes to our definition of death. It follows that as terrible as they must be to experience, these temporary "deaths" are not the real thing.

By contrast Carl's wife in *Up* and Tadashi – Hiro's beloved older brother in *Big Hero 6* – really, truly, die. And so do many, many antagonists in Disney films, often by falling from a high plateau. Gaston falls from the Beast's castle, Charles F. Muntz from the sky in *Up*, *Snow White's* Evil Queen from a cliff, Frollo from a gargoyle atop the titular cathedral in *The Hunchback of Notre Dame* – the list goes on. And although Disney rarely shows us the gruesome outcome (one of the kid-friendly reasons to kill villains this way), it is safe to say none of these baddies survives. In all of these examples, when the body goes, so does the life within it.

But Disney films are full of characters who continue to exist in some form after their physical bodies cease to be. Post-death existence takes myriad forms: guardian angels (famed chef Auguste Gusteau in *Rataouille*; Sitka in *Brother Bear*) ghosts (Zero the dog in *The Nightmare Before Christmas*), ancestral spirits (Fa family ancestors in *Mulan*), even demons (Dr. Facilier's "Friends on the Other Side" in *The Princess and the Frog*, or Chernabog's minions in *Fantasia's Night on Bald Mountain*). These characters raise the possibility that there is some life after physical death, while at the same time suggesting that human existence is not merely physical.

Plato (427–347 BCE) believed that human beings are the temporary union of souls and bodies. He argued that there are two basic kinds of existence: the things we perceive with our senses, and the things we perceive with our minds. Our bodies are material and eventually die and decay, whereas souls are immaterial and immortal. In the *Phaedo*, Plato defended this claim with what is called the "affinity argument."[3] There, he argued that the soul, which we cannot access via sensory experience, is most like intelligible being, while the body, which we do experience with our senses, is most like sensible being. The soul, being intelligible, changeless, and indivisible, rules the body like the divine rules over mortals.

Or it *should*. For some, bodily experience is too tempting and distracting. Why follow the rational dictates of one's soul when one's body promises pleasure? In *The Hunchback of Notre Dame*, Judge Claude Frollo views himself as a pious and holy man. But he lusts after Esmeralda, comparing her effect on him to "hellfire ... this fire in my skin this burning desire is turning me to sin!" Frollo's lust and rage at his own inability to tame it motivate some of his most heinous acts. It would be no surprise to Plato that Frollo's inability to control his physical urges and emotions eventually led to his undoing.

We can contrast Plato's view of the soul with that of Epicurus (341–271 BCE). For Epicurus, atoms and the void (space) comprise everything in the universe. Atoms are the elemental building block of everything that exists, including humans. Although human souls are special in *some* ways, they are, like everything else, composed of atoms, and at death they disperse. Epicurus drew on this materialistic metaphysics to make his famous argument, in his *Letter to Menoeceus*, that fearing one's own death is irrational.[4] Basically, if we exist, we are not dead, and when we are dead, we do not exist. Pain is the only thing to fear, and since being dead doesn't feel like anything, it cannot be painful. Even better, if all the world is composed of atoms in the void, there is no afterlife, so no need to fear eternal punishment.

Consider Marlin, Nemo's father. After losing his wife and 399 baby eggs to a hungry barracuda, he is so terrified of death that he can no longer enjoy his life. His mantra is, "How do you know something bad isn't gonna happen!?" His fear doesn't help him: it causes the pain of what Epicurus called "perturbation." Marlin's overprotectiveness leads to an estrangement from Nemo, which creates the dangerous situation he wanted to avoid in the first place. Luckily, Marlin has a memory-challenged friend to help. Dory's forgetfulness tends to keep her focused on the present. She could be describing every moment of human life when she tells Marlin, "So, we're cheating death now. That's what we're doing, and we're having fun at the same time."

"If you weren't you, then we'd all be a bit less we" —Piglet, *Winnie the Pooh*

"'Ohana means 'family.' 'Family' means 'no one gets left behind'" —Lilo, *Lilo and Stitch*

The kinds of philosophical questions outlined so far tend to focus on the meaning of death for an individual. But thinking about death, dying, and the dead can tell us a lot about our communities and their values. Several Disney films depict a porousness between the realms of the living and the dead. What kinds of philosophical commitments might support these beliefs?

In many indigenous philosophies, "living" is a relationship rather than a quality. As Native American philosopher Vine Deloria, Jr., explains, "everything in the natural world has relationships with every other thing and the total set of relationships makes up the natural world as we experience it."[5] To have a life is just to be related to other things in the web of existence, the entirety of which is sacred. This includes plants, animals, and other material objects, all of which are, in some way, conscious and ensouled.

It follows that "death," in the sense of total annihilation and non-existence, is not possible. Life is connected spirit or energy, and it is never destroyed. Consider this conversation in *The Lion King*:

MUFASA: Everything you see exists together in a delicate balance. As king, you need to understand that balance and respect all the creatures, from the crawling ant to the leaping antelope.
SIMBA: But, Dad, don't we eat the antelope?
MUFASA: Yes, Simba, but let me explain. When we die, our bodies become the grass, and the antelope eat the grass. And so we are all connected in the great Circle of Life.

In many indigenous philosophies, respect for all life, not just human life, is a foundational moral imperative. We can sense this in Pocahontas' song, "Colors of the Wind":

> "You think you own whatever land you land on
> The Earth is just a dead thing you can claim
> But I know every rock and tree and creature
> Has a life, has a spirit, has a name."

As Deloria puts it, "Not only is everything related, but it also participates in the moral content of events, so responsibility for maintaining the harmony of life falls equally on all."[6]

For many contemporary indigenous philosophers, anything we experience is a part of reality. Nonmaterial beings are no less "natural" than rocks or trees. Relationships with spirits help determine a person's identity. For example, Moana understands herself in terms of her role as a future leader of her island, Motunui, but also as the heir to a glorious, but buried, history of seafaring ancestors. It is a visit from her grandmother's spirit, asking pointedly, "Moana, do you know who you are?" that spurs Moana to empathically claim both identities:

> "I am the daughter of the village chief
> We are descended from voyagers
> Who found their way across the world
> They call me."

For Tala, death is not merely an end, but a change in the way she relates to the web of being.

We can see this in *Brother Bear* as well, set among a Native community in post ice age Alaska where they experience the Northern Lights as "the spirits of our ancestors" who "have the power to make changes in our world." When his older brother Sitka is killed by a bear, young Kenai kills the animal in retribution. Suddenly emerging as a spirit from the aurora, Sitka turns Kenai into a bear himself, to help him understand the interconnectedness of things. In this way, a spirit helps young Kenai appreciate the web of being, and his responsibility within it. In *Brother Bear*, as in many other Disney films, ancestors don't disappear but remain present in our lives. As Tina Turner sings in "Great Spirits": "Great Spirits of all who lived before. Take our hands. Take our hands and lead us."

Respectful relationships imply reciprocity, so it's not just the living who can be helped by the dead, but the dead can be helped – or harmed – by the living. Consider the plot of *Coco*. In a small Mexican town on Día de los Muertos, 12-year-old Miguel mistakenly enters the Land of the Dead, a Day-Glo world of spirit animals and animated skeletons. Day of the Dead originated in Mexico, combining elements of indigenous Aztec ritual with Catholicism. Miguel discovers that the famous balladeer Ernesto de la Cruz murdered Miguel's great-great-grandfather, Héctor, stealing his songs and his guitar. When Miguel returns to the land of the living, his revelations destroy

Ernesto's reputation while elevating Héctor to be recognized as one of the great Mexican artists. Ernesto is forgotten (suffering the "final death" in the film), while Héctor returns to his rightful place in the family, symbolized by his photo on the family *ofrenda*, or altar. He can now partake with both his living and dead loved ones in the traditional rituals of the holiday, dancing and feasting. His legacy is secure.

Speaking of Catholicism, Saint Thomas Aquinas (1225–1274) disagreed with Plato's view of the soul. As he puts it in his commentary on 1 Corinthians 15, the "soul is not the whole human being, but only part of one: my soul is not me."[7] For Aquinas, the body is not a prison for the soul. Rather, body and soul are intertwined as matter and form, and both are necessary. Humans are rational animals, living bodies able to do incredible things with our minds. Aquinas believed that when a person dies, they receive judgment. Those who did not repent of their sins, and who rejected God are sent to hell. Disney captures this possibility with Claude Frollo's death. Judge Frollo cloaked his evil deeds in righteousness: he "longed to purge the world of vice and sin / And he saw corruption everywhere, except within." He dies when the gargoyle he clings to comes to life and demonically roars at him. Our last image of Frollo is his plunge into a fiery lake of molten metal, one of Disney's more explicit portrayals of hell.

Epicurus's student, Lucretius (99–55 BCE), would find this whole story kind of silly. Like Epicurus, he denies that death can harm us, so events after our death – our non-existence – cannot either. As he puts it,

> Look back upon the ages of time past
> Eternal, before we were born, and see
> That they have been nothing to us, nothing at all.
> This is the mirror that nature holds for us
> To show the face of time to come, when we
> Are at last dead.[8]

In this, the symmetry argument, Lucretius is saying that just as our pre-birth non-existence doesn't bother us, so our post-death non-existence shouldn't. Put another way, "Dead men tell no tales."

And yet, it certainly *feels* like Ernesto's life was made worse by events that took place after he died. In *Coco*, belief in the existence of ancestral spirits that interact with the living helps generate this possibility. But even some philosophers who believe that death is the final and total end of a person think that posthumous harm is possible. The idea, argued most persuasively by the philosopher Joel Feinberg (1926–2004), is that certain kinds of events can retrospectively affect the well-being of a person before death, by fulfilling or frustrating the living subject's desires and ambitions.[9] Ernesto's well-being was lower in life than it might have been because of facts about his postmortem future, while the other man's is higher. In life, Ernesto wanted to be adored and celebrated, whereas Héctor wanted to be respected for his music and remembered fondly by his family. Thanks to Miguel's adventures, Ernesto's greatest desire in life has been thwarted, and Hector's fulfilled.

This view of whether either Ernesto's or Héctor's life went well assumes that well-being consists in having one's desires fulfilled, an assumption we can question. How can *irrational* desires contribute to our well-being? It's probably better for Olaf the enchanted snowman in *Frozen* if his longing for a warm summer goes unfulfilled! Whether posthumous harm is a thing or not, many of us believe that, somehow, a person is harmed, perhaps only symbolically, when their corpse is desecrated, or when memories of them are diminished by slander.

"The time has come, gypsy. You stand upon the brink of the abyss" —Claude Frollo

Death and morality connect in interesting ways in Disney movies. Disney often thematically connects the quality of a life lived with the quality of a death. Villains meet violent, unexpected deaths, which serve as fitting ends for their crimes. Clayton, who attempted to capture and sell a troop of gorillas, is hanged by jungle vines in *Tarzan*. Dr. Facilier, a trickster who practices an evil form of voodoo, is killed by the demons he invoked with his dark magic in *The Princess and the Frog*. Scar is devoured by the hyenas he allied with to kill Mufasa. It is not just death, but ghastly, painful deaths that serve as cosmic punishment for the injustice and harm the villains have caused.

On the other hand, characters who have lived a good life, marked by justice, caring, moderation, and honor, die with dignity. In the 2015 live-action *Cinderella*, "Ella's" mother passes peacefully in her home surrounded by family, but not before advising her daughter to "Have courage and be kind." In the same film, the King receives a terminal diagnosis stoically, reminding Prince Kit that death is the "Way of all flesh, boy." He too, expires tranquilly in bed. Ellie, in *Up*, dies in a more medicalized, but still quiet and peaceful, setting. Finally, Moana's grandmother Tala drifts off in a candlelit room surrounded by her loved ones, only to reappear as a glorious illuminated manta ray, guiding Moana on her great ocean journey.

In some Disney films, heroes are defined partly by their willingness to take risks that might result in death, as long as these risks are to protect or obtain good things that make human life worth living. Bambi's mother sacrificed herself to the deer hunter to save her son. *Mulan*, set mainly in fifteenth century China, tells the story of a girl who joins the Imperial Army in her ailing father's place, disguised as a man. Before the climactic battle scene, the soldiers were told to, "Prepare to fight. If we die, we die by honor." Mulan takes this to heart by charging alone, ahead of her own comrades, directly at the rushing Hun cavalry. She fires the last remaining cannon at a mound of mountain snow, creating an avalanche that buries the invaders.

Mulan's risk-taking was for a good cause: protecting her people from an invading army. The Chinese philosopher Confucius (551–479 BCE) taught that a righteous person should not choose to stay alive at the expense of virtue.[10] Mulan's respect for her father and sense of duty to her people and her ancestors are very much in line with Confucian teaching about living a good life. The Confucian good life requires developing and manifesting our moral capacities in the context of our interpersonal relationships, beginning with family (including ancestors) and then branching out to include more and more people as we develop and grow. For Confucius, every human being owes her life to her parents, ancestors, and society, so this is where moral obligation begins. A basic moral requirement is to cherish life as something of the highest value; without physical life, we could not manifest righteousness. But, recognizing that death is the way for all humans, Confucianism teaches that a dignified life includes the manner of death. If physical existence is an instrument to living a morally good life, then to preserve it at the expense of morality makes no sense. In Mulan's battlefield situation, she made the brave choice to put her mortal life at great risk to cultivate her higher nature. We can say the same for Bambi's mother.

A related ethical issue that Disney films address with regard to death is appropriate grief. Moving on after a painful loss is the major theme of *Up* and *Big Hero 6*. In *Up*, Carl's life stops when his wife Ellie dies. He sits alone, a bitter and reclusive old man, in the house they once shared, while the city grows around him. A relationship with a young explorer scout helps Carl move forward, symbolized by letting his floating house free, only to land at the exact spot, Paradise Falls, where Carl and Ellie had planned to travel before her death.

In *Big Hero 6*, Hiro's older brother is killed in an explosion set off by the movie's villain. Hiro openly scoffs at the idea that "People keep saying he's not really gone as long as we remember him. It still hurts." Instead of mourning openly and seeking emotional support, Hiro closes himself off from friends and relatives. He reprograms Tadashi's marshmallow-like healthcare robot, Baymax, into a fighting machine to seek revenge on Tadashi's killer. By the end of the film, Baymax has helped Hiro accept his loss. In exchange, Hiro reprograms the huggable robot for the role Tadashi envisioned: helping people. The moral arc of both Carl's and Hiro's characters involves learning to mourn, and to ultimately accept and move on from death of a loved one. Gusteau in *Ratatouille* put this Disney lesson best: "If you focus on what you left behind, you will never be able to see what lies ahead."

Disney films, on balance, show an awareness and respect for the cycle of human life. Perhaps that's why Disney reserves some of its worst deaths for evil characters who refuse to accept the fact of their own mortality. Mother Gothel in *Tangled* used the Healing Incantation – and, of course, Rapunzel's magical hair – to stop the aging process, to "make the clock reverse" and "change the Fates' design." She dies by falling, screaming, out of the tower where she had imprisoned Rapunzel, only to turn to dust as, wrapped in her heavy cloak, she visibly and audibly hits the ground – a rare "post-fall" image from Disney. Like Mother Gothel, The Queen in *Snow White*, who yearns to stay "the fairest in the land" regardless of time and age, also perishes from a fall off a cliff in a thunderstorm. What makes her death especially gruesome is the two vultures who look on with morbid interest, only to swoop toward her fallen body, eager for their next meal. And then there's Dr. Facilier: "No! I'm I am not ready at all! In fact, I got lots more plans! … Just a little more time!" In all of these examples, Disney illustrates the connection many philosophers maintain between courage, cowardice, and death.

I think we've all arrived at a very special place, eh? Spiritually? Ecumenically? Grammatically? – Captain Jack Sparrow

Disney films, especially the animated ones, have a reputation for being light and joyful, and many of them are. But the creative minds at the Disney studios explore themes that run the gamut from light to dark, and darkness includes death. The topic of death is addressed in so many different films in so many different ways that it is impossible to cover them all. But death is a part of life, so it's important to think about, even if only in the abstract. Disney and Pixar films are so rich and popular that we should use them to engage in difficult conversations about death and other subjects.[11] Lucretius's argument notwithstanding, it can be hard to think about our own mortality, and especially hard to think about losses we have suffered. But talking about death is a way into so many important questions about life. And as Grandmother Willow told Pocahontas, "Sometimes the right path is not the easiest one."

Notes

1. Cox, M., Garrett, E., and Graham, J. A. (2005). Death in Disney films: implications for children's understanding of death. *Omega: Journal of Death and Dying* 50: 267–280.
2. For a fascinating analysis of personal experiences that contributed to Walt Disney's interest in death, see Laderman, G. (2000). The Disney way of death. *Journal of the American Academy of Religion* 68: 27–46.
3. Plato, *Phaedo*, http://cscs.res.in/dataarchive/textfiles/textfile.2010-09-15.2713280635/file 78b-84b.
4. Epicurus, *Letter to Menoeceus*, http://classics.mit.edu/Epicurus/menoec.html
5. Deloria, B., Foehner, K., and Scinta, S., (ed.) (1999). Relativity, relatedness, and reality. In: *Spirit and Reason the Vine Deloria Reader*, vol. 34, 32–40. Golden, CO: Fulcrum Publishing.
6. Deloria, B., Foehner, K., and Scinta, S., (ed.) (1999). If you think about it, you will see that it is true, *Spirit and Reason: The Vine Deloria, Jr. Reader*, vol. 52: 40–62, Golden, CO: Fulcrum Publishing.
7. Aquinas, T. (1993). Essence and existence, In: *Selected Philosophical Writings*. (ed. T. McDermott), vol. 95: 90–114. Oxford: Oxford University Press.
8. Lucretius (1997). *On the Nature of the Universe: A New Verse Translation* (trans. S.R. Melville). 96–97. Oxford: Clarendon Press.
9. Feinberg, J. (1977). Harm and self-interest. In *Law, Morality and Society: Essays in Honour of H. L. A. Hart*. (ed. Hacker, P. M. S. and Raz, J.), 284–308. Oxford: Clarendon Press.
10. Doering, O. (2001). Euthanasia, and the meaning of death and dying: a confucian inspiration for today's medical ethics. *Formosa Medical Ethics Journal* 2: 48–66.
11. Tenzek, K. E. & Nickels, B. M. (2017). End-of-life in Disney and Pixar films: an opportunity for engaging in difficult conversation. *OMEGA: Journal of Death and Dying* EPub.

Liberty Square in the Shadow of Cinderella's Castle

Political Philosophy in Disney's Theme Parks

Timothy Dale and Joseph Foy

From humble beginnings as an animator, Walt Disney's vision for a world transformed by the power of his work was anything but modest. Disney's iconic characters have made an indelible mark on popular culture, and his ambitious branding and expansion into theme parks has also made significant impacts on marketing, engineering, and globalization. Walt Disney wanted to change the world by remaking it through his grand vision and ubiquitous influence. Beyond just being a brand, however, Disney was successful in realizing his global vision because he believed that ideas matter. Disney theme parks are explicitly driven by principles – of innovation, education, and the magic of engineered illusions. Below the surface, however, distinctly philosophical questions lie in wait. If we are free to choose our own path in life, why is Liberty Square in the shadow of Cinderella's Castle at the Magic Kingdom? If we should develop a global perspective, how is this fostered by a theme park featuring cultural caricatures? The underlying philosophical tensions in Disney's theme parks reflect those found in Disney's stories themselves: princesses who defy traditional structures while embracing hierarchy, characters who become authentic only through transformations, and a global perspective that is only gained through the cultural appropriation of particular characters.

Disney and Philosophy: Truth, Trust, and a Little Bit of Pixie Dust, First Edition.
Edited by Richard B. Davis.

We can gain a better understanding of these tensions by taking a tour of the underlying political ideas lurking inside the Epcot and Magic Kingdom theme parks.

"I Just Can't Wait to Be King": celebrating Equality and Hierarchy in the Magic Kingdom

Walt Disney is largely responsible for popularizing the "princess story" in American culture. In these stories a young female, usually from humble beginnings, encounters some form of hardship and emerges as royalty by the story's end. The characters involved, the structure of the stories, and the happy endings cause audiences to identify with the main character, and allow us all to dream of someday becoming royalty.

These stories are the centerpieces of the Disney collection and their flagship theme parks. Indeed, Cinderella's castle itself is at the heart of Disney's Magic Kingdom. The first of Disney's theme parks, the Magic Kingdom was intended to capture the magic and imagination of the Disney movies, and bring to life the settings of Disney stories. Even though visitors enter the park along a Main Street like that of any American town, there is no mistaking the fact that the park is ruled by Cinderella who lives in the castle at its center.

As visitors continue into the park, they enter the American Revolutionary era town of "Liberty Square." This path into Magic Kingdom brings into focus a tension in the core philosophy of the park and the stories themselves: Disney celebrates both the hierarchy of royalty and the equality of self-determination. For example, we can celebrate American independence from monarchic rule at *Liberty Tree Tavern* in Liberty Square by eating "Freedom Pasta with Sautéed Shrimp" or a "Declaration salad," while sitting in the shadow of a castle built to represent the elitism of monarchy. This is more than a simple irony. Philosophically speaking, a celebration of the American Revolution specifically rejects hierarchy and elitism. Dismantling the castle is what the Declaration (salad) does! A monarchy is what we have freedom (pasta) from!

A castle, on the other hand, is a symbol of royal privilege and social stratification. A castle protects the ruler and royal family from ordinary people who are not allowed to participate in political decisions. After all, the romantic attraction of being a princess is to be powerful, wealthy, and not having to serve others. Thus, the castle – in both theme park and story – pictures the princess' aspiration to elevate herself out of a miserable life. Although the Disney princess stories allow us to feel included by leading us to believe that anyone can become a princess, the appeal of the story, and what makes a princess special, is that not *everyone* can become one. Cinderella's castle at the center of Liberty Square is no less problematic than a princess with special privileges in a democracy. Regardless of how benevolent she is, the principles of freedom and democracy are incompatible with the principles of monarchy.

The philosopher John Locke, on whose work the Declaration of Independence and the American Revolution is based, argues in his *Second Treatise of Government*[1] that a society should only be ruled by the collection of people who live within it. He writes "when any number of men have, by the consent of every individual, made a community, they have thereby made that community one body, with a power to act as one body, which is only by the will and determination of the majority."[2] Locke suggests that government be based on laws created by this majority, and warns against a society containing rulers who are above these laws. He argues that the principles of consent and self-determination require that the state governs by "laws, promulgated and known to people, and not by extemporary decrees."[3]

The Lockean principles of self-government specifically count against the privileges of a princess, and indeed offer a stark alternative to it. Locke would be willing to acknowledge that we all want to be princesses, but that is precisely why we should prefer self-governance. That is, Lockean democracy promises that we all can be princesses in a political system which allows self-determination through a social contract. In this way, a liberal democracy produces a society in which we are all rulers.

Locke goes on to justify revolution when rulers exist who do not follow the will of the people. There can be no special rights, he argues, in a society attributed to rulers or families of those rulers.[4] In fact, liberal democratic principles require that any special rights that may exist be taken away from those enjoying these privileges. Perhaps we will begin the revolution as soon as we finish our Declaration salads.

If he were to visit the Magic Kingdom, Locke might be confused about how the values of monarchy could be so easily embraced in a liberal democracy committed to freedom and equality. The explanation for this, in part, has to do with producing stories for commercial purposes. In the Disney theme park, the celebration of freedom is manufactured so that it can be consumed. Similarly, stories glorifying monarchy are produced because people like to imagine that they are princesses (even in a democracy). Philosophical problems arise, however, because commercial appropriation risks these values existing merely for consumption. Consuming values this way can also lead to overlooking the ways in which these values are in tension with each other.

"I Can Show You the World": epcot as a Multicultural Experience

Epcot was the second of four parks built at the Walt Disney World Resort location in Florida. It features two separate sections: Future World, showcasing science and technology; and the World Showcase, designed to be a kind of permanent world's fair. While Liberty Square in the Magic Kingdom celebrates the independence of those who live in liberal democracies, the World Showcase at Epcot celebrates multiculturalism, and the possibility of appreciating and learning from a multitude of cultures. Adrift in a sea of culinary and cultural experiences, visitors to the World Showcase at Epcot can sample a taste of what it might be like to visit other countries. The purpose of an attraction is to provide visitors with a multicultural experience. But of course this raises the question: what *is* multiculturalism?

The term "multicultural" refers to the coexistence of groups with diverse traditions and backgrounds. Multiculturalism, the philosophical version of the term, proposes that the coexistence of these differences is good; it is a benefit to those living in a multicultural world to learn as much as possible about the different cultures existing within it. Politically speaking, a multicultural society is successful if there is sufficient common ground to sustain a conversation between cultures, and a recognition that each culture has a right to thrive. This is the basic idea behind the World Showcase at Epcot: provide each of the 11 countries represented space to demonstrate their culture and expose visitors to a slice of the experience.

So the cultural presentations at Epcot are consistent with some philosophical principles of multiculturalism. It's important for people to have choices. Multicultural citizenship means that we have a range of choices, and that we have the freedom to choose what is good for us.[5] Knowledge about these choices is also essential for being able to make a choice. Opportunities to expand our cultural horizons by encountering different art, food, and are essential for providing us with a menu of choices that define our own cultural identity. Epcot is designed in part to give visitors cultural experiences they may not otherwise have had; it broadens the range of multicultural options.

According to Seyla Benhabib, we need these experiences because our individual identities are formed in response to different cultural engagements.[6] Our culture and identity isn't something fixed; rather, this mixture of experiences helps us move away from the idea that diverse cultures cannot peacefully coexist. From a multicultural perspective, the World Showcase is useful for showing us that we can exist in the same space, and that people from different backgrounds can have productive encounters with each other. It is only through conversations across differences, says Benhabib, that we can transcend those differences. She writes that "most democratic dialogue is not about incommensurables, but about divergent and convergent beliefs, and very often we do not know how deep these divergences are, or how great their overlap may be, until we have engaged in conversation."[7]

Benhabib's arguments also suggest a potential problem for multiculturalism in the context of the World Showcase at Epcot. It reduces culture to an oversimplified experience. Recent philosophical arguments about multiculturalism, especially those advanced by Charles Taylor, have stressed the importance of recognition for the full inclusion of cultural differences within a society.[8] It is not enough to merely acknowledge that another culture exists. It must be allowed to exist on its own terms – with protections for its unique language and traditions. The commercialized experience of culture at Epcot reduces a country to a small set of restaurants, performances, and clothing. While this may afford a cursory knowledge of a culture for visitors, it works at cross purposes to multiculturalism if these experiences are portrayed as accurately representing the complexity inside these countries and cultures. Even with the best intentions, reducing a culture to a limited set of characteristics limits our celebration of that culture.

The multiculturalism of the World Showcase is restricted in an additional way. Only *eleven* countries are permanently represented (United States, Japan, Morocco, France, United Kingdom, Canada, Mexico, Norway, China, Germany, Italy).[9] From a multicultural perspective, this narrow list begs the question: why were some countries chosen and others passed over? In fact, it is a violation of the principles of multiculturalism to favor some cultures over others in terms of recognition or rights.[10] This may well be cost effective, but shouldn't we avoid privileging one culture over another, remaining as neutral as possible when representing different cultural modes of living.

"Look at This Stuff; Isn't It Neat?": disney and the Commodification of Political Values

In the 1971 dedication of Walt Disney World, Roy O. Disney attempted to capture the spirit and purpose of the Magic Kingdom with the following sentiment immortalized on the dedication plaque that rests at the base of the flagpole on Main Street:

> May Walt Disney World bring Joy and Inspiration and New Knowledge to all who come to this happy place ... a Magic Kingdom where the young at heart of all ages can laugh and play and learn – together.

More than a place for children to play and adults to relive their childhood, the Magic Kingdom was designed to be an experience that would both educate and inspire. In addition to grandeur and innovation, Disney's vision for its theme parks is to create realistic environments for capturing experiential truths (inspiration and new knowledge). But it's worth asking: Does this enrich our world, or merely offer the ultimate form of escapism? Denying the tensions between philosophical ideas like hierarchy and equality, multiculturalism and cultural appropriation, can be problematic when the parks are built for the purpose of celebrating and educating about the concepts they also obscure.

Perhaps the escapist nature of the entertainment underlying the Disney experience is best revealed in the way the term "Disney" is often used as a qualifier for a manufactured or insincere representation of something. Certain pejorative terms have even arisen within the cultural vernacular to encapsulate this very idea as it is tied to the Disney experience. Take for example the idea of "Disneyland Parent," a phrase commonly used in child custody situations to describe a "noncustodial parent who indulges his or her child with gifts and good times during visitation and leaves most or all disciplinary responsibilities to the other parent ... provid[ing] luxuries ... in an effort to gain or retain the child's affection."[11] In this use of the term, Disneyland Parenting is the "experience" of parenting without the challenges or struggles of what it means to actually raise a child.

Disney is not the only corporation to receive such treatment. Many of those large corporate entities that have become synonymous with

Western capitalist cultures (Coca Cola, Walmart, McDonald's, to name a few) are seen in a similar way. Political theorist and social critique Benjamin Barber even co-opted the McDonald's franchise term "McWorld" to describe this phenomenon.[12] According to Barber, the term "McWorld" signifies a global commodity market that blends and homogenizes cultures in a shallow manner for commercial purposes. Rapidly changing forces in technology and an interconnected global market, as well as transnational issues like environmental politics, shape the way that people think of themselves and relate to each other.

What makes Disney different here is that corporations like McDonald's, Coca-Cola, and Walmart generally don't pretend to be educating people or promoting specific values (apart from their brand). By contrast, Disney theme parks are intentionally designed to educate and promote values. That's their mission. Naturally, this forces us to ask whether Disney *is* promoting the values it seems to be advancing in its parks. It's also worth thinking about the type of education at work in the parks given their marketed representation of cultures and experiences. If it is possible to celebrate royalty and equality at the same time, shouldn't that tension at least be acknowledged in the celebrations? If cultures are to be represented in limited and simplistic ways, shouldn't that be reflected within the experience?

These questions are politically important in light of Benjamin Barber's observations about the impact of a globalized and marketed reality on our cultural identity. Barber suggests that there are two countervailing forces at work here – each operating in stark opposition to the other. First, there is the lived cultural identity so often experienced in opposition to the mass-marketed forms of culture. This experience of culture often leads to the type of tribalization that is at the root of ethno- and religious-nationalist movements. Indeed, it is so powerful that it tends to resist multiculturalism, as it dilutes the sense of belonging one feels for her own group and experience. If this is the response Disney's theme parks produce, they are actually working at a cross-purposes with their vision.

On the other side of the coin, there is "McWorld" – the marketing of cultures in shallow or blended ways to please consumers looking to purchase a commodified version of an actual experience. This might be what's occurring with Disney. We're receiving pre-packaged and commodified versions of "freedom" in the Magic Kingdom and "multiculturalism" at Epcot, resulting in our being mere spectators of these philosophical ideas. We leave the parks with the feeling of having acquired new knowledge, but without having to confront the complex, and sometimes conflictual, tensions that come with being deeply embedded in a cultural experience. If that is what's occurring at Disney theme parks, we are having a reinforcing educational experience rather than a transformative one.

The Disneyfication of experience is, therefore, similar to how Barber defines and describe the globalizing forces of "McWorld." It is a commercially packaged opportunity to tour the most palatable aspects of culture without having to confront the contentiousness of reality. Of course, the appeal of visiting a Disney park for many of us is to escape having to think deeply about reality. Philosophers, however, cannot help but question these things. But their purpose in doing so isn't to spoil the fun (philosophers also like to have fun!). It is but to remind us of the values underlying our commitments, and to reinforce the idea that the theme park experiences Disney wants us to have matter in the way they intend. We can experience culturally inspired foods, clothing, and art at Epcot, while acknowledging the deep experience and historical context underlying *true* cultural identity. We can experience freedom in Liberty Square in the shadow of a castle, while acknowledging the unacceptable political realities of hierarchy.

Is there a better alternative? For many philosophers, conversation around the nuances and tensions in the values we celebrate will alone suffice. Even better, we could add a "Vote for Cinderella" cake to the menu at *Liberty Tree Tavern*, rotate a few more countries into the World Showcase at Epcot, and display some dissenting voices when presenting political values in the Disney theme parks.

Notes

1. Locke, J. (1952). *Second Treatise of Government* (ed. T.P. Peardon). New York: Bobbs-Merrill.
2. Locke, *Second Treatise*, p. 55.
3. Ibid., p. 73.
4. Ibid., p. 95.
5. Kymlicka, W. (1996). *Multicultural Citizenship: A Liberal Theory of Minority Rights*. Oxford: Oxford University Press.
6. Benhabib, S. (2002). *The Claims of Culture*. Princeton: Princeton University Press.
7. Ibid., p. 136.

8. Taylor, C. (1994). The politics of recognition. In: *Multiculturalism* (ed. A. Gutmann), 25–74. Princeton, NJ: Princeton University Press.
9. There are up to nine additional spaces in the World Showcase for other countries, and several other countries have been rumored to be coming over the years with no development, including Brazil, Puerto Rico, Russia, Spain, and Israel.
10. Taylor, "The Politics of Recognition," p. 56.
11. "Disneyland Parent," https://definitions.uslegal.com/d/disneyland-parent (accessed July 19, 2018).
12. Barber, B.R. (1995). *Jihad vs. McWorld*. New York: Times Books.

Index

Disney and Philosophy: Truth, Trust, and a Little Bit of Pixie Dust, First Edition.
Edited by Richard B. Davis.

DISNEY AND PHILOSOPHY

The Blackwell Philosophy and Pop Culture Series

Series editor: William Irwin

A spoonful of sugar helps the medicine go down, and a healthy helping of popular culture clears the cobwebs from Kant. Philosophy has had a public relations problem for a few centuries now. This series aims to change that, showing that philosophy is relevant to your life – and not just for answering the big questions like "To be or not to be?" but for answering the little questions: "To watch or not to watch *South Park*?" Thinking deeply about TV, movies, and music doesn't make you a "complete idiot." In fact it might make you a philosopher, someone who believes the unexamined life is not worth living and the unexamined cartoon is not worth watching.

Already published in the series:

24 and Philosophy: The World According to Jack
Edited by Jennifer Hart Weed, Richard Brian Davis, and Ronald Weed

30 Rock and Philosophy: We Want to Go to There
Edited by J. Jeremy Wisnewski

Alice in Wonderland and Philosophy: Curiouser and Curiouser
Edited by Richard Brian Davis

Alien and Philosophy: I Infest, Therefore I Am
Edited by Jeffery A. Ewing and Kevin S. Decker

Arrested Development and Philosophy: They've Made a Huge Mistake
Edited by Kristopher G. Phillips and J. Jeremy Wisnewski

Avatar and Philosophy: Learning to See
Edited by George A. Dunn

The Avengers and Philosophy: Earth's Mightiest Thinkers
Edited by Mark D. White

Batman and Philosophy: The Dark Knight of the Soul
Edited by Mark D. White and Robert Arp

Battlestar Galactica and Philosophy: Knowledge Here Begins Out There
Edited by Jason T. Eberl

The Big Bang Theory and Philosophy: Rock, Paper, Scissors, Aristotle, Locke
Edited by Dean Kowalski

The Big Lebowski and Philosophy: Keeping Your Mind Limber with Abiding Wisdom
Edited by Peter S. Fosl

BioShock and Philosophy: Irrational Game, Rational Book
Edited by Luke Cuddy

Black Sabbath and Philosophy: Mastering Reality
Edited by William Irwin

The Ultimate Daily Show and Philosophy: More Moments of Zen, More Indecision Theory
Edited by Jason Holt

Disney and Philosophy: Truth, Trust, and a Little Bit of Pixie Dust
Edited by Richard B. Davis

Doctor Strange and Philosophy: The Other Book of Forbidden Knowledge
Edited by Mark D. White

Downton Abbey and Philosophy: The Truth Is Neither Here Nor There
Edited by Mark D. White

Dungeons and Dragons and Philosophy: Read and Gain Advantage on All Wisdom Checks
Edited by Christopher Robichaud

Ender's Game and Philosophy: The Logic Gate is Down
Edited by Kevin S. Decker

Family Guy and Philosophy: A Cure For The Petarded
Edited by J. Jeremy Wisnewski

Final Fantasy and Philosophy: The Ultimate Walkthrough
Edited by Jason P. Blahuta and Michel S. Beaulieu

Game of Thrones and Philosophy: Logic Cuts Deeper Than Swords
Edited by Henry Jacoby

The Girl with the Dragon Tattoo and Philosophy: Everything Is Fire
Edited by Eric Bronson

Green Lantern and Philosophy: No Evil Shall Escape this Book
Edited by Jane Dryden and Mark D. White

The Ultimate Harry Potter and Philosophy: Hogwarts for Muggles
Edited by Gregory Bassham

Heroes and Philosophy: Buy the Book, Save the World
Edited by David Kyle Johnson

The Hobbit and Philosophy: For When You've Lost Your Dwarves, Your Wizard, and Your Way
Edited by Gregory Bassham and Eric Bronson

House and Philosophy: Everybody Lies
Edited by Henry Jacoby

House of Cards and Philosophy: Underwood's Republic
Edited by J. Edward Hackett

The Hunger Games and Philosophy: A Critique of Pure Treason
Edited by George Dunn and Nicolas Michaud

Inception and Philosophy: Because It's Never Just a Dream
Edited by David Kyle Johnson

Iron Man and Philosophy: Facing the Stark Reality
Edited by Mark D. White

LEGO and Philosophy: Constructing Reality Brick By Brick
Edited by Roy T. Cook and Sondra Bacharach

The Ultimate Lost and Philosophy: Think Together, Die Alone
Edited by Sharon Kaye

Mad Men and Philosophy: Nothing Is as It Seems
Edited by James South and Rod Carveth

Metallica and Philosophy: A Crash Course in Brain Surgery
Edited by William Irwin

The Office and Philosophy: Scenes from the Unfinished Life
Edited by J. Jeremy Wisnewski

Sons of Anarchy and Philosophy: Brains Before Bullets
Edited by George A. Dunn and Jason T. Eberl

The Ultimate South Park and Philosophy: Respect My Philosophah!
Edited by Robert Arp and Kevin S. Decker

Spider-Man and Philosophy: The Web of Inquiry
Edited by Jonathan J. Sanford

The Ultimate Star Trek and Philosophy: The Search for Socrates
Edited by Jason T. Eberl and Kevin S. Decker

The Ultimate Star Wars and Philosophy: You Must Unlearn What You Have Learned
Edited by Jason T. Eberl and Kevin S. Decker

Superman and Philosophy: What Would the Man of Steel Do?
Edited by Mark D. White

Supernatural and Philosophy: Metaphysics and Monsters...for Idjits
Edited by Galen A. Foresman

Terminator and Philosophy: I'll Be Back, Therefore I Am
Edited by Richard Brown and Kevin S. Decker

True Blood and Philosophy: We Wanna Think Bad Things with You
Edited by George Dunn and Rebecca Housel

True Blood and Philosophy: We Wanna Think Bad Things with You, Expanded Edition
Edited by George Dunn and Rebecca Housel

True Detective and Philosophy: A Deeper Kind of Darkness
Edited by Jacob Graham and Tom Sparrow

Twilight and Philosophy: Vampires, Vegetarians, and the Pursuit of Immortality
Edited by Rebecca Housel and J. Jeremy Wisnewski

Veronica Mars and Philosophy: Investigating the Mysteries of Life (Which is a Bitch Until You Die)
Edited by George A. Dunn

The Walking Dead and Philosophy: Shotgun. Machete. Reason.
Edited by Christopher Robichaud

Watchmen and Philosophy: A Rorschach Test
Edited by Mark D. White

Westworld and Philosophy: If You Go Looking for the Truth, Get the Whole Thing
Edited by James B. South and Kimberly S. Engels

Wonder Woman and Philosophy: The Amazonian Mystique
Edited by Jacob M. Held

X-Men and Philosophy: Astonishing Insight and Uncanny Argument in the Mutant X-Verse
Edited by Rebecca Housel and J. Jeremy Wisnewski

DISNEY AND PHILOSOPHY

TRUTH, TRUST, AND A LITTLE BIT OF PIXIE DUST

Edited by

Richard B. Davis

WILEY Blackwell

This edition first published 2020

Registered Office(s)
John Wiley & Sons, Inc., 111 River Street, Hoboken, NJ 07030, USA
John Wiley & Sons Ltd, The Atrium, Southern Gate, Chichester, West Sussex, PO19 8SQ, UK

Editorial Office
111 River Street, Hoboken, NJ 07030, USA

For details of our global editorial offices, customer services, and more information about Wiley products visit us at www.wiley.com.

Wiley also publishes its books in a variety of electronic formats and by print-on-demand. Some content that appears in standard print versions of this book may not be available in other formats.

Library of Congress Cataloging-in-Publication Data

Names: Davis, Richard Brian, 1963– editor. | Irwin, William, 1970– editor.
Title: Disney and philosophy : truth, trust, and a little bit of pixie dust / edited by Richard B Davis, William Irwin.
Description: Hoboken, NJ : Wiley-Blackwell, 2020. | Series: The Blackwell philosophy and pop culture series | Includes bibliographical references and index.
Identifiers: LCCN 2019030287 (print) | LCCN 2019030288 (ebook) | ISBN 9781119538318 (paperback) | ISBN 9781119538288 (adobe pdf) | ISBN 9781119538356 (epub)
Subjects: LCSH: Walt Disney Company. | Animated films–United States–History and criticism. | Disney characters–Philosophy.
Classification: LCC PN1999.W27 D54 2020 (print) | LCC PN1999.W27 (ebook) | DDC 384/.80979494–dc23
LC record available at https://lccn.loc.gov/2019030287
LC ebook record available at https://lccn.loc.gov/2019030288

Cover Design: Wiley
Cover Images: © kostins/Shutterstock; © passion artist/Shutterstock

Set in 10.5/13pt Sabon by SPi Global, Pondicherry, India

Printed in the United States of America

V42346096-BFF3-4B6A-9B30-18B9E8F51512_110819

BRANDYWINE

WORKBOOK

IN

AMERICAN HISTORY

Volume I **To 1877**

Revised By

Lena Boyd-Brown, Howard Jones, and
Louis Williams,
Prairie View A & M University;

Merline Pitre,
Texas Southern University

BRANDYWINE PRESS

Cover Photo: George Washington Carver in his laboratory. *(Courtesy, Tuskegee Institute)*

ISBN 1-881089-35-5 (Volume II)

2nd Printing

Telephone Orders: 1-800-345-1776

Printed in the United States of America

Contents

Succeeding in History Courses

by John McClymer

STUDYING HISTORY AND STUDYING FOR EXAMS

The instructor who designed this course hopes you will take advantage of the opportunity to learn about the American past. Your own objectives in taking the course may be somewhat different. You may be taking it because it fulfills some requirement for graduation or because it fits into your schedule or, perish the thought, because it seems less objectionable than the alternative you could be taking.

In a better world, these differences between your objectives and those of the course would not matter. The studying you do to perform well on exams and papers would involve your learning a fair amount of history. And so your grade would certify that you had indeed left the course with a more informed and thoughtful understanding of the American past than you had when you entered it. Unhappily, in the world we must actually live in, the connection between studying history and studying for exams in history is not necessarily so clear or straightforward.

The hard fact is that many students manage to prepare themselves for mid-terms and finals without permanently adding to their understanding. There they sit, yellow hi-liting pens in hand, plodding through the assigned chapters. Grim-faced, they underline every declarative sentence in sight. Then they trace and retrace their tracks trying to commit every yellowed fact to memory. As the time of the test draws near, they choke back that first faint feeling of panic by trying to guess the likeliest question. The instructor is never, they say to themselves, going to ask us to identify George Washington. But what about Silas Deane? And Pinckney? No, wait. There were TWO Pinckneys! That means there is almost certainly going to be a question about ONE of them. So it is that some students devote more energy to Thomas and Charles Cotesworth Pinckney than they do to George Washington. By such tactics they may get ready for the exam, but sabotage their chance of gaining any insight into American history.

Life does afford worse tragedies. This one, however, is remediable. And this appendix can help. It is designed to help you do well in the course, and to help you learn some history. It is, in fact, dedicated to the proposition that the easiest and most satisfying way to succeed in a history course is to learn some history. It makes very little sense, after all is said and done, to spend your time trying to keep the Pinckneys straight or running down a fact or two about Silas Deane. What will it profit you? You may pick up a few points on the short answer section of the exam, but those few points are a small reward for hours of studying. And, in the meantime, your essay on Washington as a political leader was distinctly mediocre. Clearly something is wrong.

That something is that studying for exams is a poor way of learning history. On the other hand, studying history is an excellent way of preparing for exams. If you had, for example, thought about American relations with France during John Adams' presidency, you would very probably remember who Charles C. Pinckney was. And you would scarcely have had to memorize anything.

The object of this essay is to persuade you to make some changes in the way you study. The first is to conserve your yellow pens. All that hiliting simply lowers the resale value of the book. If you underline everything you read, you will wind up with a book of underlinings. There may be some psychological comfort in that. All of that yellow does provide visible evidence that you read the material. Unfortunately, it will not leave you with a useful guide to what to review. You have hi-lited too much.

A second drawback follows from the first. You have created a democracy of facts. All names, dates, and events are equally yellow. The Pinckneys and Silas Deane, in other words, have just become as noteworthy as George Washington or John Adams. You need, more than anything else, some way of determining what is important.

The next step may prove harder. You will have to give up trying to learn history by rote. A certain amount of memorizing may be unavoidable in a survey course, but ultimately it is the enemy of understanding. That is because many people use it as an alternative to thinking. Have you ever wished there were a better way? Well, there is. If you understand what Lincoln had hoped to accomplish with the Emancipation Proclamation, for example, you will not need to memorize its provisions. You will know why it did not promise freedom to any of the slaves in states (like Maryland or Missouri) which remained loyal to the Union. You will know why the Proclamation did not go into effect until one hundred days after it was issued. You will not, in short, stumble over a question like: "Whom did the Emancipation Proclamation emancipate?"

Facts are by no means unimportant. It is essential to have something to think about. But it is generally more fun to pay attention to ideas. Lincoln, to pursue this example, was interested above all else in restoring the Union. He was perfectly willing, he said, to keep slavery if that would accomplish his purpose; he was equally willing to abolish slavery if that would do the trick. So there is no mystery that in the Emancipation Proclamation he gave the states of the Confederacy one hundred days to return to the Union on pain of losing their slaves if they did not. The same reason explains why the Proclamation did not apply to slave states still in the Union.

If you take care of the ideas, the facts will assemble themselves. There are two reasons for this happy state of affairs. One has to do with the way in which textbooks are written and courses taught. The other has to do with the way people learn.

No historian, including the authors of the text and your instructor, pretends that history is the story of everything that ever happened. Obviously, many things happened for which there are no surviving records. More importantly, scholars use the records that have survived in a highly selective way. Even though they are always interested in finding new information, and in finding new ways of using information already known, each individual work of history—be it an article, a doctoral dissertation, a monograph, a textbook, a course of lectures—represents hundreds and thousands of choices about what to include and what to omit. Much more is known, for example, about the signers of the Declaration of Independence than you will read in any textbook. What you actually encounter in this course, as a result, is here because the text authors or your teacher decided for some reason to include it. Usually the reason is that this particular bit of information helps explain or illustrate some pattern of behavior or thought. The moral for you should be clear. Focus on these patterns. They are what you should be thinking about.

If you do, learning theorists have some good news for you. They have found that while it is difficult for the average person to recall disconnected bits of data (for example, which Pinckney was an emissary to France during the XYZ affair), it is comparatively easy to remember details of coherent stories. This is not a very startling finding. Details make sense once you see how they fit together. Let us return to the example of the Emancipation Proclamation. Lincoln's actions followed from: 1) his political priorities in which the integrity of the Union outranked achieving peace or ending slavery, 2) his analysis of the course of the war, and, 3) his perception of the choices open to him. Had Lincoln valued peace or ending slavery more highly than the Union, had easy victory or actual defeat seemed near at hand, had other inducements to the states of Confederacy to return to the Union seemed more promising, he would have acted differently. Once Lincoln's perception of the situation becomes clear to you, you will have little, if any, difficulty remembering what he did.

Neither compulsive underlining nor prodigious memorization will help you to understand these patterns. What will? We can rephrase the question: What does it mean to read and listen intelligently? For most of us, reading and listening are passive forms of behavior. We sit and wait to be told. Someone else, we expect, will provide the answers. Worse, we expect someone else will provide the questions. And, of course, they do. For our part, we limit ourselves to hi-liting and jotting notes. At best, this situation leaves us with a more or less adequate record of what someone else thinks we should know.

Most of what passes for studying involves not a conscientious effort to wrestle with the subject, but a determined effort to be prepared to answer likely questions. That is why we pay more heed to Silas Deane than to George Washington. It is why studying for exams is such a poor way to learn history. And, its chief drawback perhaps from your point of view, it is usually a recipe for earning a mediocre grade.

Letting your teacher or the authors of the text do your thinking for you also leads to tedium. The simple truth is that passivity is boring. Yet we rarely blame ourselves for being bored. It can not be our own fault. We are only "taking" the course. Someone else is "giving" it, and so we look to the instructor to liven things up a bit. Maybe some audio-visuals or a bit of humor, we think, would make the course less dreary. These hopes are misplaced for, while humor is a blessed thing and audio-visuals have their place, it is the nitty-gritty of the course that should interest us.

Boredom is almost always a self-inflicted wound. Students are bored because they expect the instructor to be interesting when it is they who must themselves take an interest. Teacher and students are equally responsible for the success of a course. Most of the students in American history courses will live out the rest of their lives in the United States. Their lives will be affected for both good and ill by what has happened in the American past. It follows that the simple desire to make sense of their own lives should lead them to take an interest in this course.

Taking an interest involves learning to read and listen actively. Intellectual activity begins with questions—Your own questions directed, in the first instance, to yourself and then to your teacher. Why is it, you might wonder, that the United States is the only industrialized country without a comprehensive national system of health care? Why did slavery last so long in the American South? Why did the Founding Fathers establish a republic? And why did a party system develop even though the founders were bitterly opposed to political parties? Why, for that matter, were they so set against parties in the first place?

You will not always find satisfactory answers. But you will have started to think about the meaning of the American past. And when you do, something quite desirable happens to all of those facts. They will take on life and become evidence, clues to the answers you are seeking. The questions, that is, will give you a rational basis for deciding which facts are important. And George Washington will finally receive his well-deserved priority over the Pinckneys.

All of this leads directly to the question of how you should study for this course. It is a truism that students do poorly when they are ill-prepared. But we too easily assume that the sole reason why we are sometimes ill-prepared is because we did not spend enough time getting ready. This is a half-truth, and a dangerous one. It ignores the critical fact that we often use the time we spend reviewing very inefficiently. And, since there is often no practical way of increasing the time we have to review (there being, after all, only so many working hours in the day), it makes far more sense to use the time we do have effectively instead of moaning about how we should have studied more.

How do you get ready for an exam? Do you get out your textbook and notes and pour over them again and again until the time runs out or the sheer boredom of it all crushes your good intentions? If so, then you have lots of company—a consolation of sorts. There is, on the other hand, a better way.

Find a quiet and comfortable spot (something not always easy to do in a dormitory). Bring along a blank pad and something to write with. Then jot down, just as they occur to you, whatever items you can remember about the course. Do not rush yourself. And do not try, at this stage, to put things in order. Just sit there and scribble down whatever pops into your mind. After a while you will have quite a large and varied mix of names, ideas, dates and events. Then see how much of this you can put together. There is no need to write out whole sentences or paragraphs. An arrow or a word or two will frequently be enough. You are not, after all, going to hand these scribbles in. You are just collecting your thoughts. Do not be concerned if this process seems to be taking up some of the limited time you have to study. It will prove to be time well spent.

Now look over what you have written. Where are the gaps? You will find that you know a fair bit about the material just from your previous reading of the text and from listening in class. But some topics will still be obscure. You may, for example, pretty well understand why Polk declared war on Mexico, but you may feel less sure about his negotiations with Great Britain over Oregon. All right. Now you know what you should be studying. There is no reason for you to go over the war with Mexico. Why study what you already know. And here is the nub of the matter, for an intelligent review is one that focuses on what you need to refresh your mind about.

You will doubtless have noticed that this strategy presupposes that you have read the textbook and taken good notes in class. Just what, you might wonder, are good notes? Many students think that the closer they come to transcribing the instructor's every word the better their notes are. They are mistaken. There are several reasons why. Unless your shorthand is topnotch, you will not succeed. Instead you will be frantically scrambling to catch up. In the process you will not only miss some of what is said, but you will pay attention to scarcely any of the lecture. At the end of class you will have: 1) a sore hand; 2) a great deal of barely legible notes; and 3) little if any idea of what the class was about.

Another reason not to attempt to transcribe lectures (taping them, by the way, is usually a poor idea) is that you will spend much of your time taking down information you either already know or can easily find in the textbook. How often do you need to see the fact that Jefferson Davis was the president of the Confederacy? A sensible person will decide once is enough.

The most important reason not to take down everything is that it prevents you from doing what you ought to be doing during class, listening intelligently. Your instructor is not simply transmitting information during a lecture but is also seeking to explain the hows and whys of the American past. It is these explanations you should be listening for, and your notes should focus on them. It is much easier to do this if you have read the relevant textbook chapters first. That way you will already know much of the factual information. And you will have, one hopes, some questions already in your mind. You will have, that is, something to listen for. And you can take notes sensibly. You can fill in explanations of points that had puzzled you, jot down unfamiliar facts, and devote most of your time to listening instead of writing. Your hand will not be sore; you will know what the class was about; and your notes will complement rather than duplicate what you already knew.

So far we have dealt mainly with the mechanics of studying—taking notes, reviewing for exams, and the like. Valuable as knowing the mechanics can be, and in terms of your grade they can be very valuable indeed, the real secret to studying history is learning how to think historically. History is both a body of knowledge about the past and a way of thinking about the human condition. You are probably familiar with the first of these two aspects of the subject. History is knowing about the Revolution, the Civil War, and so on. It is knowing, that is, that they happened, when they happened, and how they happened. It is also having some explanation of why they happened as they did, and of the differences their happening made. All of that is undoubtedly perfectly obvious to you. It may, in fact, seem to include the sum and substance of history. It does not.

History is also a way of thinking. It rests on the assumption that you understand what something is by finding out how it came to be that way. This is an assumption which, consciously or not, you share. When you ask friends how they are doing, for example, you are really asking what has happened to them since you last met. You are asking about the past—the recent past to be sure—but the past nonetheless. You accept, that is, the axiom that the past has consequences for the present and the future. If your roommate has just failed an organic chemistry final, to use a sad but not uncommon occurrence, you both know what that will mean for her chances of getting into medical school.

You also know, if you think about it for a minute, that the political beliefs of the Founding Fathers still matter. They matter not only because their beliefs continue to influence our own but also because we continue to use them as the standard against which we measure present-day political figures. You can even appreciate that the child-rearing practices of the Puritans are worth knowing about—not of course because they have been passed down unchanged from the seventeenth century nor because they provide a model for you in raising your own family, but because we can not understand changing cultural realities or social practices unless we first have a clear idea of what they were once like. Change, in short, is incomprehensible if we do not have a point of reference from which to measure it. And history alone can provide us with such a fixed point.

Learning to think historically is a simple necessity if we hope to make sense of the world around us. Fortunately, it involves nothing more than learning to employ in a disciplined way the same patterns of thought we already use on a daily basis. That your roommate failed organic chemistry is a historical fact just as Lincoln's victory in the presidential election of 1860 is. How your roommate failed, and how Lincoln won, can also be determined factually, to some degree. You can, that is, discover which questions your roommate got wrong, just as you can find out which states Lincoln carried. You can even begin to assemble facts which will help explain why your roommate missed those particular questions and why Lincoln won those particular states. With regard to your roommate, you might recall that she cut a number of classes. You could hypothesize that some of the material covered in those classes was on the exam. You might recall that your roommate had a political science paper to finish the week before the exam. Perhaps that kept her from studying chemistry thoroughly.

Similarly you could determine with some accuracy which voting blocs went for Lincoln. You could then analyze the campaign issues and speculate about how those constituencies lined up on those issues. In both cases you would be trying to marshall the facts so that they would support some interpretation. Clearly, if you could know all of the facts, and if there were only one possible explanation for them, your interpretation would be true in the same way that the facts themselves are true. You could say: it happened this way and no other.

Unfortunately, life is not so amenable to explanation. You will never have all the facts, and no explanation will ever be the only one possible. Consider your roommate's "F" in organic. You know which questions were missed. But the questions on the exam could have been different. Then your roommate's grade would, possibly, have also been different. So knowing which questions your roommate lost points on is not enough. You would also have to know why these particular questions, and not others, were on the test in the first place. Consider too that the test scores were probably "curved." A more forgiving curve might have allowed your roommate to pass. But to know why the curve was the way it was you would have to know why the other raw scores were the way they were. Your roommate's raw score, the actual points lost on particular questions, in other words, is only half the story. That score could, presumably, have become an "A" if other students in the course had done even worse than your roommate. There is no need to pursue the point any farther. It is clear that you could never be sure you knew all of the relevant facts. And if this be true for your roommate's "F", how much more obviously true it must be for Lincoln's election. There were millions of voters. Who could know why they all voted as they did?

Despite all of this you may feel—and quite sensibly—that your roommate's "F" is hardly an impenetrable enigma. You may not know everything about it, but you know enough. You can offer an explanation that fits the facts you do know and is congruent with what you know of your roommate's study habits, general intelligence, and so forth. What you have is an interpretation. So too with Lincoln's election. People may have had reasons for voting as they did that you will never know, but you can supply enough reasons to explain why he won. You can explain, that is, what is known, and your view is compatible with what is known about American elections during that period.

You can perhaps already see how to define a convincing interpretation. It is one that provides that simplest sensible account of why something happened. The goal of historical inquiry is interpretation. And while, as we have seen, interpretation is not synonymous with truth, it is something more than mere opinion.

Anyone can have an opinion. People claim that have a right to have opinions about anything and everything (some even seem to feel it is their duty to have an opinion about everything). But you have to earn the right to offer an interpretation because an interpretation is a thoughtful explanation based on a careful assessment of evidence. It follows that when you find scholars disagreeing over how to interpret the American Revolution, say, as Professors McDonald and Genovese do in one of their debates, you ought not to conclude that their dispute is "just a matter of opinion" or that the truth probably lies somewhere in the middle (an old saw that should be permanently retired) or that one opinion (yours included) is just as good as another. Rather you need to ask: how well do these interpretations accord with what I know about the Revolution? How much sense can I make of what happened before and after it by using one or another of these explanations? The debates, in short, are an invitation to you to think about the meaning of American history. They should prompt you to struggle with the issues in your own mind and to come up with your own interpretation.

You may feel somewhat hesitant about putting your own interpretation forward, particularly if it differs markedly from those offered by your instructor or the authors of the text. And, within limits, you should be hesitant. A certain intellectual modesty is becoming in a beginning student. But you have read the material; you have listened intelligently in class; and you have thought about the issues. So you have the right to a view of your own. Teaching is not indoctrination. The object of the course is not to tell you what to think. The goal is to help you learn to think for yourself. You are therefore entitled to disagree.

When presenting your own interpretation, whether or not it agrees with one you have already encountered, you should always explain clearly how you reached that particular conclusion. This means explaining what evidence you found most important; it means explaining why that evidence struck you as important; and it means explaining the logic of your position. If you can do these three things, then you need not fear presenting your own ideas.

This appendix has an additional feature designed to help you think about how historical interpretations are developed and tested. This is a section on how to read the McDonald-Genovese debates. You will quickly realize, as you read the debates, that McDonald and Genovese rarely disagree over the facts of American history. They disagree over which facts are important and over how they should be interpreted. This section contains suggested exercises you can do on your own, or which your instructor can assign, that will enable you to read the debates more critically.

It is now time to see how these general considerations about studying history apply to specific tasks you will have to undertake in this course. We will start with how to take midterm and final examinations.

HOW TO TAKE EXAMS

In the best of all possible worlds examinations would hold no terrors. You would be so well prepared that no question, no matter how tricky or obscure, could shake your serene confidence. Unfortunately, the real world normally finds the average student in a different situation. Somehow it seems one's preparation is always less than complete. And so one approaches exams with some anxiety. "Of course," one says to oneself, "I should have studied more. But I did not. Now what?" This section can not tell you how to get A's without studying, but it can suggest some practical steps which can help you earn the highest grade compatible with what you do know.

The first step is to look over the entire exam before you start answering any of it. It is impossible to budget your time sensibly until you know what the whole exam looks like. And if you fail to allow enough time for each question, two things—both bad—are likely to happen. The first is that you may have to leave some questions out, including perhaps some you might have answered very effectively. How often have you muttered: "I really knew that one!"? The other unhappy consequence is that you may have to rush through the last part of the exam. Again, there may be questions you could have answered very well if you had had more time.

How do you budget your time effectively? The idea, after all, is to make sure that you have enough time to answer fully all the questions you do know. So the best plan is also the simplest. Answer those questions first. It may feel a bit odd at first answering question #7 before #4, but you will soon enough get used to it. And you will find that, if you still run out of time, you at least have the satisfaction of knowing you are rushing through or leaving out questions you could not have answered very well anyway. You will, in other words, have guaranteed that you will receive the maximum credit for what you do know.

There is another advantage to answering questions in the order of your knowledge instead of in the order asked. Most students are at least a little tense before an exam. If you answer the first several questions well, that tension will likely go away. As you relax, you will find it easier to remember names, dates, and other bits of information. Contrariwise, if you get off to a shaky start, that simple case of pre-exam jitters can become full-scale panic. Should that happen, you may have trouble remembering your own phone number, and your chances of recalling those facts which are just on the tip of your tongue will shrink to the vanishing point. Obviously, it is very important to get off to a good start. So do not trust to luck. Do not just hope the first couple of questions are easy. You can make sure you get off on the right foot by answering first whatever questions you are sure of.

Let us suppose you have gotten through everything you think you know on the exam and you still have some time left. What should you do? You can now try to pick up a few extra points with some judicious guessing. There is not much point to trying to guess with essay questions. In all probability you will write something so vague that you will not get any credit for it anyway. Rather you should try to score on the short-answer section. Some types of questions were made for shrewd guesswork. Matching columns are ideal. A process of elimination will often tell you what the answer has to be. Multiple choice questions are almost as good. Here too you can eliminate some of the possibilities. Most teachers feel obligated to give you a choice of four or five possible answers, but find it hard to come up with more than three that are plausible. So you can normally count on being able to recognize the one or two that are just there as padding.

Once you have narrowed the choices down to two or three, you are ready to make your educated guess. There are three rules. 1) Always play your hunches, however vague. Your hunch is based on something you heard or read even if you can not remember what it is. So go with it. 2) Do not take your time. If you can not think of the answer, just pick one and have done with it. 3) Try to avoid changing answers. There are a number of studies showing that you are more likely to change a right answer than to correct a wrong one.

Identifications are the type of short-answer question most resistant to guesswork. Unless you have a fairly strong hunch about the answer, you should leave this sort of question blank. The reason is that while it is true that an incorrect answer will cost you no more points than leaving the question out altogether, it is also true that an incorrect answer says something about the depths of your ignorance which a blank space does not. You want the exam as a whole to convey what you do know. Supplying a mass of misinformation usually creates a presumption that you do not know what you are talking about even on those sections of the exam when you really do. So be careful about wild guesses. They are almost sure to do more harm than good.

These suggestions are not substitutes for studying. They may, however, help you get the most out of what you know. They may, that is, spell the difference between a mediocre grade and a good one.

HOW TO WRITE BOOK REVIEWS

One goal of book reviews is to set forth clearly and succinctly who (if anyone) would benefit from reading the work in question. It follows that a good review indicates the scope of the book, identifies its point of view, summarizes its main conclusions, evaluates its use of evidence, and—where possible—compares the book with others on the subject.

It is highly likely that you have written book reviews in high school or in other college courses so it is important that you do not approach this kind of assignment with a false sense of security. It sounds easy, after all, to write a five-hundred-or-so word essay. And you have written lots of other reviews. But did those other reviews focus clearly on the questions a good review must address? If they did not, your previous experience is not going to prove especially helpful. It may even prove something of a handicap. You may have developed some bad habits.

Easily the worst habit is that of summarizing not the book's argument but its contents. Let us suppose you are reviewing a biography of George Washington. The temptation is to write about Washington rather than about the book. This is a sure path to disaster. Washington had, to put it mildly, an eventful career. You are certainly not going to do it justice in a few paragraphs. And you are not, in all probability, going to find that much that is fresh or interesting to say about him. Meanwhile you have ignored your primary responsibility which is to tell the reader whether this biography has anything fresh or interesting to say.

So you need to remind yourself as forcefully as possible that your job is to review the book and not the subject of the book. Does the book focus narrowly on Washington or does it also go into the general history of America during those years? Is the author sympathetic to Washington, tending to see things Washington's way? Does the writer attempt to psychoanalyze Washington or stick to political and military questions? Is there a firm command of the available evidence (this requires you, alas, to read the footnotes)? And, last but not least, does the author have something new to say about Washington and his times? If so, how well documented is this new interpretation?

It is less important to evaluate how well the author writes. While it is hard to imagine a poorly written novel that is still worth reading, it is common enough (unhappily) for important historical works to be written in a plodding fashion. So you should comment on the quality of the author's prose, but you should generally not make that an important part of your overall evaluation unless it is so good or so awful that it makes reading the work sheer bliss or unrelieved torture.

You should generally not comment on whether or not you enjoyed the book. That is undoubtedly an important consideration for you, but it is of little interest to anyone else. There are some occasions when you need to suffer in silence. This is one of them.

HOW TO SELECT A TERM PAPER TOPIC

Doing research, as you may already have had occasion to learn, is hard work. Worse yet, it is often boring. Typically it involves long periods of going through material that is not what you were looking for and is not particularly interesting. It also involves taking detailed and careful notes, many of which you will never use. These are the dues you must pay if you are ever to earn the excitement which comes when you finally find that missing piece of evidence and make sense of things.

Not everything about doing research is boring. Aside from the indescribable sensation of actually finding out what you wanted to know, there are also occasional happy accidents where you stumble across something which, while not relevant to your research, nonetheless pricks your imagination. Many a historian studying an old political campaign has read up on the pennant races or fashions or radio listings for that year. These are, as one scholar put it, oases in the desert of historical evidence. But, as he quickly added, no one crosses the desert just to get to the oasis. The truth of the matter is that you have to have a good reason for getting to the other side. This means a topic you are genuinely interested in.

The point cannot be overemphasized. If you have a question you really want to answer, you will find it much easier to endure the tedium of turning all those pages. You will have a motive for taking good notes and for keeping your facts straight. If you are not truly interested in your topic, on the other hand, you may be in trouble. You are going to be constantly tempted to take short-cuts. And even if you resist temptation, you are going to find it hard to think seriously about what you do find.

So the topic has to interest you. That, you may be thinking, is easy to say. But what if your interest in American history is less than compelling? What if, perish the thought, you do not give two figs about the whole American past? Are you then going to be stuck with some topic you could care little about? The answer is "No". "No," that is, unless it turns out that you have no curiosity about anything at all; and, if that is the case, you are probably dead already or nearly so. Anything that can be examined chronologically is fair game for the historian. There are histories of sports and of sciences, of sexual practices and jokes about them, of work and of recreation. It is odd, to say the least, that students so often choose to write of war, politics, and diplomacy even when their real interests lie elsewhere. If you use your imagination, you should be able to find a topic which you are genuinely interested in and which your teacher agrees merits serious study. This being true, you have no one to blame but yourself if you wind up writing on some question you are not passionately concerned with answering.

Once you have such a topic you need to find ways of defining it so that you can write an intelligent essay. "The Automobile in American Life" could well serve as the subject for a very long book. It is not going to work as a subject for a term paper, and for two compelling reasons. First, you could not possibly research so vast a topic in the time you have to work with. Second, your paper, however long, is not going to be of book length—in fact it is not likely to exceed 5,000 words. So you would be stuck with trying to compress an immense amount of information into a brief essay. The final product will be a disaster.

You need to focus on some aspect of the general topic which can be intelligently treated in the space and time you have to work with. Students usually look at this problem backwards. They complain about how long their papers have to be. They should complain about how short they have to be. Space is a luxury you normally can not afford. If you have done a fair amount of research on an interesting topic, your problem is going to be one of finding a way of getting all you have to say into your paper. Writing consists of choices about what you want to say. And if you have done your work properly, the hard choices involve deciding what to leave out.

"Fair enough," you may be thinking, "but I do not want to get stuck researching some minute bit of trivia, the 'gear shift level from 1940 to 1953,' for example. I want to study the automobile in American life." Here we come to the heart of the matter. Your topic must be narrowly defined so that you can do it justice, but it must also throw some light on the broad question that interested you in the first place. This is easier said than done, but it can be done. The trick is to decide just what it is about your topic—cars in this instance—that really interests you. Cars are means of transportation, of course, but they are also examples of technology, status symbols, and much else besides. Because of the automobile, cities and suburbs are designed in ways very different from how they were when people traveled by trolley or train. Because of the automobile, even teenage dating patterns are what they are. Having a driver's license, and regular access to a car, has become a crucial part of growing up.

The point is that you have to think about your topic and then decide what aspect of it to examine. If you wind up doing a treatise on changing methods of changing tires, you have only yourself to blame. You could have been studying sex and sexism in automobile advertising.

HOW TO LOCATE MATERIAL

Once you have worked up an interesting and practical topic for your term paper, you are ready to begin your research. For many students this means ambling over to the library and poking around in the card catalog. This may not be the best way to begin because the librarians who catalog the library's holdings, while skilled professionals, cannot possibly anticipate the needs of every individual researcher. So they catalog books by their main subject headings and then include obvious cross-references. Much of what you need, on the other hand, may not be obvious. So, for example, if you are interested in the causes of the Civil War, you will have no trouble finding a title like Kenneth Stampp's *And The War Came* listed under "U.S. History, Civil War." But will you find Roy Nichol's *Disruption of the American Democracy*? You may not.

The point is that there may be a number of important works in your library you will not be able to find if you start by checking the card catalog. What should you do instead? The first thing is to locate the *Harvard Guide To American History*. This is an invaluable tool. It will tell you the best (in the editors' opinion) books and articles on your subject. For each title prepare a separate card listing full bibliographic specifics (i.e., the author's full name, the complete title including subtitle, the place of publication, the edition, and if a journal article the volume and issue numbers). You will need all of this information.

Now you have the beginnings of a decent bibliography. Your next step should be to introduce yourself to the research librarian. This person's specialty is helping people look for information. Yet many students never consult with a librarian. Do not pass up an opportunity to make your work easier! Ask your research librarian to help. Often he can point you to more specialized bibliographical guides, can show you where to learn of the most recent books and articles, and can help you refine your topic by indicating what aspects are easiest to get information on.

You now have a reasonably extensive set of cards. And you can now safely consult the card catalog to see which of these titles your library has. Prepare yourself for some disappointments. Even good undergraduate libraries will not have everything you need. They will have some (unless your library is very weak or your topic very esoteric). Virtually all college libraries participate in the inter-library loan system. This system, which the library staff will gladly explain to you, will permit you to get virtually any title you could wish for. The only catch is that you must give the library enough lead time. For books and articles which are not especially rare this normally means one to three weeks.

HOW TO TAKE NOTES

As you sift through the material you have found you will need to take careful notes. As you do, you should write down each piece of information which you believe might prove relevant on a notecard. You also will need to specify the full source for each piece of information.

If you follow these two bits of advice, you will save yourself much time and trouble. Finding information the first time, in your sources, is trouble enough. You do not want to have to find it all over again when you sit down to write your paper. But this is often just what students have to do because they discover that they did not bother to write down some bit of data (which, perhaps, seemed only marginally important at the time) or because they took all of their notes on loose leaf paper and now must search through every page to find this one fact. It is far easier, over the long run, to have a separate card for each piece, or closely related pieces, of information. Tell yourself that you are the last of the big time spenders and can afford to use up index cards as though they were blank pieces of paper. After all, that is what they are.

The general rule is that you should take extra pains when compiling your research notes so that the actual writing will be as trouble-free as possible. It follows from this that you should take lots of notes. Do not try to determine in advance whether or not you are going to use a particular bit of data. Always give yourself the benefit of the doubt. Similarly, do not try to decide in advance whether you will quote the source exactly or simply paraphrase it. If you take down the exact words, you can always decide to make the idea your own by qualifying it in various ways and putting it in your own words. When taking notes, in brief, your motto should be: the more the merrier.

WRITING TERM PAPERS AND OTHER ESSAYS

You have no doubt already learned that next to mastery of the subject matter nothing is more important for earning good grades than effective writing. You surely know people whose study habits are not all that they should be but whose grades are high. Nine times out of ten the secret of their success is their ability to write well. What they have to say may not always be all that impressive, but the way they say it is.

Students who are not among that relatively small group who write well sometimes think it unfair that writing skills should count so heavily. The course, some complain, is American History, not Creative Writing, and so their grade should not be influenced by their prose. Only what they know about history should count. But most teachers continue to believe that the ability to express what you know clearly and forcefully is an indispensable measure of how well you have learned the subject matter. So, like it or not, your writing is going to count. Writing well is an invaluable skill, and not only in college. Most good jobs (and most not-so-good ones) involve writing. There is correspondence, there are reports, there are memoranda. The writing will never stop.

No matter how poorly you write, you can learn to write effectively. This is not to say that anyone who desires it can become a brilliant prose stylist. Great talent is rare in every field. But anyone who can speak English effectively can learn to write it effectively. It is simply a matter of expressing your ideas clearly. This you can learn to do. It does not require genius, merely patience and practice.

Charity, St. Paul said, was the chief of all the virtues. In expository prose, however, the chief virtue is clarity. And like charity, it covers a multitude of sins. Be they ever so humble, or homely, your sentences will receive a sympathetic reading if they are clear. Why? There are a number of reasons. The first is that your papers, reviews, and essays—while they may seem very long to you when writing them—are in reality quite brief. A twenty-page paper, for example, only contains 5,000 words. This means that you do not have very much space to get your ideas across. The less space you have, the more carefully you have to choose your words. If it takes you four or five pages to get to the point, you have wasted a substantial portion of your essay. (If, on the other hand, you were writing a 500 page book, those four or five pages would not matter so much.)

It has perhaps crossed your mind that there are occasions when you are not very eager to get to the point. Sometimes you may not be sure just what the point is. Sometimes you do know, but are not convinced that your point is a very good one. At such times, a little obfuscation may seem a better idea than clarity. It is not. I can assure you, based on my experience as a college teacher (which has involved reading thousands of student papers), there is nothing more troubling than reading a paper where the author tried to hedge bets or fudge ideas. The very worst thing you can do is leave it up to your reader (also known as your instructor) to decide what you are trying to say. Teachers, as a group, have not heeded St. Paul. They conspicuously lack charity when reading student papers. They will not give you the benefit of the doubt. They will, more often than not, decide that you did not get to the point because you do not know the material. We teachers can be a heartless breed. So, no matter how weak your ideas seem to you, set them forth clearly. Something is always better than nothing.

Clarity is a virtue in part because so many papers from other students will not exemplify it. As a result, your teacher will be inclined to read yours more sympathetically. What you said may not have been brilliant, but it did make sense. And, contrary to popular reports, most teachers really are interested in helping students. It is much easier to help you if your instructor can figure out what you were trying to say.

My mistakes will stand out, you are thinking. That sounds very dangerous. We have all been conditioned to avoid detection. The last thing we want is for the teacher to find out that we do not know something. But teachers delight in watching students improve. The reason is obvious: they see it as proof that they are doing a good job. They take special pleasure in the progress of students who start off poorly but steadily get better over the course of the semester. You can do a lot worse than be one of those students.

Let us assume that you are willing to give clarify a try. How do you go about writing clearly? The first rule of thumb is to avoid complexity. You should strive to write simply and directly. This does not mean that you are limited to a basic 1500-word vocabulary. There are hundreds of thousands of words in the language and you are entitled to use any of them, provided only that you use them correctly. You should not, on the other hand, go out of your way to find esoteric words or expressions. Use words that accurately express your meaning. Wherever possible use words that are part of your ordinary vocabulary. Above all, do not try to impress your instructor by using synonyms you located in a dictionary or, worse yet, a thesaurus. You run a high risk of using these words incorrectly because they may have connotations you are unaware of.

You should also avoid complicated grammatical structures. Do you know when to use the subjunctive mood? Do you know the rules about using semi-colons? Do you know which types of subordinate clauses require commas? If you have answered any or all of these questions negatively, then you should bone up on your grammar. And, in the meantime, you should avoid writing sentences where these kinds of questions arise. There is no reason to increase the probability of making an error. Grammatical errors can often be avoided simply by keeping your sentences fairly short. Qualifications of your main idea can go into separate sentences. You do not have to fit everything into a single sentence. Furthermore, your sentences will have more pace and rhythm if you keep them relatively short.

Grammatical difficulties—be they outright errors or merely negligent constructions—are a writer's nightmare. Each time you make an error or use an awkward phrase you distract the reader. He or she stops paying attention to what you are saying and instead focuses on how you are saying it. If you distract the reader often enough (four or five times a page will do it in most cases), you will have reduced your chances of getting your ideas across virtually to zero.

So it is vitally important to eliminate grammatical problems. This is, of course, easier said than done. But there are ways to do it. Many schools have writing centers where you can get help with your papers. If your school has such a center, use it. The improvement in both your prose and your G.P.A. can be dramatic. If your school lacks a writing workshop, ask your teacher to read over an early draft of your paper. This is the reader you have to please after all. So why not go straight to the source?

You may have observed that both of these suggestions presume that you will have completed an early draft. And so you should. But let us suppose that, like most college students, you write your papers by the dawn's early light just before they are due. You do not have an early draft. If you find yourself in this all-too-common situation, you may still be able to find someone who will, as a favor, read over your paper before you type the final version. There are college students who have a good working knowledge of grammar. You need to find one and get him or her to edit your work, that is, help you get rid of the most blatant errors. This person can also tell you if your paper is easy to follow. You should write so that someone unfamiliar with the subject but reasonably well informed in other respects can understand what you are saying. Such a person makes an excellent reader and can help you pinpoint the ideas you need to explain more fully.

Once you have worked out a scheme for eliminating grammatical shortcomings, you can turn to the equally crucial chore of articulating your ideas. This means deciding the most cogent sequence in which to present them, on the one hand, and explicating the connections between them on the other. The first order of business is making sure that your opening paragraphs clearly set out what your paper is about and how you are going to approach this topic. Your opening sentences should explain: what your topic involves; why it is worth investigating; and how you are going to look into it. If your topic were, for example, "Sex and Sexism in Automobile Advertising," you might write something like the following:

> The automobile is more than a means of transportation. It is also a powerful engine of change. Highways and suburbs have altered the human and physical geography of the nation. Shopping malls and drive-ins have transformed the retail economy. Social practices—from dating customs to recreational patterns—bear the imprint of the car. Cars have also come to symbolize status and prestige. Expensive models are perceived, and marketed, as visible signs of success. As a result, changing automotive advertising campaigns provide a wealth of data about how Americans have conceptualized the "good life" in this century.
>
> Success means different things to different people, but—if the car ads are to be believed—Americans tend to think of success in terms of power and sex.

You will note that this example sets the topic in a larger context, explains what the paper will examine (power and sex as components of the American idea of success), and how it will examine them (by analyzing changing patterns of automotive advertising). Further it explains why these ads are an important source of material for this topic.

"Well begun," the adage runs, "is half done." This is especially true in writing papers and essays. A good opening tells the reader what to expect. It piques curiosity and makes one eager to read on. A poor opening (one, that is, which leaves the reader still wondering what the paper is about or why a certain topic is important) does the opposite. So work on your openings! You may not have the time to write several drafts of your paper (although you should make the time), but you must take the time to rewrite your introduction as many times as necessary for it to sparkle.

You, as the author, have the responsibility of directing your reader's attention. You do this by explaining the logical connection(s) between the points you raise. You can not assume that your reader will figure out the logic of your paper. Your reader, you should recall, is a professional skeptic who starts from the assumption that you do not know what you are talking about. So it is the height of folly to assume that your instructor will supply logical connections for you. You have to supply them, and you do this—principally—by means of topic and transitional sentences.

Topic sentences introduce ideas. They belong at the beginning of paragraphs. All too often students bury their central ideas in the middle of paragraphs. Only the most attentive reader is likely to ferret them out. And while every teacher strives to be most attentive, the unvarnished truth of the matter is that there is usually a stack of papers to go through—a prospect that inspires a certain dread and tends to make one somewhat eager to get the whole business over with. So, despite our best intentions, we teachers are often less attentive than we should be. The lesson for you is clear. Do not risk having your best notions go unnoticed.

Transitional sentences explain connections. You can put them at the end of paragraphs if you wish. Wherever you put them, be sure you write them as carefully as you do your introduction and your topic sentences. A good topic sentence may also be a transitional device and improve the flow of your writing.

These few hints will not suffice to turn you into a good writer, but they can help you avoid fatal errors. If your writing is a problem, then you owe it to yourself to seek sustained professional help either in writing courses or at your school's writing center. Remember, a serviceable prose style will not only measurably improve your grade in this course (and many others), it will also improve your chances for success in whatever career you enter.

WHEN AND HOW TO USE FOOTNOTES

Many students apparently believe that the only thing worse than having to read footnotes is having to write them. It is easy to understand why they feel that way, but they are making much ado about very little. Footnotes are used to inform the reader (including your reader) where the information being used in the body of the paper can be found. That is the sum and substance of the matter.

So, when should you use a footnote? These are two occasions when you must. The first is when you are referring to someone's exact words whether by direct quotation or by paraphrase. The second is when you are referring to some bit of information that is not already well known or is someone's interpretation of the facts. How, you might wonder, can you tell whether or not something is already well-known? There is, fortunately, a simple rule. Any thing you can find in a standard textbook (like *Firsthand America*) does not need to be footnoted. Hence, for example, you do not need to footnote that George Washington was the first president of the United States. You do need to footnote an exact quotation from his "Farewell Address." You do not need to footnote that Henry Ford introduced the assembly line to the manufacture of automobiles. You do need to footnote your source for his political opinions.

As you can see from these examples, there is no mystery about using footnotes. If you are in doubt about a particular case, you still have two steps open to you. One is to ask your instructor, the reader you are seeking to inform in the first place. The other, if you find it impracticable to contact your teacher, is to use the footnote. Having an unnecessary footnote is a minor flaw. Not having a necessary one is a serious omission. So you can simply err on the safe side.

Now that you know when to use footnotes, you can consider the matter of how to use them. There are several commonly used formats. Simply ask your instructor which one is preferred. If your teacher has no preference, amble over to your campus bookstore and invest in the University of Chicago's *Manual of Style*. It is brief, clearly written, reliable, and cheap. It is very unlikely you will encounter a question the *Manual of Style* will not answer.

WHAT TO INCLUDE IN YOUR BIBLIOGRAPHY

Early in your research you compiled a list of possible sources. The temptation is to type out a bibliography from those cards. This is fine provided that you actually used all of those sources. Your bibliography should include all the sources you consulted and only the sources you consulted. So even though you have all sorts of cards, and even though your bibliography would look far more impressive if you included sources you looked up but did not use, do not. The game is not worth the candle. Your instructor will have a quite accurate sense of what sources you used just from reading your paper. So it is most unlikely that padding your bibliography will impress. In fact, your teacher is more than likely to challenge your reliability if any part of your paper seems padded. In scholarship, honesty really is the best policy.

A WORD ABOUT PLAGIARISM AND ABOUT ORIGINALITY

Plagiarism is the act of claiming another's work as your own. It is about as serious an offense as you can commit. Many colleges require teachers to report all instances of plagiarism and, while the punishment can vary, it is always stiff. Moreover, of all the various ways of cheating teachers find plagiarism the easiest to detect.

Some students even manage to plagiarize without realizing that this is what they are doing. They either quote or paraphrase a book or article without indicating that. (They omit the quotation marks or they omit the footnote.) They have, without necessarily intending to, passed off someone else's work as their own. Sometimes this results in nothing worse than a private lecture from the instructor on the necessity of correctly attributing all information. Even so it is embarrassing, and it creates the impression that you do not know what you are doing. So, be sure you indicate the sources not only of your information but also of the interpretations or ideas you include in your papers.

Teachers will often tell their students that their papers should be original. Since scholars use this word in a somewhat different sense than you might expect, a word of explanation may prove helpful. In ordinary speech something is original if it is the first of its kind or if it is the only one of its kind. Historians and other scholars mean something less dramatic than that. We refer to research as "original" if the researcher did the work himself. We do not mean that his conclusions have never been reached before or that no one else has ever used his source materials. The way you put familiar information and ideas together may be original.

Do not hesitate to make use of ideas from other historians. No one with any sense expects beginning students to make startling discoveries or to develop radically new perspectives on the past. Of course it would be wonderful if you did, but no one anticipates that you will. It is, accordingly, perfectly legitimate for you to use other people's insights. The only hitch is that you must always acknowledge where they came from.

NAME ______________________ DATE ______________

15 "BEEN IN THE STORM SO LONG": EMANCIPATION AND RECONSTRUCTION

SUGGESTED OUTCOMES

After studying Chapter 15, you should be able to

1. Describe the economic and social condition of the South in 1865.
2. Explain the causes of the New Orleans race riot of 1866.
3. Describe the impact of slavery and emancipation on African-American family life and on the social life of the larger African-American community.
4. Provide a brief, general definition of the meaning of the term "Reconstruction."
5. Explain the major provisions of the Abraham Lincoln, the Andrew Johnson, and the Radical Republican proposals for Reconstruction, and explain the significant differences among them.
6. Describe the Radical Republican proposal to provide farm land of their own to the recently emancipated slaves, and explain why the proposal was never implemented.
7. Explain the process by which Reconstruction came to an end in the various southern states, and provide an overall explanation for why Reconstruction came to an end in the South.
8. Provide a general explanation for why historians have been critical of the presidency of Andrew Johnson.
9. Trace the major achievements (civil rights bills and the Thirteenth, Fourteenth, and Fifteenth Amendments) of Radical Republicans in promoting civil rights.
10. Explain why Andrew Johnson almost lost the presidency in impeachment proceedings.
11. Explain why the united movement for African-American voting rights and women's voting rights split in the late 1860s.
12. Describe the various groups struggling for political power in the South during Reconstruction.

CHRONOLOGY

1863 Abraham Lincoln issues the Emancipation Proclamation.
Abraham Lincoln gives the Gettysburg Address.

1864 Ulysses S. Grant assumes command of the Union Army.
Abraham Lincoln wins a second presidential term.
Congress passes the Wade-Davis Bill.

1865 Congress establishes the Freedmen's Bureau.
General Robert E. Lee surrenders at Appomattox Court House.
Abraham Lincoln is assassinated and Andrew Johnson becomes President.
The Thirteenth Amendment to the Constitution is adopted.

1866 Congress passes the Civil Rights Act of 1866.
Tennessee is readmitted to Congress and the Union.

1867 Congress passes the Tenure of Office Act.
Congress passes the Military Reconstruction Act.

1868 Congress conducts impeachment proceedings against President Andrew Johnson.
The Fourteenth Amendment to the Constitution is adopted.
Ulysses S. Grant is elected President.
Alabama, Arkansas, Florida, Louisiana, North Carolina, South Carolina, and Georgia are readmitted to Congress and the Union.

1870 Texas, Mississippi, and Virginia are readmitted to Congress and the Union.

1872 Ulysses S. Grant wins a second presidential term.
Congress passes the Amnesty Act.
Crédit Mobilier scandal is exposed.

1875 Congress passes the Civil Rights Act of 1875.

1876 The presidential election between Republican Rutherford B. Hayes and Democrat Samuel Tilden ends in dispute.

1877 The Compromise of 1877 is reached and Rutherford B. Hayes is declared President.

PHOTOGRAPH AND ILLUSTRATION ANALYSIS

1. The accompanying photograph is a collective portrait of the African-American members of the Louisiana state legislature during Reconstruction. What role did African Americans play in southern state governments during Reconstruction?

NAME ____ DATE ____________________

Louisiana was one of five southern states to have a majority of black voters after the Civil War. A total of 133 black legislators served in the state from 1868 to 1896. *(Courtesy, Louisiana State Museum)*

2. Some northerners argued that the Civil War did not really do too much damage to the South. Using the accompanying photograph of Charleston, South Carolina, how would you react to that argument?

Charleston, South Carolina. At the war's end, much of the South lay in ruins. *(Courtesy, Library of Congress)*

DOCUMENTS ANALYSIS

1. Read the following sharecropping contract. How did the contract actually trap the sharecropper into a legal and economic situation that resembled slavery?

NAME ______________________ DATE ____________

A SHARECROPPING CONTRACT

This contract made and entered into between A. T. Mial of one part and Fenner Powell of the other part both of the County of Wake and State of North Carolina—

Witnesseth—That the Said Fenner Powell hath bargained and agreed with the Said Mial to work as a cropper for the year 1886 on Said Mial's land on the land now occupied by Said Powell on the west Side of Poplar Creek and a point on the east Side of Said Creek and both South and North of the Mial road, leading to Raleigh, That the Said Fenner Powell agrees to work faithfully and dilligently without any unnecessary loss of time, to do all manner of work on Said farm as may be directed by Said Mial, And to be respectful in manners and deportment to Said Mial. And the Said Mial agrees on his part to furnish mule and feed for the same and all plantation tools and Seed to plant the crop free of charge, and to give the Said Powell One half of all crops raised and housed by Said Powell on Said land except the cotton seed. The Said Mial agrees to advance as provision to Said Powell fifty pound of bacon and two sacks of meal pr month and occasionally Some flour to be paid out of his the Said Powell's part of the crop or from any other advance that may be made to Said Powell by Said Mial. As witness our hands and seals this the 16th day of January A.D. 1886

Witness — *A. T. Mial* [signed] [Seal]

W. S. Mial [signed] — *Fenner* his X mark *Powell* [Seal]

2. Using the statements as sources for your conclusions, how did former slaves feel about their years of bondage?

____

____

____

____

____

____

BLACKS *recalling slavery decades later had a wide spectrum of memories:*

Might as well tell the truth. Had just as good a time when I was a slave as when I was free. Had all the hog meat and milk and everything else to eat.

—HARDY MILLER

De white folks wuz good ter us, an' we loved 'em. But we wanted ter be free 'cause de Lawd done make us all free.

—TOM WILCOX

There was no such thing as being good to slaves. Many white people were better than others, but a slave belonged to his master, and there was no way to get out of it.

—THOMAS LEWIS

I thought slavery wuz right. I felt that this wuz the way things had to go—the way they were fixed to go. I wuz satisfied. The white folks treated me all right. My young missus loved me, and I loved her. She whupped me sometimes—I think, just for fun, sometimes.

—JOE HIGH

Some colored people say slavery was better, because they had no responsibility. It is true, they were fed, clothed, and sheltered, but I'm like the man that said, "Give me freedom or give me death!"

—BELLE CARUTHERS

3. What does this testimony of Harriet Hernandes, a black living in Spartanburg, South Carolina, in 1871, reveal about the nature of Ku Klux Klan intimidation?

____

____

____

____

____

____

____

INTIMIDATION OF BLACK VOTERS *The following testimony was given by Harriet Hernandes, a black resident of Spartanburg, South Carolina, July 10, 1871, to the Joint Congressional Select Committee investigating conditions in the South.*

Question: How old are you?
Answer: Going on thirty-four years. . . .

Q: Are you married or single?
A: Married.

Q: Did the Ku-Klux come to your house at any time?
A: Yes, sir; twice. . . .

Q: Go on to the second time. . . .
A: They came in; I was lying in bed. Says he, "Come out here, sir; come out here, sir!" They took me out of bed; they would not let me get out, but they took me up in their arms and toted me out—me and my daughter Lucy. He struck me on the forehead with a pistol, and here is the scar above my eye now. Says he, "Damn you, fall." I fell. Says he, "Damn you, get up." I got up. Says he, "Damn you, get over this fence!" and he kicked me over when I went to get over; and then he went on to a brush pile, and they laid us right down there, both together. They laid us down twenty yards apart, I reckon. They had dragged and beat us along. They struck me right on the top of my head, and I thought they had killed me; and I said, "Lord o' mercy, don't, don't kill my child!" He gave me a lick on the head, and it liked to have killed me; I saw stars. He threw my arm over my head so I could not do anything with it for three weeks, and there are great knots on my wrist now.

Q: What did they say this was for?
A: They said, "You can tell your husband that when we see him we are going to kill him. . . ."

Q: Did they say why they wanted to kill him?
A: They said, "He voted the radical ticket, didn't he?" I said, "Yes," that very way. . . .

Q: When did [your husband] get back home after this whipping? He was not at home, was he?
A: He was lying out; he couldn't stay at home, bless your soul! . . .

Q: Has he been afraid for any length of time?
A: He has been afraid ever since last October. He has been lying out. He has not laid in the house ten nights since October.

Q: Is that the situation of the colored people down there to any extent?
A: That is the way they all have to do—men and women both.

Q: What are they afraid of?
A: Of being killed or whipped to death.

Q: What has made them afraid?
A: Because men that voted radical tickets they took the spite out on the women when they could get at them.

Q: How many colored people have been whipped in that neighborhood?
A: It is all of them, mighty near. . . .

NAME ______________________________ DATE ______________

VOCABULARY

The following words may not be part of your normal vocabulary. If their meaning is not familiar to you, you should look them up in a dictionary.

renascent	coercive	suffrage	confiscate
gender	reconciliation	paternalistic	tenancy
antebellum	magnanimous	philanthropic	impeachment

IDENTIFICATION OF KEY CONCEPTS

In two to three sentences, identify each of the following:

Abraham Lincoln's plan for Reconstruction ______________________________

Andrew Johnson's plan for Reconstruction ______________________________

The Radical Republican plan for Reconstruction ______________________________

Thirteenth Amendment ______________________________

Fourteenth Amendment ______________________________

Fifteenth Amendment ______________________________

Military Reconstruction Act of 1867 ______________________________

Freedmen's Bureau

Sharecropping

Wade Davis Bill

"Black Codes"

Carpetbaggers

Scalawags

Redeemers

Compromise of 1877

PHOTOGRAPHIC EXERCISE

1. Why might the engraving on the left on the following page, entitled "Verdict, 'Hang the D_ Yankee and Nigger,' " relate to the black suffrage convention of 1866 in New Orleans?

NAME ______________________________ DATE ______________

This engraving, subtitled "Verdict, 'Hang the D—— Yankee and Nigger,' " appeared in *Harper's Weekly*. No verifiable figures exist as to how many Republicans, white or black, fell victim to ex-Confederate retaliation during Reconstruction. *(Courtesy, Library of Congress)*

This early photograph shows black workers being led from the cotton fields. *(Courtesy, The New-York Historical Society)*

2. Can you tell whether the photograph on the right was taken before or after the Civil War?

SELF-TEST

Multiple-Choice Questions

1. Southern whites who supported Reconstruction were known as
   a. carpetbaggers.
   b. scalawags.
   c. Redeemers.
   d. Copperheads.

2. Lincoln's plan for reconstructing the Union
   a. gave blacks the vote.
   b. abolished property requirements for voting.
   c. was harsher than the Wade-Davis Bill.
   d. satisfied neither abolitionists nor northern radicals.

3. The Tenure of Office Act forbade Johnson to
   a. appoint southern sympathizers to federal jobs.
   b. remove federal officials without the consent of the Senate.
   c. issue orders to the army except through General Grant.
   d. remain in office beyond 1869.

4. Historians beginning in the late 1950s and 1960s have seen Radical Reconstruction as
   a. another phase in the search for justice on the part of African Americans.
   b. a disagreeable part of American history best forgotten.
   c. a friendly compromise between the North and the South.
   d. a backward step after the Civil War.

5. Black Codes were
   a. written by the Union army to guarantee freedom for slaves.
   b. unwritten rules among blacks.
   c. southern laws restricting the freedom of former slaves.
   d. ways to transmit secret messages to the North while the Civil War was in progress.

6. Which of the following presidential elections ended without a clear-cut victor and resulted in prolonged political negotiations to determine the winner?
   a. 1864 b. 1868 c. 1872 d. 1876

7. Which is true of the militant National Woman Suffrage Association in the 1860s?
   a. It argued that women should be given the vote because they were superior to African Americans.
   b. It emphasized the need for suffrage for both African American and white women.
   c. It accepted the status quo.
   d. It opposed the goals of the Women's Rights Convention of 1848.

8. Congress enacted the Force Acts to restrain
   a. former Confederate army units from regrouping in uniform.
   b. the violence of African Americans against whites.
   c. the police from helping white southerners.
   d. terrorist groups such as the Ku Klux Klan.

9. After the Civil War, who advocated breaking up large southern plantations and allocating them in forty-acre tracts to ex-slaves?
   a. Abraham Lincoln
   b. Thaddeus Stevens
   c. Andrew Johnson
   d. Alexander Stephens

10. During Reconstruction, African Americans formed a majority
    a. only in one state convention, that of South Carolina.
    b. that elected two black governors.
    c. that sent black congressmen to Washington.
    d. that kept whites "in their place."

NAME ______________________________ DATE ____________

Matching Questions

For questions 11 through 15, use one of the lettered items.

11. Northerners who came to the South to assist poor African Americans and to exploit the South economically.___
12. Conservative whites who took over the southern state governments at the end of Reconstruction.___
13. A term for white southerners who cooperated with northern officials during Reconstruction.___
14. Federal workers who tried to provide education and health benefits to the recently emancipated African Americans in the South.___
15. Northern politicians interested in punishing southern whites and in providing political rights to southern African Americans.___

a. Carpetbaggers
b. Scalawags
c. Freedmen's Bureau
d. Redeemers
e. Radical Republicans

For questions 16 through 20, use one of the lettered items.

16. Freed the slaves.___
17. Gave the recently emancipated slaves the right to vote.___
18. Resolved the disputed presidential election.___
19. Gave citizenship to African Americans.___
20. Imposed harsh terms on the former Confederate states.___

a. Compromise of 1877
b. Fourteenth Amendment
c. Military Reconstruction Act of 1867
d. Thirteenth Amendment
e. Fifteenth Amendment

True-False Questions

21. The Crédit Mobilier scandal occurred under President Lincoln.___
22. Abraham Lincoln's Reconstruction plan was generally considered to be very harsh on the South.___
23. The most important leaders of Radical Reconstruction were Charles Sumner and Thaddeus Stevens.___
24. The crop-lien system often kept ex-slaves in perpetual debt.___
25. Andrew Johnson became President upon the assassination of Abraham Lincoln.___

Essay Questions

1. Was Reconstruction at least partially successful? In what respects, if any?

____
____
____
____
____
____
____
____
____
____
____

2. Who really won the Civil War—the North or the South? Consider all of the questions the war was fought over, particularly the place of African Americans in the South, and explain your answer.

3. For what reasons might a President be impeached?

4. Did Elizabeth Cady Stanton, Susan B. Anthony, and the National Woman Suffrage Association support the Fifteenth Amendment? Why or why not?

Self-Test Answers

1. b 2. d 3. b 4. a 5. c 6. d 7. a 8. d 9. b 10. a 11. a 12. d 13. b 14. c
15. e 16. d 17. e 18. a 19. b 20. c 21. F 22. F 23. T 24. T 25. T

NAME ______________________________ DATE ______________

16 INDUSTRIALISM AND LABOR STRIFE 1865–1900

SUGGESTED OUTCOMES

After studying Chapter 16, you should be able to

1. Explain the meaning of the term "infrastructure" and why it is a prerequisite to industrialization.
2. Describe how Andrew Carnegie became an industrial tycoon in the steel industry.
3. Explain the major developments in retail sales in the late nineteenth century.
4. Describe the major developments in corporate organization in late nineteenth-century American business.
5. Explain "laissez-faire" and "monopoly" and describe how the federal government began dealing with monopolies in the late 1800s.
6. Explain what types of jobs were available outside the home to women in the late nineteenth century.
7. Describe how American industrial workers lived in the late 1800s and early 1900s.
8. List and briefly describe the major labor strikes in the late nineteenth-century United States.
9. Describe the major national labor unions in the United States in the late nineteenth century, and explain why the American Federation of Labor was the most successful.

CHRONOLOGY

1871 Knights of Labor is formed.

1873 Congress stops issuing the old silver dollar.
Panic of 1873 begins.
The Supreme Court decides *Munn v. Illinois*.

1877 The great railroad strike takes place.

1878 Congress passes the Bland-Allison Silver Purchase Act.

1880 Refrigerated railroad cars bring about the national distribution of fresh beef.

1886 The Supreme Court decides *Santa Clara Co. v. Southern Pacific Railroad.*
The American Federation of Labor is formed.

1887 Congress passes the Hatch Act and the Interstate Commerce Act.

1890 Congress passes the Sherman Silver Purchase Act and the Sherman Antitrust Act.

1892 Homestead Steel strike occurs.

1893 The Depression of 1893 begins.

1894 Congress passes the Wilson-Gorman Tariff.

1895 The Supreme Court decides *United States v. E. C. Knight.*

1905 The Supreme Court decides *Lochner v. New York*.

1908 The Supreme Court decides *Muller v. Oregon*.

PHOTOGRAPH AND ILLUSTRATION ANALYSIS

1. What do you think was so impressive about the Corliss steam engine pictured here? Why was it important?

NAME ______________________________ DATE ______________

2. According to the Currier & Ives sketch, what are the major ingredients of success in the United States? Do you think these qualities assured success? Why or why not?

____

____

____

____

____

____

____

THE WAY TO GROW POOR. ✢ THE WAY TO GROW RICH.

This Currier and Ives print preached that the way to grow rich was through hard work and thrift; in reality, a little shrewdness was also needed.

DOCUMENTS ANALYSIS

1. Andrew Carnegie gave the following advice to young men concerning the best way to get ahead in America. What are the key ingredients to success, at least according to Andrew Carnegie? Do you think he was correct? Why or why not?

____

____

____

____

____

____

____

ANDREW CARNEGIE *was once quite an ordinary man. While most business leaders of his and future times came from wealth, Carnegie was free to give this inspirational address, based partially on his own career, to Curry Commercial College in Pittsburgh during 1885:*

THE ROAD TO BUSINESS SUCCESS: A TALK TO YOUNG MEN

It is well that young men should begin at the beginning and occupy the most subordinate positions. Many of the leading business men of Pittsburgh had a serious responsibility thrust upon them at the very threshold of their career. They were introduced to the broom, and spent the first hours of their business lives sweeping out the office. . . . I was one of those sweepers myself, and who do you suppose were my fellow sweepers? David McCargo, now superintendent of the Alleghany Valley Railroad; Robert Pitcairn, Superintendent of the Pennsylvania Railroad, and Mr. Moreland, City Attorney. . . .

Assuming that you have all obtained employment and are fairly started, my advice to you is "aim high." I would not give a fig for the young man who does not already see himself the partner or the head of an important firm. Do not rest content for a moment in your thoughts as head clerk, or foreman, or general manager in any concern, no matter how extensive. Say each to yourself. "My place is at the top." *Be King in your dreams.* . . .

The first and most seductive, and the destroyer of most young men, is the drinking of liquor. I say to you that you are more likely to fail in your career from acquiring the habit of drinking liquor than from any, or all, the other temptations likely to assail you. . . .

Assuming you are safe in regard to these your gravest dangers, the question now is how to rise from the subordinate position we have imagined you in, through the successive grades to the position for which you are, in my opinion, and, I trust, in your own, evidently intended. I can give you the secret. It lies mainly in this. Instead of the question "What must I do for my employer?" substitute "What can I do?" Faithful and conscientious discharge of the duties assigned you is all very well, but the verdict in such cases generally is that you perform your present duties so well that you had better continue performing them. Now, young gentlemen, this will not do. The rising man must do something exceptional, and beyond the range of his special department. *He must attract attention.* . . . Some day, in your own department, you will be directed to do or say something which you know will prove disadvantageous to the interest of the firm. Here is your chance. Stand up like a man and say so. Say it boldly, and give your reasons, and thus prove to your employer that, while his thoughts have been engaged upon other matters, you have been studying during hours when perhaps he thought you asleep, how to advance his interests. You may be right or you may be wrong, but in either case you have gained the first condition of success. You have attracted attention.

Always break orders to save owners. There never was a great character who did not sometimes smash the routine regulations and make new ones for himself. The rule is only suitable for such as have no aspirations, and you have not forgotten that you are destined to be owners and to make orders and break orders. . . .

And here is the prime condition of success, the great secret: concentrate your energy, thought, and capital exclusively upon the business in which you are engaged. Having begun in one line, resolve to fight it out on that line, to lead in it; adopt every improvement, have the best machinery, and know the most about it.

The concerns which fail are those which have scattered their capital, which means that they have scattered their brains also. They have investments in this, or that, or the other, here, there and everywhere. "Don't put all your eggs in one basket" is all wrong. I tell you "put all your eggs in one basket, and then watch that basket." It is trying to carry too many baskets that breaks most eggs in this country. He who carries three baskets must put one on his head, which is apt to tumble and trip him up. One fault of the American business man is lack of concentration.

NAME ______________________ DATE ______________

2. What conclusions can you draw about consumer culture from the budget of department store workers Ellen and Sadie?

____

____

____

____

____

____

____

____

____

ELLA AND SADIE FOR FOOD (ONE WEEK)	
Tea	$0.06
Cocoa	.10
Bread and rolls	.40
Canned vegetables	.20
Potatoes	.10
Milk	.21
Fruit	.20
Butter	.15
Meat	.60
Fish	.15
Laundry	$ .25
Total	$2.42
Add rent	1.50
Grand total	$3.92
Income	$9.00
Expenses	$4.00

3. From the following congressional testimony what conclusions can be drawn about unskilled workers in the United States in the late nineteenth century?

____

____

____

____

____

____

____

____

____

____

A federal investigating committee in 1890 examined the superintendent of the Enterprise Manufacturing Company:

Q: How much help do you employ?
A: We have, I think, 485 on our pay-roll.
Q: How many of those are men?
A: I cannot answer that exactly; about one-seventh.
Q: The rest are women and children, I suppose?
A: Yes, sir.
Q: How many of them would you class as women and how many as children?
A: I think about one-third of the remainder would be children and two-thirds women. That is about the proportion.
Q: What is the average wages that you pay?
A: Eighty-two cents a day for the last six months, or in that neighborhood.
Q: What do the women make a day?
A: About $1.
Q: And the men?
A: Do you mean common laborers?
Q: Yes; the average wages of your laborers.
A: About $1 a day.
Q: What do the children make on an average?
A: About from 35 to 75 cents a day.
Q: You employ children of ten years and upward?
A: Yes, sir.
Q: Do you employ any below the age of ten?
A: No.

Eva Lunsky, an employee, testified at a later hearing:

Q: When were you born?
A: I don't know.
Q: Nobody has ever told you?
A: No, sir.
Q: Did you mamma ever tell you when you were born?
A: She told me, but I have forgotten.
Q: You don't know whether you ever had a birthday party or not?
A: Yes, sir; I have had a birthday party.
Q: When?
A: Last year.
Q: How old were you last year?
A: I was 15.
Q: Was it in the winter time?
A: It was in the summer time.
Q: And you don't know the month?
A: No, sir.
Q: Do you know when the Fourth of July is?
A: No, sir.
Q: Do you know when the summer time is when they fire off fire crackers; don't they have any down your way? (The witness gave no answer.)
Q: Did you ever go to school in this country?
A: I went only three months.
Q: When was that, Eva?
A: That was last summer.
Q: What time in the summer was it that you went there; what months, do you know?
A: No.
Q: Do you know the names of the summer months?
A: No, sir.
Q: What month is this; do you know what month this is?
A: No.

4. What conclusions can you draw about working in coal mines from the following late nineteenth-century description?

NAME ______________________ DATE ______________

ONE COAL MINER *described his working life:*

"Day in and day out, from Monday morning to Saturday evening, between the rising and the setting of the sun, I am in the underground workings of the coal mines. From the seams water trickles into the ditches along the gangways; if not water, it is the gas which hurls us to eternity and the props and timbers to a chaos.

Our daily life is not a pleasant one. When we put on our oil soaked suit in the morning we can't guess all the dangers which threaten our lives. We walk sometimes miles to the place—to the main way or traveling way, or to the mouth of the shaft on top of the slope. And then we enter the darkened chambers of the mines. On our right and on our left we see the logs that keep up the top and support the sides which may crush us into shapeless masses, as they have done to many of our comrades.

We get old quickly. Powder, smoke, after-damp, bad air—all combine to bring furrows to our faces and asthma to our lungs."

VOCABULARY

The following words may not be part of your normal vocabulary. If their meaning is not familiar to you, you should look them up in a dictionary.

industrialization
infrastructure
colossal
technology
elite
bottlenecks

entrepreneur
clientele
currency
sound money
par
remonetize

coalition
merger
monopoly
trust
opportunistic
boycott

anarchism
injunction
piecework
sobriety
laissez-faire

IDENTIFICATION OF KEY CONCEPTS

In two to three sentences, identify each of the following:

Horizontal Integration ______________________

____

____

____

Vertical Integration ______________________

____

____

____

Bland-Allison Silver Purchase Act ______________________

____

____

____

Sherman Silver Purchase Act ______________________

____

____

____

Pool

Trust

Holding Company

Hatch Act

Greenback Party

Ohio Idea

Social Darwinism

Horatio Alger hero

Homestead Strike

Pullman Strike

NAME ______________________________ **DATE** ______________

Great Railroad Strike of 1877 ______________________________

Knights of Labor ______________________________

American Federation of Labor ______________________________

Munn v. Illinois ______________________________

Santa Clara Co. v. Southern Pacific Railroad ______________________________

Interstate Commerce Commission ______________________________

Sherman Antitrust Act ______________________________

Muller v. Oregon ______________________________

IDENTIFICATION OF KEY INDIVIDUALS

In two to three sentences, identify each of the following:

Andrew Carnegie ______________________________

Gustavus Swift ____

John Wanamaker ____

Thomas Edison ____

Aaron Montgomery Ward ____

R. W. Sears ____

R. H. Macy ____

J. Pierpont Morgan ____

SELF-TEST

Multiple-Choice Questions

1. Which one of the following was not a chain store or mail order house?
   a. R. W. Sears and A. C. Roebuck
   b. A. T. Stewart's
   c. Montgomery Ward
   d. The Great Atlantic and Pacific Tea Company

2. The strike in the steel industry in 1892 was known as the
   a. Homestead strike.
   b. Pullman strike.
   c. Anaconda strike.
   d. Lincoln County strike.

3. The form of currency least likely to cause inflation was
   a. gold. b. silver. c. greenbacks. d. paper money.

NAME ____ DATE __________________

4. The "Crime of 1873" involved
   a. the seizure of Indian lands.
   b. ceasing the production of silver dollars.
   c. Andrew Carnegie's purchase of United States Steel.
   d. ceasing the production of gold dollars.

5. Which of the following incorrectly links the individual with his business career?
   a. Andrew Carnegie—steel
   b. Gustavus Swift—meatpacking
   c. R. W. Sears—retailing
   d. J. P. Morgan—oil

6. People who desired to inflate the economy by enlarging it advocated
   a. the gold standard.
   b. the withdrawal of Civil War greenbacks.
   c. the prohibition of government purchases of silver.
   d. the coinage of silver.

7. The first successful national American labor union was the
   a. Knights of Labor.
   b. National Labor Union.
   c. American Federation of Labor.
   d. Congress of Industrial Organizations.

8. Much of the increase in the nation's wealth (GNP or gross national product) in the late nineteenth century came from
   a. mining. b. agriculture. c. the steel industry. d. railroads.

9. In 1860 the United States
   a. was a greatly industrialized nation.
   b. imported few manufactured goods.
   c. was one of the richest nations in the world.
   d. abandoned textile production to European competition.

10. During the second half of the nineteenth century, American economic attitudes were influenced by all of these except
    a. laissez-faire.
    b. Social Darwinism.
    c. the claim that governmental interference in business violated the Fourteenth Amendment.
    d. communist theory.

Matching Questions

For questions 11 through 15, use one of the lettered items.

11. The transportation and communication system of an economy.___
12. The belief that the government should not interfere with business.___
13. The formation of monopolies.___
14. The belief that the social structure is the result of the "survival of the fittest."___
15. The process by which a business acquires control over suppliers and distributors.___

a. laissez-faire
b. vertical integration
c. Social Darwinism
d. horizontal integration
e. infrastructure

For questions 16 through 20, use one of the lettered items.

16. Upheld a law regulating the working hours of women.___
17. Upheld the right of states to regulate the price charged by grain elevators.___
18. Accepted the view that corporations were legally "persons" and protected by the Fourteenth Amendment.___
19. Severely weakened the Sherman Antitrust Act.___
20. Declared unconstitutional a law regulating the working hours in a bakery.___

a. *Lochner v. New York*
b. *United States v. E. C. Knight*
c. *Muller v. Oregon*
d. *Munn v. Illinois*
e. *Santa Clara Co. v. Southern Pacific Railroad*

True-False Questions

21. The Interstate Commerce Commission prohibited monopolies in manufacturing enterprises.___
22. Oliver Wendell Holmes, Jr., was a conservative Supreme Court justice who always upheld business rights.___
23. In the late nineteenth century, the Supreme Court was quite unsympathetic to the needs of big business.___
24. The novels of Horatio Alger reflected a belief in the great possibilities for success in American society.___
25. Child labor was not really a social problem in the late nineteenth century.___

Essay Questions

1. List some important causes of American industrialization.

____
____
____
____
____
____
____
____

2. List some important results of American industrialization.

____
____
____
____
____
____
____
____

Self-Test Answers

1. b 2. a 3. a 4. b 5. d 6. d 7. c 8. d 9. c 10. d 11. e 12. a 13. d 14. c 15. b 16. c 17. d 18. e 19. b 20. a 21. F 22. F 23. F 24. T 25. F

NAME ____________________ DATE ____________

THE WEST AND THE SOUTH 1865–1900

SUGGESTED OUTCOMES

After studying Chapter 17, you should be able to

1. Describe the geographical features of the Great Plains and the Great Basin and explain how they dictated settlement patterns in the region.
2. Describe the living arrangements of the Plains Indians.
3. Describe the federal and local government policies that led to the conquest of the Plains Indians and the loss of land by Mexican Americans.
4. Understand the differences between the mining frontier, the cattlemen's frontier, and the farming frontier.
5. Describe what life was like for frontier women.
6. Explain the major ideas incorporated in Frederick Jackson Turner's "frontier thesis."
7. Explain the meaning of the term "New South."
8. Describe how the "Jim Crow" system descended on the South.
9. Explain the significance of Booker T. Washington's "Atlanta Compromise" speech.
10. Describe the economic life of most southern blacks in the late nineteenth century.

CHRONOLOGY

1849 Gold is discovered in California.
1862 Congress passes the Morrill Act and the Homestead Act.
1864 The Chivington massacre occurs in Colorado.
1865 The Great Sioux War begins.
1869 The first transcontinental railroad is completed.
Wyoming gives women the right to vote.
1870 The Leadville, Colorado, gold rush begins.
1872 Yellowstone National Park is created.
1873 Congress passes the Timber Culture Act.
1874 The gold rush begins in the Black Hills of South Dakota.
1876 Custer is killed at the Battle of the Little Big Horn.
1877 Congress passes the Desert Land Act.
Chief Joseph and the Nez Percé fail in their attempted flight to Canada.
1881 Helen Hunt Jackson writes *A Century of Dishonor*.
1883 The gold rush begins in Coeur d'Alene, Idaho.
1886 Henry Grady publishes the concept of the "New South."
1887 Congress passes the Dawes Severalty Act.
1890 The massacre of Sioux Indians takes place at Wounded Knee, South Dakota.
1893 Frederick Jackson Turner presents his frontier thesis before the American Historical Association.
1894 Congress passes the Carey Act.
1895 Booker T. Washington delivers the Atlanta Compromise Speech.
1896 *Plessy v. Ferguson*
1902 Congress passes the Newlands Reclamation Act.

PHOTOGRAPH AND ILLUSTRATION ANALYSIS

1. What is the significance of what the workers are celebrating in the accompanying picture? What group of workers is missing from the picture?

Driving the Golden Spike on May 10, 1869, at Promontory Point, Utah, joining the Union Pacific and Central Pacific lines and completing the first transcontinental railroad. *(Courtesy, Union Pacific Railroad Museum Collection, Omaha, Nebraska)*

NAME ______________________________ DATE ______________

2. Using material from your textbook on black labor in the South following the Civil War, what is your interpretation of this picture?

Florida strawberry pickers in the 1890s. *(Courtesy, New-York Historical Society)*

DOCUMENTS ANALYSIS

1. Drawing on Emma New's recollections on the next page, name some of the difficulties facing women living on the frontier. Which was a greater burden: loneliness or natural disasters? Might Emma have gained some satisfactions from her hard life?

EMMA MITCHELL NEW *remembers her pioneer days, beginning in 1877, on the Kansas prairie. She and her husband were homesteaders, settling public land that became theirs for a small fee after they had lived on it a number of years.*

WE LANDED IN RUSSELL [on the prairie of central Kansas] forepart of December, 1877, with our car-load of goods, consisting of a few household goods, team of horses, a few chickens, a wagon and plow, enough lumber to build a small house, and a fairly good supply of provisions. We boarded at a hotel for two weeks and by that time the house was finished enough that we could move in out on a claim two miles northwest of Russell. Many a homesick day I saw, many a tear was shed. I couldn't bear to go to the window and look out. All I could see everywhere was prairie and not a house to be seen. . . .

I thought I was going to have a good garden, but the rain failed to come and we got nothing. In the meantime we were hunting water and hauling it in barrels. We dug a deep well and got nothing. Many a time I walked a quarter of a mile down into a deep draw with pails and carried water to wash with.

My husband broke prairie as fast as he could with the old team. One time he broke a fire guard around some grass that was quite tall and then set fire to it. The wind carried the sparks across the guards and set the prairie on fire. We worked hard to put it out to save our home and buildings, until we were completely exhausted. And many a time afterward I fought fires until I was all in, for we had so many in those days.

Years came along one after the other and also droughts. Times looked perilous to us. We finally got a cow, which helped us to live. Then there came along the Indian scare. All the people around about flocked to town for safety except me. I was all alone with my two children and knew nothing of it, as my husband was a good many miles from home trying to earn a little something. He worked out many a day for fifty cents and was glad to get it. Grasshoppers were very plentiful in those days. At times, swarms of them would shade the sun.

Our house was very poor, so my husband in a few spare minutes would saw soft rocks into bricks and lay them between the studding to make it firm, as the Kansas wind rocked it so bad. I helped carry all the bricks. We picked up and burned "cow chips" for fuel. . . .

Hardships and trials came along in their turn. Got a young team to deliver our milk to town. A baby girl came to us, making the second that came to us in Kansas without doctor or nurses and practically no help except the two older children.

We got along very well when a terrible storm and cloudburst came upon us and we lost almost everything, except the cows and an old team in the pasture. We had a nice cow barn put up and that day they put up a stack of millet the whole length of the barn. It commenced to rain in the afternoon, but in due time we started the children to town with the milk. It was a general downpour and the creeks were commencing to rise. . . .

The creek was up to the house and still pouring down. My husband investigated and found that the underpinning of the house was going and that we had to get out. We took a lantern and matches and some blankets, and started for the side hills. When we opened the door to get out, the water came up to our necks. We had a struggle to get out and I can't tell to this day how we ever made it, but the Lord must have been with us. My husband carried the baby girl in his arms as high as his head. We soon got out of the deepest water, as there was a turn in the creek. We went by way of the horse stable and found we would be safe in it. Still the water was up and it was pitch dark. The matches were wet, so we couldn't light the lantern.

We stayed there until the storm abated and the water went down. Then we started out to see if we had a home left and to our delight, even in such a mess, we found it still standing. It was still dark and we couldn't see what havoc the storm had made for us. We found some dry matches and lit the lamp. Such a deplorable sight words can't express. There was an inch of mud all over the carpets and floors. . . .

NAME ______________________________ **DATE** ______________

2. Compare Sitting Bull's 1876 statement with the description of the Ghost Dance religion of the 1880s on the next page. What similarities do you see?

SITTING BULL'S TRANCE

This secondhand account describes Sitting Bull's preparation for the famous encounter where he wiped out the forces of General George Custer at the Battle of the Little Big Horn (1876).

SITTING BULL WENT OUT one day in the hope of being able to communicate with the "Great Spirit." On the second night he was seized with a strange feeling, and near morning he met the Great Spirit, clad in a beautiful robe. His hair flowed upon his shoulders and reached almost to his feet. When Sitting Bull beheld this wonderful apparition, he fainted and had a strange dream. He related his story of the trance thus:

"The Great Spirit appeared to me with a formidable band of Sioux, who have long since been dead, and they danced, inviting me to join them. Presently I was restored to my senses, and the Great Spirit talked with me. He asked me if the Indians would not be glad to see their dead ancestors and the buffalo restored to them, and to life. I assured him that they would be deeply gratified. Then the Great Spirit told me that he once came to save the white race, but that they had persecuted him; and now he had come to save and rescue the defenseless and long-persecuted Indian race. All day the Great Spirit gave me evidence of his power and instructed me.

"He said that the white men would come to take me, but as they approached the soil would become quicksand, and the men and horses would sink. He showed me how to make medicine to put on war-shirts to turn aside the bullets of the white man. He told me the Indians had suffered long enough, and that he was now coming for their deliverance. We are to occupy the earth again, which has been taken from us. Great herds of buffalo will wander about as they did long ago, and the Indian who now sleeps in death will rise again, and forever wander over the earth. There will be no reservation; no messenger from the government to say to the Indians, come back here, stay here, starve here on this spot of ground.

"The Great Spirit said that the Indians must keep dancing; that the earth was theirs at his command, and for all this privilege, they must dance the dances which are pleasing to him. He said that all the Indians who would not listen to his words, or refuse to join in the ceremonies which are pleasing to him, will be destroyed with the white race."

GHOST DANCE RELIGION

The Ghost Dancers were a later phenomenon among Indians now tied down to the reservation.

Yet even now they were not completely subjugated. In 1890 the Teton Sioux of South Dakota faced hunger as a result of drought and congressional stinginess. They fell under the spell of a prophet, Wovoka, who told them that if they performed certain dances the dead would be resurrected, white men driven out, and Indian lands restored. The "Ghost Dancers" alarmed the local whites, who called for troops. The soldiers, in turn, frightened the Indians, who came under the influence of aggressive Sioux warriors. "If the soldiers surround you," one warrior promised, "three of you, on whom I have put holy shirts, will sing a song around them, then some of them will drop dead. Then the rest will start to run, but their horses will sink into the earth." The upshot of all this was the massacre at Wounded Knee, when soldiers armed with repeat-firing Gatling guns mowed down at least 146 Indians of both sexes, young and old.

3. In this statement, the historian Frederick Jackson Turner describes some of the traits that frontier living gave to the American character. What are those traits?

THE HISTORIAN FREDERICK JACKSON TURNER ON THE FRONTIER

From "The Significance of the Frontier in American History" (1893)

To the frontier the American intellect owes its striking characteristics. That coarseness and strength combined with acuteness and inquisitiveness; that practical, inventive turn of mind, quick to find expedients; that masterful grasp of material things, lacking in the artistic but powerful to effect great ends; that restless, nervous energy; that dominant individualism, working for good and for evil, and withal that buoyancy and exuberance which comes with freedom—these are traits of the frontier, or traits called out elsewhere because of the existence of the frontier. Since the days when the fleet of Columbus sailed into the waters of the New World, America has been another name for opportunity, and the people of the United States have taken their tone from incessant expansion which has not only been open but has even been forced upon them. He would be a rash prophet who should assert that the expansive character of American life has now entirely ceased. Movement has been its dominant fact, and, unless this training has no effect upon a people, the American energy will continually demand a wider field for its exercise. But never again will such gifts of free land offer themselves.

NAME ______________________________ DATE ______________

VOCABULARY

The following words may not be part of your normal vocabulary. If their meaning is not familiar to you, you should look them up in a dictionary.

subsidy	domesticate	beleaguered	thesis
public domain	nomadic	bonanza	authoritarian
appropriation	provincialism	speculative	philanthropic
rudimentary	militia	domesticity	

IDENTIFICATION OF KEY CONCEPTS

In two to three sentences, identify each of the following:

Homestead Act of 1862 ______________________________

Desert Land Act of 1877 ______________________________

Newlands Reclamation Act of 1902 ______________________________

Plains Indians ______________________________

"Digger" Indians ______________________________

Treaty of Fort Laramie ______________________________

Custer and the Battle of the Little Big Horn ______________________________

Nez Percé Indians ____________________

Dawes Severalty Act of 1887 ____________________

The Gold Frontier ____________________

The Cattlemen's Frontier ____________________

Chisholm Trail ____________________

The Farming Frontier ____________________

Ghost Dance ____________________

Wounded Knee Massacre ____________________

Frontier Thesis ____________________

New South ____________________

NAME ______________________________ DATE ______________

Jim Crow ______________________________

Atlanta Compromise Speech ______________________________

IDENTIFICATION OF KEY INDIVIDUALS

In two to three sentences, identify each of the following:

John Pope ______________________________

John Chivington ______________________________

George Custer ______________________________

Chief Joseph ______________________________

Sitting Bull ______________________________

Frederick Jackson Turner ______________________________

Booker T. Washington ______________________________

Henry Grady ____

____

____

____

SELF-TEST

Multiple-Choice Questions

1. The Dawes Severalty Act of 1887 provided for
   a. the division of tribal lands among Native American families.
   b. protection of the buffalo herds.
   c. the closing of Indian Territory.
   d. protection of Indian lands against further attack.

2. The most significant factor leading directly to the subduing of the Plains Indians was
   a. the brutality of the United States army.
   b. the discovery of gold in California.
   c. the Mexican War.
   d. the destruction of the buffalo herds.

3. The "frontier thesis" was the work of
   a. Charles Beard.
   b. John W. Burgess.
   c. Frederick Jackson Turner.
   d. Ralph Waldo Emerson.

4. Which census marks the end of the frontier?
   a. 1870 b. 1875 c. 1880 d. 1890

5. The Plains tribes included the
   a. Choctaws and Chickasaws.
   b. Algonquins.
   c. Mohegans and Senecas.
   d. Sioux, Comanches, and Apaches.

6. General George Armstrong Custer and his Seventh Cavalry lost their lives at the Battle of
   a. Wounded Knee.
   b. the Little Big Horn.
   c. Yorktown.
   d. Gettysburg.

7. The "long drive" was
   a. the first pony-express route.
   b. an overland cattle expedition from Texas to the nearest railroad.
   c. the springtime journey across the Badlands in search of pasture.
   d. the trail from Abilene to the Gulf of Mexico.

8. Which group supplied the most cheap labor in the building of the first transcontinental railroad?
   a. Mexicans b. Irish c. Chinese d. Indians

9. The last armed conflict between Indians and whites was the battle of
   a. Wounded Knee.
   b. the Little Big Horn.
   c. the Nez Percé.
   d. Leadville.

10. Which decade was most filled with natural disasters for western ranchers?
    a. 1860s b. 1870s c. 1880s d. 1890s

NAME ______________________________ DATE ________________

Matching Questions

For questions 11 through 15, use one of the lettered items.

11. Led to the loss of extensive amounts of Mexican-American land in California.___
12. Provided 160 acres of government land free to settlers.___
13. Broke up Indian reservation land into small, individual plots.___
14. Provided 640 acres of government land to settlers in dry regions.___
15. Provided land to state governments for reclamation projects.___

a. Homestead Act of 1862
b. Desert Land Act of 1877
c. Carey Act of 1894
d. Land Act of 1851
e. Dawes Severalty Act of 1877

True-False Questions

16. Sitting Bull was the leader of the Nez Percé Indians.___
17. Vigilante justice was sometimes an effective and democratic response to lawlessness.___
18. After 1871 millions of buffalo were slaughtered for their hides.___
19. Very few African Americans or Mexican Americans worked as cowboys in the late nineteenth-century West.___
20. The Jim Crow system did not really discriminate against southern blacks.___

Essay Questions

1. What similarities and what contrasts existed between the South and the trans-Mississippi West?

2. In what ways was the trans-Mississippi West a reflection of industrialism and its mentality?

3. Summarize the main argument of the Atlanta Compromise address.

Self-Test Answers

1. a 2. d 3. c 4. d 5. d 6. b 7. b 8. c 9. a 10. c 11. d 12. a 13. e 14. b 15. c 16. F 17. T 18. T 19. F 20. F

NAME ________________________ DATE ______________

18 CITY AND FARM 1865–1900

SUGGESTED OUTCOMES

After studying Chapter 18, you should be able to

1. Describe the standard of living in late nineteenth-century American cities.
2. Describe the changes that occurred in urban transportation in the late nineteenth and early twentieth centuries.
3. Describe the "new immigration" and how Americans of earlier stock reacted to the mass of immigrants coming to the United States in the late 1800s.
4. Describe the living arrangements of immigrants in the late nineteenth-century American city.
5. Explain the nativist discrimination that occurred in late nineteenth- and early twentieth-century America.
6. Explain the meaning of the term "urban machine" and describe how city government operated in urban America.
7. Describe what Americans did with their leisure time in the late nineteenth- and early twentieth-century American city.
8. Explain the economic plight of American farmers in the late nineteenth century and what the major farm organizations proposed to do about those problems.
9. Explain the meaning of the term "Populism" and discuss how the Populists proposed to solve American economic problems.

CHRONOLOGY

1862 Congress passes the Morrill Land-Grant College Act.
Congress establishes the U.S. Bureau of Agriculture.

1867 The Grange is established.

1877 Supreme Court upholds the Granger laws.

1882 Congress passes the Chinese Exclusion Act.

1885 Congress prohibits contract immigrant labor.

1887 The American Protective Association is formed.

1890 The First People's Party Convention is held.

1892 Grover Cleveland wins the presidential election.

1894 The Immigration Restriction League is formed.

1896 William McKinley wins the presidential election.

PHOTOGRAPH AND ILLUSTRATION ANALYSIS

1. Use the following three pictures to describe urban American living conditions in the late nineteenth century.

By the early 1890s New York City teemed with streetcars hauled by cables and elevated trains powered by steam locomotives. *(Courtesy, The H. N. Tiemann Company, New York)*

NAME ______________________________ DATE ______________

Hester and Clinton streets, New York City, ca. 1896. Immigrant neighborhoods often suffered from overcrowding and poor sanitary conditions. *(Courtesy, The New-York Historical Society, New York City)*

This unappetizing photograph of a dead horse, taken in New York City, shows the appalling sanitary conditions that persisted into the twentieth century. *(Courtesy, Library of Congress)*

DOCUMENTS ANALYSIS

1. If you wrote an advice column in a newspaper, much like Ann Landers does today, how would you react to the letter on the following page?

NAME ______________________________ DATE ____________________

Dear Editor,

Since I do not want my conscience to bother me, I ask you to decide whether a married woman has the right to go to school two evenings a week. My husband thinks I have no right to do this.

I admit that I cannot be satisfied to be just a wife and mother. I am still young and I want to learn and enjoy life. My children and my house are not neglected, but I go to evening high school twice a week. My husband is not pleased and when I come home at night and ring the bell, he lets me stand outside a long time intentionally, and doesn't hurry to open the door.

Now he has announced a new decision. Because I send out the laundry to be done, it seems to him that I have too much time for myself, even enough to go to school. So from now on he will count out every penny for anything I have to buy for the house, so I will not be able to send out the laundry any more. And when I have to do the work myself there won't be any time left for such 'foolishness' as going to school. I told him that I'm willing to do my own washing but that I would still be able to find time for study.

When I am alone with my thoughts, I feel I may not be right. Perhaps I should not go to school. I want to say that my husband is an intelligent man and he wanted to marry a woman who was educated. The fact that he is intelligent makes me more annoyed with him. He is in favor of the emancipation of women, yet in real life he acts contrary to his beliefs.

Awaiting your opinion on this. . . .

2. Compare the sentiments expressed in the Emma Lazarus poem with the anti-immigrant campaign of the late nineteenth and early twentieth centuries.

____

____

____

____

____

____

____

____

Not like the brazen giant of Greek fame,
With conquering limbs astride from land to land;
Here at our sea-washed, sunset gates shall stand
A mighty woman with a torch, whose flame
Is the imprisoned lightning, and her name
Mother of Exiles. From her beacon-hand
Glows world-wide welcome; her mild eyes command
The air-bridged harbor that twin cities frame.
"Keep, ancient lands, your storied pomp!" cries she
With silent lips. "Give me your tired, your poor,
Your huddled masses yearning to breathe free,
The wretched refuse of your teeming shore.
Send these, the homeless, tempest-tost to me,
I lift my lamp beside the golden door!"

The New Colossus by Emma Lazarus

3. How would you evaluate Boss George Plunkitt's definition of honesty as expressed on the next page?

____

____

____

____

____

____

____

____

PLUNKITT OF TAMMANY HALL

George Washington Plunkitt's reflections on his political experience were recorded, and perhaps embroidered upon, by the journalist William L. Riordan.

Honest Graft and Dishonest Graft

Everybody is talkin' these days about Tammany men growin' rich on graft, but nobody thinks of drawin' the distinction between honest graft and dishonest graft. There's all the difference in the world between the two. Yes, many of our men have grown rich in politics. I have myself. I've made a big fortune out of the game, and I'm gettin' richer every day, but I've not gone in for dishonest graft—black-mailin' gamblers, saloonkeepers, disorderly people, etc.—and neither had any of the men who have made big fortunes in politics.

There's an honest graft, and I'm an example of how it works. I might sum up the whole thing by sayin': "I seen my opportunities and I took 'em."

Just let me explain by examples. My party's in power in the city, and it's goin' to undertake a lot of public improvements. Well, I'm tipped off, say, that they're going to lay out a new park at a certain place.

I see my opportunity and I take it. I go to that place and I buy up all the land I can in the neighborhood. Then the board of this or that makes its plan public, and there is a rush to get my land, which nobody cared particular for before.

Ain't it perfectly honest to charge a good price and make a profit on my investment and foresight? Of course, it is. Well, that's honest graft. . . .

The Curse of Civil Service Reform

This civil service law is the biggest fraud of the age. It is the curse of the nation. There can't be no real patriotism while it lasts. How are you goin' to interest our young men in their country if you have no offices to give them when they work for their party? Just look at things in this city today. There are ten thousand good offices, but we can't get at more than a few hundred of them. How are we goin' to provide for the thousands of men who worked for the Tammany ticket? It can't be done. These men were full of patriotism a short time ago. They expected to be servin' their city, but when we tell them that we can't place them do you think their patriotism is goin' to last? Not much. They say: "What's the use of workin' for your country anyhow? There's nothin' in the game." And what can they do? I don't know, but I'll tell you what I do know. I know more than one young man in past years who worked for the ticket and was just overflowin' with patriotism, but when he was knocked out by the civil service humbug he got to hate his country and became an Anarchist.

This ain't no exaggeration. I have good reason for sayin' that most of the Anarchists in this city today are men who ran up against civil service examinations. Isn't it enough to make a man sour on his country when he wants to serve it and won't be allowed unless he answers a lot of fool questions about the number of cubic inches of water in the Atlantic and the quality of sand in the Sahara desert? There was once a bright young man in my district who tackled one of these examinations. The next I heard of him he had settled down in Herr Most's saloon smokin' and drinkin' beer and talkin' socialism all day. Before that time he had never drank anything but whisky. I knew what was comin' when a young Irishman drops whisky and takes to beer and long pipes in a German saloon. That young man is today one of the wildest Anarchists in town. And just to think! He might be a patriot but for that cussed civil service. . . . Nothin' doin', unless you can answer a list of questions about Egyptian mummies and how many years it will take for a bird to wear out a mass of iron as big as the earth by steppin' on it once in a century.

NAME ______________________ DATE ______________

4. What is the significance of the following table?

Freight Rates for Transporting Crops

Grand Island to Omaha (150 miles)			
Effective Date	Corn *(In cents per hundredweight)*	Wheat	Oats
January 1, 1883	18	19½	18
April 16, 1883	15	16½	15
January 10, 1884	18	19½	18
March 1, 1884	17	19½	17
August 25, 1884	20	20	20
April 5, 1887	10	16	10
November 1, 1887	10	12	10

Grand Island to Chicago (650 miles)			
Effective Date	Corn *(In cents per hundredweight)*	Wheat	Oats
January 7, 1880	32	45	32
September 15, 1882	38	43	38
April 5, 1887	34	39	34
November 1, 1887	25	30	25
March 21, 1890	22½	30	25
October 22, 1890	22	26	22
January 15, 1891	23	28	25

5. Read the description on the next page of Pittsburgh in 1868. Were nineteenth-century Americans more sensitive to environmental issues than those of today?

PITTSBURGH, *described here by a visitor in 1868, suffered worse pollution conditions than any other American city:*

"There is one evening scene in Pittsburg which no visitor should miss. Owing to the abruptness of the hill behind the town, there is a street along the edge of a bluff, from which you can look directly down upon all that part of the city which lies low, near the level of the rivers. On the evening of this dark day, we were conducted to the edge of the abyss, and looked over the iron railing upon the most striking spectacle we ever beheld. The entire space lying between the hills was filled with blackest smoke, from out of which the hidden chimneys sent forth tongues of flame, while from the depths of the abyss came up the noise of hundreds of steam-hammers. There would be moments when no flames were visible; but soon the wind would force the smoky curtains aside, and the whole black expanse would be dimly lighted with dull wreaths of fire. It is an unprofitable business, view-hunting; but if anyone would enjoy a spectacle as striking as Niagara, he may do so by simply walking up a long hill to Cliff Street in Pittsburg, and looking over into—hell with the lid taken off."

VOCABULARY

The following words may not be part of your normal vocabulary. If their meaning is not familiar to you, you should look them up in a dictionary.

trichinosis
chlorination
nativism
xenophobia
lynch
"coolie"
vice
de facto
tenement
intractable
amenity
hoodlum
repugnant
professionalization
asylum
autocracy
poignant
horticulture
tribulation
abysmal
stereotype
tribalism

IDENTIFICATION OF KEY CONCEPTS

In two to three sentences, identify each of the following:

New Immigrants ______________________________

____

____

____

Anti-Semitism ______________________________

____

____

____

Anti-Catholicism ______________________________

____

____

____

Immigration Restriction League ______________________________

____

____

____

NAME ______________________________ DATE ______________

Urban Political Machine ______________________________

Public Schools and Assimilation ______________________________

Morrill Land-Grant College Act ______________________________

Granger Laws ______________________________

Farmers' Alliances ______________________________

People's Party (Populism) ______________________________

Election of 1892 ______________________________

Patrons of Husbandry ______________________________

IDENTIFICATION OF KEY INDIVIDUALS

In two to three sentences, identify each of the following:

Leo Frank ______________________________

Oliver Kelley ____

Ignatius Donnelly ____

James B. Weaver ____

Mary Elizabeth Lease ____

William Marcy Tweed ____

George Washington Plunkitt ____

Louis Sullivan ____

SELF-TEST

Multiple-Choice Questions

1. Dennis Kearney's Workingmen's Party of California opposed the
   a. Irish immigrants.
   b. Chinese immigrants.
   c. Mexican immigrants.
   d. Swedish immigrants.

2. In the late nineteenth century most cities coped with their new urban problems through
   a. city commissions.
   b. reform-minded mayors.
   c. federal grants.
   d. city political machines led by bosses.

3. In the election of 1892, the Populist Party drew most of its support from
   a. industrial workers.
   b. the South.
   c. the farmers of the Northeast.
   d. wheat farmers and the Rocky mountain states.

NAME ____ DATE ____________________

4. The incidence of cholera declined after 1910 because of
   a. invention of the cholera vaccine.
   b. improved methods of removing sewage in cities.
   c. the use of filtered water.
   d. stricter enforcement of quarantines.

5. Who was not a Populist leader?
   a. Mary Elizabeth Lease
   b. Ignatius Donnelly
   c. James Baird Weaver
   d. Louis Sullivan

6. Which of the following regions was not a major source of immigration to the United States in the late nineteenth century?
   a. Italy b. Russia c. China d. South America

7. The first immigrant group to be barred from the United States was the
   a. Chinese. b. Italians. c. Germans. d. Irish.

8. The forerunner of the Populist Party was the
   a. Knights of Labor.
   b. Farmers' Alliances.
   c. Socialist Party.
   d. American Federation of Labor.

9. The word "xenophobia" refers to a
   a. desire for revolution.
   b. fear of foreign immigrants.
   c. demand for farm price supports.
   d. a belief in unrestricted immigration.

10. Granger Laws were
    a. designed to raise railroad freight rates.
    b. designed to raise bank interest rates.
    c. designed to set rates for the storage of crops in grain elevators.
    d. all declared unconstitutional.

Matching Questions

For questions 11 through 15, use one of the lettered items.

11. The Jewish businessman who was lynched in Georgia.___
12. The famous American architect.___
13. The boss of the New York City political machine.___
14. Founder of the Grange.___
15. Populist candidate for President in 1892.___

a. Louis Sullivan
b. James Weaver
c. William Tweed
d. Oliver Kelley
e. Leo Frank

True-False Questions

16. City political machines failed to provide any services to urban dwellers in the late nineteenth century.___
17. Crime was much more common in cities than in rural areas in the late nineteenth century.___
18. Prostitution was quite uncommon in urban America in the late nineteenth century.___
19. After 1880, most immigrants settled in the West where land was cheap.___
20. In 1882 Congress barred Chinese immigrants from entering the United States.___

Essay Questions

1. What kinds of economic relationships existed in the late nineteenth century between the countryside and more urban sectors of society: labor, industry, and finance? Is it possible to define political relationships as well?

2. Give some reasons immigrants migrated to the United States.

3. What is a silo?

Self-Test Answers

1. b 2. d 3. b 4. c 5. d 6. d 7. a 8. b 9. b 10. c 11. e 12. a 13. c 14. d
15. b 16. F 17. T 18. F 19. F 20. T

NAME ______________________ DATE ____________

19 CULTURE AND POLITICAL THOUGHT IN AN INDUSTRIALIZING NATION

SUGGESTED OUTCOMES

After studying Chapter 19, you should be able to

1. Describe the development of public school education in the United States in the late nineteenth century and its impact on American society.
2. Explain the most popular forms of sport and entertainment in late nineteenth- and early twentieth-century America.
3. Explain the origins and major arguments of American socialism.
4. Explain the origins and major arguments of American anarchism.
5. Describe the political positions of the two major parties between the end of Reconstruction and the turn of the century.
6. Describe the impact of the depression of 1893 on American politics.
7. Explain both sides of the arguments about the use of gold or silver in the monetary system.
8. Describe the major issues and the outcome of the election of 1896.
9. Describe the major institutions of urban reform in late nineteenth- and early twentieth-century America.
10. Describe the major developments in American intellectual history in the late nineteenth and early twentieth centuries.

CHRONOLOGY

1868 Ulysses S. Grant is elected President.
1872 Ulysses S. Grant is elected to a second presidential term.
1873 The Panic of 1873 begins.
1874 The Women's Christian Temperance Union is formed.
1876 In the disputed presidential election of 1876, Rutherford B. Hayes eventually becomes President.
National Baseball League is formed.
1878 Congress passes the Bland-Allison Silver Purchase Act.
1879 Henry George's *Progress and Poverty* is published.
1880 James Garfield is elected President.
1881 James Garfield is assassinated and Chester A. Arthur becomes President.
1884 Grover Cleveland wins the presidential election.
1888 Edward Bellamy publishes *Looking Backward.*
Benjamin Harrison is elected President.
1889 The People's Party, or the Populists, are established.
Hull House opens.
1890 Congress passes the Sherman Silver Purchase Act.
Congress passes the McKinley Tariff.
1892 Grover Cleveland is elected President.
1893 The Depression of 1893 begins.
Coxey's Army marches on Washington, D.C.
1896 William McKinley is elected President.
1899 The Socialist Party of America is established.
American Baseball League is formed.
1900 William McKinley is reelected President.
1901 William McKinley is assassinated and Theodore Roosevelt becomes President.

PHOTOGRAPH AND ILLUSTRATION ANALYSIS

1. How does the Ferris wheel differ from those you have been on? What bearing does that have on the history of technology?

NAME ______________________________ DATE ______________

The newly invented Ferris wheel, designed by George W. G. Ferris, was a major attraction at the World's Columbian Exposition, Chicago, 1893. *(Courtesy, Chicago Historical Society)*

DOCUMENTS ANALYSIS

1. What impact did the depression of 1893 have on businessman James Kymer? Does your history book give sufficient attention to small businessmen? Why or why not?

THE BIG SQUEEZE *An important part of American history is the story of the entrepreneur. For this businessman, James Kymer, the depression of 1893 was a shock:*

I went to work in Ohio with the rosiest expectations, only to find that there were many things about railroads that I did not know. The financing of such ventures was *terra incognita* to me. The Lancaster and Hamden [Railroad], however, was being built at a time such as I had never before experienced. Without my knowing it, the depression of 1893 was on the way. Some stock in the line had been sold, and a bond issue was to be floated. From these two sources the expense of building was to be met.

I was to do all the work, and things looked bright, but presently I was told that the money that had been raised by the sale of stock had been exhausted, while the bond issue had been delayed. I paid my men and bought my supplies, therefore, out of my own pocket. I could afford to, and thought but little of it. The following month the same thing happened, and the month after that. I was low on funds but had no trouble in borrowing what I needed. . . .

I borrowed more and more, but property values were falling, and my holdings were soon mortgaged to the very hilt. Being told that the bond issue still had not been floated, I myself went to New York to force it through. It was not until then that I realized just what had happened. Bond issues were impossible. Money could not be had.

I returned badly frightened. I pounded tables and argued. I fought and swore and fought again. But it was hopeless. I gathered up my last remaining assets—selling, mortgaging. I raised enough to pay my bills in Ohio. And finally, seeing at last the hopelessness of it all, I took a train for Omaha with barely money enough left in all the world to get me home. I could not even afford a Pullman berth. I did not buy a meal along the way, but existed instead on cheese and crackers that I had bought before I started.

I stepped onto the station platform in Omaha a tired, discouraged man. My wife had preceded me by a month or so, and when I reached home she put her arm about me and I cried.

NAME ______________________ DATE ____________

What a tower of strength she was to me! For a time I could not bring myself to do a thing, thinking that the worst of calamities had befallen me—not knowing that what had happened was a trifle beside what was still to come.

I got about at last, trying to make a little money, but none was to be made. That year of 1893 had come, and with it every opportunity was lost.

I fought with every artifice I knew to keep my home. I traded horses when I could, but a year went past and what few dollars had been left had grown still fewer. At the stockyards in Omaha sheep were offered at fifty cents a head, with few buyers. Farmers were burning their corn because they could not sell it for enough to buy fuel. The whole nation was laboring under an economic collapse of such severity as to seem to us almost unbelievable.

Horses at the stockyards were selling at such ridiculous prices that even I could buy some. I bought a carload and took them east, selling them in Pennsylvania and doubling my money. Still it amounted to nothing, and a letter from my wife telling me that she was ill brought me home as fast as I could come. . . .

She went to the hospital while holders of mortgages were hounding both of us. I fought them off—with nothing. I held them back in every way I could. To Hell with mortgages! How could I pay for the treatment my wife required?

A month passed. My wife grew weaker. The holders of those mortgages were constantly insistent. I fought with all my strength, my back against the wall. On the thirtieth of March, 1895, my wife died. . . .

I was left with two boys—one eighteen and one sixteen years of age. I had nothing. I owed the doctors, owed the undertaker, owed even for the cemetery plot where now my wife was lying.

---

2. According to Vachel Lindsay's poem on the next page, what did William Jennings Bryan, and his defeat in the election of 1896, represent to midwestern farmers?

BRYAN, BRYAN, BRYAN, BRYAN *by Vachel Lindsay*

The Campaign of Eighteen Ninety-six, as Viewed at the Time by a Sixteen-Year-Old

I brag and chant of Bryan, Bryan, Bryan,
Candidate for president who sketched a silver Zion,
The one American Poet who could sing outdoors,
He brought in tides of wonder, of unprecedented splendor,
Wild roses from the plains, that made hearts tender,
All the funny circus silks
Of politics unfurled,
Bartlett pears of romance that were honey at the cores,
And torchlights down the street, to the end of the world.
There were truths eternal in the gab and tittle-tattle.
There were real heads broken in the fustian and the rattle.
There were real lines drawn:
Not the silver and the gold,
But Nebraska's cry went eastward against the dour and old,
The mean and cold.

It was eighteen ninety-six, and I was just sixteen
And Altgeld ruled in Springfield, Illinois,
When there came from the sunset Nebraska's shout of joy:
In a coat like a deacon, in a black Stetson hat
He scourged the elephant plutocrats
With barbed wire from the Platte.
The scales dropped from their mighty eyes.
They saw that summer's noon
A tribe of wonders coming
To a marching time. . . .

Prairie avenger, mountain lion,
Bryan, Bryan, Bryan, Bryan,
Gigantic troubadour, speaking like a siege gun,
Smashing Plymouth Rock with his boulders from the West. . . .

Election night at midnight:
Boy Bryan's defeat.
Defeat of western silver.
Defeat of the wheat.
Victory of letterfiles
And plutocrats in miles
With dollar signs upon their coats,
Diamond watchchains on their vests
And spats on their feet.
Victory of custodians,
Plymouth Rock,
And all that inbred landlord stock.
Victory of the neat.
Defeat of the aspen groves of Colorado valleys.
The blue bells of the Rockies,
And blue bonnets of old Texas,
By the Pittsburgh alleys.
Defeat of alfalfa and the Mariposa lily.
Defeat of the Pacific and the long Mississippi.
Defeat of the young by the old and silly.
Defeat of tornadoes by the poison vats supreme.
Defeat of my boyhood, defeat of my dream.

NAME ______________________________ DATE ______________

VOCABULARY

The following words may not be part of your normal vocabulary. If their meaning is not familiar to you, you should look them up in a dictionary.

pragmatism	risqué	flamboyant	dilemma
curricula	dissemination	vulgar	determinism
assimilation	suffrage	dynamic	sovereignty
proliferation	militant	bedlam	

IDENTIFICATION OF KEY CONCEPTS

In two to three sentences, identify each of the following:

Vaudeville ______________________________

Chautauqua ______________________________

Socialism ______________________________

Anarchism ______________________________

Single Tax ______________________________

Coxey's Army ______________________________

Silver vs. Gold ______________________________

Election of 1896

Women's Christian Temperance Union

Settlement Houses

Hull House

Pendleton Act

Civil Service Reform

Pragmatism

Progressive Education

Legal Realism

Social Gospel

NAME ____________________ DATE __________

IDENTIFICATION OF KEY INDIVIDUALS

In two to three sentences, identify each of the following:

Henry George ____________________

Emma Goldman ____________________

Florenz Ziegfeld ____________________

Thomas Edison ____________________

Eugene Debs ____________________

Edward Bellamy ____________________

Benjamin Harrison ____________________

Jacob Coxey ____________________

Frances Willard ____________________

Mark Hanna

James Garfield

Chester A. Arthur

William Jennings Bryan

Jane Addams

Louis Brandeis

William James

Oliver Wendell Holmes

John W. Burgess

Charles Beard

NAME ______________________ **DATE** ______________

Lester Frank Ward ______________________________

____

____

SELF-TEST

Multiple-Choice Questions

1. Which political party usually favored lower tariffs?
   a. Know-Nothing
   b. Democratic
   c. Republican
   d. None of the above

2. The leader of the 1893 march of poor workers to Washington, D.C., was
   a. Eugene Debs.
   b. Jacob Coxey.
   c. Edward Bellamy.
   d. Henry George.

3. Which sport at the end of the nineteenth century was most commonly associated with metaphors of war and violence?
   a. golf b. football c. baseball d. basketball

4. The traveling program that brought lectures and plays to rural America in the late 1800s was known as
   a. Chautauqua.
   b. National Consumers League.
   c. the Grange.
   d. vaudeville.

5. Which of the following statements about American education in 1900 is true?
   a. It emphasized practical and vocational education.
   b. It emphasized classical education.
   c. It made assimilation more difficult for immigrants.
   d. It imitated British education models.

6. One of the most popular forms of recreation in the late nineteenth century was
   a. croquet. b. bicycling. c. handball. d. raquetball.

7. The central issue in William Jennings Bryan's campaign of 1896 was the
   a. truth of the doctrine of evolution.
   b. issue of women's rights.
   c. treatment of blacks in the South.
   d. free coinage of silver.

8. The first American college founded exclusively for women was
   a. Swarthmore. b. Oberlin. c. Dartmouth. d. Vassar.

9. The invention of motion pictures is most closely associated with
   a. Bell. b. Edison. c. Thompson. d. Griffith.

10. Ragtime music
    a. originated in the rural South.
    b. was mainly vocal in origin.
    c. originated in the black ghettos of American cities.
    d. had little influence on other music.

Matching Questions

For questions 11 through 15, use one of the lettered items.

11. The innovative pianist and composer.___
12. The inventor of basketball.___
13. The labor leader jailed in conjunction with the Pullman strike.___
14. The famous inventor of the phonograph and lightbulb.___
15. The prominent producer of vaudeville.___

a. James Naismith
b. Eugene Debs
c. Scott Joplin
d. Thomas Edison
e. Florenz Ziegfeld

For questions 16 through 20, use one of the lettered items.

16. The most prominent American socialist.___
17. A prominent American anarchist.___
18. Author of *Looking Backward*.___
19. Creator of the idea of the "single tax."___
20. The Democratic/Populist presidential candidate in the election of 1896.___

a. Emma Goldman
b. William Jennings Bryan
c. Henry George
d. Edward Bellamy
e. Eugene Debs

True-False Questions

21. Public schools at the end of the nineteenth century and the beginning of the twentieth century failed miserably in educating immigrant children.___
22. James Garfield/Chester A. Arthur/Grover Cleveland/Benjamin Harrison is a chronologically correct sequence of presidential administrations.___
23. Grover Cleveland served two nonconsecutive terms as President.___
24. The "Mugwumps" were radical, violence-prone coal miners in the 1870s and 1880s.___
25. Johns Hopkins University pioneered in graduate education.___

Essay Questions

1. What ideas and social characteristics distinguished the Republicans from the Democrats in the late nineteenth century?

____
____
____
____
____
____
____
____
____
____
____
____
____
____
____

NAME ______________________________ DATE ______________

2. Discuss the strengths and weaknesses of Populism.

3. What were some of the most influential ideas that originated in the United States in the late nineteenth century?

Self-Test Answers

1. b 2. b 3. b 4. a 5. a 6. b 7. d 8. b 9. b 10. c 11. c 12. a 13. b 14. d
15. e 16. e 17. a 18. d 19. c 20. b 21. F 22. T 23. T 24. F 25. T

NAME ______________________________ DATE ______________

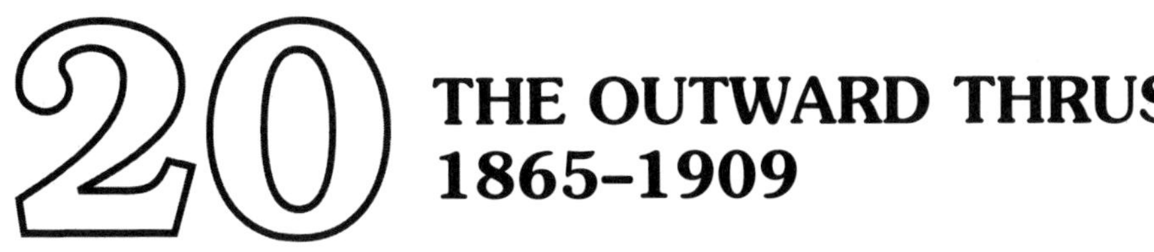

20 THE OUTWARD THRUST 1865–1909

SUGGESTED OUTCOMES

After studying Chapter 20, you should be able to

1. Explain the relationship, if any, between the closing of the frontier and overseas expansion.
2. Explain what is meant by the term "The Redeemer Nation."
3. Explain the concept of "Pan-Americanism" and its relationship to the Monroe Doctrine.
4. Explain the meaning of the term "Roosevelt Corollary to the Monroe Doctrine."
5. Explain the reasons for United States expansion overseas in the late nineteenth and early twentieth centuries.
6. List the major territorial acquisitions of the United States in the late nineteenth and early twentieth centuries and explain the strategic significance of each.
7. Explain the causes of the Spanish-American War of 1898.
8. Describe Theodore Roosevelt's foreign policy ideas and his views of the use of American military power.
9. Explain the meaning of the term "Open Door" and relate it to American economic objectives in Asia.
10. Discuss both sides of the debate over whether the United States should engage in overseas expansion.

CHRONOLOGY

1867 The United States purchases Alaska from Russia.

1887 The United States helps settle the Venezuela boundary dispute.

1889 Along with Great Britain and Germany, the United States establishes a cooperative protectorate over Samoa.

1890 Alfred Mahan publishes *The Influence of Sea Power on History*.

1893 Grover Cleveland refuses to annex Hawaii.

1895 The anti-Spanish rebellion begins in Cuba.

1898 The U.S.S. *Maine* explodes and sinks in Havana Harbor.
The Spanish-American War begins.
The United States annexes Hawaii.
Admiral George Dewey conquers the Spanish navy in the Philippines.
The Treaty of Paris ends the Spanish-American War.

1899 The United States assumes sovereignty over what becomes known as American Samoa.
The anti-American rebellion and war begin in the Philippines.
Secretary of State John Hay issues the Open Door policy.

1900 Congress passes the Foraker Act.

1901 The Supreme Court decides the Insular Cases.

1902 Congress passes the Philippine Government Act.

1903 The United States acquires the right to build the Panama Canal.

1904 Theodore Roosevelt issues the Roosevelt Corollary to the Monroe Doctrine.

1905 Theodore Roosevelt negotiates an end to the Russo-Japanese War in the Treaty of Portsmouth.
Theodore Roosevelt helps end the Moroccan Crisis with the Algeciras Conference.
The Taft-Katsura Agreement is reached.

1907 Japan and the United States begin negotiating the Gentlemen's Agreement.

1908 The Root-Takahira Agreement is reached.

PHOTOGRAPH AND ILLUSTRATION ANALYSIS

1. The photograph and the following cartoon portray Theodore Roosevelt and the Panama Canal. What role did he play in the American acquisition of the canal?

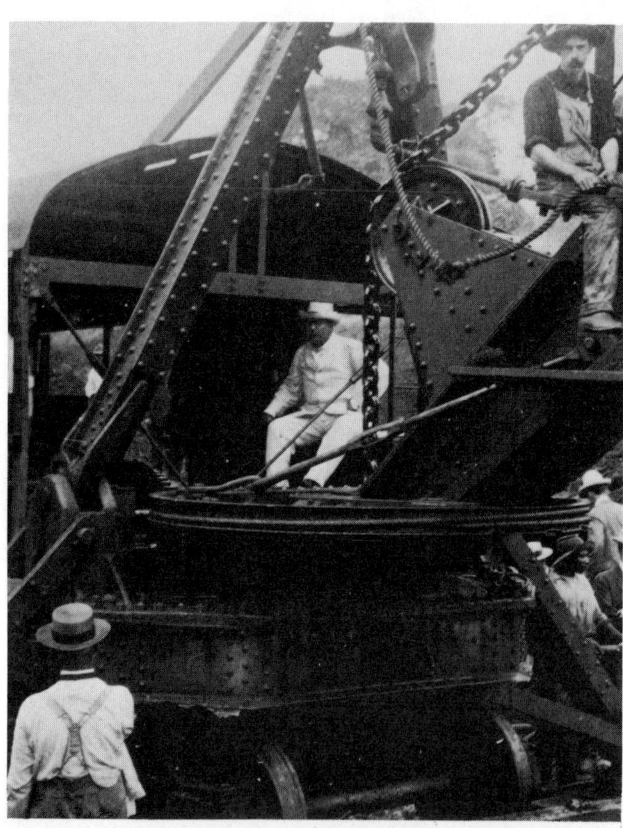

President Theodore Roosevelt operating an American steam shovel at the Panama Canal, 1906. *(Courtesy, Library of Congress)*

NAME ______________________________ DATE ______________

New York World, November 9, 1903.

Roosevelt and the Republican steamship arriving with guns and shovels to build the canal.

DOCUMENTS ANALYSIS

1. Why is the Edgar Lee Masters poem on the next page considered sarcastic and antiwar? Does it accurately reflect the war in the Philippines?

THE WAR IN THE PHILIPPINES *was the first of four the United States fought in Asia during the twentieth century. In* Spoon River Anthology *(1915) Edgar Lee Masters writes a tombstone inscription for a fictional town; the words exhibit the antiwar sentiment that has long vied in the United States with its martial opposite:*

HARRY WILMANS

I was just turned twenty-one,
And Henry Phipps, the Sunday-school superintendent,
Made a speech in Bindle's Opera House.
"The honor of the flag must be upheld," he said,
"Whether it be assailed by a barbarous tribe of Tagalogs
Or the greatest power in Europe."
And we cheered and cheered the speech and the flag he waved
As he spoke.
And I went to the war in spite of my father,
And followed the flag till I saw it raised
By our camp in a rice field near Manila,
And all of us cheered and cheered it.
But there were flies and poisonous things;
And there was the deadly water,
And the cruel heat,
And the sickening, putrid food;
And the smell of the trench just back of the tents
Where the soldiers went to empty themselves;
And there were the whores who followed us, full of syphilis;
And beastly acts between ourselves or alone,
With bullying, hatred, degradation among us,
And days of loathing and nights of fear
To the hour of the charge through the steaming swamp,
Following the flag,
Till I fell with a scream, shot through the guts.
Now there's a flag over me in Spoon River!
A flag! A flag!

VOCABULARY

The following words may not be part of your normal vocabulary. If their meaning is not familiar to you, you should look them up in a dictionary.

tsar	arbitration	flotilla	protectorate
imperialism	autonomy	guerrilla	consortium
heathen	indiscreet	archipelago	indemnity
jingoist	scapegoat	insurrection	status quo

IDENTIFICATION OF KEY CONCEPTS

In two to three sentences, identify each of the following:

Monroe Doctrine ______________________________

____

____

____

Insular Cases ______________________________

____

____

____

Lodge Corollary ______________________________

____

____

____

NAME ______________________________ DATE ______________

Treaty of Paris of 1898 ______________________________

Open Door Policy ______________________________

Russo-Japanese War and the Treaty of Portsmouth ______________________________

Gentlemen's Agreement ______________________________

Root-Takahira Agreement ______________________________

Algeciras Conference ______________________________

Roosevelt Corollary ______________________________

"Yellow Press" ______________________________

Spanish-American War in the Philippines ______________________________

Panama Canal ______________________________

IDENTIFICATION OF KEY INDIVIDUALS

In two to three sentences, identify each of the following:

Alfred Thayer Mahan ______________________________

James G. Blaine ______________________________

Grover Cleveland ______________________________

Henry Cabot Lodge ______________________________

Richard Olney ______________________________

John Hay ______________________________

George Dewey ______________________________

Josiah Strong ______________________________

Queen Liliuokalani ______________________________

NAME ______________________ DATE ______________

MAP EXERCISE

1. Draw a continuous line from the first to the last of all the possessions the United States acquired in the Pacific between 1867 and 1914.

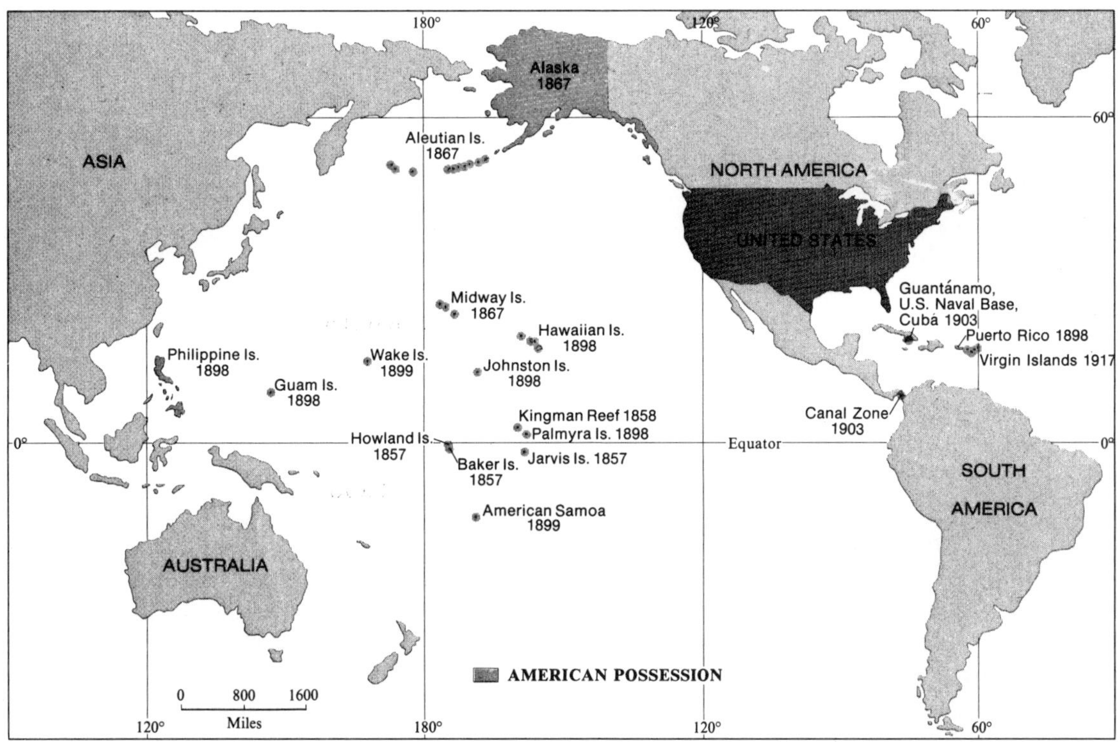

United States' Pacific Possessions.

SELF-TEST

Multiple-Choice Questions

1. Americans were interested in annexing the Philippines for all of these reasons except
   a. fear that the Germans would take the islands.
   b. the desire to spread the Protestant faith.
   c. business interests in the Far East.
   d. a desire to offer a calculated affront to Spain.

2. The President of the United States during the Spanish-American War was
   a. William McKinley.
   b. Grover Cleveland.
   c. William Jennings Bryan.
   d. Theodore Roosevelt.

3. Theodore Roosevelt is generally credited with negotiating an end to
   a. the Russo-Japanese War.
   b. the Moroccan crisis.
   c. Both a and b.
   d. Neither a nor b.

4. Which of the following territories was not acquired by the United States during or as a result of the Spanish-American War?
   a. Guam b. Philippines c. Puerto Rico d. Alaska

5. Emilio Aguinaldo led the
   a. Filipino rebels.
   b. Spanish rulers in Cuba.
   c. Panamanian revolutionaries.
   d. Cuban rebels.

6. The Jones Act and the Tydings-McDuffie Act were concerned with
   a. Cuba.
   b. the Philippines.
   c. Puerto Rico.
   d. Morocco.

7. The Teller Amendment
   a. evoked the Monroe Doctrine against Spain.
   b. was a specific case of American "dollar diplomacy."
   c. specified the United States would not annex Cuba.
   d. gave the United States control of Puerto Rico.

8. All of these justified overseas expansion except
   a. racial chauvinism.
   b. Social Darwinism.
   c. the end of the frontier.
   d. isolationism.

9. What group most strongly opposed imperialism?
   a. Republicans
   b. Mugwumps
   c. Protestant missionaries
   d. businessmen

10. The significance of the first Venezuelan boundary dispute and its settlement was that
    a. the United States began acquiring territories in the western hemisphere.
    b. from that time until World War I, Anglo-American relations were strained.
    c. Great Britain deferred to American wishes in matters concerning the western hemisphere.
    d. Great Britain decided to give the United States a free hand throughout the world.

Matching Questions

For questions 11 through 15, use one of the lettered items.

11. Settled the *Alabama* claims.___
12. Designed to maintain the territorial integrity of China so that American companies could trade there.___
13. Announced that the United States alone would act to protect the legitimate claims of European nations in the western hemisphere.___
14. Prohibited foreign companies from constructing facilities which might have a military use in the western hemisphere.___
15. Designed to promote unity among the countries of the western hemisphere.___

a. Roosevelt Corollary
b. Lodge Corollary
c. Treaty of Washington
d. Open Door
e. Pan-Americanism

For questions 16 through 20, use one of the lettered items.

16. A strong advocate of Pan-Americanism.___
17. Responsible for the purchase of Alaska.___
18. An articulate individual interested in imperialism because of the opportunities it would provide for Protestant missionary work.___
19. An advocate of naval power.___
20. The individual who developed the Open Door policy.___

a. James Blaine
b. William Seward
c. Alfred Thayer Mahan
d. John Hay
e. Josiah Strong

NAME ____ DATE ____________________

True-False Questions

21. Grover Cleveland played a key role in the United States annexation of Hawaii.___
22. In the Venezuelan boundary dispute, the United States was most concerned about the feelings of Spain.___
23. Theodore Roosevelt was hesitant in his attempts to secure the right to build a canal in Panama.___
24. The Spanish-American War lasted only three months.___
25. Philippe Bunau-Varilla favored building the canal in Guatemala.___

Essay Questions

1. Identify some specific events in expansionism from the end of the Civil War into the early twentieth century, and consider reasons for each.

2. What were the causes of the Spanish-American War?

3. Explain the process by which the United States developed the Panama Canal.

Self-Test Answers

1. a 2. a 3. c 4. d 5. a 6. b 7. c 8. d 9. b 10. c 11. c 12. d 13. a 14. b 15. e 16. a 17. b 18. e 19. c 20. d 21. F 22. F 23. F 24. T 25. F

NAME ______________________ DATE ______________

THE PROGRESSIVE SPIRIT 1900–1917

SUGGESTED OUTCOMES

After studying Chapter 21, you should be able to

1. Explain the significance of the Triangle Shirtwaist Factory fire.
2. Explain in general terms the meaning of "Progressivism."
3. List the major technological and organizational innovations in American industry during the early twentieth century and explain their social and economic impact.
4. Discuss the forces that helped bring about the assimilation of the immigrants settling in the United States.
5. Explain the meaning of the word "muckrakers" and list the main individuals involved in the movement.
6. Describe the primary concerns of woman progressives and evaluate their success in achieving their objectives.
7. Describe the emergence of a new American middle class.
8. Describe the prevalence of graft and corruption in city government and explain the major reform movements trying to eliminate those problems.
9. Describe the major developments in the labor movement in the early twentieth century.
10. Explain the philosophy of W. E. B. Du Bois.
11. Explain the reasons why African Americans began migrating from the South to the North during the era of World War I.
12. Explain the significance of the Niagara Movement.

CHRONOLOGY

1895 *The Red Badge of Courage* by Stephen Crane is published.

1901 J. P. Morgan establishes the United States Steel Corporation.

1905 Niagara Movement is founded.
Industrial Workers of the World is founded.

1907 Panic of 1907 occurs.
Congress passes the Aldrich-Vreeland Act.

1908 Ford Motor Company introduces the Model T.

1911 Triangle Shirtwaist Factory fire occurs.
Congress issues the Dillingham Report.
NAACP is founded.

1912 Pujo Committee investigation begins.

1914 Amalgamated Clothing Workers Union is formed.

1915 Margaret Sanger establishes the National Birth Control League.

1917 Congress passes a literacy test for new immigrants.

1920 The Nineteenth Amendment to the Constitution is adopted.

PHOTOGRAPH AND ILLUSTRATION ANALYSIS

1. Explain the photograph. Why was the Triangle Shirtwaist Factory fire so important to urban Americans in the Progressive Era?

NAME ______________________________ DATE ______________

Women trapped in the Triangle Shirtwaist Factory fire on March 25, 1911, had to choose between being burned alive or jumping to near-certain death from windows eight stories high. The disaster took 146 lives. *(Courtesy, Brown Brothers)*

2. Explain this political cartoon. How does it illustrate the feelings of many Americans in the early 1900s?

THE ONLY WAY TO HANDLE IT.

Cartoon delineating the movement for immigration restriction. It culminated in a congressional law of 1921 limiting new immigrants to three percent of each group living in the U.S. in 1920, and a law of 1924 setting the year at 1890.

NAME ______________________________ DATE ________________

DOCUMENTS ANALYSIS

1. Read Pauline Newman's account of working for the Triangle Shirtwaist Company. What gains and losses does she see from the movement to improve labor conditions?

____

____

____

____

____

____

____

____

____

____

____

____

____

____

WORKING FOR THE TRIANGLE SHIRTWAIST COMPANY

Pauline Newman, an organizer and educational director for the International Ladies' Garment Workers Union until her death in 1986, worked at the notorious Triangle Shirtwaist factory in New York. This is her account.

A cousin of mine worked for the Triangle Shirtwaist Company and she got me on there in October of 1901. It was probably the largest shirtwaist factory in the city of New York then. They had more than two hundred operators, cutters, examiners, finishers. Altogether more than four hundred people on two floors. The fire took place on one floor, the floor where we worked. . . .

We started work at seven-thirty in the morning, and during the busy season we worked until nine in the evening. They didn't pay you any overtime and they didn't give you anything for supper money. Sometimes they'd give you a little apple pie if you had to work very late.

What I had to do was not really very difficult. It was just monotonous. When the shirtwaists were finished at the machine there were some threads that were left, and all the youngsters—we had a corner on the floor that resembled a kindergarten—we were given little scissors to cut the threads off. . . .

Well, of course, there were [child labor] laws on the books, but no one bothered to enforce them. The employers were always tipped off if there was going to be an inspection. "Quick," they'd say, "into the boxes!" And we children would climb into the big boxes the finished shirts were stored in. Then some shirts were piled on top of us, and when the inspector came—no children. The factory always got an okay from the inspector, and I suppose someone at City Hall got a little something, too. . . .

I stopped working at the Triangle Factory during the strike in 1909 and I didn't go back. . . .

After the strike I worked with the union, organizing in Philadelphia and Cleveland and other places, so I wasn't at the Triangle Shirtwaist Factory when the fire broke out, but a lot of my friends were. . . . Of course, someone from here called me immediately and I came back. It's very difficult to describe the feeling because I knew the place and I knew so many of the girls. The thing that bothered me was the employers got a lawyer. How anyone could have defended them—because I'm quite sure that the fire was planned for insurance purposes. And no one is going to convince me otherwise. And when they testified that the door to the fire escape was open, it was a lie! It was never open. Locked all the time. One hundred and forty-six people were sacrificed, and the judge fined Blank and Harris seventy-five dollars!

Conditions were dreadful in those days. But there was something that is lacking today. . . .

Now, I'm a little discouraged sometimes when I see the workers spending their free hours watching television—trash. We fought so hard for those hours and they waste them. We used to read Tolstoy, Dickens, Shelley, by candlelight, and they watch the "Hollywood Squares." Well, they're free to do what they want. That's what we fought for.

Source: Joan Morrison and Charlotte Fox Zabusky, eds., *American Mosaic: The Immigrant Experience in the Words of Those Who Lived It* (New York: E.P. Dutton, 1980), pp. 9–14.

2. Explain the the song printed here.

IN THE CONFLICTS *between capital and labor, labor has always had the best music.*

THE PREACHER AND THE SLAVE

Long-haired preachers come out ev'ry night,
Try to tell you what's wrong and what's right,
But when asked about something to eat,
They will answer with voices so sweet:

Chorus
You will eat (you will eat), bye and bye (bye and bye),
In that glorious land in the sky (way up high).
Work and pray (work and pray), live on hay (live on hay),
You'll get pie in the sky when you die (that's a lie!).

3. Lincoln Steffens is considered to be one of the most influential of the "muckraker" writers and journalists. Explain why the following is an example of muckraking journalism.

NAME ______________________________ DATE ______________

____

____

____

____

____

____

____

____

____

____

THE SHAME OF THE CITIES *by Lincoln Steffens*

One of the most prominent muckrakers, Steffens stressed the link between business and politics, maintaining that privilege was the enemy, not city bosses alone.

"Philadelphia: Corrupt and Contented"

All our municipal governments are more or less bad. . . . Philadelphia is simply the most corrupt and the most contented. Minneapolis has cleaned up, Pittsburgh has tried to, New York fights every other election, Chicago fights all the time. Even St. Louis has begun to stir (since the elections are over), and at the worst was only shameless. Philadelphia is proud; good people there defend corruption and boast of their machine. . . .

The machine [in Philadelphia] controls the whole process of voting, and practices fraud at every stage. The assessor's list is the voting list, and the assessor is the machine's man. "The assessor . . . padded his lists with fraudulent names registered from his house. . . . The constable of the division kept a house [of prostitution]; a policeman was assessed as living there. . . . The election was held in the disorderly house maintained by the assessor. . . . The man named as judge had a criminal charge for a life offense pending against him. . . . Two hundred and fifty-two votes were returned in a division that had less than one hundred legal votes within its boundaries." These extracts from a report of the Municipal League suggest the election methods. The assessor pads the list with the names of dead dogs, children, and non-existent persons. One newspaper printed the picture of a dog, another that of a little four-year-old negro boy, down on such a list. A ringing orator in a speech resenting sneers at his ward as "low down" reminded his hearers that that was the ward of Independence Hall, and naming . . . signers of the Declaration of Independence, he closed his highest flight of eloquence with the statement that "these men, the fathers of American liberty, voted down here once. And," he added, with a catching grin, "they vote here yet."

VOCABULARY

The following words may not be part of your normal vocabulary. If their meaning is not familiar to you, you should look them up in a dictionary.

pompadour	aberration	enmities	obscenity
phenomenon	ravage	condescension	moralize
hydroelectric	acquiescence	ethos	
suburbs	muckraking	utilitarian	
pasteurize	amalgamated	graft	

IDENTIFICATION OF KEY CONCEPTS

In two to three sentences, identify each of the following:

Triangle Shirtwaist Factory fire ______________________________

Scientific Management ______________________________

Assembly line ______________________________

Pujo Committee ______________________________

McClure's ______________________________

National Monetary Commission ______________________________

Industrial Workers of the World ______________________________

New immigration ______________________________

Americanization ______________________________

Mass Culture and Assimilation ______________________________

NAME ______________________ **DATE** ______________

Muckrakers ______________________

Nineteenth Amendment ______________________

General Federation of Women's Clubs ______________________

National Birth Control League ______________________

IDENTIFICATION OF KEY INDIVIDUALS

In two to three sentences, identify each of the following:

Lincoln Steffens ______________________

Samuel "Golden Rule" Jones ______________________

Frederic C. Howe ______________________

Booker T. Washington ______________________

W. E. B. Du Bois ______________________

Henry Ford ______________________________

Frederick Taylor ______________________________

William Haywood ______________________________

Margaret Sanger ______________________________

Florence Kelley ______________________________

Samuel Gompers ______________________________

Stephen Crane ______________________________

Frank Norris ______________________________

SELF-TEST

Multiple-Choice Questions

1. Which constitutional amendment guaranteed women the right to vote?
   a. Seventeenth
   b. Eighteenth
   c. Nineteenth
   d. Twentieth

2. Which is an incorrect pair?
   a. Lincon Steffens—corrupt city governments
   b. Ida M. Tarbell—investigation of Standard Oil
   c. Samuel Hopkins Adams—insurance company fraud
   d. Ray Stannard Baker—railroads

NAME ______________________ DATE ______________

3. The suffragette movement attracted the support of all except
   a. settlement house workers.
   b. the National Consumers' League.
   c. the large corporations.
   d. the Congressional Union.

4. *McClure's* and *Collier's* were well known during the Progressive Era as
   a. muckraking magazines.
   b. opponents of prohibition.
   c. examples of yellow journalism.
   d. political magazines.

5. Membership in the American Federation of Labor consisted mostly of
   a. unskilled workers.
   b. skilled workers.
   c. both skilled and unskilled workers.
   d. African Americans.

6. In the Progressive Era of the early 1900s all but one of these might be found in a middle-class home.
   a. flush toilet b. radio c. television d. electric iron

7. The Industrial Workers of the World (IWW or Wobblies) wished to
   a. join with the AFL.
   b. organize One Big Union.
   c. supplant the AFL.
   d. organize the middle classes.

8. The name George Eastman is associated with the mass-produced
   a. nickelodeon.
   b. automobile.
   c. camera.
   d. radio.

9. Which of the following is mispaired?
   a. Booker T. Washington—*Up from Slavery*
   b. W. E. B. Du Bois—*The Philadelphia Negro*
   c. W. E. B. Du Bois—*The Souls of Black Folk*
   d. Booker T. Washington—Niagara Movement

10. Urban progressive mayors include all but
   a. Samuel M. Jones of Toledo.
   b. Tom Johnson of Cleveland.
   c. Hazen Pingree of Detroit.
   d. Robert La Follette of New York City.

Matching Questions

For questions 11 through 15, use one of the lettered items.

11. The country's major proponent of birth control and family planning.___
12. Head of the Industrial Workers of the World.___
13. Prominent black civil rights advocate of the early 1900s.___
14. Proponent of "scientific management."___
15. Author of *The Red Badge of Courage*.___

a. Frederick Taylor
b. William Haywood
c. Stephen Crane
d. W. E. B. Du Bois
e. Margaret Sanger

True-False Questions

16. Samuel Gompers was the leader of the Industrial Workers of the World.___
17. Eugene V. Debs was the prominent socialist candidate for President in the election of 1912.___
18. The Industrial Workers of the World was a conservative union.___
19. In *The Octopus,* Frank Norris praised the impact of the railroad on America.___
20. The House-Senate Dillingham Report of 1911 predicted that the new immigrants would be "unassimilable."___

Essay Question

1. Describe some of the major social and economic features of the time that historians have called the Progressive Era.

Self-Test Answers

1. c 2. d 3. c 4. a 5. c 6. c 7. b 8. c 9. d 10. d 11. e 12. b 13. d 14. a 15. c 16. F 17. T 18. F 19. F 20. T

NAME ______________________________ DATE ______________

PROGRESSIVISM IN PEACE AND WAR 1900–1918

SUGGESTED OUTCOMES

After studying Chapter 22, you should be able to

1. Explain why Upton Sinclair's novel *The Jungle* had such a major impact on America in the early 1900s.
2. Describe the major reform movements trying to solve problems in state government during the early twentieth century.
3. Explain why Theodore Roosevelt has been called the "first twentieth-century President."
4. Discuss the major accomplishments of the Theodore Roosevelt Administration.
5. Explain why the presidential election of 1912 is considered one of the most significant in United States history.
6. Discuss the beginnings of the conservation movement and explain the debate over conservation versus development.
7. Explain the difference between the New Freedom of Woodrow Wilson and the New Nationalism of Theodore Roosevelt.
8. Explain the meaning of the term "Dollar Diplomacy" and give examples of it.
9. Explain why the United States was unable to maintain its initial position of neutrality concerning World War I.
10. Explain why historians and Europeans have used the term the "Arsenal of Democracy" to describe the role the United States played in World War I.
11. Describe the military and economic contribution made by the United States to the Allied victory in World War I.
12. Discuss the role of the federal government in the economy during World War I.

CHRONOLOGY

1900 Robert La Follette becomes governor of Wisconsin.
William McKinley is elected to a second presidential term.

1901 William McKinley is assassinated and Theodore Roosevelt becomes President.

1902 The national coal strike takes place.

1903 Congress passes the Elkins Act.

1904 Theodore Roosevelt wins the presidential election.
The Supreme Court decides the *Northern Securities* case.

1906 Upton Sinclair's novel *The Jungle* is published.
Congress passes the Hepburn Act, the Pure Food and Drug Act, and the Meat Inspection Act.

1908 William Howard Taft is elected President.

1909 Congress passes the Payne-Aldrich Tariff.
Herbert Croly publishes *The Promise of American Life*.
As part of Dollar Diplomacy, the United States intervenes in Nicaragua.

1910 Congress passes the Mann-Elkins Act.

1911 Henry Cabot Lodge issues the Lodge Corollary to the Monroe Doctrine.

1912 Woodrow Wilson wins the presidential election.

1913 Congress passes the Federal Reserve Act.
The Tampico incident strains U.S. relations with Mexico.

1914 Congress passes the Smith-Lever Act, the Federal Trade Commission Act, the

Clayton Antitrust Act, and the Harrison Narcotics Act.
World War I erupts in Europe.

1915 As part of Dollar Diplomacy, the United States intervenes in Haiti.
The *Lusitania* is sunk by a German U-boat.

1916 The United States invades Mexico.
Congress passes the Federal Farm Loan Act, the Warehouse Act, the Adamson Act, the Keating-Owen Act, and the Workmen's Compensation Act.
Woodrow Wilson is elected to a second presidential term.
The *Sussex* is sunk by a German U-boat and President Wilson issues the Sussex pledge or ultimatum.

1917 The United States acquires the Virgin Islands.
Germany resumes unrestricted submarine warfare.
Congress declares war on Germany, Austria-Hungary, and Italy.

1918 Congress passes the Overman Act.
President Woodrow Wilson establishes the Railroad Administration, Food Administration, Fuel Administration, National War Labor Board, War Industries Board, and War Finance Corporation.
President Wilson issues his Fourteen Points.
The armistice ends World War I hostilities.

PHOTOGRAPH AND ILLUSTRATION ANALYSIS

1. How does the cartoon illustrate the New Nationalism of Theodore Roosevelt? Why does it not illustrate the New Freedom of Woodrow Wilson?

NAME ______________________________ **DATE** ______________

"The President's Dream of a Successful Hunt"
(Courtesy, Library of Congress)

2. Look at the World War I cartoon on the following page. Historians today consider it to be a piece of propaganda. Why?

President Wilson portrayed the Germans as "wild beasts." *(Courtesy, Imperial War Museum, London)*

NAME ______________________________ DATE ______________

DOCUMENTS ANALYSIS

1. Explain this song. What did President Theodore Roosevelt do about "trusts" and "rebates"?

Not long ago the railroads owned the whole United
  States,
Their rates were high to farmers, but a trust could
  get rebates,
Who stopped this crime of freight rebates among
  the railroad men?
Who fixed it so the railroads carry people now and
  then?
It's Theodore, the peaceful Theodore;
Of all the rulers great or small
He is the greatest of them all.

2. Read the excerpt on the next page from *The New York Times*. What can you determine from it about American attitudes toward Germany at the time?

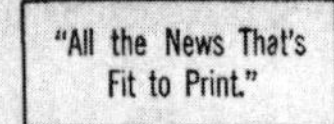

"All the News That's Fit to Print."

The New York Times.

EXTRA
5:30 A. M.

VOL. LXIV...NO. 20,923. NEW YORK, SATURDAY, MAY 8, 1915.—TWENTY-FOUR PAGES. ONE CENT

LUSITANIA SUNK BY A SUBMARINE, PROBABLY 1,260 DEAD; TWICE TORPEDOED OFF IRISH COAST; SINKS IN 15 MINUTES; CAPT. TURNER SAVED, FROHMAN AND VANDERBILT MISSING; WASHINGTON BELIEVES THAT A GRAVE CRISIS IS AT HAND

SHOCKS THE PRESIDENT

Washington Deeply Stirred by the Loss of American Lives.

BULLETINS AT WHITE HOUSE

Wilson Reads Them Closely, but Is Silent on the Nation's Course.

HINTS OF CONGRESS CALL

Loss of Lusitania Recalls Firm Tone of Our First Warning to Germany.

CAPITAL FULL OF RUMORS

Reports That Liner Was to be Sunk Were Heard Before Actual News Came.

Special to The New York Times.

WASHINGTON, May 7. – Never since that April day, three years ago, when word came that the Titanic had gone down, has Washington been so stirred as it is tonight over the sinking of the Lusitania. The early reports told that there had been no loss of life, but the relief that these advices caused gave way to the greatest concern late this evening when it became known that there had been many

The Lost Cunard Steamship Lusitania
X Where the First Torpedo Struck. XX Where the Second Torpedo Struck.

SOME DEAD TAKEN ASHORE

Several Hundred Survivors at Queenstown and Kinsale.

STEWARD TELLS OF DISASTER

One Torpedo Crashes Into the Doomed Liner's Bow, Another Into the Engine Room.

SHIP LISTS OVER TO PORT

Makes It Impossible to Lower Many Boats, So Hundreds Must Have Gone Down.

ATTACKED IN BROAD DAY

Passengers at Luncheon—Warning Had Been Given by Germans Before the Ship Left New York.

Only 650 Were Saved, Few Cabin Passengers

QUEENSTOWN, Saturday, May 8, 4:28 A. M.—Survivors of the Lusitania who have arrived here estimate that only about 650 of those aboard the steamer

3. The following notice came after the United States declaration of war. From your reading of the notice, what did the Selective Service require?

NAME ____ DATE ____________________

Attention!

ALL MALES between the ages of 21 and 30 years, both inclusive, must personally appear at the polling place in the Election District in which they reside, on

TUESDAY, JUNE 5th, 1917

between the hours of 7 A.M. and 9 P. M. and

Register

in accordance with the President's Proclamation.

Any male person, between these ages, who fails to register on June 5th, 1917, will be subject to imprisonment in jail or other penal institution for a term of one year.

NO EXCUSE FOR FAILURE TO REGISTER WILL BE ACCEPTED

NON-RESIDENTS must apply personally for registration, at the office of the County Clerk, at Kingston, N. Y., AT ONCE, in order that their registration cards may be in the hands of the Registration Board of their home district before June 5, 1917

Employers of males between these ages are earnestly requested to assits in the enforcement of the President's Proclamation.

Signed,

BOARD OF REGISTRATION
of Ulster County
E. T. SHULTIS, Sheriff
C. K. LOUGHRAN, County Clerk
Dr. FRANK JOHNSTON, Medical Officer

After the declaration of war on April 2, 1917, the Selective Service Act was passed in May.

4. World War I took large numbers of men into the armed forces, creating labor shortages at home. Women found themselves with new job opportunities. Read the following letter. What does it say about prevailing male attitudes toward women and work?

____

____

____

____

____

____

____

____

____

____

____

____

____

____

____

IN THIS ERA OF EMERGING WOMEN'S RIGHTS, *a woman wrote to a friend about the summer she did the haying:*

Dear Mrs. Coney:

Mr. Stewart had been too confident of getting men, so that haying caught him with too few men to put up the hay. He had no man to run the mower and he couldn't run both the mower and the stacker, so you can fancy what a place he was in.

I don't know that I ever told you, but my parents died within a year of each other and left six of us to shift for ourselves. Our people offered to take one here and there among them until we should all have a place, but we refused to be raised on the halves and so arranged to stay at Grandmother's and keep together. Well, we had no money to hire men to do our work, so had to learn to do it ourselves. Consequently I learned to do many things which girls more fortunately situated don't even know have to be done. Among the things I learned to do was the way to run a mowing-machine. It cost me many bitter tears because I got sunburned, and my hands were hard, rough, and stained with machine oil, and I used to wonder how any Prince Charming could overlook all that in any girl he came to. For all I had ever read of the Prince had to do with his "reverently kissing her lily-white hand," or doing some other fool trick with a hand as white as a snowflake. . . .

I almost forgot that I knew how until Mr. Stewart got into such a panic. If he put a man to mow, it kept them all idle at the stacker, and he just couldn't get enough men. I was afraid to tell him I could mow for fear he would forbid me to do so. But one morning, when he was chasing a last hope of help, I went down to the barn, took out the horses, and went to mowing. I had enough cut before he got back to show him I knew how, and as he came back manless he was delighted as well as surprised. I was glad because I really like to mow.

Elinore Stewart

VOCABULARY

The following words may not be part of your normal vocabulary. If their meaning is not familiar to you, you should look them up in a dictionary.

polyglot	trustbuster	isolationism	regeneration
moralism	aversion	reactionary	libertarian
indictment	surreptitious	rationing	reparations
ideology	hypocrisy	doughboy	militant
secular	mediation	disarmament	armistice

IDENTIFICATION OF KEY CONCEPTS

In two to three sentences, identify each of the following:

Sixteenth Amendment ______________________________

____

____

____

Seventeenth Amendment ______________________________

____

____

____

NAME ______________________________ **DATE** ______________

Initiative ______________________________

Referendum ______________________________

Recall ______________________________

Northern Securities Co. v. United States ______________________________

Elkins Act ______________________________

Election of 1904 ______________________________

Coal Strike of 1902 ______________________________

Hepburn Act ______________________________

Conservation Movement ______________________________

Pure Food and Drug Act ______________________________

Meat Inspection Act ______

______

______

______

Mann-Elkins Act of 1910 ______

______

______

______

Ballinger-Pinchot Controversy ______

______

______

______

New Nationalism ______

______

______

______

Election of 1912 ______

______

______

______

New Freedom ______

______

______

______

Federal Reserve Act ______

______

______

______

Federal Trade Commission Act ______

______

______

______

Clayton Antitrust Act ______

______

______

______

Workmen's Compensation Act ______

______

______

______

NAME ______________________________ DATE ______________

Adamson Act ______________________________

Dollar Diplomacy ______________________________

Committee on Public Information ______________________________

Unrestricted Submarine Warfare ______________________________

Preparedness Campaign ______________________________

Arsenal of Democracy ______________________________

IDENTIFICATION OF KEY INDIVIDUALS

In two to three sentences, identify each of the following:

Robert La Follette ______________________________

William McKinley ______________________________

Theodore Roosevelt ______________________________

Harvey Wiley ____

____

____

____

Gifford Pinchot ____

____

____

____

Upton Sinclair ____

____

____

____

Herbert Croly ____

____

____

____

SELF-TEST

Multiple-Choice Questions

1. The most far-reaching domestic measure of the Wilson Administration was the
   a. Federal Reserve Act of 1913.
   b. Smith-Lever Act.
   c. Adamson Act.
   d. La Follette Seamen's Act.

2. Woodrow Wilson won the election of 1912 largely because
   a. he had the most nationalistic programs.
   b. the Republican Party had split into two factions.
   c. he was the best-known candidate.
   d. the Democrats had long been a majority party.

3. Woodrow Wilson was very critical of
   a. the British form of government.
   b. racial segregation.
   c. Mexican leaders.
   d. southern society.

4. Which of the following is mispaired?
   a. New Nationalism—Theodore Roosevelt
   b. New Freedom—Woodrow Wilson
   c. Herbert Croly—*The Promise of American Life*
   d. Woodrow Wilson—The Rise of the Old South

5. Woodrow Wilson's New Freedom
   a. allowed a distinction between good and bad trusts.
   b. attacked bigness in government and business.
   c. gave new rights to African Americans.
   d. gave new rights to immigrant Americans.

NAME ______________________________________ DATE __________________

6. *Northern Securities Company v. United States* (1904) upheld
   a. President Roosevelt's attacks on an important holding company.
   b. the first child labor law.
   c. a law regulating working conditions.
   d. a law extending conservation areas.

7. A divisive issue between Theodore Roosevelt and William Howard Taft was
   a. reclamation of arid lands.
   b. the Ballinger-Pinchot dispute.
   c. labor reform.
   d. Taft's rejection of the Mann-Elkins Act.

8. The winner of the presidential election of 1904 was
   a. Hazen Pingree.
   b. Robert La Follette.
   c. William Howard Taft.
   d. Theodore Roosevelt.

9. When the war broke out in Europe in 1914 most Americans
   a. preferred neutrality.
   b. wished to come to the aid of Britain.
   c. suffered economic hardships caused by the conflict.
   d. were sympathetic to Germany.

10. During World War I Russia
    a. supported the Allies faithfully throughout the war.
    b. changed sides several times.
    c. tried to remain neutral throughout.
    d. experienced a revolution and withdrew from the war.

Matching Questions

For questions 11 through 15, use one of the lettered items.

11. Authorized Congress to pass an income tax.___
12. Overturned federal laws against child labor.___
13. Restricted the scope of the Sherman Antitrust Act.___
14. Upheld Theodore Roosevelt's decision to break up trusts.___
15. Revolved around freedom of speech.___

a. *Schenck v. United States*
b. *Hammer v. Dagenhart*
c. *Northern Securities Co. v. United States*
d. *United States v. E. C. Knight*
e. Sixteenth Amendment

For questions 16 through 20, use one of the lettered items.

16. Outlawed interlocking directorates and held corporate officials personally responsible for violation of federal antimonopoly laws.___
17. Prohibited misleading advertising of various consumer products.___
18. Outlawed child labor.___
19. Required an eight-hour workday in the railroad industry.___
20. Gave the federal government some control over fluctuations in the money supply.___

a. Pure Food and Drug Act of 1906
b. Federal Reserve Act of 1913
c. Keating-Owen Act of 1916
d. Adamson Act of 1916
e. Clayton Antitrust Act

True-False Questions

21. President William Howard Taft died in office.___
22. In the coal strike of 1902, President Theodore Roosevelt supported the interests of the coal companies against the interests of the workers.___
23. The Keating-Owen Act of 1916 was an early attempt by the federal government to outlaw child labor.___
24. "Dollar Diplomacy" had its greatest success in China.___
25. President Taft enforced the Sherman Antitrust Act with more vigor than Theodore Roosevelt.___

Essay Questions

1. Describe some of the leading characteristics of political progressivism. Are there any conflicts within it?

2. In what sense was Theodore Roosevelt a symbol of the Progressive Era? What were his strengths and his limitations as judged by today's standards?

Self-Test Answers

1. a 2. b 3. c 4. d 5. b 6. a 7. b 8. d 9. a 10. d 11. e 12. b 13. d 14. c
15. a 16. e 17. a 18. c 19. d 20. b 21. F 22. F 23. T 24. F 25. T

NAME ______________________________ DATE ______________

THE NEW ERA

SUGGESTED OUTCOMES

After studying Chapter 23, you should be able to

1. Explain the principal aims of Woodrow Wilson's "Fourteen Points."
2. Explain why the United States did not join the League of Nations, even though it was the major American component in the Treaty of Versailles.
3. Discuss the meaning of the term "Red Scare" and explain why it occurred in the United States after World War I.
4. Describe the rural-urban animosities that existed in the United States during the 1920s.
5. Describe the major elements of American popular culture as it existed in the 1920s.
6. Explain why historians have described the era of the 1920s as a period of political conservatism in the United States.
7. Describe which progressive elements survived during the 1920s.
8. Discuss the presidential election of 1928 and explain why it is considered significant in United States history.
9. Explain why the United States has been accused of being isolationist in the 1920s. Is the charge true?
10. Explain why the term "laissez-faire president" cannot fairly be used to describe the Herbert Hoover Administration. What did President Hoover do in an attempt to stimulate the economy and end the Great Depression?
11. Discuss some of the causes of the Great Depression.
12. Explain the significance of Charles Lindbergh's flight across the Atlantic.
13. Describe the Harlem Renaissance.

CHRONOLOGY

1918 President Wilson issues his Fourteen Points.
The armistice ends World War I hostilities.

1919 The United States Senate refuses to ratify the Treaty of Versailles.
The steel strike occurs.
The Chicago race riot occurs.
The Boston police strike occurs.
The Eighteenth Amendment is adopted and Prohibition begins.

1920 The Palmer Raids take place.
Congress passes the Transportation (Esch-Cummins) Act, the Water Power Act, and the Merchant Marine (Jones) Act.
Warren G. Harding wins the presidential election.

1921 The Washington Naval Conference convenes.

1922 The Supreme Court decides the *Bailey v. Drexel Furniture* case.

1923 Warren Harding dies and Calvin Coolidge becomes President.

1924 Congress passes the Johnson Act.
Calvin Coolidge wins the presidential election.
The Dawes Plan goes into effect.

1925 The Scopes Trial takes place in Dayton, Tennessee.

1927 Congress passes the Radio Act.

1928 The Young Plan goes into effect.
Herbert Hoover wins the presidential election.

1929 Congress passes the Agricultural Marketing Act.
The stock market crashes.

1930 The State Department releases the Clark Memorandum.

1931 Japan invades Manchuria.
Congress establishes the Reconstruction Finance Corporation.

1932 Franklin D. Roosevelt wins the presidential election of 1932.

1933 The Twenty-first Amendment is adopted and Prohibition comes to an end.

PHOTOGRAPH AND ILLUSTRATION ANALYSIS

1. Explain these cartoons.

____

____

____

____

____

____

____

____

____

____

____

____

____

____

Opposition to President Wilson's League of Nations mounted, and the Senate finally defeated his plan that would have allowed the United States to join. *(Cartoon by Rollin Kirby,* New York World, *April 14, 1921)*

The Teapot Dome and Elk Hills oil scandal rocked the Republican administration in 1924, resulting in the prosecution or resignation of several of Harding's appointees. *(Cartoon by Clifford Berryman, Courtesy, Library of Congress)*

NAME ______________________________ DATE ____________________

2. What is the meaning of the key symbols in this photograph of the Ku Klux Klan of the 1920s?

The Klan was active against Catholics outside the South. This picture, replete with symbols, was taken near Milwaukee, Wisconsin. *(Courtesy, FPG)*

3. How "bad" was the Great Depression judging by the "Hooverville" on the next page? Where was this picture taken? Where does the name Hooverville come from?

By the early 1930s, shantytowns had sprung up across the United States. *(Courtesy, Museum of History & Industry)*

4. From looking at the chart on the following page, can you say how much the New Deal did to cure the Great Depression?

NAME ______________________________ DATE ______________

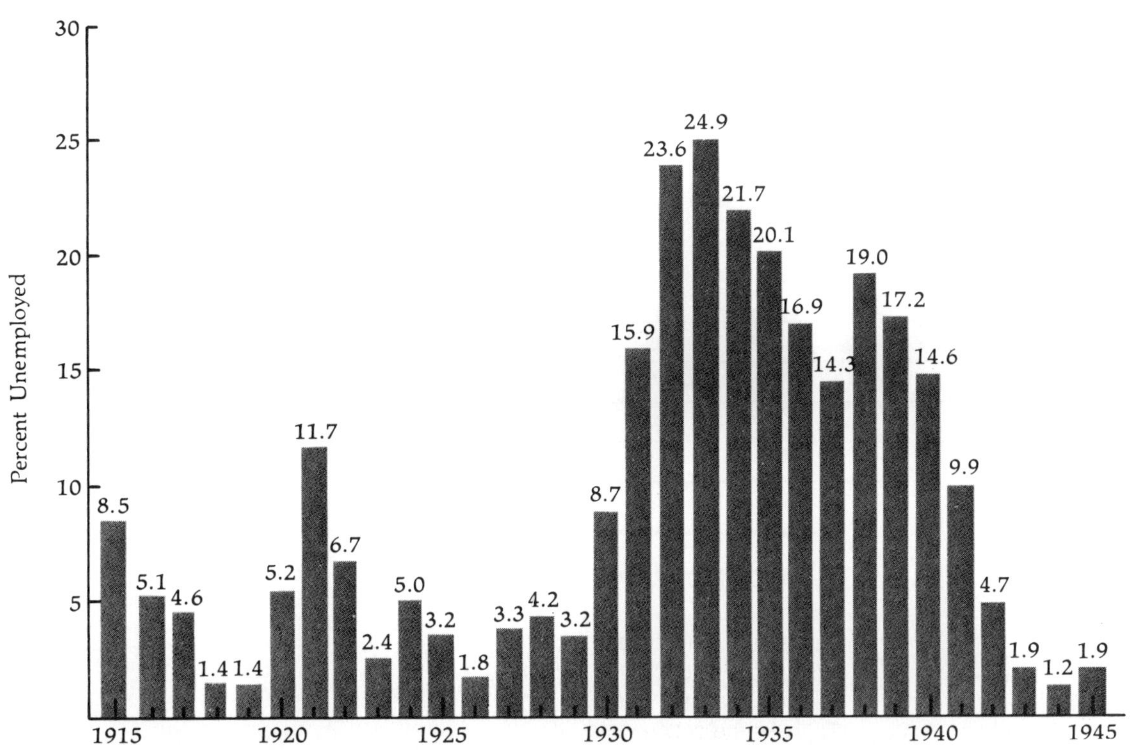

Unemployment, 1915–1945.

5. Look at the following chart. Why did labor unions grow in membership during the 1930s?

____

____

____

____

____

____

____

____

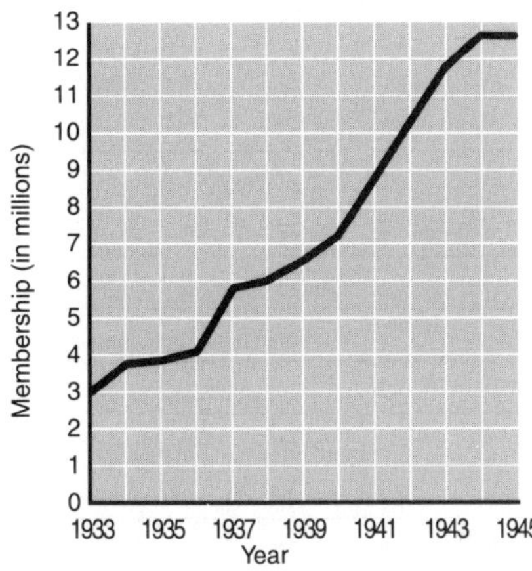

Labor Union Membership, 1933–1945

DOCUMENTS ANALYSIS

1. Read the poem by Langston Hughes. What does it say about about the life of a sharecropper in the early 1900s? Read the description of sharecropping in your textbook. What do the poem and the description have in common?

SHARE-CROPPERS *by Langston Hughes*

Just a herd of Negroes
Driven to the field,
Plowing, planting, hoeing,
To make the cotton yield.

When the cotton's picked
And the work is done
Boss man take the money
And we get none.

Leaves us hungry, ragged
As we were before.
Year by year goes by
And we are nothing more.

Than a herd of Negroes
Driven to the field—
Plowing life away
To make the cotton yield.

2. How does Frances Ridgway's account on the following page reflect the role of gender differences during the Great Depression?

NAME ______________________________ DATE ______________

____

____

____

____

ONE WOMAN'S STRUGGLE FOR AN EDUCATION DURING THE DEPRESSION

Frances Ridgway's story of life in rural Michigan speaks for the experiences of many depression-era women.

The Depression caused my family to change their way of living. There were six of us kids and in order to feed us all, my parents traded their town home for an eighty-acre farm. There was no electricity there, no running water, and no flush toilet. And the house was back off the road a half a mile.

But my father thought at least we could eat, living on a farm. And we did, even if it was only beans. My mother would put up 600 or 700 quarts of beans every year.

When I reached twelve years old, I wanted to go to high school; but back in northern Michigan they didn't encourage farm girls to get much of an education. Now, I really insisted that my parents let me go live with this family who paid me two dollars a week to take care of the house and kids.

I did that kind of work for the better part of four years. Sometimes I stayed at home, but when I did I'd have to walk almost four miles to get to the place where the school bus stopped.

I'll tell you, I washed and I cleaned and did all the dirty work, you know. Anyway, when I started that first year of high school, I had six dollars saved, and that was enough to buy all my supplies until Christmas. I supplemented my income in another way, by writing all the book reports for the boys on the football team at a nickel apiece. And you know for a nickel you could get a big, thick pad of paper.

During my senior year I got an NRA grant of six dollars a month for helping the teachers correct papers. I thought that was wonderful.

But on the whole, it was hard. I was so very poor. I had one skirt I made out of an old coat in home economics class. And I wore NRA pants. You know, my family got food supplements, and they'd come in sacks that had NRA stamped on them. My mother'd dye them a dark seal brown, but the NRA was still there. My brothers used to always call my NRA pants, "Nuts Running America." I forget . . . I think it meant National Recovery Act.

Anyway, I had no clothes and no money but I finished at the top of my class and I competed for a scholarship and won. It was to Wellesley, a big Eastern college for women. Well, of course, that was out of the question. I didn't even have the money to get there, let alone all the extras I'd need.

But I had a goal for myself. Ever since I was twelve years old there was one major goal in my life . . . one thing . . . and that was to never be poor again. I wasn't especially attractive, and I was poor. I couldn't do anything about the one, but I made up my mind I wasn't always going to be poor.

Source: Frances Ridgway, quoted in Jeane Westin, *Making Do: How Women Survived the '30s*. Chicago: Follett, 1976. 152–153.

VOCABULARY

The following words may not be part of your normal vocabulary. If their meaning is not familiar to you, you should look them up in a dictionary.

regeneration	demobilization	fundamentalism	aesthetic
mandate	chauvinism	agnosticism	rectitude
reparations	irreconcilable	bohemians	rhapsodize

IDENTIFICATION OF KEY CONCEPTS

In two to three sentences, identify each of the following:

Fourteen Points ______________________________

League of Nations ______________________________

Treaty of Versailles ______________________________

Nineteenth Amendment ______________________________

The Red Scare ______________________________

Chicago Race Riot of 1919 ______________________________

Palmer Raids ______________________________

Sacco-Vanzetti Case ______________________________

Eighteenth Amendment and Prohibition ______________________________

Election of 1920 ______________________________

NAME ______________________________ DATE ______________

Johnson Act and Immigration Restriction ______________________________

Religious Fundamentalism and the Scopes Trial ______________________________

Harlem Renaissance ______________________________

Election of 1928 ______________________________

Teapot Dome ______________________________

McNary-Haugen Plan ______________________________

Washington Naval Conference ______________________________

Clark Memorandum ______________________________

Reconstruction Finance Corporation ______________________________

Hoover Doctrine ______________________________

Transportation (Esch-Cummins) Act

Ku Klux Klan

Dawes Plan

Young Plan

IDENTIFICATION OF KEY INDIVIDUALS

In two to three sentences, identify each of the following:

A. Mitchell Palmer

Warren G. Harding

Calvin Coolidge

Al Smith

Herbert Hoover

NAME ______________________________ DATE ______________

Charles Lindbergh ______________________________

____

____

____

Andrew Mellon ______________________________

____

____

____

Charles Evans Hughes ______________________________

____

____

____

Marcus Garvey ______________________________

____

____

____

SELF-TEST

Multiple-Choice Questions

1. Woodrow Wilson believed that the key to a successful peace settlement at Versailles was
   a. reparations.
   b. the restoration of German strength.
   c. the League of Nations.
   d. supporting Communism in the Soviet Union.

2. Events of the troubled year 1919 include all but
   a. the Palmer Raids.
   b. the Boston police strike.
   c. a Chicago race riot.
   d. strikes in major industries.

3. The Hoover Doctrine was a U.S. foreign policy dealing with
   a. the Japanese invasion of Manchuria in 1931.
   b. Latin America.
   c. Africa.
   d. Cuba and the Caribbean.

4. Nativism in the 1920s played a part in all but the
   a. rise of the second Ku Klux Klan.
   b. prohibition movement.
   c. study of I.Q. tests.
   d. St. Valentine's Day Massacre.

5. The election of 1928 featured all but
   a. enormous bigotry against Al Smith.
   b. Smith's assertive display of his Roman Catholicism.
   c. Hoover's reputation for military skill.
   d. a popular sense that Hoover represented both tradition and prosperity.

6. In the 1920s Japan
   a. was dominated by Chinese and Russian influences.
   b. became an important military power with which the West had to bargain.
   c. was allied with China to oppose Russian movement into East Asia.
   d. actively aided rebels in the Philippines against American imperialism.

7. Woodrow Wilson's Fourteen Points included all but
   a. freedom of the seas.
   b. national self-determination in central and eastern Europe.
   c. the League of Nations.
   d. reparations.

8. The major works of literature of the 1920s can best be characterized as reflecting
   a. an interest in the workings of democracy.
   b. a critical attempt, favorable or unfavorable, to understand American culture and values.
   c. fascination with European cultures.
   d. the search for the values inherent in other nations and cultures.

9. The Dawes and Young Plans concerned
   a. drug addiction.
   b. treatment of Latin America.
   c. treatment of immigrants.
   d. war debts and reparations.

10. Calvin Coolidge's presidency was most closely associated with the needs of
    a. labor.
    b. immigrants.
    c. southern migrants.
    d. business.

Matching Questions

For questions 11 through 15, use one of the lettered items.

11. A decision not to recognize the puppet Japanese government in Manchuria in 1931.___
12. The treaty ending World War I in Europe.___
13. A multinational treaty outlawing war.___
14. Resulted in a substantial reduction in the number of capital ships by the United States, Great Britain, Japan, France, and Italy.___
15. Designed to finance the sale of surplus American farm products in foreign markets.___

a. Kellogg-Briand Pact
b. Treaty of Versailles
c. Washington Naval Conference of 1921–1922
d. McNary-Haugen Plan
e. Hoover Doctrine

For questions 16 through 20, use one of the lettered items.

16. A business demand for the "open shop."___
17. Made Prohibition the law of the land.___
18. A scandal during the Harding Administration.___
19. Imposed major restrictions on immigration to the U.S.___
20. Provided government loans to banks during the depression.___

a. American Plan
b. Eighteenth Amendment
c. Johnson Act
d. Reconstruction Finance Corporation
e. Teapot Dome

NAME ______________________________ DATE ______________

True-False Questions

21. The Sacco-Vanzetti case revolved around stock market fraud.___
22. The Scopes trial revolved around the teaching of evolution in the schools.___
23. *Middletown* by Robert and Helen Lynd is a sociological study of a medium-sized Indiana city.___
24. The first major sound movie was released in 1915.___
25. In the election of 1928, Herbert Hoover defeated Al Smith for the presidency.___

Essay Questions

1. Was the decade of the 1920s the stagnant period that some characterizations of it have portrayed?

2. Speculate on ways that the Harlem Renaissance was influential.

3. What were the Espionage and Sedition Acts? Why were they products of a "progressive" President?

4. Why is the 1920s sometimes called the most productive decade in American literature during the twentieth century?

Self-Test Answers

1. c 2. a 3. a 4. d 5. c 6. b 7. d 8. b 9. d 10. d 11. e 12. b 13. a 14. c 15. d 16. a 17. b 18. e 19. c 20. d 21. F 22. T 23. T 24. F 25. T

NAME ______________________ DATE ____________

THE NEW DEAL

SUGGESTED OUTCOMES

After studying Chapter 24, you should be able to

1. Describe the personality and background of Franklin D. Roosevelt and discuss how they influenced his presidency.
2. Discuss the meaning of the term "New Deal."
3. Describe the time known as the "One Hundred Days" and explain why it is considered one of the most prolific legislative periods in United States political history.
4. Describe the living conditions of unemployed people during the Great Depression.
5. Describe the major ideas of those individuals who were the most well-known opponents of Franklin D. Roosevelt and the New Deal.
6. Describe which New Deal programs have had the most lasting effect on American life.
7. Explain why Franklin D. Roosevelt attempted to "pack" the Supreme Court and how the entire controversy can be considered a victory as well as a defeat for the President.
8. Explain the significance of the New Deal in modern United States history.
9. Explain how the Great Depression affected American literature during the 1930s.

CHRONOLOGY

1932 Federal troops disperse the Bonus Marchers in Washington, D.C.
Franklin D. Roosevelt is elected President.

1933 Roosevelt declares a nationwide banking holiday.
Congress passes the Emergency Banking Act and the Economy Act.
Congress passes the Banking Act of 1933.
Roosevelt creates the Farm Credit Administration.
Congress passes the National Industrial Recovery Act and the Agricultural Adjustment Act.
Congress establishes the Federal Emergency Relief Administration, Tennessee Vally Authority, Public Works Administration, and Civilian Conservation Corps.
Congress establishes the Home Owners' Loan Corporation.

1934 Congress passes the Securities Exchange Act.
Congress passes the National Housing Act.

1935 The Supreme Court decides the case of *Schechter v. United States*.
Congress establishes the Works Progress Administration, the Rural Electrification Administration, and the National Youth Administration.
Congress passes the National Labor Relations (Wagner) Act, the Social Security Act, the Public Utility Holding Company Act, and the Wealth Tax Act.

1936 Roosevelt wins a second presidential term.

1937 Roosevelt launches his assault on the Supreme Court.
The sit-down strikes begin.
The Depression of 1937 begins.

1938 Congress passes a second Agricultural Adjustment Act and the Fair Labor Standards Act.

1940 Roosevelt wins a third presidential term.

PHOTOGRAPH AND ILLUSTRATION ANALYSIS

1. Who are the people identified in the accompanying photograph? What happened to them? Look at the next photograph. Why was this event a political disaster for President Herbert Hoover?

The Bonus Marchers of 1932. *(Courtesy, Library of Congress)*

NAME ________________________ DATE ______________

General Douglas MacArthur disobeyed President Hoover's orders and engineered a confrontation that ended in the burning of the Bonus Army shacks in the muddy Anacostia Flats of Maryland. *(Courtesy, National Archives)*

2. Explain the sketch on the next page.

The New Deal programs quickly made Roosevelt the hero of the working class. *(Cartoon by Burris Jenkins, January 30, 1934)*

3. The photograph on the next page is considered a classic. What does it tell you about the life of a migrant woman during the Great Depression?

NAME ______________________________ DATE ______________

***Migrant Mother, Nipomo, California,* by Dorothea Lange.**
(Courtesy, The Museum of Modern Art, New York)

4. Explain the cartoon on the next page having to do with the Supreme Court of the 1930s.

The American people rejected President Roosevelt's "court-packing" scheme aimed at obtaining Supreme Court rulings more sympathetic to the New Deal. *(Courtesy, F. D. R. Library)*

DOCUMENTS ANALYSIS

1. Read the selection on the next page from Thomas Wolfe's novel *Of Time and the River*. What is meant when it is described as "folk nationalism"?

NAME ______________________ DATE ____________

IN HIS NOVEL *Of Time and The River* Thomas Wolfe evoked the folk nationalism that helped America through the Depression. Wolfe sang

the thunder of imperial names, the names of men and battles, the names of places and great rivers, the mighty names of the States. The name of The Wilderness; and the names of Antietam, Chancellorsville, Shiloh, Bull Run, Fredericksburg, Cold Harbor, the Wheat Fields, Ball's Bluff, and the Devil's Den; the names of Cowpens, Brandywine, and Saratoga; of Death Valley, Chickamauga, and the Cumberland Gap. The names of the Nantahalahs, the Bad Lands, the Painted Desert, the Yosemite, and the Little Big Horn; the names of Yancey and Cabarrus counties; and the terrible name of Hatteras.

Then, for the continental thunder of the States: the names of Montana, Texas, Arizona, Colorado, Michigan, Maryland, Virginia, and the two Dakotas; the names of Oregon and Indiana, of Kansas and the rich Ohio; the powerful name of Pennsylvania, the name of Old Kentucky; the undulance of Alabama; the names of Florida and North Carolina.

In the red-oak thickets, at the break of day, long hunters lay for bear—the rattle of arrows in laurel leaves, the war-cries round the painted buttes, and the majestical names of the Indian Nations: the Pawnees, the Algonquins, the Iroquois, the Comanches, the Blackfeet, the Seminoles, the Cherokees, the Sioux, the Hurons, the Mohawks, the Navajos, the Utes, the Omahas, the Onondagas, the Chippewas, the Crees, the Chickasaws, the Arapahoes, the Catawbas, the Dakotas, the Apaches, the Croatans, and the Tuscaroras; the names of Powhatan and Sitting Bull; and the name of the Great Chief, Rain-In-The-Face. . . .

The rails go westward in the dark. Brother, have you seen starlight on the rails? Have you heard the thunder of the fast express?

Of wandering forever, and the earth again—the names of the mighty rails that bind the nation, the wheeled thunder of the names that net the continent: the Pennsylvania, the Union Pacific, the Santa Fé, the Baltimore and Ohio, the Chicago and Northwestern, the Southern, the Louisiana and Northern, the Seaboard Air Line, the Chicago, Milwaukee and Saint Paul, the Lackawanna, the New York, New Haven and Hartford, the Florida East Coast, the Rock Island, and the Denver and Rio Grande. . . .

The names of the mighty rivers, the alluvial gluts, the drains of the continent, the throats that drink America (Sweet Thames, flow gently till I end my song). The names of men who pass, and the myriad names of the earth that abides forever: the names of the men who are doomed to wander, and the name of that immense and lonely land on which they wander, to which they return, in which they will be buried—America! The immortal earth which waits forever, the trains that thunder on the continent, the men who wander, and the women who cry out, "Return!"

Finally, the names of the great rivers that are flowing in the darkness. . . .

The names of great mouths, the mighty maws, the vast, wet, coiling, never-glutted and unending snakes that drink the continent. Where, sons of men, and in what other land will you find others like them, and where can you match the mighty music of their names?—The Monongahela, the Colorado, the Rio Grande, the Columbia, the Tennessee, the Hudson (Sweet Thames!); the Kennebec, the Rappahannock, the Delaware, the Penobscot, the Wabash, the Chesapeake, the Swannanoa, the Indian River, the Niagara (Sweet Afton!); the Saint Lawrence, the Susquehanna, the Tombigbee, the Nantahala, the French Broad, the Chattahoochee, the Arizona, and the Potomac (Father Tiber!)—these are a few of their princely names, these are a few of their great, proud, glittering names, fit for the immense and lonely land that they inhabit.

2. Read the account of an enrollee in the Civilian Conservation Corps of the 1930s. What is there to praise about the work? Is there anything to criticize?

ONE ENROLLEE *in the Civilian Conservation Corps recalls:*

"I was sent to Utah. I'll never forget the ride up the mountains in this battered old truck. We had an old grizzled army sergeant in charge. When we got to the area, it was just thick woods. 'Where's the camp?' I asked. The sarge waved his hands around the trees. 'This is it. Break out the axes and chop like hell if you don't want to sleep on the ground.' We chopped and built cabins and even a mess hall. For the next three years I grew up, physically and mentally and spiritually, in that beautiful country. It was one of the most rewarding experiences of my life. Before I left I was offered a job as a ranger. To this day I wonder whether I was a fool in turning it down and coming back east. A large number of the CCCs stayed on. Some own ranches today."

VOCABULARY

The following words may not be part of your normal vocabulary. If their meaning is not familiar to you, you should look them up in a dictionary.

incumbent	sordidness	fascist	dilemma
interregnum	solace	scruples	
refinance	vagrant	boondoggle	
speakeasy	foreclose	barrage	

NAME ____________________ DATE ____________

IDENTIFICATION OF KEY CONCEPTS

In two to three sentences, identify each of the following:

Bonus Army ____________________

First Hundred Days ____________________

Second Hundred Days ____________________

Election of 1936 ____________________

Depression of 1937–1938 ____________________

Farm Credit Administration ____________________

National Industrial Recovery Act ____________________

Agricultural Adjustment Administration ____________________

Works Progress Administration ____________________

Civilian Conservation Corps

Banking Act of 1933

Wealth Tax Act of 1935

Social Security Act

National Labor Relations Act

Agricultural Adjustment Act of 1938

Home Owners' Loan Corporation

Fair Labor Standards Act of 1938

Election of 1936

Court-Packing Scheme

NAME ______________________________ DATE ______________

Sit-down strikes ______________________________

Brains Trust ______________________________

IDENTIFICATION OF KEY INDIVIDUALS

In two to three sentences, identify each of the following:

Thomas Wolfe ______________________________

John Steinbeck ______________________________

Robert Wagner ______________________________

Eleanor Roosevelt ______________________________

Frances Perkins ______________________________

Adolfe Berle ______________________________

Huey Long ______________________________

Gerald L. K. Smith ______________________________

____

____

____

Father Charles Coughlin ______________________________

____

____

____

Francis Townsend ______________________________

____

____

____

SELF-TEST

Multiple-Choice Questions

1. The right of labor to organize and bargain collectively was guaranteed by
   a. Section 7a of the NIRA.
   b. the AAA.
   c. the RFC.
   d. *Schechter v. U.S.*

2. During his First Hundred Days in office, Roosevelt took all of these actions to combat the Depression except
   a. declaring a bank holiday.
   b. establishing the Tennessee Valley Authority.
   c. establishing the FDIC.
   d. relaxing federal authority over the currency.

3. Roosevelt's Second Hundred Days resulted in all of these except
   a. the reinstatement of the draft.
   b. the social security system.
   c. legislation affecting labor-management relations.
   d. the Wealth Tax Act.

4. The Congress of Industrial Organizations
   a. was created by New Deal legislation to protect private investment in industry.
   b. organized labor not by craft but by industry.
   c. had the firm support of the AFL.
   d. opposed Section 7a of the NIRA.

5. The Supreme Court declared which of these unconstitutional?
   a. NIRA and the first AAA
   b. OPA and TVA
   c. HOLC and CCC
   d. the Butler and Schechter acts

6. Who was President when the Bonus Army marched to its destination?
   a. Calvin Coolidge
   b. Theodore Roosevelt
   c. Herbert Hoover
   d. Franklin D. Roosevelt

NAME ______________________________ DATE ______________

7. One reason Roosevelt's court-packing plan failed was
   a. the court itself changed direction and became more liberal.
   b. the chief justice resigned.
   c. new members of the court were elected.
   d. liberal senators mostly disapproved of it.

8. The depression had all of these effects on American life except
   a. a decline in the birth rate.
   b. a drop in the divorce rate.
   c. alterations in family life patterns.
   d. a movement for equal pay for women.

9. The Depression
   a. was over by 1938.
   b. ended before Roosevelt's stunning reelection victory in 1936.
   c. lessened in severity but then returned, ending only during World War II.
   d. was really over before Hoover left the White House.

10. The rate of crime in the 1930s
   a. increased in all its forms.
   b. stayed level with that in the 1920s.
   c. decreased.
   d. increased in crimes against property but decreased in assaults.

Matching Questions

For questions 11 through 15, use one of the lettered items.

11. A medical doctor who became popular in the 1930s by proposing old-age pensions.___
12. The "Radio Priest" who hated Fanklin D. Roosevelt.___
13. The famous depression-era photographer.___
14. Secretary of labor under Franklin D. Roosevelt.___
15. The Louisiana politician who proposed the "Share-Our-Wealth" plan.___

a. Charles Coughlin
b. Francis Townsend
c. Frances Perkins
d. Huey Long
e. Dorothea Lange

For questions 16 through 20, use one of the lettered items.

16. Provided flood control, irrigation, and hydroelectric power projects.___
17. Tried to deal with the farm problem by paying farmers not to raise large volumes of crops.___
18. A government relief program that put young men to work in rural areas.___
19. Provided government insurance for bank deposits.___
20. Provided new protections for organized labor.___

a. FDIC
b. AAA
c. Wagner Act
d. CCC
e. TVA

True-False Questions

21. Franklin D. Roosevelt came from a working-class background.___
22. Eleanor Roosevelt traveled and wrote about social reform.___
23. The *Schechter* decision declared the NIRA unconstitutional.___
24. During the New Deal, a minimum wage law was never passed.___
25. During the Great Depression, the American birth rate declined.___

Essay Questions

1. What were the central features of the New Deal? Did the New Deal lack direction? Who did the New Deal serve?

2. What was "conservative" about the New Deal?

Self-Test Answers

1. a 2. d 3. a 4. b 5. a 6. c 7. a 8. d 9. c 10. d 11. b 12. a 13. e 14. c
15. d 16. e 17. b 18. d 19. a 20. c 21. F 22. T 23. T 24. F 25. T

NAME ______________________ DATE ______________

25 DIPLOMACY AND WAR 1933–1945

SUGGESTED OUTCOMES

After studying Chapter 25, you should be able to

1. Explain why the United States decided to extend diplomatic recognition to the Soviet Union in 1933.
2. Describe the origins of the Good Neighbor Policy and how it was implemented during the 1920s, 1930s, and 1940s.
3. Discuss Adolf Hitler's major goals for Germany and Europe.
4. Explain why and how the United States slowly drifted into war between 1937 and 1941.
5. Explain why Japan attacked Pearl Harbor in 1941 and how the United States reacted to the attack.
6. Describe domestic life in the United States during World War II and how life changed for so many people.
7. Describe what happened to African Americans and Japanese Americans during World War II.
8. Discuss the Allied military strategies for the European and Pacific fronts during World War II.
9. Explain the diplomatic significance of the Yalta Conference of 1945, as well as its significance in the postwar world.

CHRONOLOGY

1933 The World Economic Conference convenes in London.
The United States extends diplomatic recognition to the Soviet Union.
Congress creates the Export-Import Bank.
The Seventh International Conference of American States convenes in Montevideo, Uruguay.

1934 Franklin Roosevelt withdraws the last United States troops from Haiti.

1935 Congress passes the Neutrality Act.

1936 Congress passes a second Neutrality Act.
Germany reoccupies the Rhineland.

1937 Congress passes a third Neutrality Act.
Japan invades China.
President Roosevelt delivers his "Quarantine Speech" in Chicago.

1938 Germany takes control of Austria and Czechoslovakia.

1939 Germany invades Poland and World War II begins.

1940 Congress passes the Selective Service Act.
Franklin D. Roosevelt wins a third presidential term.
The United States concludes the "destroyers-for-bases" deal with Great Britain.
Japan invades Indochina.

1941 Japan bombs Pearl Harbor and the United States declares war.
Congress establishes the Lend-Lease program.
Germany invades the Soviet Union.

1942 Allied forces invade North Africa.
Congress establishes the War Production Board, War Labor Board, and the War Manpower Commission.
Congress passes the Emergency Price Control Act.
Some Japanese Americans are placed in internment camps.
Japanese forces conquer the Philippine Islands.
American forces are victorious at Guadalcanal and Midway.

1943 Allied forces invade Sicily and Italy.
The Tehran Conference convenes.
American forces in the Pacific seize the Gilbert Islands.

1944 Allied armies invade France.
American forces in the Pacific seize the Marshall Islands and the Mariana Islands.
American forces invade the Philippines.

1945 The Yalta Conference convenes.
American forces in the Pacific take Iwo Jima and Okinawa.
Germany surrenders.
Atomic bombs are dropped on Japan.
Japan surrenders.

PHOTOGRAPH AND ILLUSTRATION ANALYSIS

1. Explain this photograph. What happened to Japanese Americans during World War II?

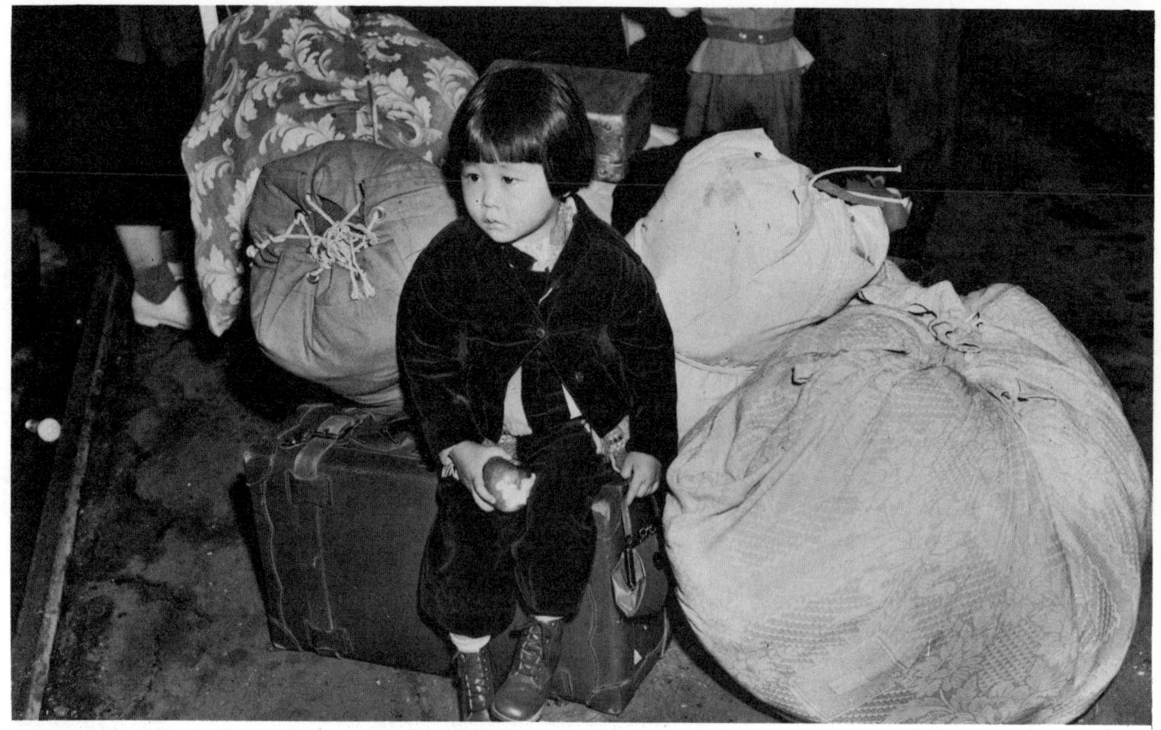

Although engaged in a war to defeat racist regimes in Japan and Germany, the United States succumbed to wartime hysteria, interned Japanese Americans living in California, and relocated them far inland.
(Courtesy, National Archives)

NAME ______________________ DATE ____________

2. Explain this photograph.

John Atherton, *A Careless Word, Another Cross.*
(Courtesy, The Museum of Modern Art, New York)

DOCUMENTS ANALYSIS

1. After reading the statement on the next page by Yoshiye Togasaki, describe life for Japanese Americans at the Manzanar relocation camp. What violations of their rights as American citizens occurred?

MS. YOSHIYE TOGASAKI, *a Californian, recalled her wartime imprisonment in a concentration camp for Japanese Americans:*

We could not go to public swimming pools in San Francisco, and they tried to segregate the schools, you know. It was not quite the same discrimination as the blacks in the South experienced, because we were not excluded from most public facilities, but we were definitely set apart. We might have white friends in school, but they did not socialize with us outside of school. We did not date whites, we did not go to parties or dances with them.

They thought of us as inferior, at least many of them did. We were called J-A-P-S. And of course there was the problem that nobody recognized you as a citizen. So we had to struggle that much harder to reach our goals. I certainly had to do my share of struggling to become a doctor. . . .

The rule was that everyone was evacuated who was at least one-sixteenth Japanese. . . .

I went to Manzanar. It was built from scratch by the military, and so it resembled a military place. Families had no privacy, and they were split apart. I was particularly upset with that aspect of it. A mother and children might be in one place, the father in another, and maybe teen-age daughters would be thrown in with four or five bachelors.

It was also a very dirty place. Manzanar at one time had been a pear orchard, before Los Angeles took over all of the water rights of the area. When that happened, the orchard went dry, and the place became very dusty. The wind would blow from the south, and then it would turn around and blow from the north, and it was a very fine grit that covered everyone and everything. It was in the beds and in the food. We took showers, of course, but that was an unpleasant task. The showers were all open, and you can imagine how the women were embarrassed with that. . . .

Many of the older people had lived in the United States most of their lives, and the nisei (second-generation Japanese-Americans) were full citizens. They were law-abiding people, they were hard-working, they loved the United States, and now they were treated like traitors. . . .

All of Manzanar was a stockade, actually—a prison. We were in jail. There was barbed wire all around, there were great big watch towers in the corners, and there were spotlights turned on during the night. You could not cross the boundaries, unless you were authorized on a work detail or something. The guards carried rifles. There was a teen-ager at Manzanar who walked out into the desert one day. He was not running away, he just walked in plain sight. Who in God's name would try to escape in broad daylight? He was mentally deranged. And he got shot. They shot him in the back. So we all knew exactly where we stood.

NAME ______________________________ **DATE** ______________

2. What does this shipyard diary of a woman welder, Augusta Clawson, tell about gender differences in employment during World War II?

____

____

____

____

____

____

____

____

____

____

____

____

____

____

____

____

____

____

____

____

____

____

THE SHIPYARD DIARY OF A WOMAN WELDER

Back to work and more welding. I "dis-improved" as rapidly after lunch as I had improved during the morning. One girl stopped to ask, "How you doin'?" and watched me critically. "Here, let me show you, you're holding it too far away." So she took over, but she couldn't maintain the arc at all. She got up disgusted, said, "I can't do it—my hand shakes so since I been sick," and I took over again. But she was right. I held it closer and welded on and on and on. . . .

We were called to another safety lecture—good sound advice on Eye Safety. . . . Only Chile has a higher accident rate than the United States. Last year the shipyard had fairly heavy absenteeism, but this year they hope to build an extra ship on the decrease in absenteeism. He cautioned us about creating hazards by wearing the wrong kind of clothing, and told us not to wear watches or rings. After it was over, Missouri was bothered about her wedding ring. It hadn't been off in fourteen years. She was willing to take it off, but only if necessary.

The lecturer brought up the rumor that arc welding causes sterility among women. He said that this was untrue, and quoted an authoritative source to prove its falsity. . . . Actually, welders had *more* children than other people. "No, thanks," said the first girl; "I don't like that either!" . . .

I, who hate heights, climbed stair after stair after stair till I thought I must be close to the sun. I stopped on the top deck. I, who hate confined spaces, went through narrow corridors, stumbling my way over rubber-coated leads—dozens of them, scores of them, even hundreds of them. I went into a room about four feet by ten where two shipfitters, a shipfitter's helper, a chipper, and I all worked. I welded in the poop deck lying on the floor while another welder spattered sparks from the ceiling and chippers like giant woodpeckers shattered our eardrums. I, who've taken welding, and have sat at a bench welding flat and vertical plates, was told to weld braces along a baseboard below a door opening. On these a heavy steel door was braced while it was hung to a fine degree of accuracy. I welded more braces along the side, and along the top. I did overhead welding, horizontal, flat, vertical. I welded around curved hinges which were placed so close to the side wall that I had to bend my rod in a curve to get it in. I made some good welds and some frightful ones. But now a door in the poop deck of an oil tanker is hanging, four feet by six of solid steel, by *my* welds. Pretty exciting!

Source: Augusta Clawson, *Shipyard Diary of a Woman Welder*. New York: Penguin, 1944, quoted in Rosalyn Baxandall, Linda Gordon, and Susan Reverby, eds., *America's Working Women: A Documentary History, 1600 to the Present*. New York: Random House, 1976. 288–289.

VOCABULARY

The following words may not be part of your normal vocabulary. If their meaning is not familiar to you, you should look them up in a dictionary.

fascism	belligerent	plebiscite	infamy
impregnable	collectivization	embargo	pincer
proletarian	martial	communique	
unilateral	bilateral	bigotry	
multilateral	rapprochement	quarantine	

IDENTIFICATION OF KEY CONCEPTS

In two to three sentences, identify each of the following:

World Economic Conference of 1933 ______________________________

____

____

____

Good Neighbor Policy ______________________________

____

____

____

Neutrality Act of 1935 ______________________________

____

____

____

Spanish Civil War ______________________________

____

____

____

NAME ______________________________ DATE ______________

Nye Committee ______________________________

____

____

____

Sitzkrieg ______________________________

____

____

____

Blitzkrieg ______________________________

____

____

____

Election of 1940 ______________________________

____

____

____

Lend-Lease ______________________________

____

____

____

Pearl Harbor ______________________________

____

____

____

Japanese Americans and World War II ______________________________

____

____

____

Battle of Guadalcanal ______________________________

____

____

____

Battle of the Bulge ______________________________

____

____

____

Pacific military strategy ______________________________

____

____

____

Tehran Conference

OVERLORD

Yalta Conference

IDENTIFICATION OF KEY INDIVIDUALS

In two to three sentences, identify each of the following:

Cordell Hull

Douglas MacArthur

Gerald Nye

Benito Mussolini

George Patton

Chester Nimitz

NAME ______________________________ **DATE** ______________

Francisco Franco ______________________________

Joseph Stalin ______________________________

Winston Churchill ______________________________

Neville Chamberlain ______________________________

Wendell Willkie ______________________________

MAP EXERCISE

1. Using the map of Europe on the next page, make a chronological list of the major Allied invasions of World War II.

2. Using the map of the Pacific on the next page, make a chronological list of the major American invasions of World War II.

NAME ______________________________ DATE ____________________

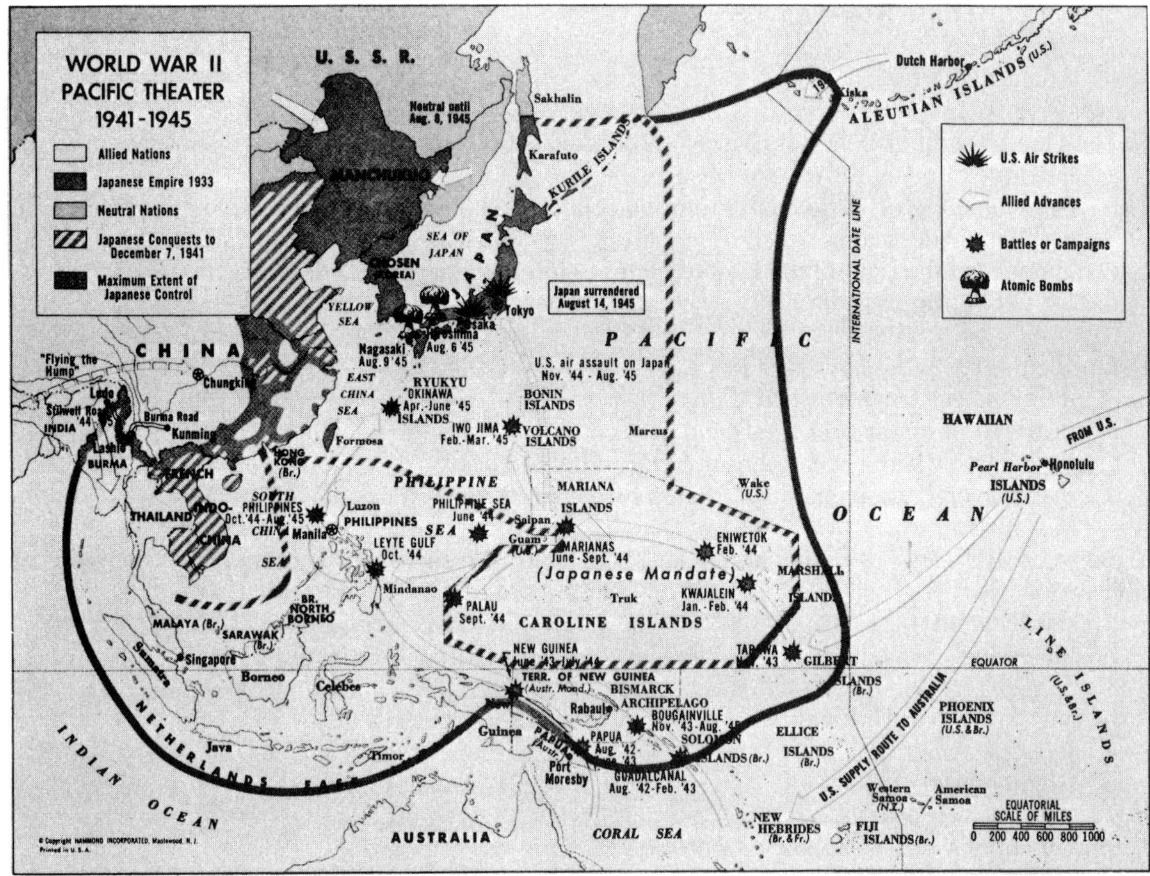

SELF-TEST

Multiple-Choice Questions

1. Recognition of the Soviet Union by the United States
   a. did not occur until Truman became President.
   b. was accompanied immediately by a military pact.
   c. was the result of the agreement of the Soviet Union to repay its debt from World War I.
   d. had as an objective the stabilization of international politics and economics.

2. Hitler's strategies in the 1930s can best be characterized as being
   a. encouraged by the weak response from democratic states.
   b. universally deplored.
   c. limited to conquest of the Sudetenland.
   d. bound by rules of traditional warfare.

3. Congress passed the neutrality acts in the
   a. 1920s. b. 1930s. c. 1940s. d. 1950s.

4. Which one of the following was not a World War II ally of the others?
   a. Germany b. Italy c. Soviet Union d. Japan

5. Which came first?
   a. Pearl Harbor
   b. Soviet-German Non-Aggression Pact
   c. Blitzkrieg
   d. Atlantic Charter

6. The Good Neighbor Policy of Hoover and Franklin Roosevelt
   a. had little effect in the case of Mexico.
   b. condemned intervention and promised cooperation in relationships between the United States and Latin America.
   c. announced the right of the United States to intervene to keep order in Latin America.
   d. led to civil war in Cuba.

7. During the 1930s the United States and Japan
   a. differed over Japan's role in China.
   b. nearly went to war over the *Panay* incident.
   c. traded freely with each other until December 7, 1941.
   d. made several arrangements to share raw materials in Southeast Asia.

8. Between 1937 and 1941 the American response to the threat of German aggression could be described as
   a. strictly neutral.
   b. increasingly sympathetic to Britain.
   c. totaly isolationist.
   d. vigorously interventionist.

9. During World War II domestic repression was directed primarily at
   a. Japanese Americans.
   b. Communists.
   c. Italian Americans.
   d. German Americans.

10. One of Hitler's most effective weapons was the
    a. submarine.
    b. fifth column in the United States.
    c. military genius of Mussolini.
    d. attacks of intuition he exhibited.

Matching Questions

For questions 11 through 15, use one of the lettered items.

11. Franklin D. Roosevelt's secretary of state.___
12. Commander of American naval forces in the Pacific.___
13. Army general who reconquered the Philippines.___
14. Commander of American military forces in Europe.___
15. British prime minister who allowed Czechoslovakia to fall into German hands.___

a. Douglas MacArthur
b. Chester Nimitz
c. Dwight Eisenhower
d. Neville Chamberlain
e. Cordell Hull

For questions 16 through 20, use one of the lettered items.

16. The British prime minister.___
17. Leader of the Soviet Union.___
18. Leader of China.___
19. Leader of Japan.___
20. Leader of Spain.___

a. Chiang Kai-shek
b. Hideki Tōjō
c. Francisco Franco
d. Joseph Stalin
e. Winston Churchill

NAME ______________________________ DATE ______________

True-False Questions

21. The Coral Sea, the Solomons, and the Marianas are scenes of naval battles in the Pacific during World War II.___
22. Kristallnacht occurred in England.___
23. Hitler launched a huge offensive against the Soviet Union in June 1941.___
24. In 1943 the Allied powers invaded Sicily and Italy.___
25. World War II formally began with the invasion of Austria in 1938.___

Essay Questions

1. How and why had the isolationist mood changed by the time of the nation's entrance into World War II?

2. Which enemy was the larger threat during World War II—Germany or Japan? Explain.

3. Why did the Allied side win World War II?

Self-Test Answers

1. d 2. a 3. b 4. c 5. c 6. b 7. a 8. b 9. a 10. a 11. e 12. b 13. a 14. c
15. d 16. e 17. d 18. a 19. b 20. c 21. T 22. F 23. T 24. T 25. F

NAME ______________________________ DATE ________________

26 POSTWAR POLITICS AND THE COLD WAR

SUGGESTED OUTCOMES

After studying Chapter 26, you should be able to

1. Explain why the United States decided to drop the atomic bombs on Japan in 1945.
2. Explain what happened to relations between the United States and the Soviet Union after World War II.
3. Describe the origins and meaning of the containment policy and why the Truman Doctrine and Marshall Plan are examples of it.
4. Describe the reaction against the New Deal that characterized American politics in the late 1940s and early 1950s. Specify one major anti-New Deal measure passed by Congress.
5. Discuss the meaning of the term "Fair Deal."
6. Describe American middle-class styles of living during the 1950s.
7. Discuss the causes of the Korean War.
8. Explain the reasons behind the Red Scare of the late 1940s and early 1950s.

CHRONOLOGY

1944 Congress passes the GI Bill.

1945 Franklin D. Roosevelt dies and Harry Truman becomes President.
Potsdam Conference is held.
Atomic bombs are dropped on Japan.
Japan surrenders, ending World War II.
The United Nations is formed.

1946 Congress passes the Employment Act.
A nationwide railroad strike goes into effect.
Republicans gain control of the House and the Senate in the elections of 1946.
Winston Churchill gives his "Iron Curtain" speech.
The Truman Doctrine is implemented.
Truman establishes the President's Committee on Civil Rights.

1947 George Kennan writes his famous article on containment.
Congress passes the Marshall Plan, the National Security Act, and the Taft-Hartley Act.

1948 The Berlin Airlift begins.
Harry Truman wins the presidential election.

1949 China falls to the Communists under Mao Zedong.
The North Atlantic Treaty Organization is formed.

1950 The Truman Administration issues National Security Council Paper Number 68.
North Korea invades South Korea.
The Second Red Scare is characterized by the Alger Hiss case and Senator Joseph McCarthy's sensational charges.

1951 President Truman relieves General Douglas MacArthur of his command.

1952 Dwight D. Eisenhower wins the presidential election.

1953 The Korean armistice is negotiated.

PHOTOGRAPH AND ILLUSTRATION ANALYSIS

1. Compare Charleston, South Carolina, in 1865 with Hiroshima in 1945. How do the two cities compare?

Charleston, South Carolina. At the Civil War's end, much of the South lay in ruins. *(Courtesy, Library of Congress)*

NAME ______________________________ DATE ______________

Hiroshima after the blast. *(Courtesy, United States Air Force Photo)*

2. Explain the illustrations on the next page.

"Give-em-hell" Harry drew increasing criticism from Republicans and others, but for the most part their efforts to control Truman were ineffective. *(Courtesy, Library of Congress)*

Stop Communism in the Philippines. A U.S. government poster. *(Courtesy, Library of Congress)*

DOCUMENTS ANALYSIS

1. When George Kennan was enunciating what became known as the containment theory, he used the following illustration. What does it have to do with the containment of Soviet communism?

COMMUNISM, *according to George Kennan, was like*

"a toy automobile wound up and headed in a given direction, stopping only when it meets with some unanswerable force . . . a fluid stream which moves constantly, wherever it is permitted to move . . . [until] . . . it has filled every nook and cranny available to it in the basin of world power."

NAME ______________________________ DATE ______________

VOCABULARY

The following words may not be part of your normal vocabulary. If their meaning is not familiar to you, you should look them up in a dictionary.

resoluteness	implacable	subversive	disdain
domesticity	collaboration	stalemate	
gender	bipartisanship	espouse	

IDENTIFICATION OF KEY CONCEPTS

In two to three sentences, identify each of the following:

Potsdam Conference ______________________________

GI Bill ______________________________

Baruch Plan ______________________________

Containment Policy ______________________________

Marshall Plan ______________________________

Truman Doctrine ______________________________

Berlin Airlift ______________________________

North Atlantic Treaty Organization

Election of 1948

Taft-Hartley Act

Fair Deal

Fall of China (1949)

National Security Council Paper No. 68

House Un-American Activities Committee

Election of 1952

IDENTIFICATION OF KEY INDIVIDUALS

In two to three sentences, identify each of the following:

Bernard Baruch

NAME ______________________________ **DATE** ____________

George C. Marshall ______________________________

Robert Taft ______________________________

Thomas E. Dewey ______________________________

Dean Acheson ______________________________

Dwight D. Eisenhower ______________________________

Joseph McCarthy ______________________________

Alger Hiss ______________________________

Adlai Stevenson ______________________________

George Kennan ______________________________

Henry Wallace ______________________________

Julius and Ethel Rosenberg ____

____

____

____

SELF-TEST

Multiple-Choice Questions

1. The Marshall Plan was urged for all the following reasons except
   a. humanitarianism.
   b. the hope that a prosperous Europe would provide American markets.
   c. the belief that capitalist advances would discourage the spread of socialism and communism.
   d. economic revenge on the Soviet Union for its takeover of Czechoslovakia in 1948.

2. The phenomenon of McCarthyism
   a. frightened many people but caused little real harm to anyone.
   b. was solely the product of McCarthy's enormous popular appeal.
   c. represented an attempt to spread Communist ideas through the mass media.
   d. offered a simplistic explanation for Soviet expansion in eastern Europe.

3. The Korean War ended in
   a. a clear-cut American victory.
   b. a clear-cut Communist victory.
   c. something resembling a stalemate.
   d. a rout of the Chinese.

4. Labor leaders of the Truman Era were
   a. Robert Taft and John Bricker.
   b. John L. Lewis and Walter Reuther.
   c. Thomas E. Dewey and Fiorello LaGuardia.
   d. Bernard Baruch and George Frost Kennan.

5. Which of the following was not a political party running a candidate in the presidential election of 1948?
   a. Progressive Party
   b. Republican Party
   c. Single Tax Party
   d. Dixiecrat Party

6. Truman's Fair Deal included all of the following except
   a. repeal of the Taft-Hartley Act.
   b. civil rights legislation.
   c. national health insurance.
   d. a drive against "creeping socialism."

7. The second atomic bomb dropped by the United States on Japan in 1945 destroyed the city of
   a. Nagasaki.
   b. Hiroshima.
   c. Kobe.
   d. Kyoto.

8. The author of the article on containment by Mr. X was
   a. George C. Marshall.
   b. George Kennan.
   c. Joseph McCarthy.
   d. John Kenneth Galbraith.

9. In the congressional elections of 1946
   a. the Republicans gained control of the House and Senate.
   b. the Democrats gained control of the House and Senate.
   c. the Republicans suffered a major defeat.
   d. the Republicans voiced disappointment over Latin America.

NAME ______________________________ DATE ________________

10. The Korean War was fought from
    a. 1947–1950. b. 1950–1953. c. 1953–1956. d. 1956–1959.

Matching Questions

For questions 11 through 15, use one of the lettered items.

11. Provided housing and education benefits for individuals who had served in the military during World War II.___
12. Provided economic and military assistance to Greece and Turkey after World War II in order to defeat Communist insurgencies there.___
13. A program to control the use of atomic energy around the world.___
14. An extensive program of United States economic assistance to the nations of western Europe after World War II in order to assist them in resisting Communism.___
15. An American commitment to preventing the Soviet Union from expanding beyond its 1945 military boundaries.___

a. Baruch Plan
b. Marshall Plan
c. Truman Doctrine
d. Containment Policy
e. GI Bill

For questions 16 through 20, use one of the lettered items.

16. President Truman's domestic program.___
17. A measure designed to curb the power of labor unions.___
18. Established the Council of Economic Advisers.___
19. Claimed that Communists were aiming at world domination.___
20. The meeting between Harry Truman, Clement Atlee, and Joseph Stalin to shape the postwar world.___

a. NSC-68
b. Taft-Hartley Act
c. Potsdam Conference
d. Employment Act of 1946
e. Fair Deal

True-False Questions

21. President Franklin D. Roosevelt made the final decision to drop the atomic bombs on Japan.___
22. Dwight D. Eisenhower won the presidential election of 1952.___
23. The Taft-Hartley Act was widely considered to be antilabor.___
24. Joseph R. McCarthy was a Wisconsin Republican.___
25. The Alger Hiss case was an important issue in the Second Red Scare.___

Essay Questions

1. What evaluations can be made about the establishment of a Western political and military opposition to the USSR and other Communist powers?

____

____

____

____

____

____

2. Would the United States have used the atomic bomb on German cities?

Self-Test Answers

1. d 2. d 3. c 4. b 5. c 6. d 7. a 8. b 9. a 10. b 11. e 12. c 13. a 14. b 15. d 16. e 17. b 18. d 19. b 20. c 21. F 22. T 23. T 24. T 25. T

NAME ______________________________ DATE ________________

CONSENSUS AND DIVISION: 1953–1965

SUGGESTED OUTCOMES

After studying Chapter 27, you should be able to

1. Explain the significance of the Greensboro, North Carolina, sit-in.
2. Describe the various components of the Hispanic community in the United States.
3. Describe the first stages of the civil rights movement as it emerged during the Eisenhower Administration.
4. Explain why the term "moderate conservatism" is applied to the Eisenhower Administration.
5. Describe the background of American-Soviet tension in the 1950s and the major events contributing to that tension.
6. Describe the judicial philosophy of the Supreme Court under Chief Justice Earl Warren and briefly discuss the major decisions reached by the Warren court.
7. Explain how the values of the "Beat" generation and "rock and roll" contradicted the values of a mass culture, consumer society.
8. Discuss the background and personality of John Fitzgerald Kennedy and how that background helped shape his presidential administration.
9. Explain the approach President John Kennedy took to the civil rights issue in the 1950s and 1960s.
10. Explain why the United States and the Soviet Union almost went to war over Cuba in 1962.
11. Explain the meaning of the terms "New Frontier" and "Great Society" and discuss the relative merits and significant of each.
12. Explain the Johnson Administration's approach to civil rights.

CHRONOLOGY

1952 Dwight D. Eisenhower wins the presidential election.

1953 The Korean armistice goes into effect.
Earl Warren is appointed chief justice of the Supreme Court.

1954 The Supreme Court decides the case of *Brown v. Board of Education of Topeka, Kansas*.

1955 The Soviet Union, United States, Great Britain, and France convene a summit meeting at Geneva.
Martin Luther King, Jr., leads the Montgomery, Alabama, bus boycott.

1956 The Soviet Union crushes the Hungarian rebellion.
The Suez Crisis erupts.
Congress passes the Interstate and Defense Highway System Act.
Dwight D. Eisenhower wins a second presidential term.
Jack Kerouac publishes *On the Road*.

1957 The Soviet Union launches Sputnik I.
National Guard troops help integrate the Little Rock, Arkansas, schools.
Congress passes the Civil Rights Act.
President Eisenhower issues the "Eisenhower Doctrine."

1958 Congress passes the National Defense Education Act.
Civil war erupts in Lebanon.

1959 Castro overthrows Batista in Cuba.

1960 The "sit-in" movement begins.
John F. Kennedy is elected President.
The U-2 aircraft is shot down over the Soviet Union.

1961 The Freedom Riders campaign for integrated transportation.
The Bay of Pigs fiasco occurs.
The Berlin Crisis begins.
John F. Kennedy launches the Alliance for Progress.

1962 The Cuban missile crisis occurs.
Rachel Carson publishes *Silent Spring*.

1963 The Nuclear Test Ban Treaty is signed.
Martin Luther King, Jr., leads the Birmingham, Alabama, civil rights protests and the March on Washington.
John F. Kennedy is assassinated and Lyndon Johnson becomes President.
The Supreme Court decides the case of *Gideon v. Wainwright*.

1964 Lyndon B. Johnson wins the presidential election.
Congress passes the Civil Rights Act and the Economic Opportunity Act.
Lyndon Johnson launches his "War on Poverty."

1965 Congress establishes the Medicare program.
Congress passes the Voting Rights Act, the Water Quality Act, and the Immigration and Nationality Act.
The Supreme Court decides the case of *Baker v. Carr*.

PHOTOGRAPH AND ILLUSTRATION ANALYSIS

1. Compare these next two photographs. Did African-American and white civil rights workers in the South have anything to fear during the 1950s and 1960s?

A black woman in a southern town during the 1950s watches Klansmen in full regalia. *(Courtesy, AP/Wide World Photos)*

NAME ________________________________ DATE ________________

This Greyhound bus carrying the first Freedom Riders into Alabama was set afire by a mob outside the town of Anniston. *(Courtesy, AP/Wide World Photos)*

2. How did the people pictured in this photograph feel about President Lyndon Johnson's Great Society programs?

____

____

____

____

____

____

____

____

The civil rights movement of the 1960s marched onward, seeking equality in schooling, voting, employment, and housing. *(Courtesy, AP/Wide World Photos)*

3. What do these photographs—the first of a popular television show *Father Knows Best*; the second an idealized family of the 1950s; and the third of another housewife with her children—tell about suburban life in the 1950s? Is it any different today?

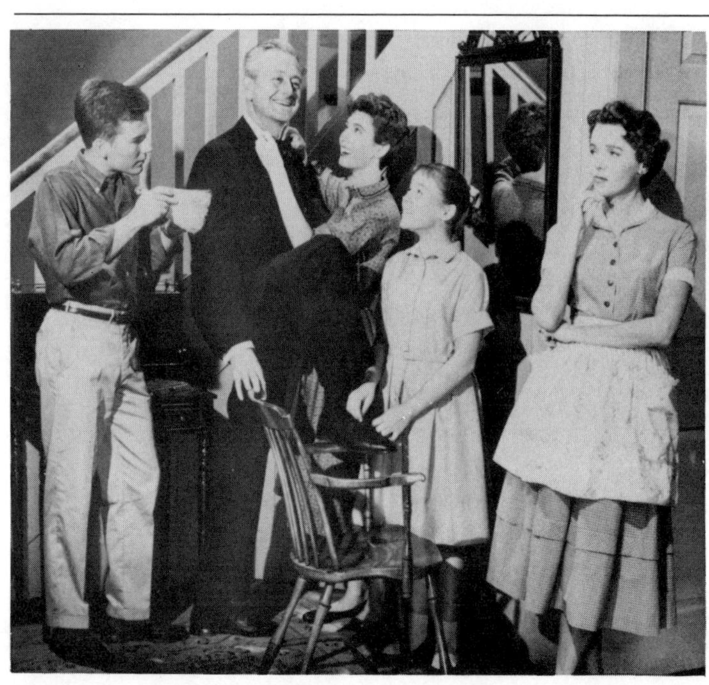

The television program "Father Knows Best" debuted in 1953. One historian described the character played by Robert Young as having "no politics, no opinions, and no connections with the world about him." *(Courtesy, Wide World Photos)*

NAME ______________________ DATE ______________

This photograph shows an idealized picture of family life in the 1950s. It suggests the theme of "togetherness," a word coined by *McCall's* magazine in 1954. *(Courtesy, Magnum)*

This young mother in New Rochelle, a suburb of New York City, was photographed in 1955. No wonder 24,000 American women responded to a 1960 *Redbook* magazine article entitled "Why Young Mothers Feel Trapped." *(Courtesy, Magnum)*

DOCUMENTS ANALYSIS

1. Read the letter on the following page from Martin Luther King, Jr.'s "Letter from Birmingham Jail." Summarize King's philosophy of non-violent civil disobedience.

LETTER FROM BIRMINGHAM CITY JAIL *by The Reverend Martin Luther King, Jr.*
King's attack on white moderates who counseled patience is a classic.

MY DEAR FELLOW CLERGYMEN, While confined here in the Birmingham City Jail, I came across your recent statement calling our present activities "unwise and untimely." Seldom, if ever, do I pause to answer criticism of my work and ideas. If I sought to answer all of the criticisms that cross my desk, my secretaries would be engaged in little else in the course of the day and I would have no time for constructive work. But since I feel that you are men of genuine good will and your criticisms are sincerely set forth, I would like to answer your statement in what I hope will be patient and reasonable terms. . . .

You deplore the demonstrations that are presently taking place in Birmingham. But I am sorry that your statement did not express a similar concern for the conditions that brought the demonstrations into being. I am sure that each of you would want to go beyond the superficial social analyst who looks merely at effects, and does not grapple with underlying causes. I would not hesitate to say that it is unfortunate that so-called demonstrations are taking place in Birmingham at this time, but I would say in more emphatic terms that it is even more unfortunate that the white power structure of this city left the Negro community with no other alternative.

In any nonviolent campaign there are four basic steps: (1) collection of the facts to determine whether injustices are alive; (2) negotiation; (3) self-purification; and (4) direct action. We have gone through all of these steps in Birmingham. There can be no gainsaying of the fact that racial injustice engulfs this community. Birmingham is probably the most thoroughly segregated city in the United States. Its ugly record of police brutality is known in every section of this country. Its unjust treatment of Negroes in the courts is a notorious reality. There have been more unsolved bombings of Negro homes and churches in Birmingham than any city in this nation. These are the hard, brutal, and unbelievable facts. On the basis of these conditions Negro leaders sought to negotiate with the city fathers. But the political leaders consistently refused to engage in good faith negotiation.

Then came the opportunity last September to talk with some of the leaders of the economic community. In these negotiating sessions certain promises were made by the merchants—such as the promise to remove the humiliating racial signs from the stores. On the basis of these promises Reverend [Fred] Shuttlesworth and the leaders of the Alabama Christian Movement for Human Rights agreed to call a moratorium on any type of demonstrations. As the weeks and months unfolded we realized that we were victims of a broken promise. The signs remained. As in so many experiences of the past, we were confronted with blasted hopes, and the dark shadow of a deep disappointment settled upon us. So we had no alternative except that of preparing for direct action, whereby we would present our very bodies as means of laying our case before the conscience of the local and national community. . . .

2. After reading the excerpt on the next page from Malcolm X on the March on Washington, contrast his approach to the problems of blacks to that of the Reverend Martin Luther King, Jr.

NAME ______________________ **DATE** ______________

MALCOLM X ON THE "FARCE ON WASHINGTON"

Not long ago, the black man in America was fed a dose of another form of the weakening, lulling and deluding effects of so-called "integration." It was that "Farce on Washington," I call it. . . .

The morning of the March, any rickety carloads of angry, dusty, sweating small-town Negroes would have gotten lost among the chartered jet planes, railroad cars, and air-conditioned buses. What originally was planned to be an angry riptide one English newspaper aptly described now as "the gentle flood."

Talk about "integrated"! It was like salt and pepper. And, by now, there wasn't a single logistics aspect uncontrolled.

The marchers had been instructed to bring no signs—signs were provided. They had been told to sing one song: "We Shall Overcome." They had been told *how* to arrive, *when, where* to arrive, *where* to assemble, when to *start* marching, the *route* to march. First-aid stations were strategically located—even where to *faint*!

Yes, I was there. I observed that circus. Who ever heard of angry revolutionists all harmonizing "We Shall Overcome . . . Suum Day . . ." while tripping and swaying along arm-in-arm with the very people they were supposed to be angrily revolting against? Who ever heard of angry revolutionists swinging their bare feet together with their oppressor in lily-pad park pools, with gospels and guitars and "I Have A Dream" speeches?. . . .

Hollywood couldn't have topped it.

In a subsequent press poll, not one Congressman or Senator with a previous record of opposition to civil rights said he had changed his views. What did anyone expect? How was a one-day "integrated" picnic going to counter-influence these representatives of prejudice rooted deep in the psyche of the American white man for four hundred years?

The very fact that millions, black and white, believed in this monumental farce is another example of how much this country goes in for the surface glossing over, the escape ruse, surfaces, instead of truly dealing with its deep-rooted problems.

What that March on Washington did do was lull Negroes for a while. But inevitably, the black masses started realizing they had been smoothly hoaxed again by the white man. And, inevitably, the black man's anger rekindled, deeper than ever, and there began bursting out in different cities the "long, hot summer" of 1964, unprecedented racial crises.

Source: Malcolm X (with Alex Haley), *The Autobiography of Malcolm X*. New York: Random House, 1965. 278, 280–281.

3. Explain the meaning of the poem on the next page by Abelardo Delgado and relate it to textbook material on Spanish-speaking immigrants.

ABELARDO DELGADO, *born in Chihuahua, Mexico, emigrated to the United States in 1943. He was a leading figure in the Chicano political movement of the late 1960s and early 1970s. His poem "Stupid America" was published in 1969.*

Stupid america, see that chicano
with a big knife
in his steady hand
he doesn't want to knife you
he wants to sit on a bench
and carve christfigures
but you won't let him.
stupid america, hear that chicano
shouting curses on the street
he is a poet
without paper and pencil
and since he cannot write
he will explode.
stupid america, remember that chicanito
flunking math and english
he is the picasso
of your western states
but he will die
with one thousand masterpieces
hanging only from his mind.

4. How does this Malvina Reynolds poem constitute a critique of modern suburbia?

MALVINA REYNOLDS, *a Californian, wrote more than 500 songs. "Little Boxes," recorded by the folk singer Pete Seeger in 1963, attacked consumerism, conformity, and political indifference. It was greatly liked by college students who had grown up in those "ticky tacky houses" and wanted to show that they had not "come out all the same." The song seems as relevant in the 1980s and 1990s as it was in the 1960s.*

Little boxes on the hillside, little boxes made of ticky tacky
Little boxes on the hillside, little boxes all the same
There's a green one and a pink one and a blue one and a yellow one
And they're all made out of ticky tacky and they all look just the same.

And the people in the houses
All went to the university,
Where they were put in boxes
And they came out all the same,
And there's doctors and there's lawyers,
And business executives,
And they're all made out of ticky tacky
And they all look just the same.

And they all play on the golf course
And drink their martinis dry,
And they all have pretty children
And the children go to school,
And the children go to summer camp
And then to the university,
Where they are put in boxes and they come out all the same.

And the boys go into business
and marry and raise a family
In boxes made of ticky tacky
And they all look just the same.

NAME ______________________________ DATE ______________

5. What is Dwight D. Eisenhower saying to his brother Edgar in this quotation?

IKE *bluntly cautioned his conservative brother Edgar:*

"Should any political party attempt to abolish social security and eliminate labor laws and farm programs, you would not hear of that party again in our political history. There is a tiny splinter group, of course, that believes that you can do those things, . . . a few Texas oil millionaires, and an occasional politician and businessman from other areas. Their number is negligible and they are stupid."

---

6. Is this quotation from John F. Kennedy's inaugural address consistent in tone with what you know of foreign policy events during his administration? Explain.

KENNEDY'S *inaugural address is the subject of much controversy. Its measured cadences suggest a belligerence at odds with his more prudent conduct of foreign policy. Here are some of his more famous words:*

"Let the word go forth from this time and place, to friend and foe alike, that the torch has been passed to a new generation of Americans—born in this century, tempered by war, disciplined by a hard and bitter peace, proud of our ancient heritage—and unwilling to witness or permit the slow undoing of those human rights to which this nation has always been committed, and to which we are committed today at home and around the world.

Let every nation know, whether it wishes us well or ill, that we shall pay any price, bear any burden, meet any hardship, support any friend, oppose any foe to assure the survival and the success of liberty.

This much we pledge—and more."

VOCABULARY

The following words may not be part of your normal vocabulary. If their meaning is not familiar to you, you should look them up in a dictionary.

civility	rhetorical	colonialism	filibuster
repression	tacitly	indigent	refugee
abstention	banal	desegregation	naturalization
doldrums	precept	boycott	apportionment
stridency	dissension	intransigent	

IDENTIFICATION OF KEY CONCEPTS

In two to three sentences, identify each of the following:

"wetbacks" ______________________________

Mexican Americans ______________________________

Cuban Americans ______________________________

Puerto Rican Americans ______________________________

The Warren Court ______________________________

The Election of 1956 ______________________________

The Election of 1958 ______________________________

Hungarian Rebellion ______________________________

NAME ______________________ **DATE** ____________

The Suez Crisis ______________________

Sputnik ______________________

Eisenhower Doctrine ______________________

Little Rock, Arkansas, desegregation controversy ______________________

Civil Rights Act of 1957 ______________________

Election of 1960 ______________________

U-2 Incident ______________________

Bay of Pigs Invasion ______________________

Cuban Missile Crisis ______________________

Berlin Crisis of 1961 ______________________

Nuclear Test Ban Treaty

Consumer society

Beats

Rock and roll

Election of 1964

Economic Opportunity Act of 1964

Civil Rights Act of 1964

Voting Rights Act of 1965

Black Power

Immigration and Nationality Act of 1965

NAME ______________________ DATE ____________

Peace Corps ______________________

IDENTIFICATION OF KEY INDIVIDUALS

In two to three sentences, identify each of the following:

John Foster Dulles ______________________

Nikita Khrushchev ______________________

Earl Warren ______________________

Martin Luther King, Jr. ______________________

Malcolm X ______________________

Thurgood Marshall ______________________

Rachel Carson ______________________

Jack Kerouac ______________________

James Meredith ____

____

____

____

Barry Goldwater ____

____

____

____

Stokely Carmichael ____

____

____

____

SELF-TEST

Multiple-Choice Questions

1. Lyndon Johnson's Great Society programs included all but
   a. retraining the unemployed.
   b. price controls.
   c. VISTA, a domestic Peace Corps.
   d. aid to education.

2. In the Cuban Missile Crisis, Kennedy
   a. threatened to place missiles in Turkey if the USSR installed them in Cuba.
   b. attempted to prevent full installation of Soviet missiles in Cuba.
   c. advised the Soviet Union that placing an ABM system around Moscow would result in a crisis.
   d. threatened to put United States missiles in Cuba if the Soviet Union installed them in Turkey.

3. Which did not occur under President Kennedy?
   a. Berlin Wall crisis
   b. Nuclear Test Ban Treaty
   c. Alliance for Progress
   d. Suez crisis

4. Kennedy established the Peace Corps partly
   a. as a response to the civil rights movement.
   b. as a foreign policy program to combat Communist influence.
   c. to aid the unemployed.
   d. as an education program for the study of war and peace.

5. The launch of the first Sputnik in 1957
   a. shook the West.
   b. was a failure.
   c. demonstrated that the Soviet Union had given up on military competition.
   d. was an essentially diversionary tactic.

6. Earl Warren was appointed chief justice of the Supreme Court by President
   a. Dwight Eisenhower.
   b. Franklin D. Roosevelt.
   c. John F. Kennedy.
   d. Lyndon B. Johnson.

7. Which one of the following was not a prominent group of Hispanic Americans in the 1950s?
   a. Argentinians
   b. Cubans
   c. Mexicans
   d. Puerto Ricans

NAME ________________________________ DATE ________________

8. Egypt's President Nasser
   a. attacked the role of the United States in the closing of the Suez Canal.
   b. nationalized the Suez Canal.
   c. sought European protection of the Suez Canal.
   d. allied with the West against the Soviet Union.

9. John Foster Dulles's foreign policy carried the threat of
   a. brushfire wars.
   b. lightning response.
   c. massive retaliation.
   d. economic sanctions.

10. A nuclear threat was at the heart of the
   a. Bay of Pigs.
   b. Cuban missile crisis.
   c. Suez crisis.
   d. Hungarian rebellion.

Matching Questions

For questions 11 through 15, use one of the lettered items.

11. Guaranteed that both houses of state legislatures reflect the actual distribution of population in the state.___
12. Outlawed segregation in public facilities.___
13. Overturned *Plessy v. Ferguson* and ordered integration of the schools.___
14. Guaranteed the right to legal representation in all felony cases.___
15. Required police to inform a prisoner of his right to see an attorney before answering any questions.___

a. *Gideon v. Wainwright*
b. Civil Rights Act of 1964
c. *Brown v. Board of Education*
d. *Miranda v. Arizona*
e. *Baker v. Carr*

For questions 16 through 20, use one of the lettered items.

16. The individual who integrated the University of Mississippi.___
17. The prominent Black Muslim leader who was assassinated in 1965.___
18. The black militant who coined the term "Black Power."___
19. The man John Kennedy appointed federal housing administrator.___
20. The most influential of the civil rights leaders.___

a. Robert Weaver
b. Stokely Carmichael
c. Malcolm X
d. Martin Luther King, Jr.
e. James Meredith

For questions 21 through 25, use one of the lettered items.

21. Finally ended the quota system.___
22. Outlawed segregation in public facilities.___
23. Provided federal marshalls to protect the right of African Americans to vote in the South.___
24. Created the "War on Poverty."___
25. Provided for federal investigation of civil rights violations.___

a. Civil Rights Act of 1957
b. Civil Rights Act of 1964
c. Economic Opportunity Act of 1964
d. Civil Rights Act of 1965
e. Immigration and Nationality Act of 1965

True-False Questions

26. John Kennedy defeated Barry Goldwater in the election of 1960.___
27. The Peace Corps was established during the Kennedy Administration.___
28. The *Plessy v. Ferguson* decision of 1896 was overturned by the *Miranda v. Arizona* decision of 1966.___
29. Rosa Parks initiated the Montgomery bus boycott.___
30. John F. Kennedy was the first Roman Catholic to be elected president.___

Essay Question

1. Discuss the civil rights movement from *Brown v. Board of Education* into the black power phase. What continuities and what changes do you detect?

Self-Test Answers

1. b 2. b 3. d 4. b 5. a 6. a 7. a 8. b 9. c 10. b 11. e 12. b 13. c 14. a
15. d 16. e 17. c 18. b 19. a 20. d 21. e 22. b 23. d 24. c 25. a 26. F 27. T 28. F 29. T 30. T

NAME ______________________ DATE ______________

AMERICAN SOCIETY AND THE VIETNAM WAR

SUGGESTED OUTCOMES

After studying Chapter 28, you should be able to

1. Describe what happened at Kent State University in 1970 and why it occurred.
2. Discuss what happened to France in Vietnam during the 1940s and 1950s and why it is relevant to an understanding of what happened to the United States there during the 1960s and 1970s.
3. Respond to a question asking why the United States became so deeply involved in the Vietnam War.
4. Discuss the primary reasons why the United States lost the war in Vietnam.
5. Describe the antiwar movement and explain its impact on American politics.
6. Describe the Tet Offensive and its impact on American public opinion in 1968.
7. Describe the process by which President Richard Nixon de-escalated the war in Vietnam between 1969 and 1973.
8. Explain President Richard Nixon's foreign policy successes in the early 1970s.
9. Explain how the Watergate scandal destroyed the Nixon presidency.

CHRONOLOGY

1954 French forces are defeated at the Battle of Dien Bien Phu.
The Geneva Accords divide Vietnam at the seventeenth parallel.
The Southeast Asia Treaty Organization is established.

1955 Premier Ngo Dinh Diem comes to power in South Vietnam.

1962 Students for a Democratic Society (SDS) is established.

1963 John F. Kennedy is assassinated and Lyndon B. Johnson becomes President.
Ngo Dinh Diem is assassinated.

1964 The Free Speech Movement begins at the University of California at Berkeley.
Lyndon B. Johnson wins the presidential election.
The controversial Gulf of Tonkin incidents allegedly occur and Congress passes Gulf of Tonkin Resolution.

1965 SDS organizes the first large-scale anti-Vietnam war protest.
Lyndon Johnson introduces regular American ground forces to South Vietnam.

1968 The Tet Offensive takes place in Vietnam.
Richard Nixon wins the presidential election.

1970 American forces invade Cambodia and precipitate the events leading up to the Kent State University massacre.

1973 The final peace agreement ending the Vietnam War is signed.

PHOTOGRAPH AND ILLUSTRATION ANALYSIS

1. What common theme runs through the following four photographs?

Confrontations between students and authorities were a hallmark of the late sixties and early seventies. *(Courtesy, United Press International Photo)*

NAME ______________________________ DATE ____________

The growing antiwar movement attacked the war's purpose and morality as well as the administration's "arrogance of power." *(Courtesy, AP/Wide World Photos)*

Cesar Chavez, leader of the United Farm Workers, whose nationwide grape boycott in 1965 brought the plight of migrant farm workers to the attention of the nation. *(Courtesy, AP/Wide World Photos)*

An Indian encampment in front of the nation's Capitol, Washington, D.C., in 1968 was part of the wider Indian movement calling for return of lands. *(Courtesy, AP/Wide World Photos)*

2. Some historians feel that the following photograph illustrates one of the great ironies of modern American politics. Why?

NAME ______________________________ DATE ______________

President Nixon's historic trip to China in 1971 and his meeting with Mao Zedong ushered in a new age of détente between the two nations. *(Courtesy, AP/Wide World Photos)*

DOCUMENTS ANALYSIS

1. Read the excerpt on the next page from "The Port Huron Statement." Summarize the early political philosophy of Students for a Democratic Society.

THE PORT HURON STATEMENT *by Students for a Democratic Society*

The SDS met in Port Huron, Michigan, in 1962, and wrote an agenda for reform. Tom Hayden was one of its authors.

Introduction: Agenda For a Generation

We are people of this generation, bred in at least modest comfort, housed now in universities, looking uncomfortably to the world we inherit.

When we were kids the United States was the wealthiest and strongest country in the world: the only one with the atom bomb, the least scarred by modern war, an initiator of the United Nations that we thought would distribute Western influence throughout the world. Freedom and equality for each individual, government of, by, and for the people—these American values we found good, principles by which we could live as men. Many of us began maturing in complacency.

As we grew, however, our comfort was penetrated by events too troubling to dismiss. First, the permeating and victimizing fact of human degradation, symbolized by the Southern struggle against racial bigotry, compelled most of us from silence to activism. Second, the enclosing fact of the Cold War, symbolized by the presence of the Bomb, brought awareness that we ourselves, and our friends, and millions of abstract "others" we knew more directly because of our common peril, might die at any time. We might deliberately ignore, or avoid, or fail to feel all other human problems, but not these two, for these were too immediate and crushing in their impact, too challenging in the demand that we as individuals take the responsibility for encounter and resolution.

While these and other problems either directly oppressed us or rankled our consciences and became our own subjective concerns, we began to see complicated and disturbing paradoxes in our surrounding America. The declaration "all men are created equal . . ." rang hollow before the facts of Negro life in the South and the big cities of the North. The proclaimed peaceful intentions of the United States contradicted its economic and military investments in the Cold War status quo.

2. Read the comment by an American observer about what took place at Dien Bien Phu. How and why did the French underestimate the Vietcong?

NAME ______________________________ DATE ______________

ONE *American observer commented of Dien Bien Phu:*

"Here you were out in the middle of a jungle, and you have extremely heavy antiaircraft fire coming from positions that we didn't believe the Viet Minh could establish or maintain. We thought no one could put heavy weapons in there except the French, who had flown them in on C-119s and C-54s. But the Viet Minh, who had no air, had somehow put in 105s and 75 millimeters, and heavy mortars and all the rest of it, in what we thought was impenetrable jungle."

VOCABULARY

The following words may not be part of your normal vocabulary. If their meaning is not familiar to you, you should look them up in a dictionary.

attrition	feminism	incumbent	vendetta
disengagement	contraception	amorphous	opportunism
incursion	escalate	diminution	holocaust
junta	immolate	partisan	

IDENTIFICATION OF KEY CONCEPTS

In two to three sentences, identify each of the following:

Students for a Democratic Society ______________________________

Free Speech Movement ______________________________

Counterculture ______________________________

Dien Bien Phu ______________________________

National Liberation Front ______________________________

Gulf of Tonkin Resolution

Rolling Thunder

My Lai massacre

Tet Offensive

Democratic Convention of 1968

Election of 1968

Kent State Massacre

Nixon Doctrine

SALT I

Black Panthers

NAME ______________________ DATE ____________

Attica ______________________

Apollo 11 ______________________

Election of 1972 ______________________

Watergate scandal ______________________

IDENTIFICATION OF KEY INDIVIDUALS

In two to three sentences, identify each of the following:

Maxwell Taylor ______________________

Ho Chi Minh ______________________

Ngo Dinh Diem ______________________

Nguyen Cao Ky ______________________

Vo Nguyen Giap ______________________

Bob Dylan ______________________________

William Westmoreland ______________________________

Eugene McCarthy ______________________________

Robert Kennedy ______________________________

Hubert Humphrey ______________________________

George Wallace ______________________________

Henry Kissinger ______________________________

J. William Fulbright ______________________________

John Dean ______________________________

John Mitchell ______________________________

NAME ______________________________ **DATE** ______________

John Sirica ____
____
____
____

Archibald Cox ____
____
____
____

SELF-TEST

Multiple-Choice Questions

1. Which of the following Presidents presided over the largest build-up of U.S. troops in Vietnam?
   a. Richard Nixon
   b. John F. Kennedy
   c. Dwight Eisenhower
   d. Lyndon B. Johnson

2. The development that first focused the attention of the United States on Indochina was
   a. the fall of China to the Communists.
   b. the French defeat at Dien Bien Phu.
   c. the crisis in the Gulf of Tonkin.
   d. the SEATO alliance.

3. As a leader, Ngo Dinh Diem
   a. enjoyed broad-based popular support.
   b. was close to several prominent Communists.
   c. was increasingly confined to an inner circle of family and friends.
   d. was avowedly anti-American.

4. For the first three years of major American combat in Vietnam, American policies there included all except
   a. increasing the number of ground combat troops.
   b. extensive air attacks on the North.
   c. a sustained and energetic effort to begin peace talks.
   d. a massive groundwar against the Vietcong.

5. My Lai was the site of
   a. an Allied victory.
   b. a Vietcong victory.
   c. "carpet bombings."
   d. atrocities by American troops.

6. The invasion of Cambodia in 1970
   a. provoked widespread protests on college campuses, including Kent State.
   b. was Nixon's response to a North Vietnamese attack on Saigon.
   c. was part of a plan to invade North Vietnam.
   d. received much popular support.

7. The Gulf of Tonkin Resolution
   a. authorized President Johnson to take "all necessary measures" to stop further aggression in Vietnam.
   b. enjoyed overwhelming support in the U.S. Senate.
   c. Both a and b.
   d. Neither a nor b.

8. The Free Speech Movement demanded
   a. free speech at the University of California at Berkeley.
   b. that Columbia University cease building its gymnasium in 1968.
   c. that Harvard University abolish its ROTC.
   d. that the Weathermen go underground.

9. Opponents of the Vietnam War include
   a. Dean Rusk.
   b. Eugene McCarthy.
   c. Maxwell Taylor.
   d. Lyndon Johnson.

10. Which is false about the Vietnam War?
    a. John Kennedy increased American personnel there to around 16,000 advisers.
    b. The Paris peace talks began under the Johnson presidency.
    c. Nixon wound down the war on taking office with a minimum of additional casualties.
    d. The Tet offensive ended in a military victory for the allies.

Matching Questions

For questions 11 through 15, use one of the lettered items.

11. Richard Nixon's national security adviser and secretary of state.___
12. Won the Democratic presidential nomination in 1968 but lost the election to Richard Nixon.___
13. The United States Senator from Minnesota who opposed the Vietnam War and challenged Lyndon Johnson for the Democratic presidential nomination in 1968.___
14. The third party presidential candidate in the election of 1968.___
15. The prominent folk and rock singer who opposed the Vietnam War.___

a. Henry Kissinger
b. Eugene McCarthy
c. Hubert Humphrey
d. George Wallace
e. Bob Dylan

For questions 16 through 20, use one of the lettered items.

16. The Harvard attorney who became the special prosecutor for the Watergate investigation.___
17. Nixon's attorney general.___
18. The federal judge who presided over the Watergate investigation.___
19. The North Carolina senator who conducted the congressional investigation of Watergate.___
20. Nixon's personal legal counsel who first exposed the Watergate scandal.___

a. John Dean
b. John Mitchell
c. John Sirica
d. Sam Ervin
e. Archibald Cox

NAME ____ DATE ____________________

True-False Questions

21. The American invasion of Cambodia in 1970 was not nearly as controversial politically as Nixon had anticipated.___
22. Although President Nixon occasionally threatened to do so, he never ordered U.S. troops to invade Cambodia.___
23. French Indochina included Laos, Vietnam, and Cambodia.___
24. The three major candidates in the presidential election of 1968 were George Wallace, Richard Nixon, and Lyndon Johnson.___
25. After the beginning of the Paris peace talks in 1968, the U.S. never again bombed North Vietnam.___

Essay Questions

1. What effects did the war in Vietnam have on American politics and society?

2. How and why did the United States get involved in the Vietnam War?

3. To what extent was the Vietnam War a natural outgrowth of the Cold War?

Self-Test Answers

1. d 2. a 3. c 4. c 5. d 6. a 7. c 8. a 9. b 10. c 11. a 12. c 13. b 14. d 15. e 16. e 17. b 18. c 19. d 20. a 21. F 22. F 23. T 24. F 25. F

NAME ______________________________ DATE ______________

NEW BOUNDARIES

SUGGESTED OUTCOMES

After studying Chapter 29, you should be able to

1. Describe the youth rebellion of the 1950s and 1960s.
2. Discuss the major elements of the feminist movement of the 1960s.
3. Differentiate between the civil rights movements among African Americans, Native Americans, Hispanic Americans, gays and lesbians, and women during the 1960s, and after.
4. Explain why Richard Nixon's foreign policy initiatives with the Soviet Union and China seemed ironic to many historians.
5. Discuss the Watergate scandal and the other problems that eventually destroyed the presidency of Richard Nixon.
6. Define the term "stagflation" and explain how it affected the presidential administrations of Gerald Ford, Jimmy Carter, and Richard Nixon.
7. Explain what is meant by the term "Reagan Revolution."
8. Explain what is meant by the term "Reaganomics" and cite examples of President Ronald Reagan's economic policies.
9. Describe the causes of the Gulf War of 1991.
10. Explain what happened to the Soviet Union in the late 1980s and early 1990s.
11. Discuss the economic recession that affected the United States in the early 1990s and how it affected the presidency of George Bush.
12. Discuss the issue of deregulation in the 1970s and 1980s and describe the major deregulation measures that Congress passed.

CHRONOLOGY

1963 Betty Friedan writes *The Feminine Mystique*.

1964 The "Freedom Summer" civil rights program comes to Mississippi.
Congress passes the Civil Rights Act of 1964.
Lyndon B. Johnson wins the presidential election.

1965 Cesar Chavez takes the United Farm Workers out on strike.

1966 National Organization for Women is established.

1968 American Indian Movement is founded.

1971 Richard Nixon freezes wages and prices.

1972 La Raza Unida is founded.
Richard Nixon wins a second presidential term.
Richard Nixon travels to Moscow and Beijing.

1973 The Watergate scandal breaks into the news.
The Yom Kippur War triggers the Arab oil boycott.
The Supreme Court makes its *Roe v. Wade* decision.

1974 Richard Nixon resigns the presidency and Gerald Ford becomes President.

1975 South Vietnam falls to the Communists.
Laos and Cambodia fall to the Communists.

1976 Jimmy Carter is elected President.

1978 Congress passes the Airline Deregulation Act.

1979 The nuclear accident occurs at the Three Mile Island nuclear power plant.

Iranians storm the American embassy in Tehran and take Americans hostage.
The Soviet Union invades Afghanistan.

1980 Congress passes the Motor Carrier Act, the Rail Act, and the Depository Institutions Deregulation and Monetary Control Act.
Ronald Reagan is elected President.

1981 Ronald Reagan crushes the PATCO strike.

1982 Congress passes the Economic Recovery Tax Act.

1983 241 Marines are killed in a car-bomb attack on their base in Lebanon.

1984 Ronald Reagan wins a second presidential term.

1986 Congress passes the Tax Reform Act.

1987 The Iran-Contra scandal becomes public.
On "Black Monday" in October, the stock market crashes, falling more than 500 points in a single day.

1988 George Bush is elected President.

1990 Saddam Hussein invades Kuwait.

1991 The United States defeats Iran in the Desert Storm campaign.
The Clarence Thomas–Anita Hill hearings take place.
The Soviet Union collapses, ending the Cold War.

1992 Bill Clinton is elected President.

1993 Congress approves the North American Free Trade Agreement.

1994 Republicans take control of both houses of Congress.

1995 Parties to the Bosnian civil war negotiate a settlement in Dayton, Ohio.

1996 Bill Clinton reelected President.
Republicans remain in control of Congress.

2000 George W. Bush, Al Gore, and Patrick J. Buchanan vie for the presidency.

DOCUMENTS ANALYSIS

1. What might have caused the decline in worker strikes illustrated by the following table?

____

____

____

____

____

____

____

____

____

____

____

____

____

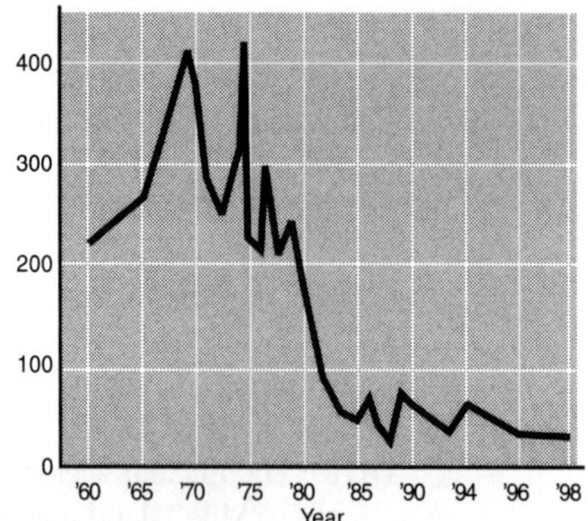

Worker Strikes, 1960–1998.

NAME ______________________ DATE ______________

2. Read the newspaper article on the next page published in 1992. How does it illustrate the continuing debate in the United States and in the world about the health of the environment?

POPULATION ISSUES LEFT OUT OF EARTH SUMMIT

A world summit meeting on environmental issues took place in Rio de Janeiro during June 1992. A Long Island, New York, newspaper spoke out about the problem underlying environmental decline.

Rio de Janeiro—The Earth Summit is ignoring population control and family planning as ways of relieving environmental stress because UN delegates caved in to pressure from the Vatican to limit such discussions, population specialists said yesterday.

Amid final preparations for today's opening of the largest environmental meeting ever, delegates, experts and politicians focused on global warming and biodiversity, in effect pushing issues on population control into the shadows. Population groups find themselves so far from the center of activity that they are holding their own meetings.

Specifically, many charge that Agenda 21, the UN document that deals with a variety of development issues to be endorsed at the summit conference, avoids any mention of family planning and contraception despite earlier drafts that explored the issues.

"What happened is that the compromise text was reached after pressure by the Holy See," said Pamela Chasek, an analyst for the independent Earth Summit Bulletin, the semi-official monitoring agency for the conference. "In the end, it became a very minor issue and nobody seemed to be tracking what was going on with population at the conference."

Pope John Paul II has criticized efforts to include mention of family planning in the document. Last week, the Vatican said that "population growth is seldom the primary cause of environment problems." It went on to say, "Policies aimed at reducing population do little to help solve urgent problems of environment and development."

U.S. policy since the Reagan administration has blocked foreign aid to organizations that provide . . . family planning information. It also has cut off aid to the United Nations population fund.

"We have come to realize that population and environment are inseparable, that being environmentalist means getting into a whole lot of other areas," said Karen Rindge of the National Wildlife Federation. Her organization, in collaboration with other major U.S. environmental groups, has called on summit conferees to deal with population. "Population is a cross-cutting issue relating to immediate concerns such as global climate change, deforestation, loss of biodiversity, status of the rights of women and economic decline."

Population is a key determinant of economic development opportunities and of how much strain an environment can handle. "People change the environment and their numbers are growing faster than ever before," said a position paper issued by the privately funded Population Crisis Committee, a Washington-based organization. "People, women must have choices for health care, for contraception—and these choices are not considered by the United Nations," committee spokeswoman Sally Ethelston said.

Many governments are loath to discuss family planning and contraception, for fear either of religious backlash or recurrent charges among nationalists in their own countries that such measures are a plot by industrialized nations to limit development.

The Population Crisis Committee estimates that the world's population of 5.4 billion will double by the year 2033, assuming the current annual growth rate of 1.7 percent. The vast majority of those increases will be in Asia and Africa, already hard-pressed to feed impoverished masses. Also, declining women's health because of early and complicated childbirth and high infant mortality rates show that population problems need to be addressed with outside help. "Yet only one percent of donor nations' foreign aid goes to population programs worldwide," said Dr. J. Joseph Speidel, president of the Population Crisis Committee.

NAME ______________________________ DATE ______________

3. What is going on in income distribution in America from 1979 to 1993, judging by the following graph? How do you account for the changes?

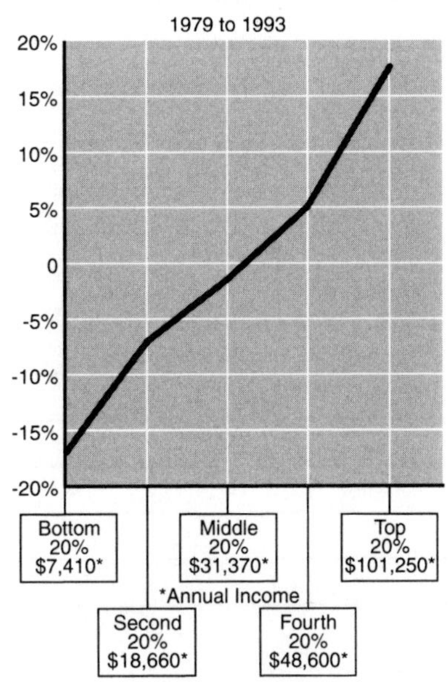

Growth in Real Family Income (in 1993 dollars, by income group).

VOCABULARY

The following words may not be part of your normal vocabulary. If their meaning is not familiar to you, you should look them up in a dictionary.

sporadic	subpeonas	extradite	recrimination
amnesty	stagflation	sacred cow	philanderer
dissident	deregulation	surrogate	
minuscule	equilibrium	cataclysmic	

IDENTIFICATION OF KEY CONCEPTS

In two to three sentences, identify each of the following:

Depository Institutions Deregulation and Monetary Control Act ______________________

Airline Deregulation Act ______________________

Rail Act ______________________

Motor Carrier Act ______________________

SALT II ______________________

Roe v. Wade ______________________

National Organization for Women ______________________

Mayaguez Incident ______________________

NAME ______________________ **DATE** ______________

Radical Feminism ______________________

Bilingualism ______________________

American Indian Movement ______________________

The Energy Crisis ______________________

Yom Kippur War of 1973 ______________________

Deregulation ______________________

New Right ______________________

Election of 1980 ______________________

Reaganomics ______________________

PATCO ______________________

Recession of 1982

Tax Reform Act of 1986

Iran-Contra Affair

Election of 1988

Desert Storm

Somalia

Election of 1992

NAFTA

Clarence Thomas–Anita Hill controversy

Bosnia

NAME ______________________________ DATE ______________

IDENTIFICATION OF KEY INDIVIDUALS

In two to three sentences, identify each of the following:

Gerald Ford ______________________________

Jimmy Carter ______________________________

Ayatollah Khomeini ______________________________

Mikhail Gorbachev ______________________________

Saddam Hussein ______________________________

Cesar Chavez ______________________________

Betty Friedan ______________________________

Reyes Tijerina ______________________________

Bill Clinton ______________________________

George W. Bush ____

____

____

____

Oliver North ____

____

____

____

Al Gore ____

____

____

____

SELF-TEST

Multiple-Choice Questions

1. Jimmy Carter's biggest liabilities in the election of 1980 were a poor economy and
   a. his liberalism.
   b. the seizing of the Tehran embassy.
   c. his "human rights" policy.
   d. Congress.

2. Which of the following incidents intensified racial issues during the George Bush presidency?
   a. the Clarence Thomas hearings
   b. the debate over affirmative action
   c. the Rodney King case
   d. All of the above.

3. The term "stagflation" refers to an economy characterized by
   a. high unemployment.
   b. high inflation.
   c. Both a and b.
   d. Neither a nor b.

4. Which of the following was not an example of federal deregulation during the Carter Administration?
   a. Airline Deregulation Act of 1978
   b. Motor Carrier Act of 1980
   c. Rail Act of 1980
   d. Television Deregulation Act of 1979

5. Which was most damaging to President Reagan's reputation?
   a. the PATCO strike
   b. the Iran-Contra Affair
   c. the appointment of Ann Gorsuch
   d. the stock market crash of 1987

6. Which one of the following was not a foreign policy challenge for the Clinton Administration?
   a. Bosnia
   b. Somalia
   c. Haiti
   d. Italy

7. The code-name "Desert Storm" refers to the Bush Administration's war to force
   a. Iran to withdraw from Somalia.
   b. Iraq to withdraw from Kuwait.
   c. Armenia to withdraw from Azerbaijan.
   d. Rwanda to withdraw from Burundi.

8. The "New Right" of the 1980s included all but
   a. disciples of Milton Friedman.
   b. supporters of Ted Kennedy.
   c. fundamentalist Christians.
   d. conservative Jews and Catholics.

NAME ____ DATE ____________________

9. During his nomination hearings for appointment to the Supreme Court, Clarence Thomas was accused by Anita Hill of
   a. racism.
   b. political corruption.
   c. sexual harassment.
   d. criminal fraud.

10. The Equal Rights Amendment
    a. was enacted into law.
    b. passed both houses of Congress.
    c. passed in three quarters of the state legislatures.
    d. was declared unconstitutional.

Matching Questions

For questions 11 through 15, use one of the lettered items.

11. The acronym referring to intercontinental ballistics carrying more than one warhead.___
12. America's leading feminist organization.___
13. The labor union representing air traffic controllers.___
14. Negotiations to limit long-range nuclear weapons.___
15. The group of countries whose major export commodity was oil.___

a. SALT
b. MIRV
c. NOW
d. PATCO
e. OPEC

For questions 16 through 20, use one of the lettered items.

16. Mikhail Gorbachev's program to relax censorship in the Soviet Union.___
17. The American merchant vessel seized off the coast of Cambodia in 1975.___
18. Mikhail Gorbachev's program to restructure the Soviet economy.___
19. Refers to the 1973 war between Israel and the Arab states.___
20. Anti-communist guerrilla groups in Central America.___

a. contras
b. glasnost
c. perestroika
d. Yom Kippur
e. *Mayaguez*

True-False Questions

21. The Tax Reform Act of 1986 substantially increased tax rates on the rich.___
22. The *Roe v. Wade* decision in 1973 outlawed early abortions.___
23. The Motor Carrier Act of 1980 reduced the power of the Interstate Commerce Commission to control market access, freight rates, and routes in the trucking industry.___
24. The Airline Deregulation Act of 1978 stopped the practice of allowing the free access of new carriers into existing routes.___
25. The real explanation behind the problem of stagflation was the dramatic increases in energy prices in the 1970s.___

Essay Questions

1. What has been the course of American foreign policy since the nation's withdrawal from the war in Vietnam? How has it varied in accordance with changes in presidential administrations?

2. Are the Democratic and Republican parties in balance in the era of the millenium? Which is more likely to emerge as the majority party and why?

Self-Test Answers

1. b 2. d 3. c 4. d 5. b 6. c 7. b 8. b 9. c 10. b 11. b 12. c 13. d 14. a 15. e 16. b 17. e 18. c 19. d 20. a 21. F 22. F 23. T 24. F 25. T